CITIZEN SOLDIERS

CITIZEN SOLDIERS

OKLAHOMA'S NATIONAL GUARD

BY KENNY A. FRANKS

UNIVERSITY OF OKLAHOMA PRESS : NORMAN

Oklahoma Horizons Series

Other Books by Kenny A. Franks

(coauthor) *Mark of Heritage* (Norman, 1976)
(coeditor) *Early Military Forts and Posts in Oklahoma* (Oklahoma City, 1978)
Stand Watie and the Agony of the Cherokee Nation (Memphis, 1979)
The Oklahoma Petroleum Industry (Norman, 1980)
(coauthor) *Early Oklahoma Oil* (College Station, 1981)
(coauthor) *Early Louisiana/Arkansas Oil* (College Station, 1982)

Jacket cartoon by Bill Mauldin, from *News of the 45th,* by Don Robinson, published by the University of Oklahoma Press.

Library of Congress Cataloging in Publication Data

Franks, Kenny Arthur, 1945-
    Citizen soldiers.

    (Oklahoma horizons series)
    Bibliography: p. 219
    Includes index.
    1. Oklahoma. National Guard—History. 2. Oklahoma.
    Air National Guard—History. I. Title. II. Series.
    UA400.F73 1984   355.3'7'09766   83-40326
    ISBN 0-8061-1862-8

Dedicated to those citizen soldiers
who died to make this nation free,
to those who still serve to keep it free,
and to the former members of
Company C, 120th Engineers
Okemah, Oklahoma

CONTENTS

ILLUSTRATIONS

PREFACE

The concept of a standing militia—citizen soldiers—took root in the early history of this nation. Citizen soldiers have played a major role in every American conflict since the time of the first colonists, when there were few regular soldiers to protect the people. The concept of a standing militia was incorporated into the United States Constitution because it was believed then —and is now—that a citizen militia is a deterrent to a militarily controlled government. Now long a part of the nation's military policy, the citizen-soldier concept has helped to make America great and has been an important factor in the nation's defense in wartime.

The history of citizen soldiers in Oklahoma began before the territorial days. Even before the establishment of the eastern colonial militias, the Indian tribes of the Great Plains utilized certain tribal members to act as soldiers or police. Their duties were to rally to the common defense of the tribe in time of need. As early as the War of 1812, members of the Five Civilized Tribes served as auxiliary troops with the American army, and in 1828 the western band of Cherokees formed a quasi-militia unit —the lighthorse. Later, when the Five Civilized Tribes arrived in Oklahoma, their tribal constitutions called for the creation of standing militias, which, until statehood, functioned as the military arm of the various tribal governments. During the Civil War, both the Union and the Confederate governments organized Indians into several military units that fought with distinction.

With the organization of Oklahoma Territory in 1890, the legislature wasted little time in forming a territorial militia, which, in 1895, evolved into the Oklahoma Territory National Guard. Later, during the Spanish-American War, two units of citizen soldiers were raised from Oklahoma and Indian territories for service. With statehood, the National Guard expanded throughout Oklahoma.

Although it had been utilized many times by state officials, the Oklahoma National Guard was first mustered into federal service for duty on the Mexican Border in 1916. The troops had barely returned home when they were again called for service, this time in World War I. Merged with the Texas National Guard, the Oklahomans became a part of the Thirty-sixth National Guard Division and served in Europe. Yet another group of citizen-soldier draftees from Oklahoma and Texas were organized into the Ninetieth, or Texas-Oklahoma, Division and likewise served in France.

During the early 1920s, Oklahoma's most illustrious citizen-soldier unit—the Forty-fifth Infantry Division—was organized, with components in Oklahoma, Colorado, New Mexico, and Arizona. After World War II, the famed Thunderbird Division became an all-Oklahoma unit. It served both the state and the nation for more than forty-five years before being reduced to brigade status in 1968. In addition, the post-World War II era saw the 125th and the 185th squadrons of the United States Air National Guard become a part of Oklahoma's citizen-soldier tradition.

Although the role of Oklahoma's guardsmen has changed with the times, the basic concept of civilian volunteers, who train near their homes but stand ready to serve their country wherever and whenever called, remains the same. These dedicated men and women, fulfilling a constitutional role, have served as the backbone of the nation's defense. Today, with the military's "Total Force" concept, the responsibility is even greater because both the National Guard and the Air National Guard serve as full partners with the regular military establishment.

As important as their role is in national defense, Oklahoma's national guardsmen are an integral part of their communities. They are the men and women to whom their neighbors turn in time of natural disasters or civil disorders. They are neighbors helping neighbors.

This book is not meant to be a completely comprehensive history of Oklahoma's citizen soldiers. I would not attempt a feat of that magnitude when others have produced multivolume works examining a single battle in which the guardsmen fought. Rather, it is meant to be an overall view of the state's National Guard from its beginning to the present. In such a work, Oklahomans and others might come to a better understanding of the contributions that the citizen soldiers have made to the state and to the nation.

I have not attempted to follow every unit of citizen soldiers raised from the state. Instead, I have drawn a broad picture of the wartime campaigns in which they participated and described the many occasions when they were summoned to aid survivors of natural disasters or to restore order during civil unrest. It would require volumes to examine every instance of valor by Oklahoma's citizen soldiers. Thus several instances of heroism by members of the Oklahoma National Guard on active duty are not covered unless they were guardsmen before the summons to federal service.

Readers unfamiliar with military parlance should have no problems with the military form of citing dates, but they may find the use of military time disconcerting. The military does not use A.M. or P.M. The serviceman quickly learns that midnight is 2400 and that 1 A.M. is 0100. As the timepiece's hands progress clockwise, 1000 is not one thousand; it is "ten hundred" or 10:00 A.M. Noon is 1200, and half-past is 1230, "twelve-thirty." One o'clock is 1300, and 6:00 P.M. is 1800. Each hour is called its place in the twenty-four hours. Many of the more complicated time designations, for example,

2245, will be parenthetically explained as (2245 is 10:45 P.M.).

The place-names used in this book are spelled the way they appear in unit reports and occasionally may vary from the spelling found on present-day maps.

I owe a great debt of gratitude to the many individuals and organizations who helped make this book possible. Major Joe E. Blackwell; Sergeant Major Jack Clapp (Ret.); Second Lieutenant Mark L. ("Beau") Cantrell; Major General John Coffey, Jr. (Ret.); Colonel William P. Grace (Ret.); Master Sergeant Dennis R. Lindsey; Colonel H. A. Meyers (Ret.); Lieutenant Colonel James R. McKinney; Colonel John W. McCasland (Ret.); Major Timothy E. Martin; Major General Hal L. Muldrow, Jr. (Ret.); Colonel Preston J. C. Murphy (Ret.); Major General Stanley F. H. Newman; Colonel Herbert C. O'Neil (Ret.); Command Sergeant Major Arthur E. Peters (Ret.); Colonel Bruce E. Rey (Ret.); and Lieutenant Colonel Roy P. Stewart (Ret.) —all were generous with their time, their personal collections, and their knowledge of the events recounted in this book. Of course, had it not been for the sacrifice of thousands of citizen soldiers from throughout the United States, such an undertaking would not have been possible.

I owe special thanks to Major General Frederick A. Daugherty (Ret.); Ralph W. Jones, former director of the Forty-fifth Infantry Division Museum; Clifton Chappell, the current director of the Museum; Katherine Yates Wright, curator of the Museum; Major General Robert M. Morgan, Jr., adjutant-general for the state of Oklahoma; the members of the Oklahoma National Guard Association; and the members of the Forty-fifth Infantry Division Association for helping make this work possible. In addition, had it not been for the technical editing of the staff of the Public Information Office of the Oklahoma National Guard and the patience of Colonel McCasland in reading and advising me on the content of the manuscript, this book would never have been finished. I thank the Forty-fifth Infantry Division Museum staff; the people of the Oklahoma Military Department; and Mary Hardin, Peggy Coe, Mary Sweeney, Geraldine Adams, Karen Fite, Steve Belen, Virginia Collier, and the other employees of the

Oklahoma Department of Libraries who devoted much time in helping me complete this work.

Without the support of Dr. Paul F. Lambert, executive director; W. R. ("Dick") Stubbs, emeritus chairman of the board; Robert A. Hefner, Jr., chairman of the board; President John T. Griffin; and the members of the Horizons Committee of the Oklahoma Heritage Association, this study of Oklahoma's citizen soldiers could never have been completed. Finally, I must thank my wife, Jayne, for being so patient with me during the months spent preparing this story.

Kenny A. Franks

CITIZEN SOLDIERS

CHAPTER 1

THE TERRITORIAL MILITIA

After the Civil War, the United States Congress began a gradual elimination of Indian sovereignty over what is now Oklahoma. The ensuing years saw the Cherokees, the Chickasaws, the Choctaws, the Creeks, and the Seminoles—the Five Civilized Tribes—agreeing to cede portions of their lands for colonization by various Plains tribes, forced by government pressures into the area. Non-Indian settlement began 22 April 1889 with the opening of the Unassigned Lands. Within a short time most of present-day western Oklahoma was occupied by non-Indians.[1]

As their numbers swelled, the new settlers petitioned federal authorities to create a territorial government. Responding to their demands, Congress passed the Organic Act, which was signed into law by President Benjamin Harrison on 2 May 1890. Under its provisions the recently elected members of the First Oklahoma Territorial Legislature convened in Guthrie on 12 August of that year. One of the first acts of the territorial legislature was to establish the Oklahoma Territorial Militia, the forerunner of the Oklahoma National Guard.[2]

Under the law, the territorial governor was authorized to organize "such military companies, battalions and regiments . . . as he may deem proper," not to exceed a total of two regiments of infantry, two battalions of cavalry, and one battery of artillery. Troops were to be mustered from male citizens between the ages of eighteen and forty-five. A regimental staff, consisting of two colonels serving as the adjutant-general and inspector general, two captains assigned as "aids-de-camp [sic]," and one sergeant general, with the rank of major, were to be appointed by the chief executive. In addition, one major was to serve as a combination quartermaster general, commissary general, and chief of ordnance. Because of his responsibility for all the funds and materiel issued to the militia, this officer was required to post a $5,000 bond with the territorial secretary. Other regimental and company officers were to be appointed by the governor as he deemed necessary.[3]

The troops were subject to the call of the governor "whenever in his opinion the safety of the inhabitants of the Territory or any part thereof is in danger." The code of conduct covering the "rules and regulations governing the army of the United States" was applied to the territorial militia, with the reservation "so far as applicable." The troops were granted the "pay and emoluments . . . allowed for the same rank . . . for officers and soldiers of the United States Army." There was one important caveat: "Provided . . . That this Territory shall be at no expense for arms and their necessary accoutrements for the equipment of the militia other than the necessary freight, expressage or carriage of such arms and accoutrements." Although eager to establish Oklahoma's first true citizen-soldier units, the First Territorial Legislature neglected to appropriate any funds to equip and maintain the men.[4]

The result was that the units were dependent on "public-spirited and martial-minded volunteers." Succeeding legislative sessions appropriated some funds for the continued existence of the adjutant-general's office, but very little money was provided "for the purchase of equipment, guns, or clothing for the guardsmen." Generally the men trained with obsolete weapons, many of which were donated, and most wore

3

cast-off uniforms. Nonetheless, one regiment of infantry was organized for service.[5]

As the territory grew, so did the militia. New and comprehensive militia legislation was enacted by the third Territorial Legislature on 8 March 1895. Under the new provisions the territorial militia was reorganized into the Oklahoma National Guard. Limited to five hundred men in time of peace, the National Guard included all able-bodied men living in the territory between the ages of eighteen and forty-five, who were either citizens of the United States or who had declared their intent to become citizens. The territorial governor was specifically allowed to exempt anyone "who has conscientious scruples against bearing arms." Individuals younger than eighteen were allowed to enlist with "the written consent of their parents or guardians." One company was reserved to be formed "from among the colored residents" of the territory. All military units formed under the 1890 militia statute were incorporated into the new Oklahoma National Guard system without reorganization.[6]

The men were organized into either infantry, artillery, or cavalry units. Any individual was allowed to form a unit, but all units had to be approved by the governor before their officers received a state commission. There were, however, severe restrictions on the number of artillery and cavalry units that could be formed. There could be only one artillery battery of two guns, with not more than eighty-one nor less than thirty men, and only one cavalry troop of not less than thirty nor more than seventy men. The infantry units were to be centered around companies of not less than thirty-four nor more than eighty men each. The governor was allowed to group the infantry companies into battalions and regiments, and to attach the cavalry to the infantry battalions or regiments as he saw fit. If any unit fell below authorized strength, it could either be disbanded or combined with another unit. No individual was allowed to belong to more than one unit at a time, and transfers between companies were allowed only with the consent of the commanders of both units, subject to the approval of the commander in chief.[7]

At the top of the command structure was the governor, who, as commander in chief, was empowered to appoint and remove members of his staff at will. Any other officer "entitled to a staff" was granted the same power. The governor's staff consisted of a brigadier general, serving as adjutant-general; one inspector general, with the rank of colonel; six majors, who were assigned as quartermaster general, paymaster general, commissary general, surgeon general, judge advocate general, and chief of ordnance; and three captains, acting as aides-de-camp. Each regiment was allotted a colonel and a lieutenant colonel, and each battalion was given a major to command the unit. Regimental colonels were authorized to form a staff consisting of a surgeon, a quartermaster, a commissary officer, an ordnance officer, a chaplain, a judge-advocate with the rank of captain, and a first lieutenant serving as adjutant. In addition, several noncommissioned officers, including a sergeant major, a commissary sergeant, a chief trumpeter, and a color sergeant, were assigned to the regimental staff.[8]

The adjutant-general assumed the day-to-day administrative tasks of the National Guard. He served as the ex officio quartermaster general, chief of ordnance, paymaster general, and commissary general. As brigadier general of the troops, the adjutant-general was charged with issuing and transmitting "all orders of the commander-in-chief with reference to the militia or military organizations of the Territory." Another duty was to furnish commissions to all officers appointed by the governor and to keep specific records of such commissions. The adjutant-general was responsible for the record-keeping of general and special orders, military regulations, militia rolls, enlistment papers, certificates of election of officers, and oaths of office for officers. He also issued requisitions for supplies needed by the various militia units. Finally, the adjutant-general was responsible for the distribution of materiel and the supervision of the various units and their equipment. He submitted a detailed report to the governor at the beginning of each fiscal year on the operations and strength of the units under his command. Because of the large amount of materiel directly controlled by the adjutant-general, he was required to post a $2,000 bond with the territorial secretary. For performing these duties and assuming these myriad responsibilities, and in addition to holding the rank of brigadier general, the adjutant-general was paid $500 a year.[9]

The quartermaster general and the chief of ordnance, subject to approval by the adjutant-general were responsible for the issuance of arms and equipment to the various militia units, "or to any civic authorities the commander-in-chief may direct." Before the weapons could be issued to the troops, the respective unit commanders were required to bond the weapons at double value. The money would be forfeited if the property was not returned in proper condition. Exceptions were made for normal wear and unavoidable loss. Stocks of weapons could be provided "to any established college, academy or school" that offered military tactics as part of its curriculum. Such institutions were exempted from the prohibition against the formation of other military organizations. The commissary general was responsible for providing "such subsistence for the National Guard, when in active service, as may be ordered by the commander-in-chief."[10]

Each infantry company was authorized one captain, one first lieutenant, one second lieutenant, one first sergeant, four sergeants, as many as eight corporals, and two musicians. Cavalry troops were assigned one captain, one first lieutenant, one second lieutenant, one first sergeant, one quartermaster sergeant, five sergeants, eight corporals, and two trumpeters. In addition to these personnel, the mounted units had three corporals that were assigned as farrier, saddler, and blacksmith. The artillery battery was commanded by a captain. Under his authority served one first lieutenant, one second lieutenant, one first sergeant, one quartermaster sergeant, two sergeants, one guidon sergeant, four corporals, one artificer, one blacksmith, one farrier, one saddler, and two trumpeters. The artillery battery also had a hospital steward and a second lieutenant serving as an assistant surgeon. The various commanders were responsible for the individual proficiency of their men and were charged with holding "drills, parades, reviews, inspections and schools of instructions" to ensure that their men received proper training.[11]

Enlistments were for three years, and all enlisted personnel were required to take an oath to support the Constitution of the United States, the Organic Act for Oklahoma Territory, and the laws of the Territory of Oklahoma. The men were to "wear the uniform of, and shall be equipped, drilled and disciplined in the same manner as the army of the United States." The only difference allowed from regular army uniforms was the authorization to substitute the coat-of-arms appearing on their buttons for that of the National Guard. Whenever the troops were called into actual service, they were to receive "the same pay and subsistence" as the members of the regular army. While on National Guard duty, the enlisted men were allowed $2 per diem and rations. Animals used by the National Guard on active duty were provided $1's worth of food per day. If on duty, Guardsmen were exempt from arrest by civil authorities, except in cases of treason, felony, or breach of the peace during, while going to, or returning from drills, parades, inspections, encampments, and tours of active duty. The property issued to the troops was exempt for the execution of debt. The men also were exempt from paying the poll tax then in effect and from jury duty, and when performing their duties had the right of way over all other vehicles other than police or fire.[12]

Individuals who were not members of the territorial militia were prohibited from wearing the National Guard uniform. Anyone who violated this regulation could be found guilty of a misdemeanor and fined $25. The money was to be applied to the contingent fund of the adjutant-general.[13]

Under the new statute there were only four means by which a commissioned officer of the Oklahoma National Guard could be discharged: resignation, disbandment of his unit, action of the territorial council, or court-martial. Enlisted men could request to be relieved of duty before the expiration of their enlistment in time of peace, and the request had to be approved by both their immediate commander and the governor. A change of residence, so that he could no longer serve with his unit, or being deemed medically unfit resulted in discharge. Of course, a court-martial usually meant being drummed out of the guard.[14]

The officers and men of the National Guard were subject to the same rules, regulations, laws, and articles of war as the regular army, except where specifically altered by the territorial legislature. The territorial governor was charged with the appointment of a committee of three officers who were to prepare additional rules and regulations "as they may deem proper for the government and orderly organization of the volunteer militia." After review by the commander in chief, these rules and regulations were to be

Company K, First Oklahoma Infantry Regiment, Oklahoma Territorial National Guard, undergoing inspection at Camp Chandler, Oklahoma Territory. *Courtesy Forty-fifth Infantry Division Museum.*

published as a part of "the military code of the Territory." The governor was also authorized to "make such changes and alterations in said rules and regulations, from time to time, as he may deem expedient."[15]

If an officer of the Oklahoma National Guard was charged with a violation of a rule or regulation governing guard actions, the territorial governor was authorized to convene a court-martial. The punishment for such violations was limited to dismissal from service or a dishonorable discharge. Violations by enlisted men were adjudged by the individual commanders of the regiments, battalions, batteries, or unattached companies. The commanding officer of the unit was authorized to convene a garrison court-martial consisting of three members of the unit, only one of which had to be an officer. All findings were subject to review by the territorial governor, and again, punishment was limited to dismissal or discharge.[16]

Although the territorial governor was commander in chief of the militia, the commanders of individual units had extensive powers. If a threat of invasion or insurrection appeared imminent, or if "a body of men acting together by force with intent to commit a felony, or to offer violence to persons or property, or . . . to break and resist the laws . . . and there is not time to inform the commander-in-chief," the commanders were authorized, "upon the written request of the sheriff," to call out their troops and suppress such activity.[17]

A contingent fund, to be paid only upon the order of either the adjutant-general or the governor, was appropriated to defray the expenses of the adjutant-general. The actual expenses incurred by the other staff officers also were paid. All expenses were audited by the territorial auditor. In addition, an auditing board was established, consisting of the territorial auditor, the secretary, and the treasurer, to "audit and allow all accounts for services and other liabilities incurred by the National Guard when called into active service."[18]

The "National Guard organization, or any subdivision thereof," was authorized to purchase, "at their own expense," property in any city or town in Oklahoma Territory for the purpose of erecting "armories, headquarters and drill halls." The title to the property would be held by the unit that purchased it, and the

Theodore Roosevelt, *right*, and other members of the Rough Riders from Oklahoma. Sergeant Major Charles W. McPherren, *center, back row*, rose to the rank of major general and became the fourth commanding general of the Forty-fifth Division. *Courtesy Forty-fifth Infantry Division Museum.*

property would be exempt from all territorial, county, or municipal taxes.[19]

The 1895 legislation provided the guidelines for the formation of the modern National Guard in Oklahoma and launched the first citizen militia in the state. The territorial militia functioned under its provisions until statehood in 1907. In 1898, during the Spanish-American War, two additional volunteer units were raised, at least partially, from the citizens of the Indian and Oklahoma territories.[20]

The United States declared war on Spain on 25 April 1898. At that time the regular army had only 28,000 officers and men, and it was obvious that a host of volunteers would have to be raised to supplement the regular troops. President William McKinley issued two calls for volunteers, one on 23 April and one on 22 May 1898. The response was overwhelming, and by August a total of 216,256 men had enlisted.[21]

The men of the Twin Territories were in the forefront of the rush to enlist. In response to the first call, troops L and M, nearly 135 men, of the First Regiment of United States Volunteer Cavalry were recruited from Oklahoma and Indian territories. They were commanded by Colonel Leonard Wood and Lieutenant Colonel Theodore Roosevelt and were commonly called the Rough Riders. Later, under the second call for volunteers, Oklahoma and Indian territories raised five companies for duty with the First Regiment of Territorial Volunteers.[22]

A group of Oklahoma volunteers of the First U.S. Regiment of Volunteer Cavalry, better known as the Rough Riders, drilling in preparation for embarking for Cuba. *Courtesy Forty-fifth Infantry Division Museum.*

The Rough Riders were sent to San Antonio, Texas, along with recruits from New Mexico and Arizona, where, in mid-May, their training was completed. Captain Allyn K. Capron, a regular army officer with the Seventh Cavalry at Fort Sill, commanded one of the Oklahoma troops and received high praise from Roosevelt. He was "the best soldier in the regiment" for getting his men "ahead in discipline faster than any other troop," and for bringing "their fighting efficiency to the highest possible pitch." Capron later became the first American officer to be killed in the fighting in Cuba. Once in San Antonio, the volunteers received their uniforms: distinctive "dusty brown blouses, trousers and leggings" topped with a dark gray, "broad-brimmed soft hat." Although the men were issued a Krag rifle, a revolver, and a sabre, several opted to use their own Winchester rifles, a substitution that was relatively easy because the Krag and the Winchester could fire the same government issue cartridge. As for the sabres, Roosevelt remarked: "We felt very strongly that it would be worse than a waste of time to try to train our men to use the sabre—a weapon utterly alien to them."[23]

On 29 May 1898 the Rough Riders left San Antonio by train for a four-day trip to Tampa, Florida, and embarkation for Cuba. "An almost inextricable tangle," Tampa was in such a state

of confusion, according to Roosevelt, that the men had to purchase their own food. Finally, after a wait of several days, eight troops of seventy men each, without their horses, were ordered to prepare to leave for the war zone.[24]

On the evening of 7 June, the troops received word to load ship at daybreak the following morning. Because of the confusion surrounding the entire mobilization, no advance arrangements for boarding the ships had been made. Midnight, the hour designated for the troops to board a train to carry them to the loading area, came and passed without the transportation arriving. At 0600 a coal train appeared and was commandeered to carry the troops. At the port, confusion again prevailed. The *Yucatan* had been allotted to two other regiments, but the Rough Riders were finally ordered aboard it. The ship's officers refused to leave port with the "wrong" troops aboard until otherwise ordered to do so, and the troops stayed on board, in port, until 14 June before the ship sailed. Eight days later the ship reached Daiquiri, "a squalid little village." Once in Cuba the Rough Riders joined the Second Cavalry Brigade, commanded by Brigadier General S. B. M. Young, and a part of the cavalry division of Major General William R. Shafter's Fifth Corps. Within two days they would be in the trenches fighting at Las Guasimas.[25]

Cannons loaded on railroad flatcars in a rail yard at Tampa, Florida, in 1898, awaiting transportation to Cuba. *Courtesy Forty-fifth Infantry Division Museum.*

Once ashore the Rough Riders were appalled at the conditions in their bivouac area. "We were camped on a dusty, brush-covered flat, with jungle on one side, and on the other a shallow, fetid pool fringed with palm-trees," according to Roosevelt. It took several days to get all of their equipment off the ship and reloaded because transportation was nonexistent. Finally, at 0430 (4:30 A.M.) on 23 June, the men began to advance toward the front lines. Their horses had been left behind when they shipped from Tampa and only the officers were mounted. With ·other members of their brigade, the Rough Riders were ordered to encamp between Juraguacito and Siboney on the road to Santiago de Cuba, the scene of the decisive land battle of the war. The heat was intense, and the troops were unaccustomed to the climate.[26]

That evening the troops bivouacked near Siboney. During the night Young received reports of a sharp engagement between Cuban and Spanish units in the vicinity, and he decided to make "a reconnaissance in force." The following day he dispatched separate columns along the two trails toward Sevilla, where he thought the enemy could be found. With orders to engage any Spanish troops encountered, Colonel Wood's regiment was sent along the western trail. Young commanded the other column. The troops moved out at 0600, and an hour and

a half later Young's column discovered an estimated 2,500 Spaniards deployed along "a range of high hills in the form of an obtuse angle, with the salient toward Siboney." Immediately Young sent word to Wood and began planning an assault.[27]

The attack was delayed until Wood deployed his men on line and coordinated the assault so that both columns, totaling 950 men, would hit the Spanish lines at the same time. In the meantime, an American Hotchkiss artillery battery began shelling the enemy. As the Americans began their advance, the enemy opened a volley fire, "executed with the precision of parade." The Rough Riders had to penetrate thick jungle foliage through which the Spanish had threaded barbed wire fencing. "Many of the men, footsore and weary from their march of the preceding day found the pace up this hill too hard, and either dropped their bundles or fell out of line."[28]

Although the attackers faced heavy fire, the terrain caused more problems than enemy gunners. Roosevelt recalled that the "air seemed full of the rustling sound of the Mauser bullets, for the Spaniards knew the trails by which we were advancing, and opened heavily on our position." The smokeless powder used by the Spanish troops made it difficult for the Rough Riders to locate them, while the acrid smoke from the black-powder American weapons made a convenient sighting point. Stubbornly moving forward, the Americans neared the crest, and the Spaniards abandoned their breastworks and blockhouses and fled toward Santiago.[29]

After routing the enemy, Young ordered a halt so the exhausted men could rest. The newly won positions were consolidated, the wounded were treated, and, because land crabs and vultures quickly attacked any fallen bodies, a thorough search was made for the missing. Thirty-four wounded men were carried to Siboney for treatment and eight dead were buried.[30]

On the next afternoon, 25 June, the Rough Riders advanced "a couple of miles" toward Santiago and then encamped along the bank of a stream. They remained there five days, spread along "one narrow road, a mere muddy track," before receiving orders to prepare for an all-out attack on Santiago. At about noon on 30 June 1898 the Rough Riders fell into column. Every man carried three days' rations and his personal weapons, while the heavy crew-served guns were loaded on borrowed mules. The heat was intense, and whenever the column halted the troops slumped at the edge of the road to rest. By nightfall the men had reached the summit of El Poso Hill, approximately three miles east of Santiago, and were dispersed in the jungle for the night. Exhausted, the troops slept as best they could, using their raincoats and saddle blankets for cover.[31]

At 0500 on 1 July, the Americans formed up. Soon an artillery battery was wheeled into position just to their front, and the men told that their task was to create a diversion while Brigadier General H. W. Lawton's Second Division launched an attack toward El Caney, a strategic town about four miles northeast of Santiago. At 0630 the artillery opened fire on the Spanish-held blockhouse atop San Juan Hill, approximately one mile east of Santiago. Again the Spaniards quickly located the American positions because of the heavy smoke from their guns, and their return fire inflicted heavy losses. Eventually, the Second Cavalry Brigade moved out in a column of fours toward Santiago behind the leading elements of the First Cavalry Brigade. Wood had been ordered to ford San Juan River and then extend his line to the right and make contact with Lawton's left flank. The orders were "of the vaguest kind," but apparently

the Rough Riders were intended to be support for the First Brigade. According to Roosevelt, confusion occurred. "No reconnaissance had been made, and the exact position and strength of the Spaniards was not known."[32]

The troops crossed the stream and deployed to the right as ordered. Almost at the same time they were joined by an observation balloon crew, who anchored near the ford and then sent the balloon aloft to observe the enemy. This, of course, attracted the Spaniards' attention, and the result "was a terrific converging artillery and rifle fire on the ford." Roosevelt was ordered to march his men "a mile or so to the right, and then halt and await further orders." The movement was "under the intense heat, [and] through the high grass of the open jungle . . . [while] the firing . . . grew steadily hotter and hotter." Eventually the men found shelter in a sunken lane. As the Rough Riders faced the Spanish, the First United States Cavalry was on their right, and behind the First was the Tenth Cavalry. Ahead, the Ninth Cavalry held the right flank; the Sixth Cavalry held the center; and the Third Cavalry was left flank—all were regular army units. Wire fencing was on either side of the lane, but the road led directly between the two hills upon which the Spanish were entrenched. The hill on the right, San Juan Hill, presented a fortified blockhouse, and the one on the left, Kettle Hill, had a series of red-roofed ranch buildings with sunken brick-lined walls and cellars.[33]

The men were under heavy fire, and Roosevelt sent a messenger to get hoped-for orders to advance. For a long time no answer was received. About the time he decided to "march toward the guns," Roosevelt received orders to take his troops "forward and support the regulars in the assault on the hills in front." Immediately Roosevelt formed the men into columns, with each troop extended in open skirmishing order. The right flank was shaped by the wire fence bordering the sunken lane. Surging forward up the sides of Kettle Hill, the Rough Riders braved a storm of Spanish shot to drive the enemy from its position at the top.[34]

Once they had carried the summit, the Rough Riders came under heavy small arms and artillery fire from Spanish units still entrenched on hills to their front. Returning the fire, the Americans supported the assault up San Juan Hill, and as the Spanish were driven from its

Colonel Roy V. Hoffman, *center front*, and officers of the Rough Riders from Oklahoma, awaiting dismissal from federal service at the close of the Spanish-American War. Hoffman commanded both the First Oklahoma Infantry Regiment and the Forty-fifth Infantry Division. *Courtesy Forty-fifth Infantry Division Museum.*

crest, succeeded in inflicting heavy casualties on the retreating enemy. The Rough Riders then rejoined the assault and attacked the next line of Spanish trenches overlooking Santiago. The fighting ended as night fell, and the Americans hastily reconstructed the entrenchments to provide shelter from the next day's enemy fire.[35]

During the following days the Rough Riders consolidated their positions. The Spanish troops made several attempts to retake the heights, but these were usually more in the form of massed fire from their entrenchments rather than direct assaults, and the American lines held. For several days the firing remained severe, but the Americans stood their ground. The campaign against Santiago turned into a siege the Spanish had no hope of lifting, and on 17 July 1898 the Spanish commander surrendered.[36]

After the victory at Santiago, the rapid spread of malaria, dysentery, and yellow fever, coupled with crumbling Spanish resistance, persuaded American officials to withdraw as many troops as could be spared as quickly as possible. As a result, the Rough Riders embarked for home on 6 August 1898. Six days later, the United States and Spain signed a peace protocol at Washington, D.C., and on 15 August the Rough Riders disembarked at Montauk Point on Long Island, New York. Here they remained for a month before being mustered out on 15 September 1898 after almost four months of service.[37]

Following the departure of the Rough Riders for Cuba, five additional companies were being raised in the Twin Territories in answer to President McKinley's second call for volunteers on May 25, 1898. In July of 1898, companies H, I, K, L, and M of the First Territorial Volunteer Infantry were formed in the towns of Guthrie, Kingfisher, Shawnee, and Stillwater in Oklahoma Territory, and in Muskogee in Indian Territory. The four companies from Oklahoma Territory were organized as the Oklahoma Battalion under the command of Major John F. Stone of Kingfisher, with captains Harry Barnes of Guthrie, Robert A. Lowry of Stillwater, Roy Hoffman of Chandler, and Fred Boynton of Kingfisher in charge of the companies. The unit raised from volunteers in Indian Territory became Company D, First Battalion, and was commanded by Captain Earl Edmonson. The remaining companies of that battalion were formed from Arizona volunteers.[38]

The men from the two territories were first assembled at Fort Reno, in Oklahoma Territory, before being moved to Camp Hamilton, Kentucky. There, they joined the recruits from New Mexico and Arizona to complete the formation of the regiment. The troops were still training at Camp Hamilton when Spain surrendered on 12 August. The troops remained in service for several months after the end of the war, and later in 1898 moved to the First Territorial Volunteer Infantry's Camp Churchman, near Albany, Georgia. The unit was mustered out of service on February 15, 1899, without ever seeing any fighting.[39]

During this early stage of development the citizen-soldier concept in Oklahoma had undergone a drastic metamorphosis. It evolved from being a paper organization with little or no monetary support from the territorial legislature, into the basic components of the organization that would lead the guard into the era of statehood. The national concept of citizen-soldier units also had changed drastically. At the outbreak of the Spanish-American War, the regular army was dangerously small and the brunt of fighting fell to the large force of volunteer troops answering the president's call. These men acquitted themselves gallantly, standing the test of battle. This pattern was to be followed by American military planners into the twentieth century—a small regular army force that could be augmented quickly by contingents of citizen soldiers whenever the need arose. The National Guard was to form the backbone of this reserve force. There was little change in the status of the National Guard in the Twin Territories until statehood in 1907, when the men of both Oklahoma and Indian territories were formed into the Oklahoma National Guard.[40]

CHAPTER 2

THE MEXICAN BORDER

In 1907 the Oklahoma National Guard passed from territorial to state control. Although Oklahoma Territory already had the basic command structure for the new statewide organization, Indian Territory had only the various lighthorse organizations of the Five Civilized Tribes. The problem was easily solved by expanding Oklahoma Territory's organization to cover the entire state. The few changes that were made by the First Oklahoma Legislature were generally designed to improve the quality of troops serving in the new statewide National Guard.[1]

Under the provisions of the National Guard Organization and the Maintenance Act of May 22, 1908, the new active militia was formed around a regiment of 945 men. A company of engineers, a hospital corps unit, and a signal corps unit were attached to the regiment for support. In addition, a reserve militia was created. It included all able-bodied males, both citizens and those foreign-born who had declared their intent to become citizens, between eighteen and forty-five years of age.[2]

The creation of a reserve militia to the National Guard organization was designed to provide a method by which additional troops could be raised should the active militia not be sufficient to fulfill a presidential requisition for troops. In such cases, the governor was empowered to issue a call for volunteers from the reserve militia. These men would be formed into new units subject to service wherever and for whatever time period dictated by the president. If, however, the reserve militia was mustered by the governor, it could only be used within the state and was to be discharged from duty as soon as the emergency had passed.[3]

The adjutant-general remained in control of the state's military department. A State Military Board was created as an advisory body to the commander in chief; the board was empowered to prepare and promulgate rules and regulations governing the organization. Members of the board included the colonel commanding the regiment of troops, the adjutant-general, and the judge-advocate. Although it was required by law to meet at least once a year, the Military Board could be convened whenever the adjutant-general believed it necessary.[4]

To help alleviate some of the previous shortages and to improve training facilities, the state agreed to pay monthly armory rent, postal costs, and other incidental expenses of all units that were fully organized and contained the minimum number of men. To ensure that the state-supported facilities were utilized, all units were required to assemble for drill and instruction at least twenty-four times a year and to assemble for at least one inspection annually. To encourage continued training, the new legislation created a special state decoration that could be awarded to all guardsmen "who excel in small arm practice." The company prize was $25; the squad prize was $15; an individual prize was $10; and a sharpshooter prize was $25.[5]

There was to be an annual muster of not more than ten days' duration, a provision that was nullified if the men were called into federal service because the duration of federal service could be indefinite. All officers and men were required to attend the annual muster, and any employer refusing to allow an employee member of the National Guard to participate in the camp could legitimately be charged with a misdemeanor.[6]

A few other minor changes were made. Any other state or territorial militia was prohibited from entering the state without permission, unless it was a unit of the United States Army. Members of the National Guard were to be immune from civil prosecution for any act performed in the discharge of their duty. District judges, county judges, and mayors were listed as officials who could request troops to support civil law.[7]

The admission of Oklahoma into the Union had not been supported by all citizens of the Twin Territories. Some factions of the Five Civilized Tribes opposed the drift away from their ancient tribal ways and resisted assimilation into the dominant culture. The most vocal group against statehood was the Crazy Snake faction of the Creek Nation, led by Chitto Harjo (often called Crazy Snake or Wilson Jones). His opposition resulted in one of the first calls to active duty for the new Oklahoma National Guard.[8]

Harjo initially expressed his displeasure at the passing of the ancient ways when the federal government began allotting land in Indian Territory to individuals before the turn of the century. Serving as a magnet for those with similar beliefs, by 1900 he was acknowledged as the spokesman for the Crazy Snake faction. Mostly full-blood Creek Indians, the Crazy Snake faction pleaded with the Creek National Council to forego further alienation of tribal customs and to return to the ways of their forefathers. At first the protests were orderly; however, as it became apparent that the council would not respond to their pleas, Harjo's followers became increasingly militant.[9]

Organizing their own lighthorse company, a quasi-military police force, the Crazy Snake Creeks began a campaign to turn the Creek Nation against its elected leaders. Although shunning violence, Harjo and his men placed posters throughout the countryside that accused tribal leaders of being traitors and urged individual Creeks to ignore the dictates of either the tribal council or federal officials. Despite Harjo's professed nonviolent beliefs, rumors swept the region of an impending Crazy Snake uprising, and, at the urging of several citizens, Troop A of the Eighth United States Cavalry was dispatched from Fort Reno to the Creek Nation to quell any disturbance. The troops quickly were joined by units of the Indian police from Union Agency at Muskogee, the United States marshal, and several marshal's deputies.[10]

Harjo and some of his supporters were arrested and taken before Federal Judge John R. Thomas. After explaining the federal government's policy of dissolving the tribal governments, Thomas released the Indians after they promised to return to their homes. The Crazy Snakes did, however, continue to gather at Hickory Ground camp near Henryetta and talk of how best to cling to their ancient ways.[11]

By 1909, Harjo's followers were again becoming concerned about the continued deterioration of their tribal heritage, and the meetings at Hickory Ground grew in number. During one of the gatherings some blacks, who lived nearby, were accused of raiding several smokehouses in the vicinity for food. Local officials believed that Harjo was behind the trouble and issued a warrant for his arrest. When the warrant was served, a fight broke out in which one of Harjo's supporters and two deputy sheriffs were killed. Harjo also was wounded during the gunfight, but managed to flee to safety in the Kiamichi Mountains.[12]

Overreacting to the events, Governor Charles N. Haskell sent two hundred national guardsmen, under Colonel Roy V. Hoffman, to Henryetta. Commanded to restore order, Hoffman supposedly entered the Crazy Snakes' camp before the troops arrived and persuaded Harjo's supporters to disband. Later, on 10 March 1910, the guardsmen began arriving. It quickly became apparent that there was little danger of an Indian uprising and that the civil authorities could handle the situation. Realizing that it was costing the state $1,500 a day to maintain the troops, Haskell recalled the militia after nearly two weeks of service. It later was learned that Harjo had died of his wounds.[13]

The development of the Oklahoma National Guard received a boost in 1916 with the passage of a broad National Defense Act by the Congress. Redesigning the regular and reserve armies of the United States, the legislation provided for better training and equipment for the National Guard. Under the new legislation, the formation of National Guard units no longer would be left up to state officials. Instead, the president was authorized to determine what branch of the

The Oklahoma National Guard's summer encampment at Fort Riley, Kansas, in the early part of the guard's history. Enlisted men occupied the conical Sibley tents; officers' were quartered in the walled tents in the foreground. *Courtesy Forty-fifth Infantry Division Museum.*

army would be organized as National Guard units in each state or territory. The new National Guard organizations would be along the same lines as the regular army. The exception was that any previously organized unit was to be allowed to retain its identity and be incorporated into the new table of organization. The various states and territories were originally allotted National Guard units equivalent to two hundred men for each United States senator and congressman; that number was later increased by 50 percent per year until a maximum force of eight hundred men per senator and representative was achieved.[14]

Nationwide, the various National Guard units were to be assigned to individual divisions, brigades, or other tactical units for organizational and training purposes. Federal funds were allocated for the training and equipping of the National Guard units, with the monies appropriated on a pro rata basis. State officials were allowed to retain the power of locating units where they deemed most appropriate; however, no units could be disbanded without the consent of the president of the United States.[15]

Enlistment in the National Guard was set at six years, with three years to be spent in active National Guard service and three years in the National Guard Reserve. Continuous service of six years with active units was allowed, however. More stringent requirements were enacted for National Guard officers, with the men required to be graduates of college-level military programs or selected from reserve lists. Should the National Guard units be called into federal service, all officer vacancies could be filled by the president.[16]

Each state and territory was authorized a National Guard Reserve, which could be called to duty if the regular National Guard and enlisted reserve troops were federalized. The number of troops was in proportion to the number of regular guardsmen. One battalion was allocated for each regiment of infantry, cavalry, or nine batteries of field artillery. The men were to be raised from the enlisted reserve or unorganized militia of the various states, and provisions were made to form the National Guard Reserve into provisional units. Should there not be enough members of the enlisted reserve or unorganized mi-

Company M, First Oklahoma Infantry Regiment parading before the offices of the *Daily Oklahoman* on Broadway in downtown Oklahoma City in 1910. *Courtesy Forty-fifth Infantry Division Museum.*

litia to fill the ranks of the National Guard Reserve, a sufficient number of men in the unorganized militia could be drafted into service to bring the units to full strength.[17]

The armament, the equipment, and the uniforms of the National Guard were to be the same as the regular army. The federal government was to equip the troops with its new weapons at no cost to the states or territories. Materiel could, however, be requisitioned by the regular army in time of actual or threatened war. Horses for the cavalry or for hauling field artillery pieces were to be purchased by the federal government, and the animals were to remain the property of the United States government.[18]

The training of National Guard troops was greatly expanded under the 1916 act. The guardsmen were to receive the same instruction and training as members of the regular army, and each unit was required to assemble for training purposes at least forty-eight times a year. This was in addition to a minimum of fifteen days of encampment annually for training. During the field maneuvers, the troops would be under federal control and would receive the same pay as regular army troops. Additional special camps for officers and enlisted men would be maintained for specialized training. Regular army officers were assigned to inspect each National Guard unit once a year to ensure that its organization and training were adequate.[19]

During periods of federal service, the National Guard was subject to the same rules and regulations governing the regular army. When not in federal service, the state National Guard units were authorized to maintain discipline through three court-martial systems—general, special, and summary. Such courts were empowered to sentence violators to confinement and fines.[20]

The National Guard could be called into federal service by the president whenever Congress authorized the use of United States troops in a number in excess of the regular army. Federal service was for the period of the national emergency, but the guardsmen could be mustered out earlier if events so warranted. Any officer or enlisted member of the National Guard was entitled to the same benefits or pensions as other members of the military if any disability was suffered while in federal service.[21]

The passage of the National Defense Act of 1916 brought the state National Guard units into line with the organization of the regular army. By providing sufficient federal funding to allow the guardsmen to be properly equipped and trained, Congress hoped to have the state militias better prepared for service with the regular army in times of national emergencies. The legislation, which was passed on 3 June 1916, proved to be timely because just fifteen days later, on 18 June, President Woodrow Wilson ordered the entire National Guard of the United States into federal service for duty on the Mexican Border.[22]

Beginning in 1910, revolution after revolution had swept Mexico, as one political faction after another vied for power. Porfirio Díaz was overthrown by Francisco Madero; Madero was assassinated by Victoriano Huerta; and then Venustiano Carranza organized the Constitutionalist party and revolted against Huerta. Mexico was embroiled in turmoil and violence, and caught up in it was Francisco ("Pancho") Villa, the United States Army, and the Oklahoma National Guard.[23]

Villa had been born in the Mexican state of Durango on 5 June 1878, the son of Augustin and Maria Arango. Changing his name to Francisco Villa, he first joined a gang of bandits when he was seventeen. Nicknamed "Pancho," he soon had a reputation as a butcher and a bandit throughout the Mexican state of Chihuahua during the late nineteenth and early twentieth centuries. When the revolution against Díaz began in 1910, Villa joined the revolutionaries and rose to the rank of colonel in Madero's forces. Villa was later imprisoned for insubordination, but he escaped and fled to El Paso, Texas.[24]

Villa was enraged when Huerta assassinated Madero, and in April of 1913 he returned to Mexico and joined the Constitutionalists' counterrevolution against Huerta. Within a short time Villa controlled much of north-central Mexico,

and by the spring of 1914 the Constitutionalists had extended their authority over three-fourths of the country. In the intervening year, the revolution had expanded beyond Mexico's borders. Germany, expecting war with Great Britain at any time, offered Huerta's beleaguered government weapons if the Mexicans would deny their oil to England in the event of war. Huerta agreed, and two ships, the *Ypiranga* and the *Bavaria,* left Germany loaded with guns and ammunition.[25]

At the same time, the United States had become embroiled with Huerta's government over the seizure of some sailors from the U.S.S. *Dolphin.* Although the men had been quickly released and and an apology offered by Mexican officials, the Americans demanded that Huerta order the hoisting of the American flag in a prominent place and salute it with twenty-one guns. The Mexicans refused, and Admiral Henry T. Mayo, the commander of the American squadron, began landing troops at Veracruz on the morning of 21 April 1913. After a brief but bitter contest, the Americans gained control of the city.[26]

Mayo also was ordered to prevent the landing of the munitions from the *Ypiranga*, which had steamed into the harbor, and he so informed the ship's captain. After being told that he could not unload his cargo, the *Ypiranga*'s captain slipped out of the harbor, sailed down the coast, and beached the weapons, which were hurriedly shipped to Huerta's troops by rail. The Mexican people in general reacted violently to the American occupation of Veracruz, and both Huerta and Carranza condemned the action. Nonetheless, United States troops remained in the city for seven months.[27]

In the meantime, the Constitutionalists continued to make steady gains against Huerta's troops, and by July of 1914 it was apparent that his regime was crumbling. On July 15 Huerta resigned and fled to Spain. Once their common foe had been vanquished, the relationship between Carranza and Villa rapidly deteriorated, and Villa began plotting with Emiliano Zapata, another leader in the war against Huerta, to overthrow Carranza. By late 1914, a revolution against the counterrevolution was under way.[28]

Villa, with his Division of the North, along with other officers loyal to Villa, launched an offensive against Carranza's troops in the northern tier of Mexican states. Along the Rio Grande

Oklahoma guardsmen operating an early wireless set, powered by a hand-cranked generator, as part of their training in war games. The men have been issued armbands to denote which side they are fighting for in the war games. The operator is utilizing a saddle as a chair. *Courtesy Forty-fifth Infantry Division Museum.*

there were many twin Mexican-American communities separated only by the river. The fighting for the Mexican towns often presented a dangerous situation to the Americans across the river, as shot and shell knew no boundary.[29]

The chaos in Mexico posed a dilemma for President Wilson. He wanted desperately to see a democratic government established in Mexico, but he did not wish to involve the United States in that country's internal affairs. In July of 1915 the United Stated did, however, recognize Carranza as president of Mexico. The decision infuriated Villa. Wilson also continued to alienate Villa with an elastic embargo policy that allowed Carranza to purchase munitions and supplies but denied Villa the same privilege. In retaliation, Villa classified all Americans as supporters of his enemy and began indiscriminately to kill Americans. More troops were dispatched to the border to protect United States citizens, and the situation bcame critical.[30]

Villa's unrestrained hatred for Americans cli-

maxed in the early morning of 9 March 1916, when he crossed the border and attacked Columbus, New Mexico and Camp Furlong, where elements of the Thirteenth Cavalry were stationed. For several days Colonel Herbert J. Slocum had received reports of Villistas activity in the region; however, he hardly expected an attack. Dividing their attack between the troops at Camp Furlong and the bank near the center of the town, the Mexicans struck shortly before sunrise. Although surprised, the Americans quickly rallied and drove the intruders back across the border. Pursuing Villa's men as far as fifteen miles inside Mexico, the cavalrymen extracted a heavy toll from the raiders.[31]

American officials were stunned by Villa's action. No one anticipated such a brazen strike by the bandits, as they were called. President Wilson, who had sought to avoid direct American involvement in the Mexican revolution, now agreed to swift and decisive retaliation—American troops would be dispatched across the border after Villa. Brigadier General John J. Pershing, the officer chosen to lead the punitive expedition, quickly began assembling men and materiel at El Paso. It would not be an easy task. There were only thirty-one infantry regiments and fifteen cavalry regiments in the entire United States Army in 1916. From these, Pershing selected the Seventh, Tenth, Eleventh, and Thirteenth Cavalry units; the Sixth and Sixteenth Infantry units; two batteries of the Sixth Field Artillery; and various supporting elements—4,800 men and 4,175 animals in all. Shortly before noon on 15 March 1916 the first units crossed into Mexico.[32]

For two months the Americans unsuccessfully scoured the rugged terrain of north-central Mexico for Villa. The use of the regular army for the pursuit had, however, left the remainder of the border poorly defended. On 5 May 1916, Villistas again struck across the Rio Grande. This time their targets were Glenn Springs and Boquillas, Texas. Clearly there were not enough troops to patrol the entire region.[33]

To stabilize the border, Major General Frederick Funston, commander of the Southern Department of the United States Army, recommended to Secretary of War Newton D. Baker a partial mobilization of the National Guard. In response, Baker called up the Arizona, New Mexico, and Texas National Guard units, a total

Company B, First Oklahoma Infantry, mustering in front of the Lincoln County, Oklahoma, courthouse after being called into federal service for duty on the Mexican border in 1916. *Courtesy Forty-fifth Infantry Division Museum.*

of about five thousand men, to guard approximately 1,250 miles of border. Their task was impossible, and when Pershing was unable to capture Villa, President Wilson called the entire National Guard of the United States—nearly 110,000 men—into federal service on 19 June 1916.[34]

Governor Robert L. Williams had been quick to offer Oklahoma troops for service when Pershing was first sent into Mexico, but Wilson had declined at that time. Now the men reacted swiftly, assembling at their local armories. Plans were made to create a central state mobilization center in Oklahoma City. Major General Frank M. Canton, the state adjutant-general, secured an agreement with Oklahoma City officials for free utilities and stable facilities at the state fairgrounds, and Camp Bob Williams was quickly

established with the men pitching tents around the fairgrounds racetrack.[35]

The mustering-in effort was confused somewhat by the inability of federal officials to decide on a permanent mobilization camp. Although approving the Oklahoma City encampment as a temporary measure, Lieutenant Colonel W. S. Scott told Adjutant-General Canton that a permanent station would be created at McAlester. At the same time, Canton was ordered by Secretary of War Baker to shift the mobilization center to Chandler, thirty-five miles to the northeast in Lincoln County, where the regular army had established a supply dump for the state's equipment.[36]

A team of inspectors sent to examine the Chandler location found the proposed camp location unsuitable because of heavy underbrush, undrained ditches, and a morass of mud. Hog pens had been built on the rifle range by local residents, and the community still used outdoor privies, many of which drained dangerously close to the water supply. As a result, it was decided that the Chandler site was unfit for use as a mobilization camp. Now totally confused, Canton suspended mobilization until army officials could reach a decision. Finally, the Oklahoma guardsmen were ordered to muster at Fort Sill, which should have been the obvious choice from the beginning.[37]

Recruits hurried to the colors as individuals, communities, and groups volunteered to raise troops. Governor Williams, however, was forced to decline all offers because the War Department refused to allow the formation of additional units until the state's National Guard regiment, under Colonel Hoffman, was up to full strength. Under the provisions of the recently enacted National Defense Act of 1916, the men were inducted for as long as an emergency existed.[38]

The deadline for reporting for muster was 0900 on 26 June. Almost immediately after arriving at Camp Bob Williams, the guardsmen were issued new uniforms: two pairs of khaki pants, two shirts, two suits of underwear, four pairs of socks, two pairs of shoes, one pair of leggings, one blouse, and a hat. All received a thorough physical examination. The regiment was nearly eight hundred men under strength when called to federal service, and the examining doctors dropped even more from the rolls. When the examinations were over, the First Infantry Regiment of the Oklahoma National Guard mustered only 924 effectives, far short of its normal 1,850 table of organization strength.[39]

As a result, there was some delay in sending the Oklahoma guardsmen to the border until replacements could be found. Refusing to waste any time, during the period between muster and the movement south, Hoffman sent the troops through a grueling routine of training. Once the men were ready, another delay resulted from a shortage of sleeping cars furnished by the railroad. Eventually, however, Company A of Clinton, Company B of Chandler, Company D of Newkirk, Company E of Pawnee, Company G of Wewoka, Company H of Durant, Company I of Stillwater, Company K of Enid, Company M of Oklahoma City, and a troop of cavalry from Okemah were ordered to southern Texas. In addition, several support units, including the field hospital stationed at Oklahoma City, the ambulance corps from Tulsa, and the regimental infirmary station at Dustin, boarded three troop trains for southern Texas on 19 July 1916. The regiment's engineers, stationed at Norman, remained at Fort Sill for nearly another month for reequipment before being ordered south on 13 August.[40]

The National Guard troops were deployed in a broad swath along and behind the Mexican border from Brownsville, Texas, to Yuma, Arizona. The First Oklahoma Infantry was stationed at San Benito, Texas, northwest of Brownsville, and the cavalry was bivouacked a few more miles up the Rio Grande at Donna. Regular army troops actually manned the border posts and were intended as the first line of defense against across-the-border raiders. The guardsmen were utilized as a second line of defense and as a reserve in case any crossing was attempted in force.[41]

It was the middle of the summer and the weather was hot but rainy. Some of the Oklahoma units were swept by a severe storm in mid-August, and the bad weather caused a lot of grumbling among the men, who spent more time battling the elements than Mexican bandits. To add to the boredom, the First Oklahoma Infantry Regiment was quarantined shortly after its arrival at the border when one man became ill with measles. Denied any contact with those outside their camp, the Oklahomans settled down to a monotonous routine until the quarantine was lifted. A part of Wilson's policy of "watchful waiting," the guardsmen's duty became a thankless, dirty task.[42]

Hoffman refused to be discouraged, however, and utilized the time for training and conditioning, both would be useful should war break out between the United States and Mexico. The national guardsmen established semipermanent tent cities, and made themselves as comfortable as possible, considering the heat, the insects, the scorpions, and the rain. Miles of sandbag fortifications were built, hundreds of listening posts were manned, and countless miles were covered by patrols. The men shot craps, tossed one another in blankets, and visited the nearby towns for whatever amusements they offered, but the dreary routine dragged on.[43]

In August of 1916 the Oklahomans were joined with troops from Louisiana and South Dakota to form a brigade for a series of war games. The Oklahoma guardsmen were given the task of defending San Benito against an assault from two regiments of infantry from the Virginia National Guard. Deployed to bear the brunt of the attack, with the regiments from Louisiana and South Dakota held in reserve, the Oklahomans beat back the Virginia assault; then, joined by the South Dakota and Louisiana troops, they counterattacked. As the Oklahoma guardsmen took the offensive, heavy rains forced a halt to the maneuvers.[44]

In autumn that year, the Oklahoma cavalry troops moved closer to the international boundary and took over part of the border patrol duty. A few suspected Villistas were captured and turned over to the proper authorities during these routine patrols. During the night of 16-17 October, one patrol crossed the border in hot pursuit of a group of Mexican raiders who had just attacked an American ranch. The raiders fled across the Rio Grande with the Oklahomans close behind, but the Villistas were more familiar with the terrain. When it became obvious that their jaded mounts would be unable to overtake the raiders, the Oklahomans returned to United States territory. This was the only time that members of the Oklahoma National Guard officially entered Mexico.[45]

Probably the only other incident in which members of the Oklahoma guardsmen came under fire during the border duty was when Company M was sent to the Rio Grande to guard a large water-pumping station on the American side of the river. The Mexicans had emplaced several artillery pieces and machine guns that threatened the facility from their side of the boundary, and the Oklahomans were ordered to protect it from damage. On one occasion the guardsmen were fired upon, either by Mexican troops or bandits. Reinforcements were hurried to the scene and the firing ceased.[46]

While the Oklahoma guardsmen patrolled the border, Pershing continued his unsuccessful pursuit for Pancho Villa deep inside Mexico. The crafty Mexican apparently vanished into the vastness of northern Mexico without a trace. Although several skirmishes were fought between the Americans and the Villistas, the majority of Villa's men easily evaded the American patrols. In the meantime, it appeared that the presence of such a large body of American troops was having little, if any, effect on the outcome of the Mexican struggle. Although an American victory over Villa would greatly increase his own power, Carranza continued to oppose the presence of Pershing's forces in Mexico.[47]

As it became obvious to Wilson that his policy of intervention in Mexico had failed, he began searching for a means to withdraw Pershing's troops. Early in January of 1917, Carranza's men inflicted a stinging defeat upon Villa's forces near Torreon. The defeat was so complete that it appeared Villa's threat to the Mexican-American border was obliterated. On 12 January 1917, Wilson ordered Secretary of War Baker to withdraw the American punitive expedition, and Pershing began leading his men out of Mexico fifteen days later. By 5 February all American troops were north of the Rio Grande.[48]

With the regular army now able to resume the task of patrolling the border, there was no longer any need to maintain such a large force of national guardsmen along the Rio Grande. Rotation of the National Guard units back to state control began soon afterward. The cavalry troops, the engineer company, and the ambulance corps of the Oklahoma National Guard arrived at Fort Sill on 17 February. The remainder of the Oklahoma guardsmen arrived at the post six days later.[49]

Although the crisis with Mexico was cooling, the international situation in Europe was rapidly heating up. On 31 January 1917, the German ambassador to the United States had informed Wilson that his government was resuming unrestricted submarine warfare. Wilson's reaction was to break diplomatic relations with Germany on 3 February. Relations between the two countries continued to deteriorate, and on 25 February, United States officials received copies of a message between the German minister of foreign affairs, Arthur Zimmermann, and the German minister at Mexico City, Heinrich von Eckhardt. In essence, Zimmermann proposed an alliance with Mexico in the event of war with the United States. Wilson was outraged, and war with Germany seemed closer than ever.[50]

The tense international situation complicated the status of the National Guard units that had served on the Mexican border. Some speculated that the troops would be retained on active duty because of the impending conflict with Germany. After the Oklahomans' arrival at Fort Sill, however, they were told to prepare to turn in their equipment and return to their home armories. The troops remained at the post for two weeks before boarding trains for the trip home.

On 1-2 March the Oklahoma guardsmen were mustered out at Oklahoma City.[51]

Most of the men were glad to get home. Their experience in the military had not been what they anticipated. Instead of chasing bandits, they had trained and drilled. Although the duty on the Mexican border had not been as exciting as they had imagined, it had been excellent training. That training would be of use, for within a few weeks the men and officers of the Oklahoma National Guard would be recalled for service in France.[52]

CHAPTER 3

WORLD WAR I:
THE THIRTY-SIXTH DIVISION

On 31 March 1917, barely twenty-nine days after being released from duty on the Mexican border, the infantry regiment of the Oklahoma National Guard was ordered back into federal service by President Wilson. War had not yet been declared between the United States and Germany, but each day seemed to bring the two countries closer to the brink. Wilson bitterly opposed the unrestricted use of submarines by the Imperial German Navy, and the German announcement of 31 January 1917, lifting the restrictions on its underseas fleet, caused grave concern in Washington. This was followed in late February with the release of the infamous Zimmermann note offering an alliance between Mexico and Germany in the event of war between Germany and the United States.[1]

As the tensions heightened, three American ships were sunk without warning during the first eighteen days of March, 1917, and Wilson began to prepare for war. He ordered the National Guard back into federal service at the end of March. Three days later, on 2 April 1917, he asked Congress to declare war against Germany. Congress promptly complied with a joint resolution that was passed in the House of Representatives on 4 April and in the Senate on 6 April. Wilson added his signature that same day. Later, on 7 December 1917, the United States declared war against Austria-Hungary, one of Germany's allies.[2]

Among the first National Guard regiments to answer Wilson's call, the First Oklahoma Infantry completed its mobilization at Fort Sill on 4 April 1917, under the command of Colonel Roy V. Hoffman. The unit remained at Fort Sill for five months while recruiting parties canvassed

the state in an effort to bring the regiment to full strength. During this interval, Hoffman maintained a rigid training schedule, concentrating on trench warfare, target practice, and physical conditioning in preparation for duty on Europe's western front.[3]

Most of the troops believed that the Oklahoma unit would be incorporated into the Forty-second Division, also called the Rainbow Division. The rumor was given more credibility when three companies of engineers were recruited from the state for duty with the Forty-second. On 30 August, though, the Oklahoma guardsmen boarded trains for Camp Bowie, Texas, to become a part of the Thirty-sixth National Guard Division.[4]

Camp Bowie, near Fort Worth, had just opened and was a camp in name only. Most of the training facilities were uncompleted and there was a severe shortage of equipment and supplies. In fact, so few weapons were available that during the early weeks they were stationed there, Oklahoma guardsmen standing guard duty were armed with clubs. Few, if any, permanent buildings had been constructed, and the troops were housed in tents, many of which lacked floors, stoves, or lights. To make matters worse, many troops were disabled by an outbreak of influenza that swept through the camp.[5]

During this early training period there were several shifts in the unit's command structure and organization. The regiment's original commander, Colonel Hoffman, was promoted to brigadier general, and the command of the infantry regiment was passed to Lieutenant Colonel Elta H. Jayne. The engineers were under Major Frank B. King; the cavalry was led by

Training in dummy trenches to condition the men to the type of fighting they would encounter on the western front in Europe as the United States prepared to enter World War I. *Courtesy Forty-fifth Infantry Division Museum.*

The Oklahoma National Guard training with a three-inch field gun at Camp Bowie, Texas, before leaving for the western front. *Courtesy Forty-fifth Infantry Division Museum.*

Major Donald R. Bonfoey; and the field hospital was commanded by Major Floyd J. Bolend. Because the First Oklahoma Infantry did not have the manpower to qualify as a regiment under the War Department's table of organization, on 15 October 1917 it was combined with the Seventh Texas Infantry to form the 142nd Infantry Regiment of the Thirty-sixth Division. The reorganization also combined Oklahoma's machine gun companies with the machine gun companies of the Third and Fourth Texas Infantry regiments to form the 131st Machine Gun Battalion; created the 111th Engineers from the Oklahoma and Texas Engineer battalions; redesignated the First Squadron of Oklahoma Cavalry into the Horse Section of the 111th Ammunition Train; and incorporated the First Oklahoma Field Hospital Company into the 111th Sanitary Train.[6]

Oklahoma national guardsmen of the Ninetieth Division on the rifle range. *Courtesy Forty-fifth Infantry Division Museum.*

The Oklahomans, in training for the war on the western front, the French-designed Benet-Merce machine gun, first adopted by the United States military in 1910. *Courtesy Forty-fifth Infantry Division Museum.*

As the guardsmen began to receive modern equipment, the 142nd's 1903 Springfield rifles were replaced with the 1917 model, and the automatic riflemen and machine gunners were equipped with French Chauchat automatic rifles and an array of Lewis, Vickers, Colt, and Hotchkiss machine guns. In the fall of 1917 a contingent of British and French officers and enlisted men arrived at Camp Bowie to instruct the troops in the trench tactics of the western front, while several Thirty-sixth Division officers visited France for battle experience. Training continued through the winter and into the spring of 1918, with four thousand draftees being added to the Thirty-sixth Division's rolls.[7]

By that time, it appeared that the stalemate on the western front would be broken, and in anticipation of the conflict developing into a

Some Oklahoma national guardsmen in their Native American dress, at Camp Bowie, Texas, in 1917, shortly before embarking for the western front. *Courtesy Forty-fifth Infantry Division Museum.*

war of maneuvers, the 142nd switched from trench-warfare training to battalion maneuvers in open ground. As their training was completed, an advance party left Camp Bowie for the east coast on 3 July to prepare for the shipment overseas. Within eight days they were followed by the rest of the 142nd. Traveling by train from Camp Bowie, first to Hoboken, New York, and then to Camp Mills, Long Island, the guardsmen were quickly loaded aboard two ships, the *Maui* and the *Rijndam,* and at 1400 on 18 July they sailed for France.[8]

Although it appeared that victory was near on the Continent, at sea the German submarine threat was still very real. The *Maui* was attacked three times during the voyage, and one enemy torpedo narrowly missed its stern. On 30 July the coast of France came into view, and that evening the convoy docked at Saint-Nazaire. Disembarking the following day, the 142nd remained near the port for five days unloading equipment and being reviewed by French officials, including President Raymond Poincare.

Finally, in early August, the troops were herded aboard French boxcars designed to hold forty men or eight horses, and referred to by the men as "A.E.F. Pullmans," for the trip to the Thirteenth Training Area centered around Bar-sur-Aube, which was about a hundred and twenty miles southeast of Paris.[9]

Arriving on 18 August, the guardsmen were distributed among several nearby towns. The regimental headquarters, headquarters company, medical detachment, C Company, and D Company were detached to Biligny; the First Battalion headquarters, A Company, and B Company were billeted at Urvill; the Second Battalion headquarters, supply company, E Company, and F Company were stationed at Couvignon; G and H companies were assigned to Bergeres; the Third Battalion headquarters and L Company were sent to Montmartin; Company I was posted to Le Puits; Company K was at Nuismont; and Company M was at Murville. All of these communities were within twenty kilometers of Bar-sur-Aube.[10]

The men's training was intensified as plans were made to hurl the troops into battle as quickly as possible. The troops were indoctrinated in the use of hand grenades, the newer models of the Browning automatic rifles and machine guns, and march discipline. Several exercises were carried out using live ammunition to acquaint the guardsmen with actual battle conditions, and a special platoon was organized to demonstrate the tactics of advance and maneuver.[11]

As the troops became more battlewise, many of the 142nd's enlisted men were transferred to the Rainbow Division as replacements. The regiment was further weakened when, on 10 September, the 111th Engineers were transferred to the American Army's First Corps. The 111th was hurriedly moved to Frouard, on the north of Nancy near the junction of the Moselle and Meurthe rivers, to support the offensive against the Saint-Mihiel salient. Later the engineers moved into the Argonne Forest and participated in the drive against Sedan. Heavily involved in keeping the Allies' road network open, the engineers were exposed to some of the heaviest fighting. Only one unit, Company D from Tulsa, had the distinction of going through the entire war without a single casualty.[12]

On 23 September, the Thirty-sixth Division was ordered to the front lines. The 142nd was dispatched to an area around Champignuel, where it remained until 4 October before entering Camp Somme Suippes at daybreak the next day. The second day there, the 142nd and 141st regiments, which composed the Seventy-first Brigade, were ordered into the trenches to relieve the Second Division.[13]

By October of 1918, German resistance was beginning to crumble. The French and the Americans were advancing in several sectors, and the Allies were keeping as much pressure on the withdrawing enemy as possible. The Thirty-sixth Division was added to the French Fifth Army to give more weight to the Meuse-Argonne offensive. Originally the offensive plans called for the French to break through the German lines east of Rheims, and for the Americans then to rush through the breech and exploit it. The key to the German defenses in the region was Blanc Mont Ridge, and it was here that some of the bitterest fighting of the campaign took place.[14]

The plan to capture Blanc Mont was simple. Set for 3 October, the attack was to be a pincers movement, with a force of United States Marines assaulting the left flank, a brigade of United States infantry attacking the right flank, and the Thirty-sixth Division, waiting in reserve, holding the center of the line. The attack went smoothly and within a day Blanc Mont Ridge was in American hands. As the fighting progressed, the 142nd Regiment and the rest of the Seventy-first Brigade took over the center of the American line during the night of October 6-7, so that fresh troops could be thrown against the weakened German positions.[15]

In moving to the front, the guardsmen were shocked by the utter desolation wrought by war. "For miles on every side there was no vegetation . . . the entire face of the earth was covered with debris." As one witness described the scene: "Mines had added their fury to the exploding shells, upheaving the ground in all directions . . . [and the] Trees had been shot away until until they were only jagged stumps sticking out of the mangled soil." Captain Ben H. Chastaine recalled that in making their way to the trenches, the men were

in and out among the barbed wire entanglements and maze of trenches which had been occupied but a short time before by the opposing forces. Thickly scattered through all parts of the former lines were "dud" shells of all calibers. Some of these were almost as large as a man and all were avoided carefully. They had been known to explode with but a slight jar after remaining in exposed positions. Here and there were the graves of both French and German dead. In that part of the field which had been "no man's land" for a long time, these graves were particularly noticeable, the dead having been buried in the night where they had fallen.[16]

To exploit the enemy's weaknesses created by earlier French and American assaults, on 7 October the Thirty-sixth Division was ordered to prepare to cross the northern slope of Blanc Mont and attack the German line that was east of Saint-Étienne-a-Arnes. At 0745 of that day, a warning order was issued to the 142nd Regiment and the other units of the Seventy-first Brigade to prepare to attack on the north toward Machault. A heavy artillery barrage was ordered, and tanks were supplied for support of the troops.[17]

German trenches in the cemetery at Saint-Étienne. During the battle for Mont Blanc, many guardsmen of the 142nd Infantry Regiment were injured by enemy machine guns firing from these trenches. *Courtesy Forty-fifty Infantry Division Museum.*

The offensive was scheduled for 0515 (5:15 A.M.) on 8 October, with the Second Battalion, composed of two companies each of Oklahoma and Texas national guardsmen, designated as the assault battalion. Companies H and G were in the first wave, and Companies E and F were in the second wave of attacking troops. After the artillery barrage, the men "went over the top" of Hill 140 in the face of heavy German machine gun and artillery fire. The northern slope of Blanc Mont was covered with trees and undergrowth that offered some cover to the advancing Americans. Once they neared the edge of Saint-Étienne and the Arnes River, however, the cover disappeared and the air was filled with "whizzing, whistling, screaming, bursting instruments of death."[18]

The 142nd's chaplain, C. H. Barnes, recorded the episode. The men moved "slowly, steadily forward into barbwire [*sic*] entanglements . . . [with] cannon . . . booming, huge shells scream-ing, . . . high explosives bursting, shrapnel whiz-zing, . . . snipers firing, . . . machine guns click, click, click, click, doing their deadly work while the air is filled with gas." The fighting, which "drove some men mad" continued for three days and nights. "Death lurked on all sides and the

field was strewn with dead." Some of the Amer-icans "literally were mowed down by fire."[19]

The national guardsmen rushed forward along a sunken road, in groups "that ran and fell and rose to advance again." The hand-to-hand fight-ing was fierce, but by early afternoon the Okla-homans had reached a small stream to the east of Saint-Étienne. Seriously short of ammunition and with their water supplies practically ex-hausted, the guardsmen threw back a heavy Ger-man counterattack. Still in control of the stream-bed as evening began to fall, the Americans hurriedly consolidated their positions.[20]

Two Oklahomans, Corporal Harold L. Turner of Company F, who had enlisted at Seminole, and Sergeant Samuel H. Sampler of Company H from Mangum, each received the Medal of Honor for their actions on Hill 140. Second in command of a platoon, which he helped orga-nize from a detachment of signal corps, bat-talion scouts, and runners, Turner led the men forward through heavy German resistance. The enemy's machine gun fire was so intense that Turner's platoon was soon reduced to only four effective personnel. Enraged at seeing his men helpless and dying, Turner rushed across twenty-five yards of exposed ground with a fixed bayonet, captured the German position, and seized fifty enemy soldiers and four machine guns.[21]

Sampler, a corporal at the time his company assaulted Hill 140, was with a group of men who had been pinned down by enemy machine guns. As the Americans began taking severe casualties, Sampler located the German gun. Rushing the enemy positions with hand grenades, he silenced the weapon, captured twenty-eight German soldiers, and allowed his company to resume the assault.[22]

It was night before the men were able to rest and eat their "Corn Willie" (canned corned beef) and hardtack. So many men had fallen in the fighting that none could be spared to bring fresh water from the rear, and the guardsmen had to make do with what was left in their canteens. Enemy artillery fire and the work of strengthening their positions kept the men awake most of the night. By 1030 the next morning, the fight had begun anew with a heavy shelling by the Germans. During the night, reinforcements from the Seventy-second Brigade and the Thirty-sixth Infantry entered the lines and relieved the 142nd. It was not until 10 October that Saint-Étienne was entered.[23]

By morning of 11 October, it became apparent that the Germans were withdrawing, but the price of victory was high. Of the 91 officers and 2,333 men in the 142nd Infantry on the morning of 7 October, only 53 officers and 1,690 men were still available for duty four days later. Taking advantage of the lull in the fighting, the Seventy-first Brigade reorganized, but because of the heavy losses the battalions were reduced "to the size of a full company while regiments were only slightly larger than full strength battalions."[24]

On 13 October all units of the Thirty-sixth Division were poised along the south bank of the Aisne River. For the next week most of the division prepared for an assault crossing, while others maintained contact with the enemy by means of extensive patrols on the north bank. Before the attack could take place, however, the Thirty-sixth was transferred. During the night of 20-21 October, it was moved to the Ninth French Corps, where it relieved the Seventh French Division. Once again, preparations were made for an attack on the far bank of the Aisne, but when the French pulled their troops out of the line the assault became impractical.

Turning their sector over to the Sixty-first French Division, the Americans were sent to the rear to prepare for an attack against the Ferme Forest.[25]

At Rilly-aux-Oies, the Aisne River made a large horseshoe curve, and along the south bank of the horseshoe was the Ferme Forest. Earlier, the French Seventy-third Division had attempted to take the German positions and had been brutally repulsed. Now the task fell to the Thirty-sixth Division.[26]

The Germans were positioned across the opening of the horseshoe and had strengthened their positions with cleverly placed wire entanglements, strongpoints, and machine gun emplacements. The Americans would have to attack directly at the German strongpoints across a wide stretch of unprotected terrain. The assault would not be an easy one.[27]

The Seventy-first Brigade was to attack with two infantry regiments abreast—the 142nd on the right and the 141st on the left. Preceding the assault was to be a twenty-minute standing artillery barrage. Then, to cover the infantry, there would be a rolling artillery barrage advancing a hundred yards every three minutes. The Third Battalion of the 142nd Infantry was to be the assault unit. The attack was scheduled for 27 October 1918.[28]

In the early morning hours, the men moved into advance positions, and at 0410 the artillery barrage began. Twenty minutes later the full attack was under way, with the men following as closely as possible behind the rolling barrage. The shellfire kept the Germans pinned down, and there was little opposition except for the wire entanglements. The Americans were in the enemy trenches before the Germans emerged from their shelters, and with the barrage preventing any counterattack, the men reached the objective and consolidated the position.[29]

During the assault the Americans uncovered many German communication lines. Suspicious as to why the enemy would leave them in such an exposed area, Colonel A. W. Bloor, the commander of the 142nd Infantry, reasoned that they had been left behind deliberately. The Germans, he thought, hoped that the Americans would tap into the lines for their own communication network. They, in turn, would be able to monitor the American conversations.[30]

Colonel Bloor was correct, and although the Americans utilized the captured enemy telephone lines for their own communications system, Bloor prevented any leak of information by using Choctaw members of Company E to transmit messages in their Indian dialect. The tactic was a resounding success, and later a captured German officer confessed that his intelligence personnel were completely confused by the Indian language and gained no benefit whatsoever from their wiretaps.[31]

The assault was a complete victory. Of those captured by the Americans, 4 were officers, 5 were noncommissioned officers, and 185 were enlisted men. Thirty-one machine guns and huge supplies of enemy ammunition and equipment were also taken. The assault battalions of the 142nd remained in the captured positions until 28 October, when the sector was turned over to the French and the Americans ordered to the rear. It was not until 3 November that the Oklahoma guardsmen reached the vicinity of Bar-le-Duc, about a hundred and twenty miles east of Paris, where they were attached to the American First Army. The 142nd Infantry was billeted near Loupe-le-Petit. Eight days later the war ended.[32]

On 18 November the Oklahoma guardsmen left Loupe-le-Petit on the long journey home. Ten days later, though, the regimental headquarters was established at Flogny nearly a hundred miles southeast of Paris, where they would spend the next five months. While here, the men who had been sent with the 111th Engineers rejoined the division.[33]

The camp at Flogny was not the best. Billets for the enlisted men were of poor quality, and there was a shortage of equipment, especially boots. The hard campaign and march to the rear had left most men's boots worn out. Good morale was important, so a vigorous training schedule was maintained to keep the men busy, and Company A of the 142nd was cited as the "most proficient in close order drill" of the First Corps. The Oklahoma guardsmen organized a troupe of entertainers to tour the division and put on shows. Schools were established for the men, and several members of the division enrolled in French and English universities. By December, regular leaves were being granted to all personnel wishing to see southern France, England, or Italy. A division football team was formed, with most of the players from Oklahoma and Texas. They had First Army Corps victories, as well as winning the First Army championship. Despite all these efforts to keep them occupied, the men, of course, were anxious to return home.[34]

On 17 May 1919, the national guardsmen entrained for Brest, where two days later they boarded ship. They sailed on 20 May for New York City and arrived on 31 May. The 142nd disembarked at Boston, Massachusetts, and moved into Camp Merritt. Finally, on 8 July, the Oklahoma guardsmen entrained for Camp Bowie and home. The journey carried them through Oklahoma City, where they stayed long enough to parade through the streets. The mustering-out process was completed on 17 July 1919.[35]

The Oklahoma guardsmen had fought in two campaigns: the men of the 142nd Regiment were in the Meuse-Argonne offensive, and the men of the 111th Engineers had fought in the Saint-Mihiel offensive. In twenty-three days of combat, the Thirty-sixth Division had 23 officers and 1,450 men killed and 35 officers and 427 men gassed. Eighty men were listed as missing. The Seventy-first Brigade, of which the Oklahoma National Guard was a part, had borne the brunt of the fighting and had suffered the greatest number of casualties. With these sacrifices, there was pride because the Thirty-sixth Division was credited with capturing a large number of enemy weapons: 3 heavy pieces of artillery, 6 pieces of light artillery, 4 howitzers, 17 trench mortars, 277 machine guns, and large quantities of rifles and small arms.

For their valor under fire, the men of the Thirty-sixth were awarded three Medals of Honor, two of which went to Oklahomans who were in the assault on Saint-Étienne, thirty-nine Distinguished Service Crosses, one Distinguished Service Medal, and several French awards.[36]

The national guardsmen of the Thirty-sixth Division were, however, only a part of Oklahoma's contribution to the war effort. By order of the War Department, the T-O, or Ninetieth Division, of the national army was formed mostly of men from Oklahoma and Texas. These citizen soldiers also saw duty on the western front.[37]

CHAPTER 4

WORLD WAR I:
THE NINETIETH (TEXAS-OKLAHOMA) DIVISION

The National Guard units called to active duty with the regular army were still not enough to supply the manpower needed to field an American Expeditionary Force. To fill the ranks, Congress enacted the Selective Service Act, which was signed into law by President Wilson on 18 May 1917. Little time was wasted in implementing its provisions, and, by 5 June nearly 10 million men had been registered. From these registrants would come the bulk of the national army. By the end of the war, 1,971,000 men had served in the expeditionary force.[1]

The men inducted from Oklahoma and Texas were formed into the Ninetieth, or T-O, Division; the T for Texas and the O for Oklahoma, but the designation was more commonly referred to by the troops as the "Tough 'Ombres." Within the division, the 179th Brigade was designated the Oklahoma Brigade, with its two regiments, the 357th and the 358th, composed of draftees from the Sooner State. The 357th Regiment was mostly the men from western Oklahoma, and the 358th's recruits were from the eastern part of the state. The 180th Brigade, formed by the 359th and 360th regiments, was the division's Texas Brigade, and, like the Oklahoma unit, the 359th's men were from northern and western Texas, and the 360th's troops were from the southern and eastern parts of the state. As often as possible, these geographical divisions were used in determining individual assignments. Recruits from both Oklahoma and Texas were used to fill out the 165th Field Artillery, the 315th Engineers, and the 315th Signal Battalion.[2]

Commanding the 179th Brigade was Brigadier General J. P. ("Patsy") O'Neil. The 357th Infantry was led by Colonel Edward T. Hartmann, and the 358th Infantry was commanded by Colonel Edward C. Carey. Prior to shipping overseas, however, Carey was replaced by Colonel Edmond M. Leary. Most of the division's senior officers were regular army, but nearly all of the junior officers were Texans who had completed Officers' Training Camp.[3]

The division, commanded by Major General Henry T. Allen, was officially created at Camp Travis, Texas, on 25 August 1917. One of sixteen national army cantonments, the post adjoined Fort Sam Houston, which was northeast of San Antonio in the south-central part of the state. The first recruits arrived from Texas on 5 September, but by 3 October men from Oklahoma were pouring into the post. Between 19 and 24 September, 18,400 men reported for duty, and the next month, between 3 and 8 October, the division received another 10,000 troops.[4]

Told not to bring any unnecessary clothing, many of the draftees from small towns reported for duty wearing only their "heavy boots on sockless feet and the all-embracing blue overalls," with a toothbrush rounding out their baggage. Others arrived with huge steamer trunks filled with clothes. Training began almost immediately in the sandy, mesquite-covered area around the post. To relieve a serious shortage of noncommissioned officers, many NCOs were selected from the recruits. The cadre that was assigned was furnished by the regular army and most of them were barely out of training themselves. To complicate matters, just as the promising NCOs were prepared for duty, many were transferred to other units, and in early January of 1918 many of the Ninetieth's NCOs were sent to Officers' Training Camp.[5]

While the enlisted men were undergoing basic training, the division's officers were attending a multitude of trench warfare schools to prepare them for duty on the western front. Experienced British and French officers were brought to the United States and some were assigned to the unit to indoctrinate the Americans. In turn, several Ninetieth Division officers visited the front in France to gain firsthand knowledge. Classes were held for the trainee officers in gas defense, communications, physical exercise, French, hygiene, sanitation, and the training of enlisted personnel.[6]

By the second week of January, 1918, the training program at Camp Travis was well under way. As the training period neared its end, however, the Ninetieth Division was stripped of its best NCOs and officers to fill out National Guard and regular army units preparing to leave for France. The majority of these transfers occurred on 25 March, with some of the men being sent to Camp Doniphan, Oklahoma, some to other posts in the United States, and some sent directly to a port of embarkation. In order to rebuild the roster, several contingents of draftees from Illinois, Minnesota, North Dakota, and South Dakota arrived in April of 1918.[7]

Once again, the military training cycle began to bring the new recruits up to fighting standards. Officers and men alike worked around the clock. Most holidays were ignored, and Sunday training was implemented to get the draftees ready for combat. It was not uncommon for the men to be loaded onto trucks and hauled to the rifle range, there to spend fifteen hours firing their weapons, and then to be trucked back to their barracks in time to go to bed for the night. This hectic pace paid off, and by 5 June 1918, the division was ordered to Camp Mills, Long Island, New York, for shipment overseas.[8]

The division's advance party departed for England on 14 June, and by 6 July all remaining troops had boarded ships and sailed. Some of the men were fortunate and were assigned to government commandeered luxury liners such as the *Olympic;* however, most of them were crowded aboard the many small steamers that had been pressed into wartime service. Although there were several attacks by German submarines, no ships were sunk nor lives lost in the crossing. Some of the men were landed in France, but most disembarked at either Liver-

pool or Southampton in England before being shuttled across the English Channel.[9]

Once in France, the men were herded aboard the infamous French boxcars for a thirty-hour journey to either Recey-sur-Ource or Latrecey, where they were billeted. The divisional headquarters was at Alais, and the training area was about one hundred fifty miles southeast of Paris and north of Dijon on a plateau in the Cote-d'Or Mountains, which were between the Seine and Saone rivers. The headquarters of the Oklahoma Brigade—the 179th—and one battalion each of the 357th and 358th Infantry regiments arrived in the training area on 2 July. The brigade headquarters and the 357th Infantry were billeted at Aignay-le-Duc, while the 358th Infantry headquarters was at Minot.[10]

The Ninetieth Division was at the training area for five weeks as every attempt was made to complete its preparation for battle. The stateside training period had been so brief that many of the troops had not even mastered close order drill; thus eight hours each day was devoted to drill, bayonet training, trench warfare, rifle practice, and tactics. The problem was compounded by the absence of many officers who were attending indoctrination schools. To help relieve the situation, a group of newly commissioned second lieutenants from the Officers' Training Camp that had been established in France was assigned to the division. In addition, several French officers were attached to the division to assist the preparations for trench warfare.[11]

The training ended on 15 August 1918, when the Ninetieth Division was ordered to replace the First Division at the front lines north of Toul along the Moselle River. The men were transported in trains specifically designed to carry a full battalion and its equipment. The trains were composed of seventeen boxcars, thirty flatcars, one passenger coach for the officers, and two service cars.[12]

General O'Neil and the Oklahoma Brigade entered the trenches near Martincout. The 358th Infantry Regiment relieved the Sixteenth Infantry, and the 357th Regiment replaced the Twenty-eighth Regiment. One battalion of each regiment took positions in the front lines, while a second battalion occupied a position about four kilometers to the rear. The third battalion waited in reserve. The Third Battalion of the

357th was the first to enter the lines and was in position shortly after 0100 on 22 August. That same night the Oklahomans in the Third Battalion of the 357th and in the First Battalion of the 358th marched into the trenches. The Third Battalion of the Texas 359th was held in reserve at Villey Saint-Étienne. In total, the division was responsible for nine kilometers of the front.[13]

Most members of the T-O Division realized that their arrival in the trenches was the forerunner of the long-promised "big American push" to break the stalemate on the western front and end the war. Wisely, in order not to arouse German suspicions, this part of the line was kept quiet. Only normal activity was allowed.[14]

Nightly, each regiment dispatched a patrol across the no man's land to locate enemy outposts to their front. In addition to gathering intelligence, these patrols helped to acquaint the men in them with the terrain over which they were expected to advance. These nightly excursions often entailed scattered clashes with the enemy. In one such instance, on the night of 10 September, Corporal William R. Ball and Private Andy Keeton of G Company, 357th Infantry, who had been separated from their patrol, happened upon fifty enemy soldiers. During the ensuing fire fight, the Americans not only held off the Germans but killed eight of them. Ball and Keeton were each awarded the Distinguished Service Cross for their actions.[15]

Preparations for the massive attack proceeded with frenzy. Artillery, tanks, and supply dumps were moved forward. Huge 9.2-inch guns were hauled into camouflaged positions. Horse-drawn and motorized transports crowded the roads. Slowing the preparations was an almost constant rainfall that made it extremely difficult for the drivers to keep the vehicles on the slick muddy roads in the dead of night when no lights were allowed.

For more than a week preceding the attack, patrols had laboriously cut paths through the enemy's wire entanglements. During the final nights before the attack, men were sent forward to some old French trenches in no man's land to prepare the fortifications for use as a jumping-off point. The work had to be done quietly with nothing left exposed to enemy observers, for

Some of the German trenches encountered in the Saint-Mihiel offensive were very elaborate. This one was lined with stone and camouflaged with branches. *Courtesy Forty-fifth Infantry Division Museum.*

such preparations could only be interpreted as a forthcoming attack. Finally, on 11 September, the infantry moved to the jumping-off positions.[16]

The Saint-Mihiel offensive was the first carried out by an American army under the separate and independent control of the American commander in chief. It was designed to remove the Saint-Mihiel salient, a German bulge in the western front that threatened the eastern flank of the Allied fortifications at Verdun and which had cut the important double-track Verdun-Toul-Belfort Railroad. Removal of the salient also would strengthen the American lines and would prepare the way for future offensive operations.[17]

It would not be an easy task, for the Germans had heavily fortified their positions. Two enemy-occupied hills—Loupmont and Montsec—provided them excellent observation posts and natural defensive obstacles. In addition, two strong German positions had been built across the base of the salient. These had been strengthened by elaborate trench systems, barbed-wire entanglements, bomb-proof shelters, and machine gun positions. The French already had tried to reduce the salient and failed. Now the Americans would try.[18]

The Ninetieth Division was a part of the American First Corps, which together with the Fourth Corps, was to attack the south side of the salient. The five divisions of First Corps were deployed with the Ninetieth on the right, the Fifth in the center, the Second on the left, the Eighty-second holding the front, and the Seventy-eighth in reserve. Within the Ninetieth Division, each brigade was to fight side by side, and within each brigade the regiments were placed side by side. While the 180th (Texas) Brigade held the right flank, the Oklahomans of the 179th Brigade were to attack. Preceding the assault was to be a four-hour barrage of artillery followed by a creeping barrage by eighteen batteries of French and American 75-mm. guns. Designed to provide cover for the attacking Americans, the creeping barrage was to advance one hundred meters every four minutes. Unfortunately, this rate proved too fast for the men to maintain as they struggled across the pockmarked battlefield.[19]

At 0500, 12 September 1918, the irregular bombardment by Allied guns was replaced by the regular, rhythmic roll of the creeping barrage. At that moment the men of the 179th Brigade jumped from their trenches to take their place in a 23-kilometer-long wave of advancing Americans. Both flanks of the assault moved forward rapidly with the 357th Infantry reaching its objective in record time. Unfortunately, the center of the line, occupied by the Third Battalion of the 358th Infantry, was hindered by rough terrain and strong German positions. The Second Battalion of the 358th Infantry suffered the heaviest losses in the assault during its advance through the wooded terrain. The Germans had stationed snipers throughout the area, and the advance began to slow. Many of the Oklahomans were experienced squirrel hunters,

though, and the American sharpshooters quickly silenced the snipers. Two Oklahomans distinguished themselves in the fighting. Corporal Wilbur S. Light of Oklahoma City shot three Germans out of the trees and three others on the ground, and Private Joseph A. Buffalo of Big Cabin silenced a number of enemy snipers. Both were awarded the Distinguished Service Cross.[20]

By 1400 the Americans had reached the first day's objectives and were mopping up enemy resistance. There was little time to rest because work was begun almost immediately to establish defensive positions to resist a German counterattack. The following morning the Third Battalion of the 357th Infantry moved through the lines to renew the assault. Almost immediately the men encountered a strong German force massing for an attack on the new American positions. The American assault upset the enemy's plans, however, and the Allies remained on the offensive.[21]

By the morning of 14 September, it was apparent that the Germans were abandoning the salient and were withdrawing in force toward the Hindenburg Line. Seizing the opportunity, General O'Neil hurriedly ordered the 179th to attack. Two battalions from each regiment were committed to the assault, but before the attack started First Corps' headquarters ordered that only a strong reconnaissance be pushed forward to the Hindenburg fortifications. Although some units of the 357th Infantry succeeded in crossing the valley and gaining the woods on the other side, they were ordered to withdraw to the previous night's positions. It was not until the afternoon of 15 September that the Second Battalion, 357th Infantry, resumed the advance and reoccupied the woods against little opposition.[22]

On 16 September, the Ninetieth Division began to probe the Hindenburg Line in earnest. At the same time, the division's defensive positions were strengthened. Twice in the following days the T-O's sector was widened. During the night of 16-17 September, all the territory on the right flank to the Moselle River was taken over from the Eighty-second Division, and on 4 October the Seventy-eighth Division was withdrawn from the left flank and its sector absorbed by the Ninetieth and Eighty-ninth divisions.[23]

Throughout this period of stabilization, patrols constantly probed at the enemy. In return the Germans would often shell the American lines. Enemy gas shells were a major problem. On 2 October, the Second Battalion of the 357th Infantry was struck hard with mustard gas. The "effects . . . were horrible beyond description." Some of the troops were "blinded for life," and others were "disfigured by the effects of the acid on parts of the skin which the liquid had touched." Nearly every man was weakened by the gas, and three hundred troops were rendered ineffective.[24]

On the night of September 23-24, the First Battalion raided the German lines and returned with five prisoners and valuable intelligence. Another raid scheduled for two days later, during the night of September 25-26, was not so successful. Timed to coincide with the launching of the Meuse-Argonne offensive east of Verdun, the 179th Brigade sent five hundred men into no man's land. Unfortunately, the Germans had apparently learned of the plan, and the Americans were met with heavy artillery and machine gun fire and were attacked by a large enemy patrol.[25]

Although the Americans succeeded in probing the enemy defenses before returning to their own lines, every company officer of the 357th Infantry that participated in the raid was a casualty. In retaliation for the attack, the Germans heavily shelled the Americans with gas, and some of the trenches became so saturated with mustard gas that they had to be abandoned. The raid did, however, succeed in convincing the enemy that an attack was forthcoming from the Ninetieth Division, and thereby tied down many German troops that otherwise would have been shifted to the Meuse-Argonne front.[26]

Between 8 and 10 October, the Ninetieth Division was relieved by the Seventh Division and pulled back to almost the same staging area it had occupied before the Saint-Mihiel offensive. The men were not withdrawn for a rest but for operations along the Meuse River. A week later the division was moved to the Blercourt area, about twelve miles east of Verdun, and assigned to the Third Army Reserve.[27]

The American offensive along the Meuse was part of a new Allied policy of "no more quiet fronts." Instead, the Germans would be attacked "from the North Sea to Asia Minor" in an effort to crack their lines, to initiate a war of movement, and to end the war. The 357th Infantry was spread out along the main line of resistance between Nantillois and Drillancourt, while the 358th Infantry occupied the second line of resistance. This placed the 179th Brigade in a position for either defensive or offensive operations. Throughout the Meuse-Argonne offensive the Ninetieth Division continually moved forward to serve as a reserve for the various attacking units. Finally, during the night of 21-22 October, the division reentered the front-line trenches.[28]

The 179th Brigade relieved the Tenth Brigade of the Fifth Division, with the 357th replacing the Sixth Infantry and the 358th occupying the positions of the Eleventh Infantry. Enemy artillery fire was severe during the rotation of units, but the transfers were accomplished without unnecessary casualties. The Ninetieth Division had the Eighty-ninth Division on its left, and the Third Division, later relieved by the Fifth, on its right. To the front was a German strongpoint between Bois des Rappes and Bois de Bantheville. The Oklahomans' first task was to eliminate the enemy pocket and straighten the line.[29]

The 179th Brigade was ordered to the attack, with the First and Third battalions of the 357th Infantry carrying the assault. The attack began at 0300 on 23 October. Bantheville was quickly occupied, but once past the town the Oklahomans came under heavy enemy artillery fire. Even so, the men succeeded in capturing their main objective, Hill 270, which dominated the region.[30]

The following day patrols were sent out to maintain contact with the enemy. At the same time the Germans were pushed off the crest of another nearby ridge. Reacting to the American attack, the Germans retaliated first with a concentration of mustard gas and then with a heavy counterattack. The assault, which began about 0530 on 25 October, was preceded by a heavy, forty-minute artillery barrage before enemy infantry rushed the American positions. The German attack was broken by intense rifle and machine gun fire.[31]

For a week the Third Battalion held its position against furious German assaults, and by the time of the huge Allied offensive scheduled for 1 November 1918, the 179th Brigade was "pretty well spent." One of its battalions had only eight officers remaining, and the other units were just as depleted. Because of this, the task of carrying the division's share of the assault fell to the 180th or Texas Brigade.[32]

The assault began on schedule, with the 180th moving forward against enemy fire. The attack was so successful all along the Allied lines, that by 2 November, the Germans were in full retreat. To maintain pressure on the withdrawing enemy, the Oklahoma Brigade, the 179th, was ordered into the attack on 3 November. At 0800 the men moved forward behind a gas and rolling barrage toward the dense woods on the Halles-Montigny heights. Much to their surprise, the troops entered the woods without being fired upon by the enemy, which had fled. Obviously the Germans were rapidly abandoning their front lines. Seizing the opportunity, General O'Neil ordered the 357th to cross the Meuse River at Sassey and the 358th to advance toward Stenay; however, higher headquarters rescinded the order and commanded the Ninetieth Division to hold its troops on the heights at Halles-Montigny.[33]

It was nearly a week later before the T-O Division was ordered to cross the Meuse River in pursuit of the enemy. Quickly preparations were made for an assault crossing, and the infantry and artillery moved into advance positions. Active patrolling was maintained up and down the stream as the Americans probed the enemy fortifications on the other side for weak points. Finally at 0400 on 9 November, the Oklahoma Brigade moved out as the division's advance guard. The 358th Infantry was to seize Stenay, while the 357th assaulted the wooded area called Bois du Chenois.[34]

The First Battalion, 179th Infantry, started across the Meuse bridge at Sassey at 0500. Almost at the same time, the troops received word that the kaiser had abdicated. Although it appeared that the war would soon be over, the fighting of 10 November was "both severe and costly." The German High Command realized the importance of the Ninetieth Division's sector and was determined to oppose its advance bitterly. As a result, probably "no other division in the Expeditionary Forces met with such stubborn resistance during the last hours preceding the cessation of hostilities." It was not until the morning of 11 November 1918 that the Germans abandoned the town.[35]

At 0720 that same day, the Ninetieth Division's headquarters was informed that "hostilities will cease along the whole front at 11[00] hours on November 11, 1918, Paris time." The war was over. The last man killed in the division was a mechanic, Carl Sheffield, of Company B, 360th Infantry, who was struck by German shellfire at 1030, only thirty minutes before the official end of the fighting.[36]

Although the armistice had taken effect, the division remained on the alert should renewed fighting break out. According to the terms of the cease-fire, several detachments of the Ninetieth Division began to gather enemy war materials. Between 16 and 21 November, the division was a part of the American Fifth Corps, but on 21 November it was assigned to Seventh Corps. The following day it passed to control of the Third Army.[37]

Unhindered by enemy activity, the Allied armies began moving toward the Rhine River. On 24 November, the Ninetieth Division started for the enemy's homeland, and on 6 December the 180th Brigade crossed the Moselle River at Remich and entered Germany. The 179th Brigade followed the next day.[38]

Now a part of the Army of Occupation, the Ninetieth Division took up positions near Berncastle, with the Oklahomans of the 357th and 358th regiments headquartered at Hillesheim and Gerolstein, respectively. Efforts were made to secure a bed for every man, and indeed every trooper at least received a bunk with a bed-sack of clean straw. A total of 110 towns were occupied by divisional troops in an area 74 kilometers from the Rhine along the Moselle Valley.[39]

The only active military duty during this period of the occupation was guarding railroad stations, bridges, and other sensitive points along the railroad. Otherwise, most of the troops' time was spent in training, interior guard, and routine duties. Within a short time the division began to stand down. A divisional football team was fielded, and both elementary and secondary schools were opened. Vocational training also was available. Several officers and enlisted men attended French and English universities as well as the A.E.F. University, and a liberal pass policy was initiated to allow the men to visit parts of the Continent and England.[40]

On 29 April 1919, General Pershing inspected

the division for the final time near Wengerohr. The fifth American division to sail for home, the Ninetieth Division departed Germany by train between 17 and 22 May for Saint-Nazaire, France. By 25 May all troops had reached the port of embarkation, and the first units sailed the next day. Throughout the ensuing weeks the remainder of the men departed for New York City; Boston, Massachusetts; Newport News, Virginia; and Charleston, South Carolina. The last of the troops to reach America landed at Charleston on 15 June. Once back on American soil the men were sent to several posts, including Camp Bowie; Camp Pike, Arkansas; Camp Travis; and Camp Dodge, Texas, to be mustered out.[41]

Throughout its service on the western front the division suffered a total of 37 officers and 1,042 enlisted men killed, 185 officers and 5,928 enlisted men wounded, 81 officers and 2,094 enlisted men gassed, and 7 officers and 336 enlisted men missing. During its tour of duty, the Ninetieth Division captured 32 German officers and 1,844 enlisted men, 25 pieces of heavy artillery, 17 pieces of light artillery, 36 trench mortars, 122 light machine guns, 72 heavy machine guns, and 902 rifles. The men had spent 42 days in quiet sectors and a total of 26 days in active sectors.[42]

The Thirty-Sixth National Guard Division, the T-O Division of the national army, and those Oklahomans in the regular army served with pride during the First World War. Three men from the state were awarded the Medal of Honor during the conflict—two of the recipients came from the Oklahoma National Guard—and many others received lesser decorations from either the United States or other Allied powers. One thousand and forty-six Oklahomans had been killed in battle, another 502 were missing in action, 710 died from disease, and 4,154 were wounded. Now that World War I was over, work began on the formation of a new Forty-fifth National Guard Division within the state, which would become one of the most famous units in the American army.[43]

CHAPTER 5

THE FORTY-FIFTH INFANTRY DIVISION

After the Oklahoma National Guard was incorporated into the Thirty-sixth Infantry Division, the state was left without its allocated infantry regiment. As a temporary replacement, Oklahoma Governor Robert L. Williams authorized the formation of several units of "home guards." Later, in March of 1918, nearly one year after the First Oklahoma Infantry was ordered into federal service, Governor Williams, at the urging of the War Department, ordered the formation of a new National Guard for the state.[1]

Two new regiments of infantry, the Second and the Third, were to be formed as replacements for the First. There were to be eighteen companies, each of one hundred enlisted men, in each regiment. Little time was wasted in organizing the new units, and throughout the spring and summer months of 1918 recruiters were busy across the state. The new regiments were granted federal recognition in late summer of 1918, after passing a regular army inspection. The following year another unit, the First Separate Infantry Battalion, was formed. The First Oklahoma Infantry Regiment was never reorganized after World War I, and the Second and Third regiments, together with the Separate Battalion, formed Oklahoma's National Guard until 1920, when the Forty-fifth Infantry Division, also called the Thunderbird Division, was authorized by Congress.[2]

The National Defense Act of 1920 was to be the bulwark of the nation's National Guard organization for thirty years. The legislation divided the United States into nine army corps areas, with Oklahoma assigned to the Eighth Corps, together with the states of Texas, Colorado, New Mexico, and Arizona. Each corps area was authorized one division of regular army troops, two divisions of national guardsmen, and three reserve divisions. As far as possible, however, the National Guard units were to retain the "names, numbers, flags, and records of the Divisions and subordinate units that served in the World War." Such an organization focused on divisions instead of regiments, and Oklahoma, combined with Arizona, Colorado, and New Mexico, provided the Forty-fifth Infantry Division.[3]

Under the 1920 legislation, the National Guard was made a part of the Army of the United States, which consisted of the regular army, the National Guard, and the organized reserve. The president was authorized to call the National Guard to federal duty in time of national emergency. Once the men were released from active duty, however, they returned to state control and to their former National Guard units. National Guard officers, who had graduated from either the Army War College or the Staff School before 1 July 1917, or who had demonstrated their fitness for General Staff assignment by service before 6 April 1917, were admitted to the General Staff eligibility list. All National Guard policies were to be made by the General Staff, and a Militia Bureau, headed by a National Guard officer with at least ten years of commissioned service as a guardsman, was established within the War Department. The head of the Militia Bureau was given the rank and pay of a major general.[4]

National Guard units had to have a minimum of fifty men, with the original enlistment for three years and subsequent enlistments for one year. Pay for the guardsmen while on field duty

Between the two world wars, Forty-fifth Infantry Division command exercises were often conducted on the Fromme Ranch, about twenty miles from San Antonio, Texas. *Left to right:* Major Albert Tucker, Major John P. Donovan, Captain J. E. Moorhead, Captain B. W. Nolen, and Lieutenant William P. Lively. *Courtesy Forty-fifth Infantry Division Museum.*

was equal to that of regular army troops. Otherwise, their remuneration was to be one-thirteenth the initial monthly pay of the same regular army rank for each drill attended in excess of one and one-half hours. This generally amounted to one dollar per drill for privates; however, during the administration of President Herbert Hoover, the pay was slashed in half, with a private receiving only 50 cents per drill. Even so, most of the men remained with their units, and the pay scale was later revised upward. Captains commanding National Guard units were granted $240 per year in addition to their drill pay as added incentive to be financially responsible for the equipment issued to their troops. Drills were

limited to sixty per year, and the guardsmen were required to attend at least 60 percent of the scheduled drills.[5]

While improving the capabilities of the National Guard, the 1920 legislation imposed a limitation of 17,700 officers and 280,000 men in the regular army. The total nationwide strength of the National Guard, including a large number of reservists to supplement the guardsmen, was pegged at 450,000. Obviously, Congress intended to create a small cadre of highly trained regulars that could swiftly be supplemented with reservists and guardsmen in time of national emergency.[6]

The reorganization of the National Guard under the provisions of the National Defense Act of 1920 was to have far-reaching effects in Oklahoma. Under its provisions, the state's recently formed Second and Third Infantry regiments were reorganized into the 179th and 180th Infantry regiments of the Ninetieth Brigade, Forty-fifth Infantry Division. The division's other brigade, the Eighty-ninth, was formed by the 157th Infantry Regiment from Colorado and the 158th Infantry Regiment from Arizona. Later, New Mexico would contribute one component of the division's artillery—Battery A, 158th Field Artillery Regiment. The First Separate Infantry Battalion was integrated into the two regiments of the Ninetieth Brigade. This was the birth of the state's most renowned military unit—the Forty-fifth Infantry Division, later known as the Thunderbirds.[7]

Between the time the division was organized in 1923 and its call to federal service just before the outbreak of World War II, it had five commanders: Major General Baird H. Markham (15 February 1923 to 6 April 1931), Major General Roy Hoffman (13 June 1931 to 13 June 1933), Major General Alexander M. Tuthill (14 June 1933 to 21 October 1935), and Major General Charles E. McPherren (25 November 1935 to 29 July 1936). The Forty-fifth's last post-World War II commander, Major General William S. Key, led the division during its federalization in 1940 and into the early months of World War II. Key remained divisional commander until 13 October 1942.[8]

For several years after the passage of the 1920 National Defense Act, the nucleus of what became the Forty-fifth Division continued to expand. The Seventieth Field Artillery Brigade was soon added. In 1923 the elements of the 158th Field Artillery, originally composed of the 160th and 189th Field Artillery, were added, along with the 120th Medical Regiment, the 120th Engineer Regiment, the 120th Ordnance Company, the Forty-fifth Signal Company, the Forty-fifth Military Police Company, a veterinary company, and a motor transportation company. Fourteen years later, in 1937, the 120th Quartermaster Regiment was formed from a portion of the motor transportation company. The following year, the veterinary contingent was reorganized into the Second Collecting Company of the 120th Medical Regiment.[9]

Throughout the organizational period, the newly formed units worked hard to achieve federal ranking and to maintain an acceptable training level. Many units, with the cooperation of their local business community, helped finance their own training facilities. Sergeant (later Colonel) John H. McCasland's unit, Company B, 180th Infantry, stationed at Atoka, constructed its own rifle range so the troops could get adequate marksmanship training. The Forty-fifth's training facilities were vastly improved during the Great Depression when Adjutant-General William S. Key, administrator of Oklahoma's Work Projects Administration programs, ordered fifty-two armories constructed across the state.[10]

There was a great feeling of pride among both the guardsmen and the townspeople about the local guard unit. The officers and senior NCOs were usually local civic or business leaders, and the enlisted men were nearly always residents of the community. The closeness between the guardsmen and the local citizenry became one of the great strengths of the National Guard in Oklahoma. Again and again, in times of civil unrest, natural disasters, and man-made catastrophes, the National Guard stepped in to control the situation. Local residents depended upon the guardsmen in time of emergencies, and in return they wholeheartedly supported their guard unit. The same feeling of camaraderie existed in the units, with each man and officer feeling a special loyalty to his unit and to the men with whom he served.[11]

The two-week summer training camps were usually held at Fort Sill, near Lawton, Oklahoma. Jack T. Conn, who in 1926 joined Ada's 160th Field Artillery Band, recalled that the trip, which "is now a two-hour drive . . . took us all night by train." Their uniforms, according to Conn, were "GI shoes, wool wraparound puttees, khaki pants, and dark brown wool shirts . . . topped by a campaign hat," which, because of the nearly constant wind, had to be held on by chin straps. This clothing was appropriate for protection from the cold, but it was completely unsuitable in "the blazing 110° Ft. Sill weather."[12]

One of Conn's most humorous recollections of his duty with the National Guard occurred at Fort Sill. According to Conn, no one had an alarm clock, and the unit's first sergeant, Beucey Lambert, depended on the battery's cooks to wake him up in time to form up the band, which, immediately following reveille at 5:30 A.M., marched down the division's street playing their instruments. One morning, a "very inebriated cook" got Lambert out of bed at 3:00 in the morning instead of the usual 5:30. Falling-in his men, Lambert waited in vain for reveille to be blown. Growing impatient, he led the bandsmen down "Division Row lustily playing 'The Field Artillery Song.'" Unfortunately for Lambert, Colonel (later major general) William S. Key was one of the officers rushing up to see what was happening.[13]

Throughout the 1920s and 1930s, Oklahoma's National Guard was used extensively to quell civil disturbances, to enforce the orders of the chief executive, and to aid in disaster relief across the state. Calling out the militia to implement the executive decisions of the governor began shortly after statehood. Lee Cruce, governor from 1911 to 1915, when faced with the failure of local officials to enforce selective state laws, used the guardsmen to force their compliance and gained the distinction of being the first Oklahoma governor to declare martial law.[14]

A moralist, Cruce was determined to end the state's reputation as "a resort" for prizefighters, bootleggers, and gamblers. Although there were state statutes prohibiting such activities, in several localities little was being done to enforce the laws. After attempting to persuade local officials to clean up their communities, to convince the legislature to tighten the statutes, and to use special enforcement laws, Cruce turned to martial law in his righteous crusade.[15]

To circumvent the law against prizefights, promoters often organized local athletic clubs and then promoted sparring matches between boxers as a demonstration of their skills. These, of course, were nothing but prizefights. When local authorities refused to intervene, Cruce called out the National Guard five times to stop such contests.[16]

The guardsmen also were used to enforce morality when Cruce thought local citizens stepped beyond the law. In March of 1914 the Panhandle and Southwestern Stockmen's Association planned its annual convention for Oklahoma City. Arrangements were made to provide the delegates with a large supply of beer, and

"Queenie," a Chicago stripper, was retained for entertainment. When Cruce learned that the arrangements committee had made preparations for an "open town," he quickly informed the members that he would declare martial law to prevent such an occurrence.[17]

Gambling was another target of Cruce's crusade. Most communities closed their racetracks after the governor's stand became obvious, but several Tulsa racing promoters persisted in scheduling a racing card for April of 1914. After local officials ignored Cruce's warnings, he dispatched Adjutant-General Frank M. Canton to the community. When the races began as scheduled, Canton called out two companies of guardsmen.[18]

The racing association had obtained an injunction from the state supreme court prohibiting the use of troops in stopping the event, but Canton replied, "Governor Cruce is my commander," and announced the races were over. As preparations were made to continue the contest, two guardsmen fired five volleys over the heads of the horses as they stood at the starting line. Canton then told the startled crowd that the next shots would be "to kill." The races were suspended.[19]

Another of Cruce's objectives was compliance with the state's Sabbath law, which prohibited the "useless and serious interruptions of the repose and religious liberty of the community . . . [and] Servile labor" on Sundays. Near the end of his administration, several McAlester citizens organized a Sunday roping contest. Local ministers appealed to Cruce to put a stop to the activity, and the governor responded by sending Canton to McAlester to put an end to the festivities.[20]

In the two decades between the end of World War I and the beginning of World War II, Oklahoma guardsmen were called out frequently to enforce executive authority and to put down civil disturbances.[21]

Their first disturbance duty, a labor riot at Drumright, took place shortly after the end of World War I. There had been an earlier minor confrontation between the International Workers of the World (the IWW or "Wobblies") and local authorities in protest of the World War I draft. Feelings were still running high against the IWW when, on 20 September 1919, the IWW backed a strike by telephone workers in Drumright. The strike quickly turned into a riot.[22]

Jack Ary, the Drumright chief of police, was seized by several strikers. In response, local authorities raised twenty special officers, armed them with Winchesters, and sent them into the streets to restore order. Tempers flared, and the strikers threatened to put the town to the torch. Drumright's mayor fled, fearing for his life, and the county judge appealed to Governor J. B. A. Robertson for troops. A hundred men from companies H, I, M, G, and the supply company of the Second Oklahoma Infantry, and companies B and D of the First Separate Battalion were summoned and hurried to Drumright during the night of 23 September. With their arrival the Wobblies quickly dispersed and order was restored.[23]

Later that same year America was swept by a national coal strike. Most of the state's miners walked off their jobs in support of the strike, and Governor Robertson ordered the National Guard into six southeastern coal-producing counties to preserve order. More than two thousand men from the Second and Third infantries, as well as components of the First Separate Battalion, were stationed at Henryetta, Colgate, and Haileyville to keep the mines operating. The national strike was settled on 10 December 1919, and the guardsmen departed after nearly sixty days of martial law.[24]

Labor trouble continued to plague the state's coal industry. An extended strike took place between 1924 and 1927, in which a large number of strikebreakers were imported in an attempt to crush the labor movement. The length of the walkout taxed even the most fervent labor organizers, and the miners themselves split into contending factions. Twice, once in 1924 and again in 1925, national guardsmen were dispatched to the state's coal-mining region to preserve order.[25]

Although the troops were used extensively to maintain peace between labor and management during the post-World War I era—including the bricklayers' strike of 1920, the packinghouse employees' strike in 1921, and the railroad workers' in 1922—their most difficult task was restoring order following the 1921 Tulsa race riot. The riot was touched off on 31 May by an alleged assault on Sarah Page, a white

elevator operator, by a local black, Dick Rowland. Apparently, Rowland stumbled against Page as he was getting on her elevator in a Tulsa building. When Page screamed, Rowland ran from the building.[26]

Later that day Rowland was arrested for assault, and the next edition of the *Tulsa Tribune* reported the "attack" on its front page. Within a short time of the paper's distribution, a crowd of white men began to gather at the jail and demanded that the police turn Rowland over to them. When word of what was obviously a threatened lynching reached "Little Africa," the black section of north Tulsa, groups of alarmed blacks, some of whom were reported to be armed, gathered near the Tulsa courthouse, where Rowland had been taken for safety. Whites, some of them armed, had already begun to congregate near the jail, and by 3:30 in the afternoon, nearly three hundred had gathered.[27]

As the day wore on, rumors circulated that made the confrontation even more tense. Inflated estimates of the crowd's size further alarmed the officials. Inevitably, a gun was fired and a full-fledged riot was soon under way. Despite efforts by the Tulsa police, assisted by concerned citizens who volunteered to help, officials determined that the militia should be called out and the governor was so notified. When the riot began, the Tulsa units of the National Guard were preparing to leave for their annual summer camp, and Lieutenant Colonel L. J. F. Rooney, of the First Battalion, Third Infantry Regiment, which was based in eastern Oklahoma, had kept state officials informed of the increasing tension.[28]

Robertson received the plea for troops at 0146 (1:46 A.M.) on 1 June, and he immediately ordered Adjutant-General Barrett "to proceed at once with all the troops available, take charge of the situation, and restore peace at all costs." Units from Bartlesville, Muskogee, Oklahoma City, Vinita, and Wagoner were assembled, and a special train prepared to hurry the troops to the riot area. Shortly after 0500 the first troops from Oklahoma City were on their way to Tulsa.[29]

Colonel Rooney was placed in command of the situation until Barrett arrived and, although he immediately positioned his troops around the banks, water works, electric plants, and major downtown businesses, he did not have enough men to control the mob of an estimated 15,000 to 20,000 (later reduced in official reports to 500) white rioters and an estimated 1,000 blacks. Barrett and reinforcements arrived at 0800. Upon his arrival, he reported seeing "trucks, loaded with scared and partially clothed negro men and women . . . parading the streets under heavily armed guards. . . . In all my experience I have never witnessed such scenes," the Adjutant-General remarked. "Twenty-five thousand whites, armed to the teeth were ranging the city in utter and ruthless defiance of every concept of law and righteousness. . . . Motor cars, bristling with guns, swept through . . . [the] city firing at will."[30]

Once the troops arrived, Barrett paraded them through the streets to the Tulsa City Hall where he met with civilian officials. Convinced that local authorities could not control the situation, Barrett asked Governor Robertson to declare martial law. Robertson complied and placed all of Tulsa County under military rule. When the guardsmen took to the streets the fighting had ceased, but Little Africa was in flames. The troops assisted the firemen in controlling the conflagration, and they jailed looters and confiscated weapons. Troops continued to pour into the city throughout the day, and with their presence the situation gradually returned to normal.[31]

On 2 June 1921, Governor Robertson and Attorney General S. Prince Freeling visited the city. After inspecting the troops and examining the situation, Robertson ordered martial law to end the next day. Several Tulsa civic and business leaders protested, but the order stood and all out-of-town troops were withdrawn. Tulsa guardsmen, numbered at 325 men, remained on call until 0900 on 4 June, when they departed for summer camp at Fort Sill.[32]

Within two years the National Guard would be at the center of another confrontation involving Governor Jack C. Walton, the Ku Klux Klan, and the legislature. The KKK's involvement in Oklahoma had increased steadily since the end of World War I, and in the 1922 gubernatorial election the Klan actively supported R. H. Wilson, one of Walton's opponents in the Democratic primary. Walton won the primary and the November general election, and took office in January, 1923.[33]

Although Walton did not immediately challenge the Klan's power, eventually they clashed when the KKK was accused of dragging some young men and women from automobiles near Henryetta and flogging them. Walton responded by declaring martial law in Okmulgee County and ordering Adjutant-General Baird H. Markham and 250 guardsmen into Okmulgee and Henryetta to preserve order. The troops stayed through June and July of 1923 before returning to their homes.[34]

Less than a month later, on 10 August 1923, the Klan reportedly kidnapped Nate Hantaman in Tulsa, took him to a deserted area on the edge of town, and whipped him for two hours. Hantaman's wife telephoned Governor Walton and accused the Tulsa police of being accomplices in the crime. Walton had Hantaman brought to Oklahoma City and launched an investigation into the matter. When it appeared that the police had been involved, Walton issued an ultimatum: arrest Hantaman's assailants within three days or he would declare martial law. When nothing happened by 13 August, the National Guard was ordered into the community.[35]

Walton made no mention of the KKK in his proclamation of martial law, but instructed Markham to convene a military court charged with investigating Klan activities in the region. State newspapers took a dim view of the use of troops, and Walton reacted by censoring the press. On 31 August, the governor suspended the writ of habeas corpus, and the next day martial law was extended throughout Tulsa County. At the same time, an additional two hundred guardsmen were sent to Tulsa.[36]

By 6 September criticism of Walton was widespread. In reaction to it, the governor threatened to place the entire state under martial law. Working quickly, the governor's enemies circulated an initiative petition calling for a special session of the legislature. They had the initiative filed and ruled valid by the State Election Board in time to have it placed on the October 2 ballot. The other issue on the ballot was a soldiers' bonus bill called for in the special election by Walton himself. Fearing that the legislature planned impeachment proceedings against him if the initiative were adopted, Walton fired the members of the State Election Board and appointed another group, with orders that it was to stop the election. This tactic failed when the courts overturned the election board's ruling.[37]

Campbell Russell, who had circulated and filed the initiative petition, now agitated for a grand jury investigation of the governor's actions, and his plea was gaining support. Walton placed the state under martial law on 15 September. Oklahoma County was placed under "absolute martial law," additional guardsmen were ordered to duty, and a large number of special deputies were sworn in. This effectively prevented any grand jury probe of the governor. At the same time, in an attempt to shift criticism to KKK activity, Walton created a special military court in Oklahoma City to investigate the Klan throughout the state.[38]

His attempt failed. There was an immediate backlash to the martial law proclamation, and the clamor for Walton's removal became louder. Although Walton had prevented the convening of a grand jury, several members of the state legislature began impeachment proceedings. While the state constitution allowed the legislature to convene in special session only upon the call of the chief executive, several of the solons, led by William D. McBee, contended that the House of Representatives could convene itself to investigate illegal acts by the governor. By the second week of September, a majority of house members supported Walton's impeachment.[39]

On 20 September 1923, sixty-five members of the house of representatives—eleven more than a majority—announced they would convene at noon on 26 September at the state capitol to begin impeachment proceedings. Walton reacted by calling the gathering an "unlawful Klan assembly," and he ordered the National Guard to prevent the meeting. When the legislators arrived at the capitol, they were ushered out of the building by the military. Although the solons left the capitol, they reassembled briefly on the building's steps before they were again dispersed by the guardsmen.[40]

Both sides now concentrated on the scheduled special election. After the courts ruled in Russell's favor and ordered the initiative petition placed on the ballot, Walton called off the election. George Short, the state attorney general, overruled him, and most county election officials sided with the attorney general. The proposal for a special session passed 209,452 to 70,638. Although Walton made an attempt to persuade the State Election Board not to certify the results, a spokesman for the legislature declared the election valid and announced that the legislature had called a special session to convene on 17 October.[41]

Walton attempted another delaying tactic that involved investigation of the KKK, and the solons agreed to convene, but they thwarted the governor once more by taking up impeachment proceedings against him first. One charge leveled at Walton in the proceedings was alleged abuse of martial law. He was impeached on eleven of the twenty-two counts and removed from office on 19 November.[42]

Although several governors since statehood had utilized the National Guard to enforce executive decisions, the practice reached its peak during the depression-era administration of William A. ("Alfalfa Bill") Murray. During his term in office, from 1931 to 1935, Murray called out the National Guard thirty-four times in an unprecedented display of gubernatorial power. His first use of guardsmen came on 1 May 1931, during a May Day celebration in Henryetta. Several oil companies in the area had reported the loss of nitroglycerine used to shoot oil wells, and many citizens feared that the explosive had been seized by Communists who would use it during the May Day parade. Murray responded by proclaiming martial law over the area and banning Communist activities.[43]

The following year, on 18 November 1932, Murray ordered the National Guard to rescue his friend, Colonel Zack Miller, who was threatened with imprisonment for debt. On 1 March 1933, Murray proclaimed martial law around an Enid bank that had refused to respect his bank moratorium. In May of 1933, Alfalfa Bill used guardsmen to prevent blacks from using Hassman Park in Oklahoma City. On several occasions martial law proclamations were used in at least eleven counties to prevent the sale of homes and farms for nonpayment of taxes. Perhaps Murray's most unusual use of the National Guard was on 30 November 1933, when he declared martial law around Owen Stadium at the University of Oklahoma in Norman. The troops collected tickets for a football game after alleged irregularities were discovered in the school's Athletic Department.[44]

One of Murray's most publicized uses of the

Governor William A. ("Alfalfa Bill") Murray inspecting guardsmen patrolling one of the bridges involved in the "Red River Bridge War." *Courtesy Forty-fifth Infantry Division Museum.*

National Guard was in the so-called Red River "Bridge War" in July of 1931. Forming the boundary between Oklahoma and Texas, the Red River was spanned by a number of toll bridges. To allow the free passage of individuals and commerce, Oklahoma and Texas officials had agreed to underwrite the cost of constructing several free public bridges parallel to the privately owned bridges at Durant, Marietta, and Ringling. By 1931 the bridge connecting Durant with Denison, Texas, had been completed with the exception of the approaches.[45]

At this point one of the toll bridge owners went to court to seek damages under the terms of his contract with Texas. A federal court granted him an injunction, and it appeared that the issue would be in litigation for years. In the meantime, the owners of the private bridges would keep collecting tolls and the public bridges would remain closed. Murray, infuriated by what he believed to be a usurpation of authority by minor federal courts, would not tolerate such interference. In response, on 16 July Murray ordered the free bridges opened. Eight days later he placed the toll bridges and the free bridges under martial law and ordered Adjutant-General Barrett to enforce his decree with troops.[46]

State Highway Department workers hurriedly completed the access roads, and then the guardsmen built barricades to close the toll bridges and direct traffic over the free ones. The bridge companies sought redress from federal marshals, but General Barrett refused to accept the injunction. Murray himself visited the bridges on 25 July, to inspect the troops and ensure that there would be no interference with his orders to "arrest any federal judge, United States marshal or any other official who attempts to take charge of the situation." When Texas Governor Ross Sterling attempted to close the Texas side of the free bridges with Texas Rangers, Murray, pointing out that, according to the Louisiana Purchase Treaty of 1803, Oklahoma's southern boundary was the south bank of the Red River, declared martial law over seventy-five feet of the south end of the bridges and ordered the troops to dismantle the Texas barricades. "You fellows be easy on Mr. Sterling's Rangers. . . . Just . . . give them a light kick in the pants if you have to," Murray told the guardsmen.[47]

By the use of troops, Murray successfully defied the federal courts, closed the toll bridges, and opened the free ones. His opponents had clearly been checkmated. Later, on 6 June 1932, his actions were upheld by the Federal Court of Appeals and later by the United States Supreme Court.[48]

Murray's other use of the National Guard was in the state's oil fields. When the huge Oklahoma City Pool was opened in December of 1928, the first wells were to the south and east of the residential and commercial area of the community. Then the derricks began a relentless march toward the more settled regions. As the wells began to encroach upon residential areas, some Oklahoma City citizens began to cry for protection from the wells, and, on 10 May 1929, the City Council created a special U-7 Zone for oil well drilling.[49]

The regulation seemed to have little effect upon the oilmen, however, as "Derricks, slush pits, and steel and ground tanks invaded industrial and residential areas." The uproar from concerned citizens increased, as oilmen moved into more and more residential areas in the following years. Finally, Murray reacted to the cries of outrage, and, on 5 May 1932, declared martial law over the community and prohibited the drilling outside of U-7 Zones. Characterizing the continued invasion of residential areas by derricks as a "danger to homes and the business section," Murray authorized Adjutant-General Barrett to use troops, if necessary, to enforce the drilling zoning laws. The governor made it

clear that the guardsmen would only be used if violations of the zoning ordinance continued. On 6 May, he announced that the martial law proclamation would be lifted if city officials would enforce their own drilling regulations. Oklahoma City Mayor C. J. Blinn and City Manager Albert L. McRill complied and the martial law proclamation was rescinded.[50]

The most important use of the National Guard in the Oklahoma oil fields was Murray's effort to drive up the price of crude after it had plunged to new lows during the Great Depression. The price the major oil companies were willing to pay for a barrel of Oklahoma crude had dropped so drastically with the onset of the economic depression that the industry was in desperate straits. Most oilmen realized that the quickest way to raise the price was to decrease the output; however, every voluntary plan put forth had failed. As a result several oilmen urged Murray to take drastic action. In response, on 28 July 1931, Murray issued an ultimatum to the big oil companies: a dollar a barrel for oil or shut down.[51]

Nothing happened, and on 4 August 1931, the governor ordered in the troops. Martial law was proclaimed within a fifty-foot zone around every well in the state. Basing his action on legislation prohibiting the extraction of oil when there was no market, Murray contended that the state was not receiving a just share of revenue when the oil was sold so cheaply, that one oil company had tried to bribe legislators to keep the price down, and that several "monopolistic" oil companies had conspired to decrease the price and thereby increase their profits. The guardsmen reacted quickly, and in general encountered little resistance from the oilmen. Twenty-seven Oklahoma oil fields were closed within a few days. Although some oilmen contended that Murray's action would throw thousands of men out of work, the governor kept the troops in the fields. Eventually his action was upheld by a three-member Federal Court meeting in Guthrie.[52]

By 19 August, the price of oil had risen to 75 cents per barrel and by September there was talk of 85-cent-per-barrel crude. Now that the price had increased, many oilmen wanted Murray to lift the martial law proclamation, but the governor refused. Oklahoma oil began to be replaced on the market by cheap Texas crude, though, and Murray relented on 10 October.

Governor E. W. Marland, *center*, called out the Oklahoma guard and defied a city prohibition against drilling oil wells on state land around the capitol building. Here he oversees the location of the first well site, east of the governor's mansion, on 6 April 1936. The officer is First Lieutenant Ross H. Routh, Adjutant-General Office. *Courtesy Oklahoma Publishing Company.*

The majority of the troops returned home and the state's wells resumed production. Even so, the fields were prorated under the direction of the Corporation Commission, which limited the state's production to 546,000 barrels of crude daily; however, rumors of "hot" or illegal oil were common.[53]

By June of 1932, Murray began to doubt that the Corporation Commission was capable of enforcing the pro-rationing orders, and on 21 June, the National Guard was sent back into the fields, under the command of the governor's cousin, Cicero I. Murray. This time some of the guardsmen and oil-field workers "engaged in free-for-all fights and 'knuckle-dusting'" as the troops enforced the governor's edict. On several occasions tear gas was used to disperse the oilmen. With oilmen generally opposed to the governor's action, the guardsmen, most of whom had no knowledge of oil-field work, found little help in mastering oil-field machinery. Stories abounded of gauges being reversed, so that when they read closed they were in reality flowing open, and of miles of secretly buried pipelines to carry illegal oil. In addition, the troops did not watch every well. The men were generally assigned selected wells to guard, while the others were left unattended.[54]

Both the governor and the oilmen believed that when the legislature convened in January of 1933 a new oil code would quickly be enacted to bring order to the state's oil fields. As a result the martial law edict was relaxed. When the legislation became bogged down and chaos returned to the drilling sites, however, Murray sent the National Guard back into the Oklahoma City Field from 4 to 10 March to enforce Corporation Commission edicts. Once the guardsmen were back in force, the solons, on 10 April, quickly adopted the new code, and after 618 days of duty in the oil fields the guardsmen were finally sent home.[55]

E. W. Marland succeeded Murray in the governor's mansion and continued the policy of using the National Guard to regulate the state's petroleum industry. By early 1936, the Oklahoma City field had expanded to the grounds of the state capitol, and, on 24 March, the residents of the region voted to open the area to drilling. Once the drilling started, though, a howl of protest arose over the "unsightly derricks . . . slush pits and smell of crude oil and gas about the executive mansion and capitol grounds." At the same time, the point was made that the oil under the capitol grounds was the property of the state and not local property owners. As a result, Marland decided that it was the state and not local officials who would control drilling activities on the capitol grounds.[56]

Ignoring Attorney General Mac Q. Williams, who contended that the city officials were within their power, Marland declared martial law on 1 April 1936. The National Guard reported for duty, and a state drilling superintendent was named. State officials then awarded the oil leases to companies of their choice.[57]

City officials almost immediately challenged Marland's actions in court; however, the governor stationed troops throughout the capitol grounds and ordered that no court process servers were to be allowed on state property. One managed to elude the guardsmen and place a summons on Marland's desk, but he ignored it. On 3 April 1936, Marland drove the first stake marking a well on the capitol grounds. Eventually Judge Ben Owens ruled in Marland's favor and the matter was settled.[58]

The National Guard's activities involved more than enforcing gubernatorial edicts. The guard was called out for humanitarian missions and disaster aid. For example, the guardsmen were called out for disaster relief in February, 1938 when Muddy Boggy Creek topped flood stage near Atoka in southeastern Oklahoma. Company B of the 180th Infantry and the ambulance company of the 120th Medical Regiment were stationed at Atoka and, even before being officially mobilized by state leaders, the guardsmen gathered at the local armory and began organizing relief efforts.[59]

While the flood raged around Atoka and other nearby communities, the guardsmen took to the water in military assault boats, provided by the 120th Engineers, to rescue men, women, and children from the high ground to which they had fled to escape the rampaging creek. Sergeant (later colonel) John H. McCasland of Company B recalled that some victims were literally plucked from their rooftops by guardsmen who braved the swirling current. The most hazardous rescue efforts took place after dark, when the guardsmen set out across the mile-wide creek in search of stranded victims.[60]

As the flood victims were pulled from the water, they were hurried to the Atoka armory, where doctors of the 120th Medical Regiment and local physicians worked frantically to treat the injured. With the aid of the Red Cross, the guardsmen set up dormitories, nurseries, kitchens, latrines, and even isolation wards when the measles broke out, to care for the refugees. One baby was delivered by a guardsman during the emergency. It was five or six days before the waters receded and the flood victims could return to their homes.[61]

As the 1930s came to an end, world events were beginning to focus the attention of the state's National Guard on Europe and Asia. Hitler had come to power in Germany, and Japan was beginning to threaten the United States' Pacific interests. Before long, America would no longer be able to rest secure behind its ocean barriers. In the years between the wars, the Forty-fifth Division had completed its organization. By the end of the 1930s it consisted of a divisional headquarters, three brigade headquarters, and seven regimental headquarters. At the same time, under the ten, twenty, thirty, and forty series—army courses designed to train officers up to the rank of colonel—most of the division's officers continued to upgrade their training to the maximum level. The training would soon be put to use, for the guardsmen would be sent overseas for the second global conflict of the twentieth century.[62]

CHAPTER 6

MOBILIZATION, 1940

Reacting ever so slowly to Japan's expansion in Asia and to Germany's blitzkrieg in Europe, the United States began to awake from its sleep of isolationism in the late 1930s, and the National Guard began to play a greater role in the nation's defense planning. One change for the Forty-fifth Division was the redesigning of the divisional insignia. Originally, the shoulder patch worn by the Oklahoma, Arizona, New Mexico, and Colorado guardsmen was a stylized version of the Indian symbol of the thunderbird, a mythical bird that caused thunder by flapping its wings and lightning by blinking its eyes. To many, though, the symbol closely resembled the Nazi swastika, with the major difference being that the thunderbird appeared to look to the left and the "arms" of the Nazi emblem were clockwise. In April, 1939, the new insignia was adopted: a red diamond, with each side representing one of the four states from which the guardsmen came. The red color represented the Spanish heritage of the region, and in the center was a golden thunderbird, representing the guardsmen's Indian heritage. Within a short time the men of the division were known as the "Thunderbirds."[1]

To upgrade the guardsmen's fighting capabilities, an accelerated training program was implemented during the weekly drill meetings and annual summer encampments. In addition, as part of America's preparedness program, in the spring of 1940 the War Department announced that the annual two-week summer camp would be expanded to three weeks. The plan was to pit several National Guard and regular army divisions against one another in the Louisiana maneuvers.[2]

A keystone to America's rearmament pro-gram, the Louisiana maneuvers constituted the largest peacetime exercise ever undertaken in the United States. A total of 460,000 men, divided into two armies, faced off along a sixty-mile front. The Red Army was commanded by Lieutenant General Ben Lear, and the Blue Army was led by Lieutenant General Walter Krueger. The exercise was designed to experiment with the new tactics of mobile warfare. Although the Blues outnumbered the Reds, Lear had better mechanized equipment, which in theory should allow him to outmaneuver Krueger and "win."[3]

Oklahoma's guardsmen, the Forty-fifth Infantry Division, were a part of the Blue Army, which numbered 330,000 men organized into ten infantry divisions: eight National Guard and two regular army, a tank group, three antitank battalions, one cavalry division, and one cavalry brigade. They were pitted against the 130,000-man Red Army, which was formed into five infantry divisions, three of them National Guard and two regular army, one armored division, and one cavalry division. In addition, each army had three hundred aircraft at its disposal.[4]

By 4 August 1940, the Oklahoma units of the Forty-fifth Infantry were camped near Pitkin in the southeast corner of Vernon Parish, Louisiana. The following day the division's Colorado, New Mexico, and Arizona contingents arrived, 9,373 officers and men. With the arrival of these troops, Major General William S. Key oversaw for the first time the mustering of the entire division at a single encampment.[5]

Suffering from years of foreign policy dominated by isolationism, the National Guard was not equipped to fight a modern war. As one

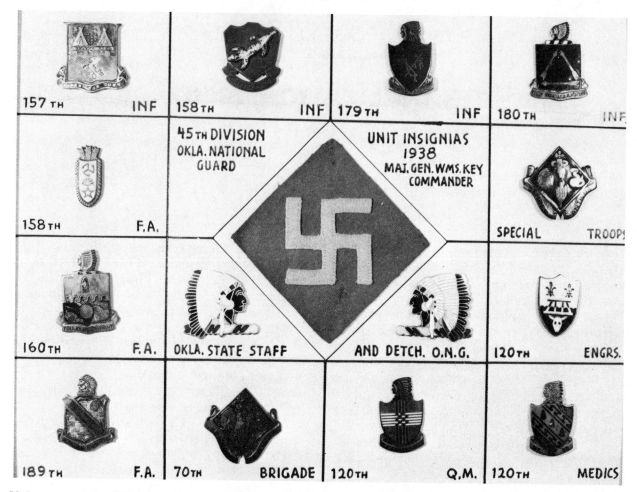

Unit crests of the Oklahoma National Guard ca. 1938. *Center:* Forty-fifth Infantry Division insignia. *Top row, left to right:* 157th Infantry, 158th Infantry, 179th Infantry, and 180th Infantry. *Second row, left to right:* 158th Field Artillery, and Special troops. *Third row, left to right:* 160th Field Artillery, Oklahoma State Staff troops, Oklahoma National Guard Detachment, and 120th Engineers. *Bottom row, left to right:* 189th Field Artillery, 70th Infantry, 120th Quartermaster, and 120th Medics. *Courtesy Forty-fifth Infantry Division Museum.*

Thunderbird officer remarked, "It is a pity the dumb public could not get down and see the feebleness of the nation's second line of defense." Although ill-prepared, the guardsmen were eager to prove their worth, and ingenuity took the place of equipment: tanks were created from canvas and paint and trucks carrying logs became antitank guns.[6]

The Oklahoma guardsmen were concentrated in the Ninetieth Infantry Brigade under Brigadier General Louis A. Ledbetter. Colonels Phillip S. Donnel and Roy Cox commanded the 179th and the 180th infantries, respectively. Brigadier

General W. E. Guthner commanded the Eighty-ninth Infantry Brigade. The Arizonans of the 158th Infantry were commanded by Colonel Prugh J. Herndon, and the Colorado troops of the 157th Infantry were led by Colonel Rudolph J. Seyfried. The support units were commanded by Colonel Grover C. Wamsley, 158th Field Artillery; Colonel Charles A. Holden, 160th Field Artillery; Colonel George A. Hutchinson, 189th Field Artillery; Colonel Roger G. Maus, 120th Quartermaster; Colonel Uil Lane, 120th Engineers; and Colonel Rex G. Bolend, 120th Medical. Major Harrison Wellman commanded the

Unit crests of the Oklahoma National Guard ca. 1939. *Center:* Forty-fifth Infantry Division (Thunderbird) insignia. *Top row, left to right:* 179th Infantry, 180th Infantry, and 160th Field Artillery. *Second row, left to right:* Seventieth Infantry Brigade, Special Troops, 171st Field Artillery, and 189th Field Artillery. *Third row, left to right:* 120th Medics, 120th Quartermaster, 145th Antiaircraft Artillery, and 245th Tank Battalion. *Bottom row, left to right:* 120th Engineer Battalion, 700th Ordnance, Oklahoma National Guard Detachment, and Seventieth Infantry Brigade. *Courtesy Forty-fifth Infantry Division Museum.*

125th Observation Squadron, a forerunner of the Oklahoma Air National Guard but a part of the Forty-fifth Infantry Division at the time.[7]

Soon after arriving at Pitkin, the men were drenched in a torrential rainstorm that turned the area into a sea of mud. The entire encampment schedule was upset. For nine days, the storm, the remnant of a hurricane, lashed the troops. It was so wet that the cooks were unable to prepare hot meals, and the guardsmen put wooden boards beneath the legs of their cots to prevent them from sinking into the mud. The wind blew so hard that on one occasion First Lieutenant Frederick A. Daugherty, who later rose to the rank of major general and Forty-fifth Division commander, looked up to see sea gulls, trying to make their way against the wind, flying *backwards.*[8]

Lieutenant Colonel Hal L. Muldrow, who retired in 1965 as a major general after commanding the division, was serving as S-3 with the artillery brigade in the 1940 exercise and recalled

Called to federal service when the United States joined the Second World War, the combined bands of the 160th Field Artillery and the 179th Infantry performed at the studios of WKY Radio in Oklahoma City. *Back row, left to right:* drums, George Y. Allen; trumpet, unknown, Gene Cunningham, and Harold Graham; trombone, Myers Cornelius, Norman Hubbard, and J. R. Nichols. *Front row, left to right:* bass, Homer Wadlington; piano, Ralph Piper; saxophone, Eugene Welch and Dean Thompson; clarinet, Cleston Gabbard; saxophone, Ralph Milsap and Floyd Holcomb. *Courtesy Forty-fifth Infantry Division Museum.*

that the gunners' trucks often sunk to their axles in the mud when left parked overnight. The entire division was water-logged for nine days; then as quickly as the storm began, it ended. When the sun reappeared, the humidity rose dramatically and hordes of mosquitoes swarmed out of the swamps.[9]

It was not until 16 August that the war games began in earnest. The Blue Army, which was to launch an attack against the Reds, was spread from Beaumont, Texas, to Bayou Teche, Louisiana, with its headquarters at Lake Charles, Lou-

isiana. The Red Army was deployed in Louisiana north and east of the Red River from Alexandria to Shreveport and Caddo Lake.[10]

Almost immediately, Lear advanced across the Red River and threw his tanks against Peason Ridge, in the Kisatchie National Forest, a key to the Blue Army's defenses. The Red Army's flanking movement failed, however, and the Blue Army seized the initiative. Although in theory Lear should have been the more mobile of the two armies, Krueger compensated for his lack of equipment by utilizing a plan developed by Forth-fifth Division personnel. Under the Thunderbird plan, a part of each division was "grounded," and the freed transport vehicles used to move the remaining Blue infantry quickly into the attack. The tactics allowed Krueger to use the guardsmen to fight their own war on their own front.

Eventually the umpires ruled that the Blue Army had destroyed the Red Army's gasoline supplies, and the end was inevitable.[11] The battle ended in a victory for the Blue Army on 20 August, and two days later the Oklahoma guardsmen started the long trip back to their armories. Within five days the troops were home, but only for a short time.[12]

The nation was shocked by the German successes in Europe. The French army had been broken, and it seemed that England would fall next. Galvanized into action, the Congress and the president began to take long-overdue steps to increase America's military might. On 27 August 1940, a joint resolution passed by Congress called the entire National Guard into federal service for a twelve-month period. On 15 September, the 125th Observation Squadron of the Oklahoma National Guard was called to active duty. On 16 September, code-named M-Day, the Forty-fifth Division was mobilized under a presidential executive order. At the same time, the nation's first peacetime draft legislation was approved.[13]

The September call was to be the first of twenty-two increments of mobilization for the nation's National Guard. The Forty-fifth Division, together with the Thirtieth, the Forty-first, and the Forty-fourth divisions, eighteen coast artillery units, and several observation squadrons composed the first call of 63,646 men. The other mobilizations stretched through June of 1941; however, the first increment was the largest.[14]

When the Forty-fifth was called into federal service, it lost the Forty-fifth Tank Company. As war loomed on the horizon in the late 1930s, the War Department had hurriedly organized additional National Guard armored and aviation units. Later, when the guardsmen were called into federal service in the fall of 1940, the tank companies were withdrawn from their divisional units for separate service.[15]

As soon as the mobilization notice was received, Major General Key established a divisional headquarters at the Lincoln Park Ar-

mory in Oklahoma City, while other guardsmen throughout the state assembled at their home armories. Key's chief of staff, Colonel James C. Styron, who later rose to the rank of major general and commanded the division, recalled that there were "no typists or trained people to handle the paperwork, not even any typewriters." The shortages were so acute that Styron had to use the typewriters at the adjutant-general's office in the state capitol at night to "peck out the movement order taking the division to Fort Sill."[16]

Although many of the men could have received exemptions from duty, by far the majority believed it was best to "go with those you know." Plans were made to induct the troops into federal service at Fort Sill, and barely a week after the mobilization order, Colonel Styron arrived at the post. On 23 September the divisional headquarters was transferred to Fort Sill, and throughout the next seven days guardsmen poured into the facility by truck and train from Oklahoma, Colorado, New Mexico, and Arizona. The first of the eighteen National Guard divisions to reach Fort Sill was the Forty-fifth, and on 1 October 1940 its commander reported that the 13,109 officers and enlisted men were ready for duty.[17]

Like all National Guard units called into federal service, the Forty-fifth was plagued by a shortage of supplies and equipment. Jack Clapp, who enlisted as a private nine days before mobilization and retired thirty-five years later as a sergeant major, recalled that the guardsmen practiced firing mortars by substituting stove pipes for mortar tubes and using empty beer cans for shells. By November the Thunderbirds began to receive 105-mm. howitzers to replace the old "French 75s," new 37-mm. antitank guns, and 60-mm. mortars.[18]

The efforts to provide the men with adequate training led the War Department to decree that all the guardsmen undergo an initial thirteen-week basic training period. Unfortunately, Fort Sill could handle only 6,500 troops in its permanent buildings. In order to accommodate the new trainees, thousands of tents were erected on the open ground. some men's tents were staked on bare earth, and some lucky ones had concrete floors. Row after row of stakes marked imaginary streets, with a kitchen at one end and a latrine at the other. Stumbling over freshly dug ditches awaiting water and sewer lines, the guardsmen hurriedly began building their own facilities, with mess halls and latrines receiving priority. Shortly after the Forty-fifth's arrival it was announced that "more than a million [dollars] will be spent in 300 buildings" for the division by 1 January 1941.[19]

Exacerbating the shortages in housing and other facilities was the unusually cold winter of 1940-1941, which caused one Thunderbird to remark after a particularly cold night that "my two blankets felt like cotton sheets." He considered himself lucky, though, for "our outfit has mattresses," while "those Colorado guys had to sleep in their clothes." Many of the guardsmen were issued decrepit blouses and "the all too short 'stand alone' overcoats" of World War I vintage that offered little protection against the bitter wind. "The overcoats were issued in bales," Major General Muldrow recalled. "They'd drive down the company streets and throw them out." In the scramble for the coats the men took any size they could get and later traded to find a better fit.[20]

Most of the rest of the uniforms were also war surplus: "high necked blouses, spiral puttees instead of leggings, laced breeches that often would split at the knee the first time a man fell forward to the ground." Newly commissioned Second Lieutenant John H. McCasland recalled: "I can remember the infantry boys hopping along in ranks on the march, trying to catch the loose ends of one of those old-style leggings." Blue denim fatigues, with "doughnut-style" denim fatigue hats, called by McCasland the "silliest and most impractical headgear ever issued," completed the ensemble.[21]

Many of the tents were heated with old-fashioned "funnel type" Sibley stoves, which, in addition to consuming huge quantities of wood, had to be cleaned twice a day to prevent them from burning holes in the tent canvas. Later, in an attempt to prevent the fires, the stoves were fitted with spark arresters. They were of little use, however, and the hot soot residue continued to burn holes in the tents. To make matters worse, the camp was swept with an influenza epidemic in December of 1940 that hospitalized 2,500 of the 22,000 troops on the post.[22]

The supply problem was helped somewhat when Key was made commander of Fort Sill, as well as of the National Guard units. From then

on proper equipment was rushed to the men. As supplies became available, a "Fit to Fight by February Plan" was implemented, and the basic training program pushed to the utmost. Throughout this period the division's ranks were filled out with six thousand draftees, who first began arriving at Fort Sill on 3 January 1941. Many of the men were from the Oklahoma-Colorado-New Mexico-Arizona region, and whenever possible they were assigned to National Guard units from their own locale. Because of these and other hardships, it took the Oklahoma guardsmen sixteen weeks, instead of the thirteen prescribed by the War Department, to complete basic training. Nevertheless, the Forty-fifth was ready by 17 January 1941—the first National Guard division to finish the training cycle.[23]

Shortly after mobilization, Lieutenant Colonel Walter M. Harrison, the division's assistant chief of staff and a former managing editor of Oklahoma City's *Daily Oklahoman* and *Oklahoma City Times,* approached Major General Key with a proposal to create a divisional newspaper. Quickly recognizing the value of such a proposal, Key wholeheartedly endorsed the project. Although there were no official funds available for such a newspaper, Key turned over a portion of the Forty-fifth's share of Fort Sill's post exchange profits to help finance the effort and authorized the recruitment of an adequate staff from divisional personnel. Roy P. Stewart, a member of the Forty-fifth and later a colonel with the division, was the *Daily Oklahoman*'s correspondent assigned to the Thunderbirds and one of Harrison's former reporters. Stewart immediately joined the effort and began screening applicants for the paper's staff. The Oklahoma Publishing Company offered its complete cooperation and provided much of the necessary equipment, and Ned Shepler, owner and publisher of the *Lawton Constitution,* made that paper's facilities available. Utilizing stories that Stewart wrote, Harrison and Stewart hurriedly completed Volume I, Number 1, of the *45th Division News* which rolled off the press on 4 October 1940. It was the first divisional newspaper published in the era of World War II.[24]

The paper went on to become one of the most famous military publications in the European theater of operations (ETO), and was recognized as the "best overseas printed Army newspaper." Many of the newspaper's staff became some of the foremost journalists in America. Private A. Y. Owens, a nationally known photographer, and Sergeant (later warrant officer) George F. Tapscott, were the paper's photographers. Often Owens would catch a ride in the 125th Observation Squadron's planes and hang over the edge of the rear cockpit to get aerial photographs of the division's maneuvers. Private Bill Mauldin applied for the job of cartoonist for the paper and was accepted. Later, Mauldin's cartoon portrayals of the war from the enlisted man's point of view in the famous "Willie and Joe" series led to his reassignment to *Stars and Stripes* and launched a career that earned him a Pulitzer Prize.[25]

Throughout the remainder of the Thunderbirds' active duty, the *45th Division News* was issued weekly. By 1941 a divisional public information office was created and regular funding was available; however, it remained the enlisted mens' publication throughout its life. Gathering copy for the newspaper was not always easy. During the 1941 Louisiana maneuvers, the staff kept pace with the division in a half-ton truck and traveled more than ten thousand miles in a two-month period. Later, at Sicily, Italy, it was discovered that American script could not be read by the Italian printers, and the Italian typewriters had no w's, k's, or y's. Imagine trying to write stories for Americans using words with no w's, k's or y's. Another adventure for the newspaper's staff occurred at Salerno when the newspaper was published within range of the Germans' artillery.[26]

Once the division completed its basic training, rumors flew about the camp. Most centered on a movement to a new training area in Texas, but some were as exotic as reassignment to the Caribbean. Texas proved to be the correct guess, and on 28 February 1941 the first of the Thunderbirds were transferred, mostly in borrowed Third Army vehicles, to Camp Barkeley near Abilene. By 7 March the entire division had arrived.[27]

At the time, Barkeley was nothing but an undrained tent city with exposed sewers. On the south of the camp a series of low mesas dominated the landscape, but on the north there was only open prairie, with nothing to break the cold winds. Side tracks for the railroad had not yet been completed, and there was little in the way of comfort. Nonetheless, training resumed as realistically as possible as every effort was made

to condition the new draftees and work them into the Forty-fifth's organization.[28]

Command post exercises were held, field training problems organized, and war games implemented. Extensive maneuvers that pitted companies against companies or brigades against brigades were carried out. In some exercises as many as 23,000 men from several Eighth Army Corps divisions might be involved, and, in June of 1941, more than 70,000 troops conducted battle maneuvers near Brownwood, Texas.[29]

There were many stories associated with the rivalry of divisions when facing one another during the maneuvers. Once some Forty-fifth Division Indians were defending their position against an attacking force from an east coast regiment. Each time the Indian machine gunner fired a burst of blanks at the attackers, his companions would "let fly BB bullets from long, rubber-band sling shots." As one witness recalled: "With the pellets rattling among the twigs and leaves overhead, the attackers . . . and the Umpires beat an unorthodox retreat to spread the general alarm that 'those damned Indians think this is a real war!'" The assault was called off long enough for the umpires to search the Indians for live ammunition.[30]

On 2 August 1941, the Forty-fifth began leaving Camp Barkeley for Third Army maneuvers in Louisiana. Trucks hauled the men part way, off-loaded near either Denton or Dallas, Texas, and then returned to Barkeley for more troops, while the first contingent continued on foot. After hauling the second group to either Denton or Dallas, the trucks picked up the first group, completed the journey to the divisional bivouac near Mansfield, Louisiana, and then returned for the second group, which had been continuing the trip on foot. The war games began on 10 August, just as the last of the Thunderbirds arrived, with the guardsmen opposing the First Cavalry Division of the regular army near Pitkin, Louisiana.[31]

The troops were still short much of their equipment and turned to their own imagination. Pop bottles were filled with diluted sorghum to simulate Molotov cocktails and hurled against "enemy" tanks. Much to the surprise of many military observers, the Forty-fifth succeeded in surrounding a large portion of the First Cavalry. The key to the guardsmen's success was an expansion of the ride-walk method of movement used to transport the Thunderbirds from Barkeley to Mansfield. This had been devised by Brigadier General Raymond S. McLain, divisional artillery commander and temporarily in charge of the Eighty-ninth Infantry Brigade during a portion of the maneuvers. In order to give the infantry maximum mobility, McLain gathered all possible transports and then marched a portion of the troops, while shuttling the others in trucks. The two groups would periodically exchange places; this way the men who were afoot remained fresh and capable of maintaining a fairly rapid pace. Throughout this phase of the war games, General Krueger referred to the Forty-fifth as his "Foot Cavalry."[32]

Another phase of the 1941 Louisiana maneuvers pitted the Third Army, which contained the Forty-fifth Division, against elements of the Second Army. During the exercise a unit of the Ohio National Guard succeeded in surrounding a lieutenant and about twenty men of the 180th Infantry. The Ohio troops were surprised when the Oklahomans announced the Ohioans were their prisoners. The umpires were undoubtedly impressed when upon command a large group of Indians rose from the tall grass that encircled the Ohio guardsmen.[33]

The Forty-fifth had been called into federal service for one year in September of 1940, and many believed that at the conclusion of the 1941 Louisiana maneuvers the guardsmen would be returned to their home units. In August, 1941, however, the Service Extension Act was approved by Congress, and in early September of 1941, as the war games were coming to an end, word was received that the War Department had extended the original one-year tour of federal service. Although the guardsmen remained on duty, the 1940 draftees, who also had been called for one year's duty, were withdrawn from the division, returned to Camp Barkeley, and released. One regiment, the 180th, lost five hundred men. Their departure left major gaps in the division's ranks.[34]

When the maneuvers ended on 29 September, the Forty-fifth returned to Camp Barkeley. Soon afterward, the division's strength was reduced again when all enlisted men with dependents or who were more than twenty-eight years of age were transferred to the Enlisted Reserve Corps. Although most of these men had been transferred as of 1 December 1941, they were quickly

called back into service after the Japanese attack on Pearl Harbor in December, 1941. Unfortunately, when recalled to active duty they were usually assigned to different units, and once again the Forty-fifth lost valuable trained troops.[35]

The outbreak of war in December, 1941 was received at Camp Barkeley with shock and bitter emotion. This too was to cost the division additional manpower. For several months the War Department had been in the process of reorganizing the old "square" National Guard divisions, each with four regiments, along the lines of the regular army's triangular divisions by eliminating brigades and organizing the divisions around three regiments. The reduction in regiments would mean a corresponding reduction in officer slots.[36]

Previously the Forty-fifth Division had consisted of the Ninetieth Infantry Brigade, containing the 179th and 180th Infantry regiments; the Eighty-ninth Infantry Brigade, containing the 157th and 158th Infantry regiments; the Seventieth Field Artillery, containing the 158th, the 160th, and the 189th Artillery regiments; the 120th Quartermaster Regiment; the 120th Engineer Regiment; the 120th Medical Regiment; and a unit of special troops containing the headquarters, military police, ordnance, and signal companies. In late 1941 the various infantry regiments, which had already been depleted by the release of draftees and transfers to the Enlisted Reserve Corps, were called upon to contribute men to bring the 158th Infantry, Arizona's regiment, up to full strength in preparation for reassignment.[37]

A few days before Christmas of 1941, the 158th left Camp Barkeley for the Panama Canal Zone to bolster the defenses of that strategic waterway. Later, on 1 February 1942, it was joined with the Second Battalion, 158th Field Artillery of the Forty-fifth Infantry Division to form the 158th Regimental Combat Team (RCT). Later, those Oklahomans who found themselves in the new 158th RCT, or the "Bushmasters" as the unit was nicknamed, shipped out for the southwest Pacific theater, where they compiled a fine combat record.[38]

With the departure of the 158th, the Forty-fifth was left with three infantry regiments: the 157th, the 179th, and the 180th. The other units of the Forty-fifth also were reorganized along the new table of organization, which went into effect on 27 February 1942. The artillery regiments were realigned as battalions; the medical regiments were restructured as battalions; and the 171st Artillery Battalion was activated.

At the same time, the two battalions of the 120th Engineer Regiment were separated. The old Second Battalion, 120th Engineers became the 120th Engineer Battalion for the new Forty-fifth Infantry Division. Likewise, the pre-triangularization First Battalion, 120th Engineers was reorganized as the 176th Engineer Regiment (General Service) on 31 January 1942. Later that same year, on 1 August, the unit was redesignated the 176th Engineer General Service Regiment, with most of the Oklahoma guardsmen assigned to the First Battalion.

The old 120th Quartermaster Regiment was reduced first to a battalion and later to a company, with the excess men being organized into the 145th Quartermaster Company, General Headquarters Reserves. Ironically, those Oklahoma guardsmen in the newly formed 176th Engineers and 145th Quartermaster Company followed Arizona's 158th RCT to the Pacific.[39]

In February of 1941, the engineers were ordered to Alaska to build lend-lease facilities for the Russians. Working conditions in the Arctic cold were grueling, according to First Lieutenant, later colonel, Herbert C. O'Neil. O'Neil had originally enlisted in the 120th Engineers, Oklahoma National Guard, as a private in 1938, only to be assigned to the 176th Engineers at the time of triangulization. He and his platoon were stationed at Galena on the Yukon River, approximately half-way between Fairbanks and Nome, Alaska, where they built a 6,000-feet-long runway and garrison facilities for a thousand troops. Outside work schedules were maintained in temperatures as low as −40° F., but during the long winter the thermometer often plunged lower and temperatures of −60°F. were common.[40]

In addition to the cold, Galena was so isolated that supplies had to be brought in by boat up the Yukon River, which was open only about two-and-a-half months during the summer. Although the river was the guardsmen's lifeline in the warmer months, when the weather turned cold the ice-choked waterway could become a deadly peril. During the winter of 1943 a nearby ice jam forced the Yukon out of its banks and sent the engineers fleeing to their "sandpile" for safety. The men were stranded for two weeks

until the Army Air Corps could get there and drop 500-pound bombs on the jam to break the ice free.[41]

Later the 176th was transferred to the Aleutian Islands to help counter the Japanese thrust into the northern Pacific. O'Neil and his men were sent to Adak, near the western end of the Aleutian string, where they worked on the largest earth-moving project up to that time: 20 million yards of earth had to be moved to create a runway. On 12 March 1945 the First Battalion, 176th Engineers General Service Regiment was reorganized as the 176th Engineer Construction Battalion and sent to the Ryukyu Islands to participate in the battle for Okinawa. Landing on the Japanese stronghold on D + 2, O'Neil and the other Oklahomans remained there until November of 1945, when they were ordered home. Once released from federal service, O'Neil helped organize a new 120th Engineer Battalion for the Oklahoma National Guard. He retired in 1970 after serving as that battalion's commander.[42]

The 145th Quartermaster Company, of which approximately 75 percent of the men were Oklahoma guardsmen, was commanded by Captain Bruce E. Rey, who had entered the Forty-fifth as a private in 1932. He retired thirty-six years later as a lieutenant colonel and the Forty-fifth's G-4 (supply and logistics officer). Rey and his men were ordered to Charleston, South Carolina, in early 1942, and from there boarded a transport destined originally for Rangoon, Burma. By the time the ship made its way across the southern Atlantic Ocean around the tip of Africa, and into the Indian Ocean, the Japanese had seized the area, and the 145th was diverted to Karachi, India, which it reached in May of 1942.[43]

After landing, Rey's men helped establish a United States Army base, and then were parceled out as replacements throughout the China-Burma-India (CBI) theater. As the guardsmen were transferred to different assignments, Rey, in July of 1942, was sent to Kunming, China, as an acting air freight officer on the Burma Road, the main supply route to China after the Japanese had cut off all regular trade routes. Three units, code-named Forces X, Y, and Z, were trying to open the road as quickly as possible, with Force X working eastward from Burma toward central China, Force Y moving westward from central China toward Burma, and Force Z beginning in central China and heading east.[44]

Rey was soon moved to Yunanyi, about one hundred miles west of Kunming, and assigned as the transportation officer of Force Y. His task was to advise the Chinese army on the proper use of transport. In addition, he oversaw the construction of seventeen supply depots along the road. Later, beginning on 18 April 1943, Rey made a reconnaissance of a possible alternate route from Kunming south to Puerh in French Indochina. Rey, with two other Americans, a Chinese interpreter, and twenty-one Chinese officers and enlisted men, moved southward on foot and horseback for thirty-four days. Averaging between eighteen and nineteen miles a day over the rugged trail, the party reached Puerh on 5 May. Obviously, Rey reported, before the route could be used to any great advantage, substantial improvements would have to be made.[45]

Although Rey and his men were bombed several times by the Japanese during their tour on the Burma Road, their major problem was the lack of adequate supplies. Uniforms quickly became ragged, and the Americans once ate rice and cauliflower three times a day for a week when food ran low. A lack of fuel for his vehicles also plagued Rey's work, and he often purchased alcohol for $35 per gallon to keep the trucks rolling. Rey remained in the CBI theater for two-and-a-half years before returning to the United States.[46]

Upon completion of the triangularization process in early 1942, the reorganized Forty-fifth consisted of the 158th, the 179th, and the 180th RCTs; the 120th Engineer Battalion; the Forty-fifth Cavalry Troop; the 120th Medical Battalion; the 45th Military Police Company; the 189th Medium Field Artillery; the 160th, the 171st, and the 158th Light Field Artillery battalions; the 700th Ordnance; the Forty-fifth Quartermaster, and various other support units. In addition, the 106th Antiaircraft Battalion, the 191st Tank Battalion, and the 645th Tank Destroyer Battalion, though not an organic part of the division, were attached to the Forty-fifth.[47]

At the same time the triangularization took place, the old brigade concept was replaced by the Regimental Combat Team (RCT) concept. The idea was to perfect a more mobile and self-sufficient organization around the nuclei of the three remaining infantry regiments. For example, the 179th Infantry was combined with the 160th Field Artillery, Company B of the 120th Engineers Battalion, and Company B of the 120th Medical Battalion to form the 179th Regimental Combat Team.[48]

Through the remaining early months of 1942, the division continued its training routine at Camp Barkeley. Finally, on 5 April it was ordered to Fort Devens, Massachusetts. The trip began on 20 April, and by the first week in May most of the troops had arrived at their new assignment. Unlike Camp Barkeley, Fort Devens was a well-established army post that had existed for years. It was located on a 1,000-acre reserve northwest of Boston and not far from Concord.[49]

Many in the division expected Devens to be a jumping-off place for overseas assignment. Instead, the Forty-fifth received several contingents of new draftees, and the training process began again. Another change occurred on 13 October 1942 while the Thunderbirds were at Devens. Brigadier General Troy H. Middleton, assistant divisional commander, replaced Key as commander of the Thunderbirds. A few days later, on 27 October, Middleton was promoted to major general; however, it was not until 11 November, after the division had left Devens for Pine Camp, New York, that Middleton was notified of his new rank.[50]

While still at Devens the Thunderbirds got a preview of their future assignment, when in July some units were moved to Camp Edwards, Massachusetts, for shore-to shore amphibious operations. The guardsmen saw the division's antitank capabilities increased with the formation of cannon companies armed with 75-mm. and 105-mm. guns mounted on tracked vehicles. Throughout the summer months and into the fall, the Oklahomans worked the new draftees into the division's table of organization.[51]

Finally, on 8 November, the Forty-fifth was moved to Pine Camp, New York. Located near Watertown, Lake Ontario, and the Canadian border, this camp was a drastic climatic change from the Southwest. Although the camp's facilities were excellent, the temperature fell to 54° below zero. The snow was more than three feet deep, and, to make matters worse, many of the guardsmen did not have adequate cold weather equipment. Still the training went on.[52]

That same month a detachment was sent to North Africa to observe the Tunisian campaign, and expectations were that the division was finally going to see combat. Emotions were heightened in December of 1942, when the Forty-fifth was alerted for possible overseas duty. The orders were suddenly canceled in January of 1943, however, and the Oklahoma guardsmen moved to Camp Pickett in southern Virginia. Although the move south was somewhat of a disappointment to the men, Pickett, only sixty miles from Richmond, offered a much milder climate than New York and was a welcome relief.[53]

There was no relief from the training. It was obvious that it would not be long before the guardsmen shipped out for the war zone, and the troops entered a final three-month program of intensive training. "Running obstacle, bayonet and infiltration courses, 5 mile timed marches and 25 mile endurance hikes . . . all became part of each day's routine." In March the Oklahomans left Camp Pickett for the pine forests of the Blue Ridge Mountains for mountain training. Late March and early April saw the Oklahomans moved to Norfolk, Virginia, for amphibious landing exercises. Several assaults were made on King Island in Chesapeake Bay, and by the end of the 95-day cycle, the division was at its peak of efficiency.[54]

Preparations were now well under way for overseas duty. Special invasion equipment was issued; old, worn-out equipment was replaced with new models; nonessential equipment was discarded; and historical files were stored. Vehicles were water-proofed, and the division was streamlined for action. With the final preparations for embarkation under way, the troops scrambled for furloughs to visit their families one last time before shipping out.[55]

Under the strictest cloak of secrecy, the Forty-fifth Division was moved to Camp Patrick Henry, Virginia, on 24 May. This was to be the jumping-off place, and the censorship of mail was increased to ensure that word of the impending sailing would not leak out. This crossing was to be different from those yet experienced by the United States Army. The troops were to sail directly from the United States in a separate task force and assault an enemy beachhead. Because of this, the ships were combat loaded. Every inch of space was utilized to store equipment, and on 4 June 1943 the troops began filing aboard the transports.[56]

To protect the twenty transports carrying the division overseas, the navy had assigned several cruisers to the convoy, including the U.S.S. *Brooklyn,* the U.S.S. *Boise,* and the U.S.S. *Philadelphia,* and a large number of destroyers and other escort vessels. For four days, the navy warships rendezvoused with the transports in the harbor. Then, almost suddenly, at 0830 on 8 June 1943, the convoy weighed anchor and eased out of the harbor. Its destination was Sicily.[57]

The decision for the Anglo-American landing in Sicily had been made at the Casablanca conference between President Franklin D. Roosevelt and British Prime Minister Winston Churchill in January of 1943. The move was a natural continuation of the Allied thrust at the "soft underbelly" of the German army across the Mediterranean and through Italy. The seizure of Sicily was the second of a three-pronged offensive and would provide a steppingstone for the invasion of Italy once the enemy was driven out of North Africa. The Forty-fifth Division, together with the First Infantry Division, the Third Infantry Division, the Second Armored Division, and the Eighty-second Airborne Division, was to be a part of Second Corps of the Seventh Army. The Ninth Infantry Division formed the reserve. These troops, together with the British Eighth Army and the First Canadian Division, were to assault the southern part of Sicily and begin the return of Allied troops to Europe. Operation Husky, as the Sicilian invasion was code-named, was to be the largest initial amphibious operation attempted up to that time, with more than three thousand ships taking part.[58]

When the Thunderbirds departed the east coast of the United States most were unaware of their final destination. The voyage across the Atlantic was uneventful. Some time was given to abandon ship and debarkation drills, but generally the men were free to entertain themselves as best they could. Many of the troops had never seen the sea before, and they stood along the rails of the transports as if transfixed by the vastness of the ocean. Within a few days of sailing the convoy passed Bermuda and entered the dangerous hunting grounds of the German submarine fleet. Blackout regulations were rigidly enforced, and radio silence isolated the men from the rest of the world.[59]

There were submarine alarms on June 13, 15, 18, and 21, which sent the convoy zig-zagging wildly to avoid the enemy, as the destroyers and destroyer escorts rushed to the reported loca-

tion. Depth charges were rolled from their decks and huge waterspouts shot into the air when the underwater bombs exploded. When the ships approached the coast of Africa they were within range of Nazi aircraft. Battle stations were fully manned from dusk to dawn to prevent a surprise attack, but no enemy aircraft were sighted. On 21 June the coast of Tangier came into sight, and at 1400 the Forty-fifth sailed through the Strait of Gibraltar into the Mediterranean. As the convoy passed through the strait, a small white boat left the British garrison and pulled beside the U.S.S. *Ancon,* a command ship, and sent aboard top-secret plans for the Thunderbirds' destination. A flight of British fighters flew overhead for protection; however, the only action was a warning shot fired from neutral Spanish Morocco when one of the planes strayed over the border.[60]

At 0900 on June 22, the convoy dropped anchor in the harbor at Oran, Algeria. The bay was filled with Allied warships of every size and description. This was not the end of the voyage, and the men were kept aboard. Two days later the convoy again sailed to a point off the Algerian coast near the city of Mostaganen for a final training exercise before the battle. After completing the assault exercise on the beach and capturing their objectives, the Thunderbirds camped nearby. The training continued until 1 July, when the men were trucked back to Oran and reboarded their transports.[61]

The transports sailed again on 5 July, and the following day the troops were told their destination—Sicily. Maps were distributed to key officers and enlisted personnel, and every man received "A Soldier's Guide to Sicily." At twilight on 8 July, the transports reversed their heading and steamed west-northwest. The following day the troops were told that the landing would take place the next morning. The transports slowed and then began cruising in circles to mark time until then. Mine sweepers, corvettes, motor torpedo boats, and other invasion support vessels joined the convoy. Finally, during the night of 9-10 July, the invasion force dropped anchor six miles off the coast of Sicily.[62]

The men shed their khaki-colored cotton clothing and put on their wool, olive-drab combat uniforms. Each man received one day's issue of both K and D rations, and each made a final check of his equipment. The seas began to rise, and the transports rolled in the heavy waves. Many of the men became seasick, and the heavy seas delayed some of the ships in arriving on station. At midnight the landing was set back one hour to 0345 on 10 June. About 0100 flares began falling over the assault beaches as Allied aircraft started their attacks. In response, enemy searchlights probed the darkness.[63]

At 0345 the preinvasion bombardment by the ships began. Just offshore two American submarines, code-named "Nickle" and "Dime," rose just far enough out of the water to expose colored lights to the invasion force and guide the landing ships ashore. Under the cover of naval gunfire, the transports moved to within 11,000 yards of the beaches (out of range of artillery) and lowered their landing craft into the water. With the order to "Lay into the boats," the Thunderbirds began to struggle over the rails, climb down the nets, and take their places in the assault craft. The invasion of Sicily was under way, and the Forty-fifth was about to enter its first battle of the Second World War.[64]

CHAPTER 7

BAPTIZED IN BLOOD: THE INVASION OF SICILY

In the early morning hours of 10 July 1943, the Thunderbirds' landing craft circled to mark time. Then, at 0345, the boat handlers formed a V pattern, turned the landing craft toward the shore, and gunned the engines. Navy guns poured salvo after salvo into the landing zone, firing over the landing craft, as the boats rushed toward the coast of Sicily. The fire-support vessels, a scant thousand yards offshore, blasted the beach area with their rocket launchers.[1]

The Allied plans called for the Forty-fifth to land at Scoglitti on the left flank of the British Eighth Army and on the right flank of the American invasion force. The 180th RCT was to occupy the code-named Red Beach, and was to be put ashore just southeast of the Acate River. From here the troops were to move northeast toward their primary objective, the Biscari air field. The 179th RCT was to land on Green and Yellow beaches south of Red Beach, seize the towns of Scoglitti and Vittoria, and then become half of a pincer attack on Cosimo Airport. The 157th RCT was to assault other beaches, code-named Blue, Green, and Yellow beaches, between five and eight miles southeast of Scoglitti, and then form the other half of the pincer attack on Cosimo Airport.[2]

As the landing craft neared the assault beaches, the troops discarded their life vests. One hundred yards from the shoreline the landing platforms slapped the water. At 0425 the first units of the Forty-fifth stepped ashore on European soil. It was a chaotic scene. Some of the landing boats were broached; others had dropped their ramps too far offshore and the troops were struggling for their lives in the deep water. To complicate matters even more, in the confusion several units had landed on the wrong beaches.[3]

Of the Forty-fifth, the 180th RCT had the most trouble getting ashore. Because of navigation errors the RCTs landed all along a twelve-mile stretch of beach instead of in the planned landing zone. Several boatloads of troops were landed on sandbars almost six hundred yards offshore, and most were forced to abandon their equipment. As a result, it was late in the afternoon of D day before the 180th's scattered and disorganized units were reunited.[4] Once on the beach, enemy reaction varied. The First Battalion of the 180th landed unopposed, but the Second Battalion was greeted with machine guns firing at them from pill-box defenses.[5]

The troops of the 179th RCT had an easier time. To their surprise, they landed virtually unopposed. Instead of gunfire, they were met by considerable numbers of Italian troops hurrying from their bunkers to surrender. In less than one hour all of the 179th was on the beach.[6]

Apparently the enemy believed that the 157th's assault beaches were impregnable, for there was little barbed wire or gun emplacements to impede its landing. Unfortunately, the reefs and rocks took their toll, and several men drowned as their landing craft collided with a reef and overturned in the swirling water. Once on the beach, in the face of only light Italian resistance, the troops quickly moved inland.[7]

The Forty-fifth was spread between Scoglitti on the south to Gela on the north. The 157th RCT was on the right flank, the 179th in the center, and the 180th on the left. While the 180th was hurriedly attempting to reorganize after its chaotic landing, the 179th and the 157th were moving rapidly inland, hampered at first by German aircraft that swept over the landing beaches shortly after dawn. The First Battalion of the 179th moved southward to secure the seven miles of beach between the landing zone and Scoglitti. At the same time, the Third Battalion moved to the high ground overlooking the beaches and then hurried along Highway 115 for eight miles to seize Vittorio. By 1400, Scoglitti had been captured, and forty minutes later the Thunderbirds held Vittorio.[8]

By the end of D day the Forty-fifth had succeeded in capturing all its initial objectives. As night approached, the troops consolidated their positions and prepared for possible enemy counterattacks. About one hour after dark, the divisional command post (CP) was shelled by naval gunfire. The unfortunate accident was the result of an incorrect gunfire plot on the part of the naval fire control center. In addition, almost as soon as this shelling stopped, German aircraft began the first of a number of bombing raids against both the landing beaches and the ships offshore. During the day's fighting many of the men had either lost or discarded much of what they considered nonessential equipment. It had been hot and dusty and their heavy clothing seemed an unnecessary burden; however, once darkness fell a chill covered the land.[9]

That night the 180th sent a patrol toward Biscari, northwest of Vittorio. The men left the American lines at about 2100, and as they penetrated the town's limit a German motorized column of Hermann Goering's elite SS Panzer Division entered from the opposite direction. The German forces consisted of infantry, mobile artillery, and an armored group containing both Mark IV and Mark VI tanks. The Mark IV weighed 26 tons and carried a 75-mm. gun, and the Mark VI, or Tiger Tank, weighed 60 tons and mounted an 88-mm. Both weapons systems presented an extreme danger to the Forty-fifth's beachhead. As the enemy continued through Biscari toward the American lines, the patrol quickly warned the 180th's CP of the impending counterattack.[10]

The Americans and the Germans clashed about three miles south of Biscari. The brunt of the attack was taken by the First Battalion of the 180th, which was still plagued by the confusion of its scattered landing. The Americans were supported by a single battery of artillery,

but they had no antitank guns with which to challenge the German armor. At first the guardsmen were able to hold off the attack with rocket launchers and rifle grenades; however, just as it seemed as if the 180th could weather the assault, the Germans called in air support.[11]

Under an almost continuous strafing attack, and with its rocket launcher ammunition exhausted, the battalion began to give way under enemy pressure. The Thunderbirds began withdrawing to the high ground south of Highway 115. The chaos of battle was heightened when the Germans began shelling the regiment's headquarters. Hurriedly the Third Battalion was rushed to reinforce the beleagured First. This move blunted the German assault, stabilized the American lines, and bought enough time for the regiment to complete its reorganization.[12]

The Americans again took the offensive on the morning of 11 July. Artillery began firing on enemy positions surrounding the beachhead. Offshore, the navy resumed fire support, and the entire division struck inland over a broad front. The 157th and 179th RCTs assaulted Cosimo Airport, the air arsenal for the entire island. By 1640, after bitter fighting, it was declared secure and proved to be a rich prize. "There were thousands of tons of bombs ranging from 50 to 2,000 pounders, piled high in the fields about, . . . also thousands of barrels of gasoline." More than a hundred enemy aircraft were captured, and one was shot down as it took off by an infantryman using a Browning automatic rifle. Still, as its sister regiments continued the assault, the 180th was bogged down.[13]

When the 180th launched its attack on the morning after D day, it met stiff German resistance. Within a short time enemy artillery and sniper fire slowed the advance to a standstill. As the fighting continued, several German tanks moved toward the Thunderbird lines over Highway 115 and closed to within a hundred yards of the hilltop positions before they were thrown back. That night the 180th launched another assault against the Germans, but it too failed.[14]

It was while the Thunderbirds were in this battle that one of the most unfortunate episodes of the battle for Sicily occurred. About 2330 (11:30 P.M.) on 11 July the Germans staged a heavy air raid on the Allied shipping standing

Barbed wire and minefields on the enemy-held beach at Scoglitti, Sicily, on 10 July 1943. *Courtesy Forty-fifth Infantry Division Museum.*

offshore. Immediately after the bombing attack, with antiaircraft fire still heavy and German flares still burning, a large flight of American planes carrying members of the Eighty-second Airborne Division flew over the area on their way to a night drop. Almost immediately, the Allies, thinking that the planes were another raid by enemy aircraft, opened fire on the paratroopers. Several American planes were shot down and some of the surviving paratroopers fell in front of the Forty-fifth's lines. The Thunderbirds and the paratroopers, each thinking the other was the enemy because each sector had a different password, opened fire. Before communications could identify them, both the Forty-fifth and the Eighty-second suffered several casualties.[15]

On 12 July the Allies began to push out of the beachhead and move inland. The 180th had been able to reorganize after beating off the earlier enemy counterattacks, and on the morning of July 12 it launched a strong attack to-

ward Biscari. Although the fighting was bitter, the assault moved forward rapidly, scattering enemy Italian troops before it. The town was quickly seized, and during that night the enemy began destroying its supply dumps and all bridges between the town and Biscari Airport. It became apparent that the Axis, as the Germans and their allies were called, were in general retreat all along the Forty-fifth's front, and Major General Troy Middleton, the division's commander, ordered an immediate pursuit.[16]

Led by the 180th RCT, the assault on Biscari's air field began at 0700 on 13 July. The enemy occupied the high ground around the airport and poured heavy artillery, machine gun, and small arms fire on the advancing Americans as they crossed the valley separating the town from the air field. Along the airport's edge, the Germans had taken shelter in a Sicilian cemetery where the massive, high-walled tombs offered good cover. As the guardsmen pressed forward, the Germans threw several of their Mark VI

Elements of the Forty-fifth off-loading from LSTs near Scoglitti, Sicily. A smaller craft, and LCM, part of an earlier landing wave, has been swamped in the center background. On the left, engineers are grading a road along the beach. *Courtesy Forty-fifth Infantry Division Museum.*

tanks into the battle. In some of the heaviest fighting to that time, possession of the air field changed hands twice. Once the Thunderbirds destroyed or threw back the enemy tanks, the Germans withdrew, and by the late afternoon of 14 July the airport was permanently in American hands.[17]

While the 180th RCT was securing Biscari Airport, the 179th and 157th also were moving inland. The Second Battalion of the 179th was given the task of protecting Cosimo Airport while aviation personnel and combat engineers hurriedly worked to make the facility operational. While the Thunderbirds were screening the air field, they were counterattacked by enemy in-

fantry, but these were only localized assaults. The Germans and Italians had given up their plans of forcing the beachhead assault back into the sea and were in general retreat, making only small harassing counterattacks to delay the American advance.[18]

Originally the Forty-fifth's last objective of the initial attack plan was the code-named "Yellow" line, which stretched in a crescent from Palma di Montechiaro on the east to Vizzini on the west. As the Thunderbirds neared the Yellow line, however, the decision was made to shift the division's operations some fifty-eight miles northwest to a point near Mazzarino. That would place the Thunderbirds in the center of

Members of the 179th RCT entering Scoglitti, Sicily, 10 July 1943. By this time most front-line troops had been equipped with the famous .30 M1 (Garand) rifle. *Courtesy Forty-fifth Division Museum.*

the American forces with the First Division on their right and the Third Division on their left.[19]

The move began on 15 July, and within fifteen hours the Thunderbirds were back in the line. Two days later, the 157th RCT led the division's attack to the north toward Pietraperzia against light enemy resistance. By nightfall the Thunderbirds had advanced thirty-two miles, and within a short time Pietraperzia and Caltanissetta had been captured and San Caterina, near the center of the island, occupied. During the advance the 157th destroyed six self-propelled 88-mm. cannons that the Germans had hidden deep within the hills along well-camouflaged roads.

As the Thunderbirds advanced, the Germans would rush out of their hiding places, fire several salvos, and then return to safety before the American artillery could locate them. Once some local inhabitants plotted the locations of the German guns for the Americans, the cannons were quickly destroyed.[20]

With enemy opposition melting before the advancing Americans, and aware that the German and Italian troops were hastily withdrawing eastward, Middleton implemented his "leapfrogging" tactics. The plan called for attack forces to be constantly pressing the enemy. To maintain this initiative, a fresh RCT was moved

Members of a Forty-fifth Division Artillery unit move forward across Sicily in high-speed M-5 tractors, towing artillery pieces. The M-5 was capable of maintaining contact with the rapidly retreating German troops. *Courtesy Forty-fifth Infantry Division Museum.*

up into the line every two or three days, passing through the regiment that was currently engaged. The plan was much like earlier methods used to transport troops by always having some on foot and some in the trucks. The continual infusion of fresh and rested troops into the battle enabled Middleton to maintain constant pressure on the withdrawing enemy. All movement was forward; there was no removal to rest areas and no opportunity for the enemy to regroup.[21]

On 19 July, the pursuit of the fleeing Germans was taken over by the 180th, which immediately launched an attack spearheaded by its Second Battalion moving north along Highway 117. The

farther north the Americans moved, the more rugged and mountainous the terrain became. As the Thunderbirds approached the intersection of Highway 117 and Valledolmo Road, the advance units of motorized infantry and anti-tank guns were attacked by several German light and medium tanks; however, the assault was beaten off and several of the enemy tanks were captured. As the advance continued, the main thrust of Axis resistance came from a series of pill-box bunkers and natural strongpoints designed only to delay the American advance along the region's winding, rocky roads.[22]

On the night of 20 July, the 180th moved along

Highway 117 in a column of battalions, keeping the pressure on the Axis troops. The Thunderbirds seized Roccapalumba Station, one of the richest hauls of the entire campaign: there were acres of gasoline casks, vast stores of engine equipment, thousands of barrels of oil, and countless mines.[23]

On 21 July a patrol under First Lieutenant Robert L. Roye entered Palermo, the capital of Sicily, several hours before the advance guard of the Second Armored Division, which received official credit for the capture of the city. That same day the division's direction of attack was shifted east in order to take control of the Termini Imerese-Cefalù road. Three days later troops of Company G of the 180th reached Termini Imerese on Sicily's northern coast. The Forty-fifth Division had cut the island in half.[24]

German resistance began to stiffen. When the 157th reentered the line on 22 July, its orders were to advance under cover of darkness to Station Cerda and cut the railroad. Although an attempt was made to move the troops by motor transport, the destruction of key bridges made this impossible, and the Thunderbirds struck out on foot. Encountering only light resistance, the Americans advanced to a point about one mile west of their objective by the early morning of 23 July. Suddenly the Germans sprang a trap, catching the Second Battalion in an ambush along an open road. Enemy machine guns and mortars opened fire with deadly effect. For fifty minutes the GIs hugged the ground as the heavy enemy fire continued. At one point the Germans blew up a large bridge to the front of the Americans, showering them with chunks of cement. The ambush was finally broken up by heavy artillery fire from the 158th Field Artillery, and the Americans withdrew. By the time the battalion flanked the enemy positions, the Germans had escaped.[25]

Cefalù was occupied the following morning, and the 180th passed through the 157th on 24 July to resume the attack. The Thunderbirds were now out of the hills and moving along the coastline, where the narrow roads ran along the beach with the water on one side and steep hills on the other. At first the Americans made rapid progress east along Highway 113; however, by midnight the fighting became heavy. To halt the American advance, the Germans planted explosives in the cliffs above the roads

"Hit th' dirt, boys!"

and showered the Thunderbirds with falling rock. As the advance slowed and the roads were destroyed, pack mules were used to carry ammunition and supplies to the front and to remove the wounded to the rear.[26]

The terrain became as much an enemy as the Germans. Barren mountains plunged to within a few yards of the beach, and often the only road available had been cut out of the mountainside. There was very little level ground, and the swollen streams rushing out of the mountains during the rainy season had left behind deep, rock-strewn gullies in the dry season. Such terrain was perfect for defense, and a small force could often hold off a much larger force with ease.[27]

The Americans were forced to adopt a constant series of outflanking movements through the almost impassable hills to push the Germans out of their defenses. Such movements "required exertions well nigh beyond human endurance." To impede the advance, the enemy had destroyed all bridges and mined all possible detours. It was a grim, bloody, slow fight.[28]

In the early morning hours of 25 July, the Second Battalion of the 180th began an attack to take Capo Raisigelta Telegrapho. Known as Telegraph Peninsula to the Americans, the spit of land reached into the sea for about a kilometer just to the west of Finale. By 0345 it was obvious that the peninsula would have to be taken before daylight or the advancing troops, trapped on the narrow coastal road, would be exposed to heavy enemy fire. The initial assault did not repulse the Germans, though, and bitter fighting raged throughout the day. Unable to overrun the enemy position by nightfall, the Americans consolidated their positions. The following morning the First Battalion joined the battle, and, weakened by the previous day's assault, the Germans were thrown off the peninsula.[29]

The following days would witness some of the most bitter fighting of the Sicilian campaign. Castel di Tusa, scene of the initial fight, became "Bloody Ridge" to the Thunderbirds. Bloody Ridge was one of five ridges lying between Cefalu and San Stefano. The Germans had heavily fortified the high ground, especially Hill 335 which overlooked the Tusa River and its valley, and ordered them held at all costs. Early on the morning of 27 July, the 157th and the First Battalion of the 180th began the attack.[30]

Castel di Tusa fell without much of a struggle, and the First Battalion of the 157th moved on to the next objective—Motta D'afformo, which was located high on the ridge overlooking the town—while the First Battalion of the 180th crossed to the east bank of the Tusa River. Suddenly, "all Hell broke loose." The 180th was forced to withdraw to the west bank in the face of murderous enemy fire, and the 157th, inching its way up the steep slope of Motta D'afformo, encountered ferocious enemy resistance. From dug-in artillery and mortar emplacements the Germans rained heavy fire on the Americans, and enemy machine guns swept the slopes from the surrounding high ground. Only after the Third Battalion of the 157th was rushed up to help were the Americans able to occupy the high ground to the northwest of Bloody Ridge.[31]

Throughout the night of 27-28 July the men of the 157th formed a circular guard, with each man deployed not more than ten feet away from the next and all facing outward toward the enemy. The Thunderbirds made themselves as comfortable as possible in the rough terrain, but it was almost impossible to get food and water to the front. "Commandeered mules loaded with supplies dropped dead in their tracks as they were led over the trailless mountainside. . . . Only men were hardly enough to act as burden bearers."[32]

The next morning the Americans renewed the assault. Because of the difficult terrain, the fighting soon became disorganized. Communications were fouled, and the assault became a series of small-unit fire fights. Bayonets and hand grenades were frequently used to drive the Germans from their emplacements.[33]

After bitter fighting, the Thunderbirds seized Hill 335's summit, only to have a German counterattack drive them off soon after. Once again, the GIs scaled the slope and threw the enemy back, this time to stay. The Americans continued to advance from ridge to ridge, encountering stubborn pockets of German resistance. Navy fire-support destroyers standing offshore aimed their five-inch guns to rout the die-hard defenders from their positions.[34]

Once the Thunderbirds held the heights, they continued the attack down the reverse slopes toward San Stefano. Although the Germans did not offer much resistance on the far side of the ridge, they left behind hundreds of booby traps and mines that extracted a fearful toll. During the night of 30 July the Americans entered San Stefano, and by 0745 of the next day the Second Battalion of the 157th completed its occupation of the city.[35]

While fighting for San Stefano, the Forty-fifth received word that it would be relieved by the Third Infantry Division. At 1530 on July 31 the Thunderbirds began leaving the front lines, and by 1 August, the entire division was on its way to a rest camp near Cefalù. Assigned responsibility for defending the coastal road in their sectors, the 180th and the 179th spent the remainder of the Sicilian campaign in the rear areas as a part of the Provisional Corps of the Seventh Army.[36]

While the men of the 179th and 180th regiments had reason to celebrate, the troops of the 157th RCT were not so fortunate. They had been selected, along with the Third Division, for an amphibious assault against Messina on the eastern tip of Sicily. The plan called for a landing well behind the German lines in an attempt to trap the enemy before they could withdraw to the Italian mainland. On 14 August the Thunderbirds moved to Termini Imerese, and the following day boarded the LCTs and LCIs that would carry them to the assault beach two miles west of Spadafora.[37]

Unfortunately for the Allies' plan, the Germans and the Italians had begun to abandon Sicily by 10 August. In an effort to trap the escaping enemy, the 157th's beach objective was changed in the early morning hours of 16 August to be two miles northwest of Termini. The effort proved futile; by the time the Thunderbirds rushed to the new landing the last of the Axis troops were gone, the final contingent—eight men of an Italian patrol—departed at 0735 on 17 August. When the Thunderbirds stepped ashore they found the beach in friendly hands but heavily mined. Moving toward Messina, a contingent from the First Battalion of the 157th entered the town on 18 August. Afterward, the 157th was then moved by boat, truck, and train to an area near Traba, Sicily, for a rest.[38]

The battle for Sicily ended. The enemy had fled to the Italian mainland, and the Forty-fifth had concluded the first of its six battle campaigns of World War II. The division had been in the front lines for twenty-two days of continuous combat and had covered more ground than any other Allied force. In so doing, it earned the praise of Lieutenant General George S. Patton, Jr., commander of the American Seventh Army, who declared, "Born at sea, baptized in blood, your fame shall never die." Described as "one of the best, if not the best division, in the history of American arms," the Forty-fifth had faced and defeated some of the best-trained German units.[39]

While the Thunderbirds rested after the Sicilian campaign, Allied headquarters planned the division's next operation. The Americans, at the urging of the British, had agreed to attempt to knock Italy out of the war before the invasion of occupied Europe began. It was known that Allied officers had met secretly with Italian officials in an attempt to arrange a surrender, but it was apparent that a direct assault upon the Italian mainland would be necessary to force Italy's surrender.[40]

On 3 September 1943, British troops began crossing from Sicily to the "toe" of the Italian boot. That same day an armistice was signed between the Allies and the Italians, but it was not made public. The Allies wanted to keep the surrender a secret until they were on the Italian mainland in force. The Italians had begun to have second thoughts, not about their surrender to the Allies but about the reaction of the Germans. Finally, on 8 September, Italy's surrender was announced.[41]

It was hoped that the invasion by the two British divisions across the Strait of Messina on 3 September would draw the Germans southward to meet the assault. Once this happened, the Allies planned to land a large combined British and American force to the north, near Salerno, and catch the enemy in a trap. Another Allied attack was to be directed against the Italian naval base at Taranto. The Salerno invasion force included the Eighty-second Airborne Division; the American Sixth Corps, which contained the Third, the Thirty-fourth, and the Thirty-sixth infantry divisions, along with the Forty-fifth; and the British Tenth Corps, which included the Forty-sixth and the Fifty-sixth divisions, the Seventh Armored Division, the Twenty-third Armored Brigade, the First, the Third, and the Fourth Ranger battalions of the U.S. Army, and the Second and the Forty-first British commandos. After sailing from North Africa and Sicily, the units were to converge on the beaches south of Salerno.[42]

Major General Middleton was informed of the forthcoming invasion on 21 August, when he and his staff were called to Algiers to confer with the Allied headquarters and Lieutenant General Mark Clark, the commander of the American Fifth Army. Shortly afterward, the Forty-fifth was transferred to the Sixth Corps of the Fifth Army, and preparations began for the division's second major combat assault against enemy beaches. By 7 September the Thunderbirds were ready to board their landing craft.[43]

Operation Avalanche, the code name for the Salerno landing, was somewhat confused from its beginning. At first, the only American contribution to the assault was to be the Thirty-sixth Division. This was later changed to include one RCT of the Forty-fifth. Then the plans were altered again to include two RCTs of the Forty-fifth. Finally, the Thunderbirds were told that they would be the floating reserve for the Fifth Army's assault waves. Although the exact time

LSTs disgorging troops from the Forty-fifth at Paestum, twenty miles south of Salerno, on the Italian boot. Temporary causeways have been constructed from the beachfront to deeper water to facilitate the operation. The assault waves have already poured ashore and moved inland. *Courtesy Forty-fifth Infantry Division Museum.*

and place of the division's "initial employment" was "purposely indefinite" because of its role as reserves, General Middleton knew that he had to be ready to put his men ashore on any one of the assault beaches should the need arise.[44]

Although Italy, for all practical purposes, was out of the fighting, there was still a formidable German army on the peninsula, and every effort was made to make the invasion a surprise. Divisional headquarters was set up in an old school building at Termini Imerese, and, it was hoped, to confuse the Germans, the division was to embark from there. While navy personnel prepared for the loading of the troops, the 540th Engineers did whatever was possible to improve the beaches, and minesweepers combed the sea for enemy mines.[45]

Thirty-two transports—sixteen LSTs and sixteen LCIs—arrived, and throughout the day of 7 September 1943 the men of the 157th and the 179th clambered aboard. The 180th remained behind in its bivouac area near San Nicoli. The next day the fleet sailed.[46]

The brief voyage to Salerno was almost without interruption. The sea was placid and blue, and the troops were allowed to loll on deck. That evening the men were informed of Italy's surrender, but their spontaneous cheers were quickly silenced by the sudden appearance of German bombers. Fortunately, the aircraft released their bombs too soon and they completely missed their targets. By the early morning hours of 9 September, the transports carrying the Thunderbirds were lying offshore in the Gulf of Salerno.[47]

Although every precaution had been taken to keep the enemy from learning of the landing, the Germans were ready. Several panzer units had been moved south from Rome to take positions in the hills overlooking the assault beaches. Artillery and mortars were placed in a wide semicircle to cover the entire landing area, and a heavy concentration of antiaircraft guns were

Private First Class Alfred Johnson, Captain John W. Armstrong, and Sergeant John W. Smith, of Seminole, Oklahoma, treat one of the many wounded in the bitter fighting on the Salerno beachhead. The military censor obliterated Smith's Thunderbird patch but missed the patch on Johnson's helmet and another on the wounded man's shoulder. *Courtesy Forty-fifth Infantry Division Museum.*

moved into the area. The beach defenses, however, were not well organized. Mines had been laid at random and barbed wire barricades hurriedly placed but the Germans pegged their successful defense of the Salerno region on many small units of tanks that could rush to any landing zone and drive the invaders into the sea.[48]

When the British and American assault units stormed ashore at 0330 on 9 September, they met diverse resistance. To maintain secrecy, there had been no preinvasion bombardment, and thus the enemy entrenchments were intact. The ran-

ger units landed on the left flank and faced little opposition as they moved inland. The British divisions occupied the center of the Allied lines, and they encountered fairly strong German resistance. It was a different story for the Thirty-sixth Division, which landed on the right flank. These troops met a determined and well-organized enemy.[49]

Although the beaches at Salerno were excellent for amphibious landings, behind the narrow coastal plain were steep hills that overlooked the invasion area on three sides and offered excellent protection for the defending troops. Because of the distance from the Sicilian air fields to Salerno, it was difficult for the Allies to maintain sufficient air cover over the beaches with land-based aircraft, and this meant that the carrier-based planes, few in number, had to assist. Nonetheless, once on the beaches, the Allies continued to pour men ashore, with a new wave landing every eight minutes. The Germans refused to give ground and met each new wave with point-blank tank and artillery fire. At dawn the Germans again sent their tanks against the beachhead, but the sortie was thwarted with the help of navy gunfire and hastily landed artillery units.[50]

With desperate fighting under way onshore, the first of the Thunderbirds entered the action. Approximately fifty men from the Third Battalion of the 157th were loaded aboard an American destroyer, the U.S.S. *Knight,* at Salerno Bay. Joining a group of American rangers, they were told to destroy a German radar and radio station on the island of Ventotene, forty miles west of Naples. Commanded by Navy Lieutenant Douglas Fairbanks, Jr., the Thunderbirds and the rangers stormed ashore during the night of 9-10 September. As it turned out, elements of the Eighty-second Airborne Division had already destroyed the facility, and the Thunderbirds returned to their parent unit.[51]

Because of the stiff German resistance facing the Thirty-sixth—a former Texas National Guard division—it was decided to use the 179th and a portion of the 157th to reinforce the right flank of the Allied line. Originally scheduled to disembark at 0300 on 10 September, the Thunderbirds were forced to postpone their landing because of bad weather. Daybreak found the men still aboard their ships, staring at the enemy coastline. Without warning, the ship was attacked by German aircraft. The first pass occurred so quickly that the antiaircraft gunners did not have time to bring their weapons to bear, but when the planes returned for a second run they were quickly routed, and preparations for the landing continued uninterrupted.[52]

At 1140 landing platforms were lowered from the transports and the great steel doors of the landing ships swung open. MPs were waiting on the beach to direct the troops to their assembly points as the Thunderbirds hurried ashore. The Forty-fifth engaged its second battle campaign, Naples-Foggia. It would be a long, hard fight up the Italian boot.[53]

CHAPTER 8

SALERNO

The 180th remained in Sicily on reserve, but the 157th and the 179th RCTS, together with the 158th, the 180th, and the 189th Field Artillery battalions, one battalion of the 540th Engineers, and a part of the 242nd Quartermaster Service Battalion were quickly hurled into the battle. The 157th was without its Second Brigade, which had taken heavy casualties. By the time the Thunderbirds entered combat, the situation at the Salerno beachhead was becoming critical. The Germans had amassed a powerful assault force to drive the invaders into the sea, and the Allies were by now too weakened to do anything other than hold what ground they had seized during the initial landing.[1]

After landing on 10 September, the 179th hurriedly moved to its assembly area about three miles north of Paestum, where it formed the onshore corps reserve. At the assembly area, the men had a brief respite, with some time to eat K rations and rest. Throughout the landing and the following day the Thirty-sixth Division took a terrific pounding from the Germans. Enemy armored units continually pressed the American lines and threatened to push the GIs into the sea. By midafternoon of the landing day the situation was so critical it forced Sixth Corps headquarters to commit its reserves. At about the same time, because of a mistake on the part of the troop carrier commander, the 157th began to land its troops ahead of schedule. The premature landing would shortly help save the beachhead because the 157th was now available to shore up weak points.[2]

Once committed to the battle, Colonel Robert B. Hutchins, commander of the 179th, was ordered to move his men eastward to Highway 8

where he planned to turn north and block any German push from the direction of Eboli. By 1925 hours the men had assembled and were making their way inland. The Thunderbirds were held up briefly at the Calore River, but once the engineers constructed a pontoon bridge, they quickly crossed into a no-man's-land.[3]

Because of the critical situation, there had been no reconnaissance of the area. The only thing that Colonel Hutchins could do was push on until he made contact with the enemy. The 179th advanced twenty-two miles inland that night before encountering any opposition. It was still dark when the regiment's lead elements ran into the Germans. Once contact was made, the Thunderbirds quickly formed a defensive perimeter. It was none too soon, for just as dawn was breaking the enemy launched a massive attack.[4]

Throwing all available men and materiel against the beachhead, the Germans were determined to sweep past the 179th and push on to the sea. Enemy tanks, self-propelled artillery, and machine guns began a withering fire, and two panzer divisions trapped the 179th on the north side of the river, while its supporting armor was still on the south shore. By 1000 it was obvious that this was a major German attack, and the 179th was in a precarious position. To the regiment's rear an enemy armor column had swung across the Sele River and was moving toward the Thunderbirds. German 88-mm. cannons—their all-purpose field gun—continually shelled crossroads in the region to prevent the shifting of Allied troops, and forward observers counted two hundred enemy tanks moving toward the beach area. The Americans seemed to

The Thunderbirds landed on Salerno beach on 10 September 1943. Although the beachhead shows little sign of battle, one of the supply ships burns offshore after being hit by German fire, while an LST off-loads onto the shore. *Courtesy Forty-fifth Infantry Division Museum.*

be trapped, with the enemy closing in from the north, the west, and the south.[5]

With German artillery and machine guns raking them from one end of their line to the other, the Thunderbirds fought back. The 160th Field Artillery fired shell after shell into the advancing Germans, but still the tanks rumbled forward. All the battalions were hotly engaged, with savage fighting reported in every section.[6]

Lieutenant Colonel Hal L. Muldrow, commander of the 189th Field Artillery, rushed forward with his executive officer, Major Otwa T. Autry, to assess the situation at the Calore River. One battery of the 189th had already crossed the stream, but it was hurriedly withdrawn to the friendly bank in the face of advancing German tanks. Because the bridge across the stream had been destroyed, the German armored force was forced to stop. Once the enemy paused, American artillery began to exact a deadly toll.[7]

Driving to a nearby deserted barn, Muldrow and Autry climbed to the top of the structure to get a better view of the situation; they began to call down firing orders to their driver, who in turn relayed the messages to the battery commanders. The 189th's gunners opened up with the unit's 155-mm. howitzers at a range of seven hundred to eight hundred yards. Firing over open sights, the artillerymen devastated the

German tanks and forced the survivors to withdraw.[8]

In the face of the onslaught, the First and the Third battalions of the 179th threw up all-around defenses. The First Battalion managed to hold its own, but the Third Battalion, after taking terrific punishment, was forced to pull back about one mile to the south, along Highway 19. The Second Battalion of the 179th was pushed back across the Calore River, with some of its men barely escaping over the last remaining pontoon bridge just ahead of German tanks. The Second Battalion was quickly isolated.[9]

Although a valiant attempt was made to reestablish contact with the beseiged 179th using tanks and tank destroyers, the Americans were unable to force a crossing of the river. Both the regiment's CP and aid station were under enemy artillery fire, and many of the wounded were being killed. In an attempt to draw the enemy's attention away from the beleaguered 179th, Major General Middleton ordered the 157th and the 142nd Infantry to launch feint attacks. The Germans were strong enough to meet these attacks and to continue to pressure the 179th. Middleton then turned to Allied airpower to relieve the pressure against the 179th, but when informed the requested air strikes were denied because of a lack of aircraft, he decided to plan

As supplies piled up on the beaches, they offered a tempting target to German aircraft based in Italy. A crew on one of the Forty-fifth's 40-mm. M-1 light antiaircraft guns watches for enemy planes. *Courtesy Forty-fifth Infantry Division Museum.*

for the worst. Just south of the 179th's position, there was a mile-wide gap in the German pincers along the Calore River. At 1845, another pontoon bridge was ordered constructed over the stream; if the 179th was overrun there would be an escape avenue for survivors.[10]

Throughout that afternoon the battle swarmed relentlessly about the men. Artillery fire from both sides was merciless, and machine gun and small-arms fire rattled incessantly. German tanks fired point-blank into the American positions, but the Thunderbirds held. By 1700, the 160th Field Artillery reported it had only five rounds per gun remaining and they were being saved for a final stand. The infantry was running critically short of ammunition, and in several in-

stances the men were forced to resort to using their bayonets. Water was in short supply, with some units completely out. When night fell, the First and the Third battalions tightened their lines and made what defensive improvements they could. Unaware of the 179th's precarious situation, the Germans did not launch another attack.[11]

While the men of the 179th were fighting for their lives, the 157th RCT was completing its landing. By the next morning, in an attempt to relieve the pressure on the 179th, the 157th had rushed to a position to launch an attack on the German flank. The key to the region was the Grataglia River plain, and the key to holding the plain was to gain control of five stone tobacco-storage buildings called the Tobacco Warehouse. Control of this point would turn the German flank.[12]

By midnight on 11 September, the 157th had fought to within five hundred yards of the Tobacco Warehouse before German machine guns and tanks had slowed its advance. On the following morning the assault on the warehouse was resumed with the support of a tank company sent to help the infantry. For two hours a brutal fight raged. The Germans entrenched in the stone buildings and nearby tall grass maintained a deadly fire on the attackers. The Americans replied in kind. More than two hundred tank shells were poured into the strongpoint, while the 158th Field Artillery "threw shells like hail storms into the buildings." The battle was fought at such close quarters that the 158th and the 189th field artillery took German tanks under direct fire.

Over a two-day period, in the face of superior firepower, the enemy began to weaken and the pressure on the 179th was relieved as the Germans were forced to throw more and more men and materiel into the threat to their flank. The battle for the Tobacco Warehouse seesawed back and forth, with the Americans and the Germans trading possession of the strongpoint. On the evening of the thirteenth, the Germans were driven out for good. The 189th Field Artillery was awarded a distinguished unit citation for its actions on 13 September 1943.[13]

While the 157th was fighting for control of the Tobacco Warehouse, troops led by Brigadier General Raymond S. McLain opened a supply route to the beseiged 179th. As the 645th Tank Destroyer Battalion struck at the enemy in the 179th's sector, reconnaissance units quickly discovered that the Germans were pulling back into the hills. At 2000 on September 12, the 179th was relieved by the Thirty-sixth Division, and the Thunderbirds marched out of the "Persano Trap."[14]

During the savage German counterattack, there was some concern among Allied leaders that it might be impossible to hold the beachhead against the onslaught. Acutely aware of the precarious situation, Sixth Corps headquarters alerted the navy to prepare for a possible evacuation. Upon hearing of the preparations, Major General Middleton, the Thunderbird commander, replied, "Put food and ammuni-

tion behind the 45th. We are here to stay."[15]

For the next few days the Thunderbirds strengthened their defenses. Although the enemy continued to probe the Forty-fifth's lines, the ground fighting slackened somewhat. The artillery was kept busy, however, with both ground-support fire missions and antiaircraft work. To bolster the beachhead's perimeter, on 13 September the 180th RCT was loaded onto navy landing craft at Sicily and transported to the Italian mainland. By 0130 the following day, advance units of the regiment were landing at Salerno. Within a short time the Forty-fifth's three RCTs were reunited.[16]

By nightfall of 16 September it was apparent that the Germans were withdrawing, although a well-fortified and heavily armed delaying force was still facing the beachhead. The Allies increased their patrol activity, and the remainder of the enemy troops abandoned their positions during the night of 17–18 September. The Forty-fifth took up the pursuit the following morning.[17]

The "break from the beachhead was like a breath of fresh air after a long stay in a small prison," recorded one Thunderbird. By 19 September, the division was pushing toward its next objective—the high ground along the Ofanto River near San Andrea di Conza and Teora. Unfortunately, the rugged terrain, the enemy mines left behind, and the destroyed roads and bridges made it difficult to keep up with the fleeing Germans.[18]

Contact was regained with the enemy on 20 September, when the Second Battalion, 180th Infantry, came under heavy mortar and artillery fire west of Oliveto. It was a natural defensive position and the Germans used the terrain to the utmost. By the following day the Thunderbirds were once more in the thick of battle as the 180th began its attack against Oliveto.[19]

Throughout the night of September 21–22 the GIs pushed the Germans back. For his heroism in the fighting around Oliveto, an Oklahoma guardsman, Second Lieutenant Ernest Childers of Broken Arrow, was awarded the Medal of Honor. On 22 September, Childers, limping from the pain of a broken bone in one foot, led eight enlisted men in an attack against several German machine-gun emplacements. Although his foot was so painful that he finally had to crawl, Childers almost single-handedly eliminated several German snipers, overran two machine-gun nests, and captured a mortar observer. He then established a defensive position and ordered up litter bearers to carry back the wounded before hobbling to an aid station to have his own injury tended.[20]

With German resistance disintegrating, the Thunderbirds continued to press forward. The enemy was withdrawing so rapidly that at times it was not possible to maintain contact, and by 24 September no units of the Forty-fifth were engaged with German infantry. Nonetheless, enemy artillery fire continued. As one commentator described the American advance, the Allies "pushed hard after the German rear guards but 'without hurrying them appreciably.'"[21]

At this time of the year a new enemy loomed— the weather. The fall rains were beginning and Italy's dusty fields were quickly turning into mud. The inclement weather, combined with the effectiveness of the Germans in destroying roads and bridges during their retreat, slowed the Allied advance to a crawl. The delay allowed the German army to reestablish its defensive lines behind the Volturno River where it awaited the Allied attack.[22]

Throughout the Allies' advances, Major General Middleton had continued to alternate his units at the front to maintain pressure on the retreating Germans. By 26 September, however, when the 180th became the division's spearhead, the condition of the roads made movement extremely difficult, and by the next day the Thunderbirds were halted by heavy rain. For the remainder of the month the Forty-fifth merely slogged its way forward, liberating many small Italian towns.[23]

On 2 October the division headed northwest. The British Eighth Army was on its right flank, and the American Thirty-fourth and Third divisions were on its left. The division's goal was Benevento and a bridgehead across the Calore River north of the town. Once the Calore River barrier was breached, the Thunderbirds were to turn north and west to clear the upper Volturno valley. At the same time the Thirty-fourth and Third divisions were to breach the Germans' Volturno River line.[24]

Throughout October the American advance was painfully slow. The Germans were as skillful in retreat as they were in the attack. Their heavy mining of roads as they retreated made using the roads extremely hazardous and inflicted many casualties. In addition, almost continuous enemy artillery fire interdicted the American supply lines. There was also a reemergence of German airpower that constantly harassed the Allies.[25]

The continuous enemy contact, the weather, and the rough terrain began to have a devastating effect. Casualties were depleting the ranks of the battle-weary troops. In the 179th, "scarcely enough trained non-coms and riflemen remained to form a nucleus in any one platoon." To offset the losses replacements were hurried to the front, but as one soldier said, the Forty-fifth was "losing veterans with 2 years' training and 2 compaigns' experience" and replacing them with "soldiers most of whom had . . . only the basic 13 weeks training." This policy "worked a terrible, brutal hardship on the fighting regiments and on their individual fighting men." It also resulted in unnecessary casualties among the replacement troops, who were forced to learn "a soldier's trade" the "hard way."[26]

Some of the objectives encountered in the advance proved to be a ready teaching ground. The fight for Mount Acerno was especially bitter. The attack began at 0045 on 14 October with the First and the Third battalions of the 179th RCT starting up the mountain slope in the face of heavy machine-gun fire. Although the Thunderbirds managed to gain a tentative foothold along the mountain's southern slope, the hand-to-hand struggle for the summit continued all day and all night. It was not until sunset on the fifteenth that the Germans were thrown off the heights.[27]

While the 179th was struggling up Mount Acerno, the 157th seized Faicchio and forced a crossing of the Titerno River. During the October 14 battle, the Thunderbirds came face to face with a new German weapon—the *Nebelwerfer*—a six-barreled rocket launcher. They quickly nicknamed its rockets "screaming meemies." All six rockets were fired at once, with the projectiles screaming through the air "like dying banshees." The *Nebelwerfer* proved to be a terribly effective weapon, and the Americans referred to it as a "six barrel organ playing the Purple Heart Blues." Opposed by enemy tanks, the 179th fought a bitter seesaw battle for the high ground around Faicchio before, as one GI proclaimed, they "booted the bastards off."[28]

Shortly after the battle for Faicchio, Sixth Corps altered the division's sector so that by

A thunderbird loads supplies onto a Dodge 7214-WC51 weapons carrier for transport to the front. Popularly called a "Beep," even this four-wheel-drive vehicle had difficulty traversing the rough terrain, especially in the wet winter weather. *Courtesy Forty-fifth Infantry Division Museum.*

the time the Thunderbirds reached Piedmonte on 18 October, they were pinched out of the front line. Three days later, after forty combat days—the longest of any division serving in the European theater of operations—the Forty-fifth was relieved and sent to the rear for a rest.[29]

Most of the Thunderbirds were withdrawn to the west of Piedmonte for refitting. The First and Second battalions of the 157th Infantry, the divisional artillery, and the Forty-fifth Reconnaissance Troop continued to outpost the area near the town. Patrols were maintained to determine the enemy's strength, and combat problems were practiced in the mountains around Piedmonte. Most of the time at the rear was devoted to rest and reequipping, however. Although the rest was well deserved, it was short-lived and within nine days the Thunderbirds were fighting for their lives again.[30]

On 30 October, the Thunderbirds began to move back to the front. The inclement weather continued, and the rains turned every road into a mud bog. Between 8 November and 30 November there were only three days without rain, and much equipment was lost and the troops made miserable. Moreover, when the Forty-fifth emerged from the broad, low valley of the Volturno River it entered some of the worst mountain terrain it was to face. Hidden high in the

mountains west of the Volturno River valley was the infamous German Winter line; it had been prepared well in advance and the enemy troops had been ordered to hold the line at all costs.[31]

Moving into the area around Venafro, the division began preparations for an assault on the German strongpoint. A "rugged, bald rocky mountain" area, the region was traversed by trails so narrow that they could be traveled only by pack mules, and former "farm boys" were recruited from various units to drive the animals up the steep trails. Eventually the terrain became so bad that the pack mules gave out, and supplies had to be hauled to the front with back packs that allowed each man to carry a hundred pounds. The Thunderbirds quickly named the region "Purple Heart Valley."[32]

The German commander, Field Marshal Albert Kesselring, was determined to stop the Allied advance up the Italian boot, and the harsh terrain in the mountains beyond the Volturno River provided the perfect defensive position. Reinforcements were brought up and positioned among the huge boulders, on rocky ledges, in caves, and on the back slopes so that they had excellent cover from Allied fire. To strengthen these natural defenses, a system of reinforced slit trenches and stone-covered natural dugouts were incorporated into the Winter line. An ex-

A squad of Thunderbird infantrymen enter Benevento, Italy, in October, 1943. The division's main objective in this campaign, the town had been virtually destroyed by the time the guardsmen entered it. *Courtesy Forty-fifth Infantry Division Museum.*

tensive minefield was laid, and demolitions destroyed all land approaches. Artillery was registered in predetermined patterns so that every "road, sheep trail and bivouac site or possible assembly area" was covered. The German machine-gun emplacements were planned so that the men and the weapons could quickly be withdrawn to other emplacements if the Americans threatened to overrun them. Then, after the machine-gun crews had been withdrawn, artillery and mortar fire could be used to break the attack. Kesselring also took care that the Germans occupied all possible observation points to ensure that any Allied attack could be taken under directed artillery fire.[33]

The American reaction to the fortifications, which heavily depended upon artillery, was to attempt to reduce them with their artillery. The Germans countered with further battery fire, and the battle became a series of artillery duels, with the infantry of both sides dug in for protection. The Forty-fifth entered the battle on 1 November, as its troops were moved to the banks of the Volturno. Flanking the Thunderbirds on the right was the Thirty-fourth Division; on its left was the Third Division.[34]

The actual river crossing began on 2 November when several patrols were sent across. Throughout the ensuing days the remainder of the division followed. Enemy opposition was mostly artillery fire; however, several German armored vehicles threatened to assault the bridgehead until they were forced to withdraw. By 4 November, the engineers had completed a pon-

"My God! There we wuz an' here they wuz."

Fresh, spirited American troops, flushed with victory, are bringing in thousands of hungry, ragged, battle-weary prisoners. (News item)

toon bridge across the Volturno, and the division's light vehicles began to pour across to reinforce the troops.[35]

Throughout the following days the Americans pressed forward against stubborn German resistance. Advancing on Venafro, the 179th forced the enemy to withdraw to higher ground. Quickly following, the Thunderbirds entered the mountains near Venafro where the fighting became a struggle from ridge to ridge in what the GIs called the "Mountains of Blood."[36]

The Italian campaign had become a war of attrition. Men collapsed under the strain and the inhuman conditions. The Forty-fifth's commander during much of the Italian fighting, Major General Troy Middleton, considered the long Italian campaign to be harder on the men than any battle of World War I. In a communication Middleton noted that there was almost "continuous rain and snow. . . . [The] front line troops are cold all the time and wet more than dry." To prevent the complete deterioration of the troops, the attacking units were rotated as much as possible.[37]

When it finally appeared that the Forty-fifth was beginning to crack the German Winter line, the Thunderbirds were suddenly withdrawn from the high ground around Venafro on 10 November. Morale sagged as the men left the ridges for which such a high price in blood had been paid. Although the Forty-fifth was relieved by rangers and paratroopers, its replacements were neither strong nor experienced enough to prevent the Germans from reclaiming the heights.[38]

By 15 November, Lieutenant General Clark decided that his forces were not of the necessary strength to break the Winter line, and he ordered an end to the advance. The battle lines became more or less static and the fighting stalemated. Sickness and fatigue began to weaken the troops, and the weariness had no respect for rank. On 22 November 1943, Major General Middleton was replaced by Major General W. W. Eagles as commander of the Forty-fifth after Middleton was stricken with arthritis in his elbows and knees. Middleton later became the commander of the U.S. Eighth Corps and played a prominent role in defeating the Germans at the Battle of the Bulge.[39]

It was the dead of winter, and trenchfoot plagued many of the men. In an effort to relieve

"Purple Heart Valley" near Venefro, Italy. The infamous German Winter line was in the mountains around the valley, and any movement brought a hail of enemy fire. *Courtesy Forty-fifth Infantry Division Museum.*

some of the harshness of the fighting, the troops generally spent only eight days at a time in the line, but during this time they were always soaking wet. This usually led to illness and trenchfoot. They would be returned to the rear for four days of rest, but that wasn't enough time to get well or for their feet to heal. Although such a schedule might have been appropriate for any other campaign, it was not ideal for the mountains.[40]

"Four days off, Hell; it took us over two days of mountain-goat climbing coming off and getting back to those damned rocks," one member of the 157th RCT remarked. "If we had one full day to thaw out we were lucky." To make matters worse the quartermasters were slow in getting cold weather clothing to the troops. In an attempt to speed things up, rear area troops were stripped of cold weather gear so it could be sent to the front.[41]

Staff Sergeant Jack Clapp, who had served with the division's G-3 section since mobilization, spent nearly a year fighting in Italy without living in a house. Instead, whenever his unit paused, he dug a hole in the ground, lined it with whatever he could find, and slept in the bottom of the pit. Although he was out of the harsh wind, he often awoke covered with snow. Because of a shortage of hot water, Clapp would

December, 1943. Because of the harsh weather the combat units were frequently rotated to the rear lines for rest and warm food. These men from the Forty-fifth are being served by American Red Cross volunteers. *Courtesy Forty-fifth Infantry Division Museum.*

rush to the mess tent every morning, fill a canteen cup with coffee, and hold it in his hands to warm them. Afterwards, before the coffee lost all its heat, he used it to shave.[42]

On 29 November the offensive was renewed, but with much the same result. The weather and the terrain greatly handicapped the advancing troops and gave the Germans every advantage. Through the following weeks the fighting again was reduced to being a struggle up a hill, seize the high ground, hold it against enemy counterattacks, and then attack the next ridge. All too often the Germans simply withdrew to even more favorable positions to await the next assault. The impasse continued.[43]

Obviously the campaign was not receiving the men and materiel needed to break the German lines. Later the surgeon general would sharply criticize the army's policy of "retaining the troops in the line for such interminable periods without a break." Instead of giving the Sixth Corps sufficient forces to be able to rotate the troops frequently between the front and the rear, and thus preserve the men to fight longer, the men serving in Italy were "being worked until, if not casual-

ties, they dropped from exhaustion." To some it appeared that the Third, the Thirty-fourth, the Thirty-sixth, and the Forty-fifth divisions were expendable. The price in men and materiel was becoming too high. Moreover, the longer the Germans delayed the Allies along the Winter line the more time they had to prepare defenses in central and northern Italy. Obviously something had to be done to break the stalemate.[44]

The solution took the form of an end run, with plans to land a large Allied force to the rear of the German lines. Originally the move was viewed as a subsidiary operation on the left flank in which the Allies would send only enough troops ashore to create the danger of encirclement and dislocate the German defenses that had been blocking the Allied march up the Italian boot. It quickly became apparent, however, that instead of a mere diversion, the plan could be developed into a huge pincer movement that would trap most of the German army in Italy. When this idea took root, preparation for Operation Shingle, as the landings at Anzio were code-named, began to take form.[45]

On 4 November 1943, General Dwight D. Eisenhower, commander in chief of the Allied forces, authorized the formulation of plans for an amphibious operation designed for the area around the city of Rome. At the same time he approved the retention of enough LSTs in the Mediterranean theater until January of 1944 to allow the operation to be carried out. Even so, there would be only eighty-eight LSTs available for the Anzio operation, and this was insufficient to place the entire force ashore at once. Instead, the troops would have to be landed piecemeal while the ships shuttled back and forth between the beachhead and Naples.[46]

Despite the shortage of shipping, General Sir Harold R. L. G. Alexander, deputy commander in chief, issued orders for the operation. Clark and the Fifth Army were to break through the German lines, penetrate into the Liri Valley to Fronsinone, and then launch an amphibious force toward Anzio. There, the troops would storm ashore and seize the Alban Hills—the last natural defensive barrier before Rome. At the same time, the rest of the Fifth Army would launch an attack from Fronsinone, join with the Anzio beachhead, and catch the Germans in a huge pincer movement.[47]

The area selected for the assault was a narrow stretch of coastal plain near Anzio running north from Terracina across the Tiber River. An area roughly fifteen miles wide and seven miles deep was to form the initial Allied landing area. This gave the assault force a perimeter of approximately twenty-six miles, which was the maximum Allied leaders believed it could hold. In addition, it incorporated the best natural defensive terrain of the region into the line. On the northwest were the Moletta and Incastro rivers, natural barriers of ravines as deep as fifty feet that would block any enemy armored counterattack; on the southeast were the Pontine Marshes; and in the center of the beachhead was the Anzio-Albano road leading to Highway 7 and Rome.[48]

Sixth Corps was selected by Lieutenant General Clark to make the landing. In addition to the Forty-fifth and the Third Infantry division, the American contribution also included the First Armored Division, the 751st Tank Battalion, the 509th Parachute Infantry Battalion, the 504th Parachute Infantry Regiment, and a force of rangers. The First British Infantry Division, the Forty-sixth Royal Tank Regiment, and a

The Forty-fifth's field artillery battalions were heavily relied upon in the fighting along the German's Winter line. *Left to right:* Captain Howard P. Rice; Lieutenant Colonel Hal L. Muldrow, Jr., commanding officer of the 189th Field Artillery Battalion; Captain Harry Lane, commanding officer of the Service Battery, 160th Field Artillery; Lieutenant Colonel John Embry (wearing patch of the 102nd Division), commanding officer of the 160th Field Artillery Battalion. *Courtesy Forty-fifth Infantry Division Museum.*

group of commandos rounded out the landing force.[49]

The Anzio operation was scheduled for 22 January 1944, and early in the month the Forty-fifth began withdrawing from the "Mountains of Blood." The 179th began moving out of the lines to the vicinity of San Potito on 1 January, and the 157th was replaced on 10 January. On 9 January the division gave the responsibility for its combat sector to the French Expeditionary Corps. The 180th, which was attached to the French command, remained in the line until 15 January. At the time of its relief the division had accumulated 110 days of combat of the 121 days that had passed since it first had landed in Sicily.[50]

Replacements were hurriedly worked into

the division's organizations as the RCTs were brought up to strength. So bitter had the fighting been that one regiment, the 157th, received 411 replacements during the lull. Near the end of the month all three regiments were moved to a staging area three miles west of Naples. Here the division's vehicles were waterproofed and its equipment packed for loading on troop carriers.[51]

While the Thunderbirds were making final preparations for boarding the transports, the plan to trap the Germans got under way. At dawn on 12 January the Allies launched a furious attack at Cassino to break through the Winter line and begin their march northward to join with the planned invasion force. Ten days later the American Third Division and the British First Division, accompanied by a multitude of special service troops and rangers, stormed ashore in an arc between Anzio and Nettuno.[52]

It would not be long before the Thunderbirds joined them in battle. The same day as the initial landing near Anzio, the 179th Regimental Combat Team, which was the division's leading element for the operation, began boarding transports at Naples. Two days later they were disembarking at Anzio. The remainder of the division followed quickly. The 157th landed on 29 January and the 180th the next day.[53]

The Allied landing caught the German defenders by surprise. The first waves of troops stormed ashore without any opposition. The Third Division pushed inland rapidly, while Allied air forces completely minimized the effectiveness of German airpower. For several days men and materiel poured ashore unhindered, and it looked as if the operation would accomplish all that was hoped for. Very quickly, however, German resistance began to stiffen as reinforcements were rushed to the region and artillery batteries in the surrounding hills began to take the beachhead under fire. The advance slowed and then halted on 1 February, with the Allies controlling a semicircle with a radius of approximately ten miles from the original landing area. The events that transpired at Anzio resulted in some of the most costly fighting of World War II.[54]

CHAPTER 9

ANZIO

While the Anzio area offered an ideal beach for a landing, some Allied officers were apprehensive about the surrounding terrain. The flatness of the beach area, though useful in moving men and equipment from ship to shore, offered little cover for the troops once on land. Moreover, some distance beyond the initial beachhead objectives were the steep slopes of the Alban Hills from which German observers could watch all movement within the Allied lines. Recalled one Thunderbird, it was "like fighting on a stage with the enemy for an audience."[1]

Aside from the lack of cover to protect the troops from enemy observation and artillery fire, the Anzio beachhead was bounded by natural defensive positions. Along the northern portion of the beachhead was a pine woods, the Padiglione Forest (named after a town close by), which terminated in a mass of scrub oak and undergrowth. Along the woods' southern border was Nero's Pike, which led from the beachhead toward Padiglione. East of the Padiglione Forest was another woods called Campo Morto. Near the center of the beachhead was a third clump of forest. On the far eastern flank of the Anzio landing area was another pine forest. The southern boundary of the beachhead was formed by the Mussolini Canal, which stretched in a wide arc from Padiglione to the sea. Northeast of the landing area, at the foot of the Alban Hills, was Cisterna and to the southeast was Littoria.[2]

The first of the Forty-fifth's combat teams ashore was the 179th, which disembarked at Anzio on 25 January 1944. It was, however, four days later before the 179th relieved the 504th Parachute Infantry Regiment on Anzio's right

flank, where it was to fight a holding action to protect the beachhead's flank from positions south of the Mussolini Canal. Once at the front most of the troops were appalled at their exposed positions on the "naked unbroken prairie."[3]

The 157th also came ashore on 25 January, and over the next two days it moved into position in Anzio's left coastal sector. To the 157th's right was the British Second North Staffordshire Regiment and on its left flank, the sea. Almost immediately the men began to dig in, but a scant two feet below the surface they struck water—a foxhole only two feet deep did not offer much protection. At noon on 30 January the 180th RCT began landing, and took up a position to protect the middle sector of the beachhead against possible German counterattacks.[4]

After storming ashore the Americans and British concentrated on consolidating their positions, building reserves of men and stockpiles of materiel, and awaiting a German counterattack. Major General John P. Lucas, the Sixth Corps' commander, had planned to occupy a "corps beachhead line" in a methodical manner around Anzio, instead of launching immediate offensive operations beyond the beachhead. With hindsight, such a policy was disastrous because at the time of the initial landing there were only two German battalions between the Allied beachhead and Rome. By 24 January, however, more than forty thousand German reinforcements had arrived and more were pouring in daily. When Lucas finally did order an advance on 29 January, there were 92,000 American and British troops assaulting 98,000 Germans; the Allies were trapped on a beachhead three miles deep and eight miles long.[5]

Although designed as an off-the-road, four-wheel-drive command reconnaissance vehicle, it still was not easy to get a "peep" (later commonly called "Jeep") through the thick beach sand and into action. This Jeep has been waterproofed and equipped with an exhaust extension in the event it landed in deeper water during an amphibious assault. *Courtesy Forty-fifth Infantry Division Museum.*

Much criticism has since leveled against the Allied decision to consolidate the beachhead instead of pushing rapidly into the Alban Hills and on to Rome immediately after the Anzio landing. Although it was true that a rush to take Rome would have seemed the logical course in light of what was learned after the war, at that time no one knew the weakness of the German defenses. If the Allies had plunged into the hills and suffered a serious defeat, there would have been nothing to stop the Germans from pushing the Allies into the sea. At the time the German army was still a powerful force, and a careful buildup of men and materiel seemed the most prudent course to those officers actually on the scene. Such reasoning was echoed by three regimental commanders, Colonel H. A. Meyers, Colonel Preston J. C. Murphy, and Colonel William P. Grace, who fought with the Forty-fifth in Italy and who were in excellent positions to ascertain the situation at the time.[6]

As part of the buildup against possible German counterattacks, on 1 February the Forty-fifth was made a "roving center" to be used against any enemy attempt to drive the Allies back to the sea. As the early days of February passed, it became apparent that such an effort would soon be forthcoming. German artillery fire was becoming heavier and enemy air attacks were increasing.[7]

Of particular concern to the Thunderbirds were the "butterfly bombs," which the Germans first used on 6 February. The "butterflies," each nearly as powerful as a 60-mm. mortar shell, were fired in a hollow, bomb-like container that broke apart just before it struck the ground. Scattered over a wide area, the smaller bombs struck the ground within seconds of each other. Sounding like popping popcorn when they exploded, the butterfly bombs were deadly against exposed men. Casualties from the bombs were particularly heavy until adequate overhead protection could be constructed for the men.[8]

In addition to the butterfly bombs, the Germans kept the beachhead under almost continuous artillery bombardment. The best-known of these guns were "Anzio Annie" and "The Anzio Express," two 280-mm. railroad rifles that each fired 561-pound shells. On the beachhead, the Thunderbirds could hear a "distant, almost discreet cough, a way [*sic*] behind the enemy lines," when the weapon was fired. There would be "a slight pause, during which you knew the shell was on its way . . . [then] came the sicken-

Chaplain W. E. King holds church services on Christmas Day, 1943. The service was held in a gully hidden from enemy view. In the background are camouflaged front-line positions. *Courtesy Forty-fifth Infantry Division Museum.*

ing crump of the explosion and the sound echoed away like a tube train pulling out of the station and racing down a long, black tunnel." Later, when the Allies broke out of the Anzio beachhead and raced toward Rome, the Germans were forced to abandon these monstrous weapons. The Thunderbirds captured both of the huge guns.[9]

Although Allied aircraft maintained daylight superiority over the beachhead area, the night belonged to the enemy. As dusk began to fall, German planes stalked the Allied lines. Suddenly, "the whole beachhead . . . become naked in the unreal light" of flares. "An angry drumming sound would fill the air, turning into a high-pitched whine," as the bombers attacked in steep dives, one participant recalled. Then, "the savage crump of the bombs would shake the earth like a terrier shaking a rat." Later, a single enemy plane, called "Bed Check Charlie" by the troops, made repeated bombing runs over the beachhead area during the night in an effort to provoke Allied gunners into opening fire — an action that would allow German artillery spotters to locate their positions easily.[10]

Under the artillery and aerial onslaught, Allied reinforcements being hurried ashore diminished and then stopped as the saturation point was reached. There was simply no more room within the boundaries of the original beachhead to continue the massive buildup. The British and Americans would have to fight with what they had. As one historian explained: "The Allies, unwilling to commit their reserves, were poking at the German stronghold with one unit at a time."[11]

At 2100 on February 7, the Germans struck at the coastal sector held by the British and the 157th. The attack opened with a jolting artillery and mortar barrage, followed by a tank-supported infantry assault against the British and the adjoining Third Battalion of the 157th. The enemy succeeded in piercing the Allied lines, and by 0300 the next morning scores of Germans were pouring through the break. Both the British and the Americans were forced to give ground, and it was not until daylight that the fighting died down enough to allow them to move back into their previous positions.[12]

After this initial German counterattack, the remainder of the Forty-fifth entered the fighting.

"Anzio Annie" was a 280-mm. railroad-transported weapon that pounded the Allied beachhead at Anzio with 500-pound shells during the bitter fighting of early 1944. The gun was heavily camouflaged and often hidden in railroad tunnels, making it virtually impossible for the Allied observers to determine its location. *Courtesy Forty-fifth Infantry Division Museum.*

On 9 February, the day after the 157th threw back the attack against the coastal sector of the beachhead, the 180th, under Colonel Robert L. Dulaney, moved into the front lines as reinforcements. A day later the 179th, commanded by Colonel Malcolm R. Kammerer, relieved the British 168th Brigade, just south of "the factory."[13]

A focal point of the fighting on the right flank of the beachhead, the factory was a cluster of three- and four-story brick buildings originally built as a farm settlement in 1936. Located on a slight rise, it dominated the surrounding countryside. It also commanded the road junction over which any armor operating in the area would be forced to travel. The Germans had turned it into a fortress, which the British had tried several times to capture. Now it would be the Forty-fifth's turn.[14]

The British had attempted to take the factory by storm. Ludicrous as it seemed, they assaulted a vastly superior enemy concentration supported by tanks with an outmanned force that was doomed to failure before the attack ever started. "The Brigade battered futilely time and again at the enemy strongpoint until, decimated almost to extinction, it had to be withdrawn." With an apparent inability to learn from previous mistakes, the American high command insisted on repeating the error. The First Battalion of the 179th Infantry was given the task of clearing the factory, and as one historian recorded, "The odds were 1,000 to 1 against it before it jumped off."[15]

Supported by two companies of the 191st Tank Battalion, the First Battalion attacked on 11 February. The plan was simple: one tank company—Company A, 191st Tank Battalion—and Company A, 179th Infantry, were to attack through an overpass near Carroceto and approach the factory from the west, while B Company, 191st Tank Battalion, and B Company, 179th Infantry, were to advance up the north-south road just east of the German strongpoint and attack from the southeast.[16]

At 0630 the assault got under way after a fifteen-minute artillery and bomber bombardment. Company A's tanks reached the overpass before its first vehicle was destroyed; a second tank blew up two hundred yards beyond. The remaining tanks shelled the southwest corner of the factory until 0830 and then withdrew behind a smoke screen. Company B's tanks reached the road junction southeast of the enemy strongpoint and from there shelled the German positions until their ammunition was exhausted. At 1030, Company A sent six tanks back to the overpass to continue the shelling. Despite the armored support, the Germans, from well dug-in positions, poured such a withering fire on the advancing infantry that the assault sputtered to a halt.[17]

The attack was resumed at 1300. By now the concentrated shellfire of the tanks and artillery was beginning to have an effect. Several enemy tanks were destroyed, and others, together with some self-propelled guns, were forced to withdraw. Under the covering fire, Company A, 179th Infantry, fought its way into the buildings along the southwest edge of the factory. Almost immediately the infantry was engaged by an overwhelming number of Germans who had been lurking deep within the factory's basements, safe from both artillery and machine-gun fire. In the ensuing bitter, almost hand-to-hand fighting, the Thunderbirds were forced to withdraw. The infantrymen of Company B also reached the factory, but were driven back by a counterattack supported by tanks and artillery.[18]

At 0200 on 12 February another attack was ordered. This time Company B would attack from the south, Company C from the southwest, and Company I from the east. Company C's tanks again were in support, but were stopped at the road junction by a minefield. The tanks continued to shell the German positions, and by 0430 companies B and C had again penetrated the factory's defenses. Two hours later, however, they were thrown back by a German counterattack; they organized a new line approximately five hundred yards south. On the 179th's

right, the 180th and the British hurried into position, while the left flank was held by the 157th.[19]

By now, defeating the Anzio landings had become a matter of pride to the German army, and the enemy high command was determined to drive the Allies into the sea. While the Thunderbirds were attempting to seize the factory, the Germans were completing preparations for a major offensive against the beachhead. The main thrust was to be along the Anzio-Albano Road—right at the 179th's defenses. The plan was to break the Allied line with massed infantry, supported by tanks, and then follow up with armored reserves. Once the defensive lines were breached, the armor would divide the beachhead into two parts by driving to the sea. Each part's defenses would then be dealt with separately. The time for the assault was set for 0630 on 16 February 1944.[20]

On the night of 15 February the First Division was relieved of responsibility for its sector, which had been divided between the Forty-fifth and the Fifty-sixth divisions. The right portion of the First Division's old sector was occupied by the 157th Infantry, commanded by Colonel John H. Church. The 179th held the center and the 180th the right flank of the Forty-fifth's front. Through the Forty-fifth's front-line sector passed the Anzio-Albano Road, which, along with the factory, became the focal points of the German attack.[21]

At 0600 on the morning of 16 February, German artillery opened fire at the central beachhead front. For thirty minutes the artillery barrage continued unabated, and then waves of German assault troops moved forward. The brunt of the attack was directed toward the Forty-fifth Division's 157th and 179th Infantry regiments. During the battle the importance of the factory became apparent. From it, German artillery observers could call down artillery fire on any American position that revealed itself, and periodically groups of between four and eight tanks would sally forth from the fortifications to pour point-blank fire into the Thunderbirds' foxholes.[22]

The 157th had taken an area three kilometers in front of the overpass known as the Caves of Pozzolana. The region was honeycombed with shepherds' caves carved into a ridge line. Connected by tunnels thousands of feet long, the caves were a haven from enemy shelling. Impervious to artillery fire, within them the Thunderbirds established supply points, first aid stations, command posts, machine-gun and mortar nests, and rifle positions.[23]

In front of the caves' entrances were "miles and miles of flat, open terrain, broken only by draws and ditches barely deep enough to conceal a crawling soldier." Across this open area wave after wave of enemy troops and tanks surged toward the entrenched Americans. "All morning long the German infantry attacked, coming across the open field . . . to be cut down by rifle and machine gun fire." The Germans had tank after tank destroyed by artillery fire or antitank guns, but regardless of their casualties, "as fast as one wave of the attackers was broken it was replaced by another." The entire Second Battalion of the 157th was awarded a distinguished unit citation for its actions during the bloody struggle that became known as the "Battle of the Caves."[24]

Companies G and E of the 157th were hardest hit. Company E was the most forward of the Allied units at Anzio, and as both British and American troops on its flanks were forced back Company E was nearly cut off. Company G was on its left flank, and much of the German assault spilled over into G Company's sector. Ignoring their losses, the Germans plunged into the Americans' foxholes as the attack turned into a series of hand-to-hand battles. Nonetheless, the Thunderbirds held their lines throughout the morning, and often the Germans were thrown back at great sacrifice. In some instances, the Americans called down artillery fire on their own positions to prevent them from being overrun.[25]

During the afternoon of 16 February, several of the American units were forced to withdraw as the enemy attacks continued. Nightfall brought no relief. Under the cover of darkness the Germans began infiltrating through the 157th's positions.[26]

At the same time Company I of the 157th had been ordered to protect a vital supply route crossroads. Originally, the company was to man the positions for only twenty-four hours, and therefore only enough ammunition, rations, and other supplies had been provided for a limited action. Once the Thunderbirds had taken up their positions, however, the German onslaught began. At daybreak on 17 February, Company I came under an intense enemy artillery bombardment that quickly cut all communications with battalion headquarters. Six German infantry attacks, often supported by tanks that approached to within three hundred yards of the Thunderbirds' lines, were thrown against Company I. All were repulsed as the men stood fast until relieved on 21 February. For its contribution to the disruption of the German assault on the beachhead, Company I, 157th RCT, was presented a distinguished unit citation.[27]

In another battle, at the center of the Fortyfifth's line, what amounted to nearly two full German divisions assaulted the 179th on the morning of 16 February. By 0815 the regiment was under a combined infantry-tank attack that was described as "rolling, wave upon wave, a grey blur, a flesh-and-steel tide." Established lines disintegrated as the fighting became disorganized. Several units began pulling back or called down artillery fire on both themselves and the enemy. When the Second and Third battalions began to withdraw, the Germans, in an attempt to force a rout and effect a major breakthrough, threw the full weight of their remaining infantry and armor at the retreating Americans.[28]

The various units of the 179th were becoming scattered and disorganized. Communication lines were cut, and MPs established straggler lines to direct those who had been separated from their units back to the front. Gradually American artillery and tank destroyers began to slow down the German armor. Then the Germans paused to regroup. This was a key to the battle because despite appalling casualties and disorganization, the lull allowed the 179th to organize a new defensive position about two-and-one-half kilometers south of the factory. Then, "with awe-inspiring courage," and doubtlessly as a complete surprise to the Germans, the 179th counterattacked to seize a stream bed due north of its new position. Both the 180th and the 157th joined in the general assault until darkness slowed the fighting.[29]

The shelling continued all night as the Germans tried to infiltrate the American lines. Many of their units had been greatly reduced in the day's fighting, and they hurried to reorganize before daylight. The next day the Germans renewed their assault. Hundreds of enemy infantrymen, supported by a large number of Mark

IV and Mark VI tanks, hurled themselves at the Thunderbirds. Wave after wave followed the initial assault, only to be "melted down before the accurate fire of our artillery, rifle and machine guns."[30] Somehow, during the night, a dangerous gap had been opened between the 179th and the 157th. Quickly exploiting the break in the American lines, the Germans poured through the gap. Within a short time a wedge two miles wide and more than a mile deep had been driven into the division's front.[31]

On the 157th's front the battle of the caves continued as the Germans tried to seize the crossroads. The fighting seesawed back and forth, and some officers began to question whether the beachhead could be held. The 157th's line was broken on its right flank, and the Germans began to move straight down the Anzio-Albano Road. In response to the threat, all available artillery and naval guns were brought to bear on the salient. Even antiaircraft guns were shifted to ground targets. Scores of Allied bombers and fighters ranged over the battle area in an attempt to stem the German advance. Likewise, the Germans threw everything they had into the effort to split the Allied lines and reach the sea.[32]

By late afternoon of the seventeenth, the Germans had penetrated down the Albano road dangerously close to the beachhead's final line of defense. To establish a more defensible line and to blunt the enemy advance, Major General Eagles ordered the Thunderbirds to attack. The assault failed. Throughout the night the Germans moved up fresh units and continued to shell the final defensive line. Under cover of darkness, enemy troops penetrated the Allied lines and, at one point, the 157th's supply route was cut by German infiltrators. Confident of delivering a knockout blow the next morning, the Germans were poised to push the Allies into the sea.[33]

The fighting raged day and night. Water and rations began to run short as supply parties found their way to the front blocked by German artillery fire or infiltrators. The men filled their canteens from streams that were red with blood, boiled the water, and then quenched their thirst. Each K-ration serving had to be shared by three men. Efforts at resupply by air were made, but often the supplies fell into German hands.[34]

The fighting was extremely bitter along the 180th's front. On 15 February, G Company of the 180th had been rushed into the line to plug a gap between the 180th and another regiment. Deployed along the Ficoccia River, morning found G Company under heavy attack by enemy infantry and tanks supported by artillery. Although the Thunderbirds fought back viciously, the German attack continued all day and all night and into 17 February. The enemy pressure was so great that the Americans barely managed to keep from being overrun. Later that day, six Mark VI tanks attempted to puncture the Thunderbirds' defenses but were thrown back.[35]

Then, however, adjoining units withdrew and Company G was encircled. Only fifty men remained effective and they had only about ten rounds of ammunition each. There was only one box of machine-gun ammunition per gun, and eleven mortar shells remained. Slowly forced to give ground, the Thunderbirds moved back, recrossed the Ficoccia, and reentered Allied lines at 1430 on 18 February. For its actions on 17-18 February, 1944, Company G, 180th Infantry, was awarded a distinguished unit citation.[36]

By the afternoon of the eighteenth the battlefront was in shambles. The 179th had been driven back to its positions covering the final beachhead. On its right flank the 180th was under heavy attack but still intact. On the left side of the German salient the beleagured 157th still held its ground, but everyone wondered how much longer the troops could stand up to the tremendous punishment. Just as it appeared the beachhead was lost, the German push began to run out of steam.[37]

Many enemy units had become as disorganized as the Allies' were, and others had been decimated. Even so, late on the afternoon of the eighteenth the Germans made another attack. Twelve tanks lumbered down "the bowling alley," as the Anzio-Albano Road and the surrounding open area was known to the Americans. Only the destroyed bridge over Carroceto Creek kept the Germans from breaking through to the sea. Ranging almost unopposed up and down the road, the enemy armor poured point-blank fire into the American foxholes. Under this cover German infantry again surged forward. By six o'clock that evening, fighting was widespread along the entire front of the salient. Both the

179th and the 180th were heavily engaged. Several small enemy units managed to penetrate the American lines, but they were too few in number to exploit their success. Now advancing over open country, the German infantry was again subjected to heavy casualties by Allied machine-gun and artillery fire.[38]

The situation was critical. The Thunderbirds reinforced their front-line units with rear-area troops in an attempt to stem the enemy advance. At the battle under way at the caves, the Germans penetrated to the very mouths of the caverns and poured deadly rifle and machine-gun fire into the defenders inside. Several units were cut off and surrounded. Shortages cropped up everywhere. There were no supplies, no grenades, no mortar shells, and, in some instances, only a few remaining rounds of rifle and machine-gun ammunition. Communications between the front and rear-area headquarters were cut, and most radios were out of commission. In anticipation of an airborne enemy attack the beachhead was divided into zones of defense, with a mobile force in each zone assigned the task of eliminating any attempted assault.[39]

Finally, at 2130, the Germans began pulling back. Never again in the Italian campaign was the enemy to come so close to breaking Allied lines and reaching the beach. That night the Germans attempted to regroup for a last-ditch assault on the following morning. The attack began at 0400 on 19 February with a heavy concentration of artillery fire on the leading edge of the salient. Ten minutes later enemy infantry and tanks moved forward. This time they were greeted with a massive concentration of prepared defensive artillery fire. Some of the Germans managed to reach the defensive wire, but were quickly cut down by rifle and machine-gun fire. The attack faltered and the Germans began to withdraw. By evening it was evident that the Allies had won the battle. The peak of the enemy offensive had passed. The Thunderbirds had held.[40]

The staunch defense by the Thunderbirds was one of the major reasons that the Germans were unsuccessful in their effort to breach the beachhead and throw the Allies back to the sea. Although the enemy assault against the five miles of front held by the division was supported by as many as eighty Mark VI and twenty Mark IV

tanks, the Thunderbirds yielded ground grudgingly. It was a costly battle, however, with many of the Forty-fifth's casualties resulting from German infiltration of the American lines.[41]

The following day several small enemy attacks were made against the Allied lines, but they were mostly to mask the German withdrawal and were not a serious threat. The Allies launched a counterattack, but it also failed. Both sides were spent after the fighting and neither would attempt another large-scale assault for months.[42]

With the lull in activity, the campaign to take Anzio became monotonous. Lieutenant Colonel Hal L. Muldrow recalled that the 189th Field Artillery only moved twice during the entire four and a half months that it spent on the beachhead. The artillerymen spent most of their time either aimlessly firing their guns or in a complex of bunkers called "Shellhole City." "The days dragged by with the same . . . nerve-racking sounds and sights and smells—the repetitious tomptom [sic] of big guns firing; the whine and boom and explosion of falling shells; the daily—and nightly patrolling." According to William R. Wilson, who joined the Forty-fifth as an enlisted man in 1940 and later rose to the rank of brigadier general, the entire beachhead was exposed to German artillery fire. The shelling affected everyone, but on one occasion it served a useful purpose when the divisional artillery chaplain converted a shell hole, forty feet across and five feet deep, into a baptismal.[43]

The shelling also made it difficult to off-load supplies, and often the task was interrupted by German artillery fire. On one occasion, Colonel Ross H. Routh, the divisional finance officer during World War II and later a brigadier general, arrived at the beach to receive the Forty-fifth's payroll. Routh had prided himself on the fact that, unlike other divisions, the Forty-fifth had always managed to pay its troops on time. This time, however, the landing craft bringing the money ashore encountered heavy enemy artillery fire and the crew dumped the safes overboard a short distance from land. Determined to maintain his record, Routh ordered his men into the water to retrieve the money. Manhandling the safes ashore, Routh spread the wet money along the rooftops of several nearby buildings to dry before turning it over to the regimental paymasters for distribution to the troops.[44]

"170-mm. Lane, Shellhole City," the nickname for the G-2 (Intelligence) Section of the Forty-fifth Division Headquarters, on the Anzio beachhead. *Courtesy Forty-fifth Infantry Division Museum.*

During the lull enemy activity was generally limited to infiltration and artillery fire; however, opposing patrols sometimes clashed. With artificial smoke released from canisters to prevent enemy artillery spotters from locating targets, the Allied beachhead took on an eerie atmosphere. As the lines stabilized the same situation developed that had existed at the Winter line and Cassino—stagnation. It was the very thing that the Anzio campaign was conceived to eliminate.[45]

This stagnation did not mean an end to the fighting. The struggle continued and often the clashes were bitter. On 22 February, 1944, First Lieutenant Jack C. Montgomery, a guardsman from Sallisaw, was in an action near Padiglione, at the center of the Anzio beachhead at the eastern end of the Mussolini Canal. Montgomery was commanding a rifle platoon that came under a heavy enemy attack about two hours before daybreak. Despite the American fire, two groups of Germans succeeded in entrenching themselves about fifty and one hundred yards in front of the Thunderbirds, and in occupying

a farmhouse about three hundred yards to the Americans' front.[46]

The nearest German position, protected by four machine guns and a mortar, was the most immediate problem and threatened to overrun Montgomery's platoon. Reacting quickly, Montgomery personally assaulted the enemy position and silenced the German fire with his rifle and hand grenades. Returning to his platoon, he then directed artillery fire on the nearby farmhouse sheltering some of the attacking enemy. Then, armed this time with a carbine, he rushed the second group of Germans entrenched about one hundred yards to the front of his command. In so doing, he captured seven enemy soldiers and two machine guns.[47]

Now it was daylight, but despite the visibility Montgomery continued to press the attack. When the artillery fire on the farmhouse lifted, he rushed forward. Ignoring the steady stream of sniper fire directed at him, Montgomery stormed the farmhouse and forced the enemy to withdraw. By his own actions he had accounted for forty-two enemy dead or captured and the taking

From *News of the 45th*, by Don Robinson, published by the University of Oklahoma Press.

of all three German strongpoints. That night, when his platoon ran short of ammunition, Montgomery returned to the rear and was carrying several bandoleers back to his men when he was wounded by German mortar fragments. He received the Medal of Honor for his heroism.[48]

Throughout this period of active defense, the Allies continued to build up their concentration of men and materiel in anticipation of a breakout. The Germans remained concealed, generally unaggressive and defensive. Their artillery capabilities, however, made every daylight move within the Allied lines subject to an almost immediate artillery barrage. "Dig or die" was the rule. Because of the artillery fire on the LSTs off-loading supplies, the Thunderbirds would send their ammunition trucks by ship to Naples for loading and then bring them back to the beachhead where they could drive directly from the LSTs to the ammunition dumps and firing batteries.[49]

March and April passed with almost a habitual routine on both sides. Night brought "Popcorn Pete" and his "damned anti-personnel bombs" or "Butterfly Bill's" attacks on the artillery; sunrise brought incessant shelling. At some points the opposing forces were "separated only by barbed wire and spent hours hurling insults at each other from the bottom of their respective holes."[50]

Only a small percentage of the men were actually able to leave the battle area. For the others, the only rest was "in the rear," but there was no rear at Anzio. Even so, when the division was pulled out of the line after seventy-nine days of fighting for a few days of recuperation in the pine forest, the men were elated. Because of the overhead cover the pine forest offered a haven from enemy observation and shelling. It was pitch dark in the woods at night, but Special Services provided a supply of magazines and recreational equipment, and a movie was shown every night. "Coming back to the Pines was like coming back to a different world," one Thunderbird recalled. "It was peaceful and quiet and cool there among the big trees and the war seemed far away."[51]

Such a respite made life at Anzio a little more bearable. To maintain morale the men were pulled out of the lines at regular intervals and sent to rest camps where they could spend a few days sleeping on a cot and eating hearty meals. Arthur E. Peters, the mess sergeant of Headquarters Company, 179th Infantry, established an officers rest center in a beach-front hotel at Naples, where, after an extended stay at the front, various officers were sent for relaxation. For six days the men escaped the horrors of war before returning to combat.[52]

In answer to the German shelling, the Allies poured thousands of artillery pieces onto the Anzio beachhead. Brigadier General Raymond S. McLain, one of the Forty-fifth's most able officers, commanded the division's artillery, which, as recalled by Forrest G. Munson, a technical sergeant in the S-2 section of Headquarters Battery, Forty-fifth Division Artillery, was augmented with many batteries of corps artillery. In addition, an extensive liaison system was maintained so that the guns of various other units could also be called upon for support. Literally hundreds of guns ranging in size from 90-mm. anti-aircraft weapons to 240-mm. howitzers were on call. At one time, seventeen battalions of artillery were on call to the Thunderbirds.[53]

This huge concentration of artillery was particularly effective against the German tactics used at Anzio. Placing great reliance on the ability of their tanks to break the Allied lines, time and again the Germans sent armored assaults against the Americans. Fortunately, the terrain at Anzio funneled any armored attacks into specific corridors, and McLain countered with devastating artillery fire that demolished hundreds of enemy armored vehicles and played a key role in holding the beachhead.[54]

According to Munson, McLain also placed great emphasis on counterbattery fire. The S-2 section spent hours pouring over aerial photographs of the German lines searching for wheel tracks, changes in vegetation indicating the use of camouflage, anything that would betray an enemy gun position. Any suspicious site was brought under immediate fire and destroyed.[55]

As the Allies became stronger, McLain developed to a fine science the tactic of "time-on-target" shelling, which was first implemented at Anzio. The idea was to surprise the enemy with unexpected saturation bombardment. First, McLain preselected a target and then every available gun concentrated its fire on the enemy position. To ensure that the Germans were literally buried under a hail of shells, the firing was regulated. The guns farthest from the target timed their fire with those nearer the front so that all the shells landed at once.[56]

It was a devastatingly effective tactic. In one instance, Munson recalled, a German battalion was caught moving through a section of the Mussolini Canal. McLain ordered a time-on-target fire mission along a 400-yard length of the waterway and destroyed the entire enemy column. Then, in response to the Germans' shelling of Allied hospitals, McLain ordered the artillery to wait thirty-five minutes and repeat the mission. This caught another enemy detachment attempting to clean up the effects of the first bombardment. Later, Italian civilians reported that the Germans suffered so many casualties that they buried their dead with bulldozers.[57]

Time-on-target missions became one of the keys to the successful breakout of the beachhead area by Allied troops. Because the enemy never knew when a fire mission would hit them, and because of the seemingly random selection of targets, it was impossible to differentiate between a time-on-target mission and a preparatory bombardment for an attack. The result was confusion among many enemy commanders when the Allies launched their breakout attack.[58]

McLain, an Oklahoma national guardsman called into federal service in 1940 with the remainder of the division, went on to become the assistant division commander of the Thirtieth or "Old Hickory" Division. He later commanded the Ninetieth (T-O) Division and the United States Nineteenth Corps. He was the first National Guard officer since the Civil War to reach the rank of lieutenant general, and served as the first statutory comptroller general of the U.S. Army.[59]

Finally on 7 May, more than three months after the initial landing, the troops at Anzio received word that a huge offensive was planned to break the German lines in southern Italy, push past Cassino, and link up with the beachhead. By 18 May, Cassino had fallen and the Allies were advancing up the Italian boot. At the same time, preparations were being made for a breakout from Anzio. A vigorous rehabilitation and training schedule was implemented, and special "small unit 'schools'" were established throughout the beachhead.[60]

At 0600, on 23 May, the breakout began. The assault was preceded by a huge artillery concentration, with fire support missions planned so carefully that "all enemy positions, houses, fences, ditches, and any other obstacle which might be used for the enemy in his defense were thoroughly and completely pounded or destroyed." Thirty minutes later the infantry moved out. The Rome-Arno campaign, the Forty-fifth's fourth of the war, was under way.[61]

Although the artillery fire had reduced many of the enemy defenses, German minefields took a heavy toll of infantry. At first the assault caught the Germans by surprise, and many hurried to surrender rather than fight; however, as time passed enemy resistance stiffened. Tanks were thrown into the fight in a vicious counterattack. A few tanks penetrated the Allied lines and roamed almost at will in the rear. It took several days to destroy them and the assault bogged down in the meantime.[62]

At 0730 on 25 May 1944, the Anzio beachhead ceased to exist as an isolated position when two patrols, one from the beachhead and the other from the troops pushing northward from Cassino, met at Borgo Grappa, five miles east of the Mussolini Canal, on Highway 7 in the Pontine Marshes. The following day the Forty-fifth made contact with forward elements of the advancing Fifth Army. As the Allies began to roll forward, German opposition varied. Sometimes the Germans surrendered; other times they counterattacked. Day after day the Thunderbirds threw the enemy back as they advanced through the Alban Hills, which for so long had confined them to the Anzio beachhead. After five days of fighting, the Forty-fifth was in a headlong rush toward Rome.[63]

In assessing the American victory at Anzio, Colonels Meyers, Murphy, and Grace all agreed that the campaign's success was largely due to the differences between the combatants. The average American GI was simply better than the German soldier. They also had more confidence in their officers and supporting branches. While the German commanders at Anzio recklessly used their infantry in what amounted to a waste of manpower, American commanders relied more on firepower. According to the colonels, no American troops were ever deployed when firepower could accomplish the same ob-

Thunderbirds relax at the "Hi Hat Bar" near Battipaglia, Italy, after the Rome-Arno campaign following the Anzio breakout. *Courtesy Forty-fifth Infantry Division Museum.*

jective. The Thunderbirds had proven their worth.[64]

The final push on the eternal city began on 3 June 1944. Lieutenant General Clark altered the American advance and swung the Thunderbirds toward Rome instead of allowing them to cut Highway 6. Although this permitted the Americans to liberate Rome sooner than expected, some officers believed it allowed many Germans to escape northward.[65]

At first, the attack on Rome encountered stiffened enemy resistance, but as the Americans pressed forward the German lines crumbled completely and spontaneously. The battle turned into "a track meet without field events" as the Tiber River was crossed and the last German line of resistance before Rome deteriorated. Allied armor surged forward, and in many instances the Thunderbirds were loaded on trucks to speed their advance and maintain contact with the fleeing enemy. By 5 June the Forty-fifth was closing in on Rome. The next day they learned of the Normandy invasion.[66]

That same day, 6 June 1944, the Forty-fifth was withdrawn from the fighting, and by 10 June the men were busy training in several rear-area rest camps. Although the Forty-fifth did not take part in the final push for Rome, once the city had fallen one combat team at a time was transported to the eternal city for a tour. As Brigadier General Wilson recalled, it was the first city in Italy that the Thunderbirds saw that had not been destroyed. On 16 June the Forty-fifth was detached from Sixth Corps and reverted to Fifth Army control.[67]

Throughout the following weeks the Thunderbirds rehearsed amphibious landings at an invasion training center at Salerno beach. Then on 17 July the division was moved to Qualiano, north of Naples, where the troops were given intensive instructions in offensive tactics. At the same time, Staff Sergeant Clapp and the remainder of the division's G-3 section feverishly worked in "the blockhouse" at Naples, where they had been moved before the Anzio breakout. The building was just what the name implied, a huge

Fifth Army Planning Headquarters, Naples, Italy, where the Forty-fifth's G-3 Section worked out the division's plans for the landings in southern France. Only those on a "need to know" basis were admitted to the facility. *Courtesy Forty-fifth Infantry Division Museum.*

blockhouse with no outside windows. There was only one entrance and all inside doors faced a central courtyard. The entrance was patrolled by MPs, and admittance was restricted to a "need-to-know" basis. Here Clapp and the others were busy planning for the Forty-fifth's next operation, the division's fifth landing since the war began.[68]

Early in August, the Thunderbirds moved to Naples and began to board landing craft. At 0800 on 12 August the troop convoy sailed to the southern coast of Corsica, where it waited for two days. Once the troopships were sealed, another "soldier's 'Guide Book' was distributed, invasion maps were unrolled, and the now familiar process of assault orientation" began. This time it was to be the southern coast of France.[69]

Operation Dragoon, as the Thunderbird landing had been code-named, was a part of the larger Operation Anvil, the invasion of southern France by the Seventh Army. The assault was planned to take advantage of the Allied breakout in northern France. As the name "Anvil" implied, the southern operation was to be the anvil against which the German army in Europe would be pinned while it received lethal blows from the north.[70]

CHAPTER 10

VICTORY IN EUROPE

The battles in which the Forty-fifth Division participated in southern France were drastically different from the ones fought in Sicily and Italy. In the latter campaigns, determined resistance by a still-powerful German army, extensive demolition of the regions' road systems, and difficult terrain in those areas combined to make the offensives slow and costly. In southern France, however, the Germans did not have enough troops to impede the Allied assault to any great degree, and the fighting was characterized by rapid advances and mobility.[1]

For the French landing, the Thunderbirds were assigned to Kodak Force, which consisted of Sixth Corps Headquarters; the Third, the Forty-fifth, and the Thirty-sixth infantry divisions; and a French armored combat command. The entire operation was under the direction of the Seventh Army, of which Sixth Corps was a part, commanded by Lieutenant General Alexander M. Patch. The Forty-fifth's landing area was just east of Saint-Maxime along four beaches code-named Red, Green, Yellow, and Blue. Red was closest to the town and Blue the most distant. Sixth Corps' task was to capture Saint-Maxime, to seize the high ground near the Argens River, to occupy Villepey, and to extend the beachhead to "Blue line," which stretched in a crescent from the western edge of Cap Negre to just west of Cannes. The Forty-fifth was in the center, flanked by the Third and Thirty-sixth divisions.[2]

Two hours before H hour on D day, 15 August 1944, the army air corps began bombing operations against enemy positions in the landing zones. Between 0700 and 0730 waves of heavy bombers attacked the area while the navy bom-barded the beaches. At 0800 the Forty-fifth began landing.[3]

American intelligence had discovered a fatal weakness in the German defenses. Heretofore, all Allied landings had taken place shortly before daybreak. As a result the local German commanders had the beach defenses manned during the early morning hours, and then either released their men or sent them to training schools in the rear. Armed with this insight, American planners coordinated the beach landings with paratroop and glider landings deeper inland; this strategy cut vital road arteries and prevented the Germans from remanning their beach defenses. This time when the Americans stormed ashore, there was little enemy opposition.[4]

Everything seemed to move like clockwork. Initial objectives were quickly seized, and the Thunderbirds began a rapid advance inland. Enemy opposition consisted chiefly of scattered pockets of resistance utilizing antitank guns and uncoordinated infantry assaults. To further confuse the Germans, the Allies, who were usually honest in their news releases, announced that they had landed in force on the Atlantic side of southern France. After hearing this, the Germans were unsure if the landings on the Mediterranean shore were the main assault or a diversionary attack, and they hesitated in rushing reinforcements to the area. The Allies' honesty had the result that within a week of the initial assault the Germans no longer had any realistic plans for holding southern France and were rapidly withdrawing northward, with the hope of establishing a new defense line.[5]

The battle quickly turned into a race, with

Forty-fifth Division vehicles lined up for waterproofing at Bagnoli, Italy, in August, 1944, before the assault on southern France. *Courtesy Forty-fifth Infantry Division Museum.*

the Allies trying to catch the withdrawing Germans before they could establish a firm line of resistance. In such a battle, American armored forces would push far ahead of the infantry in pursuit of the Germans, and then the infantry would follow to mop up any remaining enemy resistance. According to Brigadier General William R. Wilson, advances of thirty to forty miles a day by special task forces were not unusual. To keep up with the onrushing armor, the Thunderbirds were often loaded aboard trucks and then rushed forward under the protection of

several tanks. Such a fluid situation resulted in the organization of the combined arms into temporary task forces (TF) instead of RCTs. Like an RCT, a task force was based around an infantry regiment; however, unlike an RCT, a task force's makeup was constantly being changed depending upon the situation. By 23 August, elements of TF-179 had reached Grenoble, 225 miles from the initial beachhead. By the end of the month, though, stiffening enemy resistance, in addition to the many destroyed roads and bridges, began to slow the Allied advance.

Private Kenneth G. Compav, a medic, dresses the finger of Private First Class Hildie H. Sheets, while they wait to board an LST for the landing in southern France. *Courtesy Forty-fifth Infantry Division Museum.*

The weather had become a factor, with daily showers turning into steady rain that rendered the roads nearly impassable.[6]

The extraordinary distances the Thunderbirds had covered created a complicated supply problem. By 24 August, the division was operating along a 100-mile front with its leading elements almost three hundred miles inland. Even though supply vehicles ran twenty-four hours a day in an effort to keep men and materiel moving forward, the situation was becoming critical. To alleviate the problem, the "Thunderbird Railroad"—the first railroad operated by an infantry division while still engaged in combat—was or-

ganized. Sufficient fuel and rail equipment was hurriedly located, and the rail line between Saint-Julien and Grenoble was quickly repaired. Troops from various replacement companies were drafted to man trains, and the divisional G-4 section detached officers to oversee the operation. By 26 August everything was ready. Supplies were off-loaded at Saint-Maxime, carried by vehicle to Saint-Julien, and then loaded aboard railroad cars and hurried north to Bourgoin, where the divisional supply dump was located.[7]

With their supply situation somewhat relieved, the Thunderbirds hurried forward to maintain contact with the retreating Germans. Care was taken to keep the enemy from withdrawing into the nearby mountains, and several roadblocks were established near Grenoble to deny the Germans access to Alpine passes. On 28 August 1944, Task Force 179, which was spearheading the Seventh Army's drive, crossed the Rhone River on a route parallel to that of the escaping Germans.[8]

Because TF-179 threatened to block their escape routes, the Germans launched a vicious counterattack in the Meximieus vicinity on 31 August. Obviously the enemy hoped that by throwing a large-scale offensive against the American flank they could slow the Allied advance long enough to allow their troops to reach safety. F Company, Second Battalion, 179th, together with approximately one hundred men of the French Forces of the Interior (FFI) were overrun in the initial onslaught, and by 1 September the fighting around Meximieus was extremely bitter. On several occasions the Germans breached the American defenses, but reinforcements were hurried forward, and in vicious house-to-house fighting the enemy was thrown back.[9]

The counterattack at Meximieus slowed but did not halt the Forty-fifth's advance, which continued to push toward the German border. On 7 September, the Thunderbirds forced a crossing over the Daubes River, 318 miles from the landing beaches, after the Germans had destroyed both bridges in the division's sector. Four days later the 157th was closing in on the Belfort Gap, the only remaining escape route open to the Germans. It was at this point in the campaign that Lieutenant Almond E. Fisher of the 157th was awarded the Medal of Honor in an engagement near Grammont on 14 September.[10] Although wounded in both feet, Lieutenant Fisher singlehandedly destroyed four German machine-gun emplacements, and then, refusing to be evacuated, deployed his platoon against a vicious enemy counterattack. Only after the fighting ended was Lieutenant Fisher taken to the rear for medical treatment.

By mid-September the German army was beginning to recover from its initial setback in southern France. The enemy high command realized that a stand had to be made to stop the Allied advance while there was still room for the Germany army to fall back to the German frontier and the Siegfried line. The region offering the best natural defense for such a stand was the Moselle River-Vosges Mountains area.[11]

As German resistance stiffened, the Thunderbirds were relieved by Free French troops on 18 September, and shifted north to an area near the Moselle River. Here it occupied the left flank of Sixth Corps. On the division's left flank was the Third Division, and on the north was its next objective, the fortress city of Epinal.[12]

Built on both banks of the Moselle River, Epinal was the center of the region's road and communication network. West of the city were the Vosges Mountains and the German border. It was here that the Germans planned to make their stand. Eighty feet wide with twenty-feet-high banks, the Moselle River itself was a formidable obstacle, and the enemy had destroyed all bridges across the stream. Inside Epinal, three battalions of infantry reinforced by artillery, mortars, and antiaircraft units were well dug in, with mines, booby traps, and roadblocks covering all major thoroughfares.[13]

The battle for the city began on 20 September when the 179th took up positions around the town. The next day Colonel Harold A. Meyer sent the Second Battalion of the 179th to seize the high ground near the river and search for a suitable crossing point. During the night of 21-22 September assault boats and bridge materials were brought to the riverbank, and at 0400 on 22 September, the 179th and the 157th forced a crossing against stiff resistance. At the same time the 180th moved against Epinal, and in two days of heavy fighting the town was cleared of the enemy. In the meantime, the 179th and the 157th continued to push the Germans into the Vosges Mountains; the division was entering its sixth battle campaign of the war—the Rhineland.[14]

The fighting in the mountains varied from light to intense; however, the terrain made all movement difficult. For the infantry, fighting in the forest was extremely hazardous. Enemy artillery or mortar shells would explode after striking the overhead trees and spray shrapnel downward in such a way that even foxholes offered little protection. Not only did the rough terrain make the effort tough but rain and fog cut down

The French Forces of the Interior (FFI) fought alongside the Thunderbirds during the liberation of southern France. An American soldier, *left*, and a member of the FFI, identified by his armband, *right*, escort a captured collaborator of the Germans. *Courtesy Forty-fifth Infantry Division Museum.*

on visibility. In addition, a steady procession of delaying obstacles—minefields hidden in the dense undergrowth and blocks of fallen trees booby trapped with explosives—hindered the advance. Fortunately for the Thunderbirds, the Germans hurriedly withdrew the bulk of their troops westward to a new defensive line behind the Meurthe River.[15]

To cover its retreat, the enemy launched a strong delaying force against the advancing Americans. Often when the two forces clashed there was bitter fighting. At Girecourt, for example, the Second Battalion of the 180th RCT first occupied the city without resistance on 27 September, but the Germans launched a vicious counterattack that night and drove the Americans out of the town. Renewing the battle the following morning, the Americans brought up the 191st Tank Battalion to aid the infantry, and only after reducing "pocket after pocket of . . . resistance" was Girecourt retaken.[16]

Given the opportunity to regroup, the Germans hurriedly built heavy fortifications in the region around Grandvillers and Rambervillers.

Fresh troops were brought up to man the strategically placed, well-camouflaged positions. It would take a bitter fight to dislodge the enemy.[17]

The struggle for the cities began inauspiciously on 30 September when the 157th launched an attack against Rambervillers. Little enemy resistance was encountered and the city was easily occupied. When the Thunderbirds approached the carefully prepared defenses beyond the town, though, they ran into heavy artillery and mortar fire. The advance ground to a halt.[18]

While the 157th seized Rambervillers, the 179th RCT assaulted Grandvillers. Known as "little Stalingrad" to the Americans, it took a bloody four-day struggle to secure the town. Grandvillers had been heavily mined by the Germans, and interlocking fields of antitank fire forced the supporting armor to withdraw. The infantry was left to take the city with rifles, machine guns, and hand grenades. Often the opposing armies were only fifteen yards apart. The fighting was furious before the Germans abandoned the city on 3 October.[19]

With its sister regiments fighting at Grandvillers and Rambervillers, the 180th pushed into the Vosges Mountains, where its advance quickly bogged down in the forest. Obviously stiffening German resistance was halting the rapid advance of the previous weeks, and when the Thunderbirds reached the enemy's Mortange River defense line on 15 October the fighting took on the aspects of trenches, patrolling, shelling, and raids. The Germans were displaying a stronger resistance, and the Allies were exhausted. According to one historian: "Their [the Americans] attacks were often beaten off not for lack of will but for lack of physical and mental strength to keep on." Added to these factors, winter was at hand; rain fell steadily, and the wind was sharp and biting.[20]

During this phase of the fighting, advances were measured in yards instead of miles. The impasse was not broken until 23 October, when the First Battalion of the 180th forced a crossing of the Mortange River. The assault began at 0530, and by 0745 most of the battalion was across. The bridgehead was quickly expanded. The town of Mortange was taken by the 179th on 24 October, and the entire division was thrown through the break in the German lines. For its actions during the bitter fighting to break the German defensive line along the Mortange River near Fremefontaine, France, between 15 and 25 October 1944, the First Battalion of the 180th RCT received a distinguished unit citation.[21]

As the Thunderbirds neared the German border several stiff fights developed along the divisional front as the enemy again stiffened its resistance. On 1 November, Sixth Corps headquarters ordered the Forty-fifth replaced by the 100th Division and moved to the Bains les Bains area for a well-deserved rest. The movement began the following day, and by 9 November the infantry had completed its withdrawal. Several support units and artillery batteries were left behind to aid the 100th Division. At the time of its replacement, the Forty-fifth had accumulated a total of eighty-six consecutive combat days in southern France.[22]

After a rest, on 22 November the Thunderbirds were alerted to move to the Seventh Army's front for their seventh campaign of the war—Ardennes-Alsace. The Vosges Mountains defenses had been pierced, and the Germans had fallen back to a new front running in a semi-circle from Mulhouse to Mutzig and anchored on the French Maginot line. Known as the Colmar pocket, the Germans had thrown a miscellaneous collection of troops into the breach to halt the Allied advance. Aiding the enemy was the severe winter weather.[23]

By 24 November, the 179th RCT was heavily engaged near Mutzig, a fortified town just to the east of Strasbourg and the German frontier. During the battle, the Germans unleashed their latest secret weapon—the V-1 rocket—against the Thunderbirds. Although it was more advanced than anything the Allies had, it did not really slow down the American advance, and within two days the fighting had shifted westward toward Strasbourg and Germany.[24]

All three RCTs were in the line and pressing forward by 28 November. The 179th was on the left, the 180th was in the center, and the 157th was on the right. On the Forty-fifth's flanks were the 100th and the 103rd infantry divisions. Unfortunately, just as the Thunderbirds were preparing to push into the German homeland on 30 November, Major General Eagles was injured by a mine explosion. Incapacitated, he was replaced as divisional commander by Major General Robert T. Frederick. Known as "a front line general," Frederick and his headquarters staff were often well in advance of the main body of troops during the race across Germany.[25]

The early days of December, 1944 saw some of the most difficult campaigning of the entire war. The rains were almost constant and roads turned into quagmires. As the Americans neared the enemy's home soil, German resistance stiffened. Each village was defended in bitter house-to-house fighting; when the enemy was forced to retreat, he generally launched a vicious counterattack to retake the lost ground.[26]

Despite the bitter weather and heavy fighting, the Forty-fifth continued to press toward the Rhine. By 5 December, the German strongpoints of Nieberbronn les Bains, Reichshoffen-Gundershoffen, and Mertzweller were under attack. Nine days later the Maginot line was breached, and at 1245 the next afternoon, 15 December, the Forty-fifth crossed the German border. The distinction of being the first unit of the Seventh Army to penetrate the enemy's homeland belonged to a patrol from Company L, Third Battalion, 180th Infantry.[27]

Members of the 180th RCT cross a footbridge over the Blies River, which forms the boundary between France and Germany, near Frauenberg, France, on 15 March 1945. *Courtesy Forty-fifth Infantry Division Museum.*

Although the outer portion of Germany's border defenses had been penetrated, the Americans had not pierced the concrete and steel pillboxes of the enemy's in-depth fortifications. Nonetheless, the capture of Bobenthal, the first German city to fall to the division, by the 180th on 16 December was cause to celebrate. The following day the advance elements of the division reached the strongpoints of the Siegfried line.[28]

The line had been designed to provide its defenders with excellent fields of fire and perfect observation of any attacking force. Each strongpoint had to be seized separately in a multitude of small but deadly battles. Before attacking the German pillboxes it first was necessary to call down a heavy concentration of artillery or mortar fire against the positions. This shellfire kept the defenders pinned down while the infantry slowly worked its way into rifle range. Then the covering fire was lifted and a soldier would creep to the pillbox and drop a phosphorous grenade into one of the firing slits. It was a slow, costly battle that called for the utmost courage, and the 180th managed to advance only twelve hundred yards during its first five days on German soil. For its part in the bitter fighting around Bobenthal between 17 and 19 December

1944, Company K, 180th Infantry received the distinguished unit citation.[29]

In an effort to halt the American advance, the Germans launched a series of surprise counterattacks on 16 December. The most spectacular of these was the Battle of the Bulge in the U.S. First Army's area of the Ardennes. To counter the enemy onslaught, the 103rd Division was withdrawn from the Forty-fifth's left flank and shifted to replace an armored division being hurried toward the Bulge. The Thunderbirds stretched their lines across the vacated sector. Faced with such a broad front, the division halted and began to dig in. Strong entrenchments were constructed, and an active patrol network maintained to keep track of the enemy's movements. For the remainder of the month few offensive operations were launched.[30]

During the lull a serious situation developed at Bundenthal. On the sixteenth, the day of the German counterattack, the Third Battalion of the 157th had been sent into the town to secure the road junction. The going was slow and bloody, but in the early morning darkness four companies succeeded in penetrating the town. Almost immediately they came under heavy enemy fire and were forced to organize a 200-yard-square defensive perimeter. While the Americans huddled in half-demolished buildings the Germans poured a devastating rain of machine-gun and artillery fire on their positions.[31] For the next week the Thunderbirds remained trapped. Any movement during the daylight hours brought immediate enemy fire crashing down on the besieged men. Their water and food supplies began to run low. Finally, one night the men were able to find some hog meal to eat, but the shortage of water remained a problem. It was not until the night of 23 December, under the cover of a tremendous artillery barrage, that the survivors of the Third Battalion were rescued.[32]

By New Year's Day of 1945 the Thunderbirds were still holding their positions just inside the German border. Beginning on 2 January, however, the division's lines were reshuffled, and the Forty-fifth was moved to the Low Vosges sector. To give it added strength and help the division to cover its extended front, several new units were attached to the Forty-fifth. Eventually divisional headquarters had twenty-six infantry and ten artillery battalions under its command.

Unfortunately, the troops were spread over an extensive area.[33]

It was too tempting a target. For several days in early January, the Germans' Sixth SS Mountain Division and elements of their 256th and 257th Volkssturm Grenadier divisions probed the Forty-fifth's lines. Then on 11 January the Germans launched an all-out assault against the 180th Infantry. The enemy's attack was, of course, directed at that portion of the line that had been most weakened to reinforce the embattled First Army in the Ardennes. The fighting began at 0700 with one of the heaviest concentrations of artillery and mortar fire encountered during the war. Guns as large as 280-mm. bombarded the American defenses before the first wave of fresh SS troops, secretly moved into the sector from Finland, struck. Eventually the major portions of five enemy divisions struck at the Forty-fifth's lines. The battle-weary Thunderbirds gave ground before the fresh enemy soldiers, and the initial German push carried six hundred yards into Allied territory before the Americans held.[34]

The next day the Thunderbirds launched a counterattack. The Americans pressed forward in the face of repeated German assaults. The bloody fighting seesawed back and forth until all three of the Forty-fifth's combat teams were engaged. During the battle the Germans infiltrated several units behind the American lines, and often rear-area troops found themselves under attack or front-line units began receiving fire from the rear.[35]

Much of the fighting fell on the 157th in the forest south of Mouterhouse. Here the Germans were successful in infiltrating large numbers of troops behind the American lines. As a result, when the Third Battalion pushed approximately fifteen hundred yards in front of its adjoining units during a counterattack, companies I, K, and L of the Third Battalion, Company C of the First Battalion, and G Company of the Second Battalion, 157th Infantry, together with two light tanks of Company D, 191st Tank Battalion, suddenly found themselves surrounded when the enemy fell on their exposed flanks. Several attempts were made to relieve the trapped men, and a provisional force from the Second Battalion's headquarters was hurriedly thrown into the fighting. Because of the bitter winter weather, the rugged terrain, and stiff enemy resistance,

An officer searches for the enemy while two soldiers provide cover at Bobenthal, Germany. Bobenthal was the first German town to be captured by the Americans. It fell to the 180th Infantry on 16 December 1944. *Courtesy Forty-fifth Infantry Division Museum.*

the reenforcements were prevented from reaching the embattled troops.[36]

By 18 January the situation was critical. One company attempting to support the trapped Third Battalion troops was overrun and only thirty men escaped. The next day the enemy launched a series of constant attacks against the besieged Thunderbirds who were now fighting for their lives. Again several attempts were made to break through, but nearly a full company of German soldiers had entrenched themselves between the trapped men and the relief force, and the breakthrough assault failed. The fighting had been so heavy that some of the 157th's front-line units were reporting 75 percent casualties.[37]

As the men's plight worsened, plans were made to resupply them by air, but the bad weather grounded all available aircraft. Left to their own devices, on the twentieth the trapped Thunderbirds attempted again to break out by launching an attack to their rear at 1530. Although ammunition was scarce, considerable progress was made until German artillery began to rain shells on the fleeing troops. "Some of the men were blown to bits, and I saw one officer get a direct hit and just disappear," Private First Class Benjamin Melton recalled. When it became obvious that they could not make it, the men crawled back into their foxholes.[38]

The same day, at 1700, the Germans called on the Thunderbirds to capitulate. Escape was impossible. Not more than 125 men remained from the five companies that had originally been trapped. That evening radio contact with the besieged Thunderbirds was broken. Unwilling to surrender, their officers ordered the men to break up into small units and attempt to make it back to Allied lines. Of the 125, only two made it, Private First Class Melton and Private Walter Bruce. The next day, 21 January, the 157th was pulled off the line to an assembly area near Zittersheim to reorganize.[39]

By now the severe weather and stiffening German resistance had slowed the Allied advance drastically. Earlier in the new year, several men of the Forty-fifth who had been in combat since Sicily were sent home on a goodwill tour. Flying to England, they made a high-speed run across the Atlantic on the *Queen Mary* and toured Oklahoma as heroes. Thirty days later, however, they were back in combat.[40]

As the lines became static, most of the fighting was in the form of patrols that continually harassed the enemy. As the winter wore on, the Forty-fifth was relieved by the Forty-second Infantry Division and sent to a rear-area rest camp for replacement of both men and equipment. The 179th began the rotation to the rear on 16 February; the 157th followed the next day; and the 180th left the front on 18 February. For the next month the Thunderbirds remained in the rest camp preparing for their eighth and final campaign of the war—central Europe.[41]

For the coming offensive the Forty-fifth was attached to the Seventh Army and given the task of reducing the Saar pocket to help pave the way for an Allied drive deep into the German heartland. First, however, the Siegfried line would have to be cracked, a task that would not prove easy. The attack began on 15 March 1945, with the 180th on the left flank, the 157th on the right, and the 179th in reserve. The Blies River was forced and a bridgehead seized. Hurriedly the 120th Engineers threw a bridge across the stream, and men and materiel began pouring across. Enemy strongpoints were bypassed and left to be captured later, as the Thunderbirds

rushed forward, pushing the Germans back toward their main defensive positions.[42]

Within two days the Forty-fifth was poised before the vaunted Siegfried line once again. The going was no easier than when they had first attacked the wall in October of 1944. The fighting was bloody. Each pillbox had to be reduced individually under heavy enemy fire. An intense artillery barrage was directed against the German positions to blind the defenders, while the infantry and armor attacked. Rushing forward, the infantry and the engineers blew a gap in the antitank dragon teeth. Then the tanks quickly moved through the opening to the antitank ditch and poured a deadly fire at the pillbox while the infantrymen assaulted the strongpoint and the engineers filled the ditch. It was a slow and costly process.[43]

For his actions in the fighting to breach the Siegfried line, First Lieutenant, later colonel, Jack L. Treadwell, a guardsman from Snyder, Oklahoma, was awarded the Medal of Honor. Commanding Company F, Second Battalion, 180th Infantry, Treadwell was leading his men against the fortifications at Nieder-Wurzbach inside Germany. As the Thunderbirds pushed forward, they came under heavy rifle and machine-gun fire that pinned them down at the base of a fortified hill. After eight men had been hit trying to make their way up the slope, Treadwell, armed with a submachine gun and hand grenades, assaulted the German positions by himself.[44]

Advancing without any natural cover, Treadwell rushed the nearest pillbox and tossed hand grenades at the entrenchment. Once the grenades had exploded, he thrust the barrel of his gun through its aperture and forced the strongpoint to surrender. Repeating his tactics, he captured five additional pillboxes in the face of heavy enemy fire. Following their leader, the remainder of Company F overran the entire hill, drove a wedge into the Siegfried line, and allowed the 180th to pour through the gap.[45]

Knowing that the Siegfried line was all that remained between the Allies and the German homeland, the enemy viciously opposed each American thrust. In an attempt to regain the captured fortifications, the Germans launched a furious counterattack on 19 March against the 157th's sector, but their assault was beaten back.

An M-10 gun motor carriage of the 645th Tank Destroyer Battalion burns enemy snipers out of a building in Aschaffenburg, Germany. *Courtesy Forty-fifth Infantry Division Museum.*

Once the massive fortifications were broken and the counterattacks thrown back, the Germans had no choice but to withdraw.[46]

The enemy's retreat began that night. To cover their movements a screening force was left behind to hinder the Forty-fifth's advance. The small force was easily brushed aside, and the retreat turned into an unrelenting pursuit, with the Thunderbirds pressing hard upon the rear and flanks of the fleeing Germans. Large columns of enemy vehicles and infantry were caught on the open roads and destroyed.[47]

As the retreat turned into a rout, the Thunderbirds commandeered bicycles, motorcycles, trucks—vehicles of every kind—in an attempt to maintain contact with the enemy. Hundreds of German prisoners continually moved toward the rear searching for someone who would take the time to process them. Many enemy troops "appeared disappointed because no one paid any attention to them," one soldier recalled. By 23 March intensive preparations were under way for the anticipated crossing of the great Rhine River, the last major natural obstacle standing before the Thunderbirds.[48]

The assault began on 26 March with the 179th and 180th Infantry leading the attack. For added firepower, fifteen battalions of artillery had been assigned to the division. At 0230 the troops pushed their assault boats into the heavy fog and began making their way across the river. Even before the boats' motors were started, the Germans, who were as yet unable to see the Americans, began probing the mists with streams of fire. As the craft neared the east bank, the Thunderbirds came under intense 88-mm., 20-mm., and machine-gun fire. Undeterred, they continued the attack.[49]

By nightfall on the 26th, the bridgehead was secure and the Thunderbirds pressed forward immediately. Racing east, the riflemen climbed aboard tanks, tank destroyers, jeeps—any vehicle they could—to speed the advance. By 28 March, the 179th had reached the Main River and captured an undamaged railroad bridge across the stream. Hurriedly the 180th joined the steady flow of Thunderbirds across the structure. Because there was neither the time nor the troops to spare to guard them during the rapid advance of forty miles in thirty hours, thousands of surrendering enemy troops had simply been directed toward the rear.[50]

It was not until the Americans reached Aschaffenburg and the "little Siegfried line" that sustained enemy resistance was again encountered. Here the local Nazi commander, a "stern fanatic who ruled with hobnailed military despotism," forbade surrender even though the town's defenders faced a "lost and hopeless cause." Many of Aschaffenburg's inhabitants, who seemed willing to die for the fuehrer, joined the town's military defenders, SS troops, and Volkssturm units, for a last-ditch attempt to stave off a German disaster. Any citizen attempting to flee or surrender was quickly shot by the fanatics.[51]

The 157th launched the attack against the city on 29 March by assaulting Schweinheim, east of Aschaffenburg. The fighting was bitter, often "room to room, house to house, street to street," and "to cross a street or lean out a window was to flirt with death," one Thunderbird recalled. "Old men, women, and children threw grenades from rooftops," and "young German soldiers stayed in their foxholes until blasted out." By nightfall the heavily fortified barracks at the eastern edge of Schweinheim had been reached, but the attack against Aschaffenburg stalled.[52]

The next morning, Allied aircraft were called in to bomb and strafe the defenders into sub-mission, but to no avail. For the next two days the fighting continued, with Allied airpower and artillery relentlessly pounding the Germans. By 1 April, it was clear that the Germans in Aschaffenburg would hold out to the last, and the 157th was left to isolate the town, while the rest of the division swung northeast. Aschaffenburg surrendered two days later.[53]

Again the advance became a race to maintain contact with the disorganized German army and prevent it from forming a new defensive line. The pursuit was kept up without a halt until 6 April, when the Forty-fifth paused briefly to close the gaps between its units. On 8 April, the direction of the attack was shifted to the south, and the Thunderbirds halted again on 10 April to rearrange their lines. They then renewed the assault.[54]

The division continued to advance between eighteen and forty kilometers a day. On 12 April a bridgehead over the Main River was seized, and the Thunderbirds turned south toward Bamberg. Located on both sides of the Main, Bamberg was the key to the region's road and communications network as well as being a major German supply center. Although its defenders had "sworn defense of the area to the death," the town was assaulted on 13 April by the 180th RCT and captured after one day's fighting.[55]

While the 180th fought at Bamberg, the 157th and 179th bypassed the town and headed for Nuremberg—one of the Nazis' most famous shrines. Suddenly the German high command threw everything it could muster into the battle for the city. Beginning on 15 April the Luftwaffe deployed the Messerschmitt 262—its latest jet fighter—and attacked the Thunderbirds time and again in an effort to halt the American advance. The German attempts failed, however, and by 16 April the division was ready to strike for the city.[56]

The assault began the next day with an enveloping operation directed against the eastern and southern edges of the city. As they attacked, the Thunderbirds were met with a heavy concentration of artillery fire from guns that had been gathered from throughout the region specifically for Nuremberg's defense. The enemy artillery was joined by renewed Luftwaffe attacks, and though slowed, the American advance continued forward.[57]

By the night of 17 April elements of all three

Survivors of the Nazi concentration camp at Dachau, which had been liberated by the Thunderbirds. The men and women in this photograph are in better health after having been cared for by Forty-fifth Division medics and having proper food for several weeks. *Courtesy Forty-fifth Infantry Division Museum.*

infantry regiments were inside the city. Two strong enemy counterattacks were thrown back, and on the eighteenth the battle turned into a series of savage house-to-house fights. By 19 April the Germans had been pushed in to the inner walls of the old city, where they made a final stand. Nazi resistance was finally crushed by the 157th and the 179th on 20 April. Because of their efforts in the fierce fighting for control of Nuremberg, Company L, Third Battalion, 180th Infantry, was awarded a distinguished unit citation for its actions.[58]

It was obvious that the Germans were defeated, and after a day's rest the Forty-fifth renewed its advance. This time the division headed south toward Munich. As the Thunderbirds rolled forward they met only sporadic enemy resistance. The Altmühl River was crossed with little opposition; however, once on the other bank the division ran into a strong German delaying force that skillfully used demolitions, minefields, roadblocks, and strongpoints to hinder the advance.[59]

Still the Americans moved forward at a dizzy pace, and on 26 April reached the north bank of the Danube River. In the face of heavy German fire, the crossing began almost immediately and the next day the Forty-fifth was on the southern side. By then, in the words of one Thunderbird, "the division was using tanks, tank destroyers, 'Long Tom bulldozers,' anything that was motor propelled."[60]

Although the war was nearing an end, the 157th and elements of the 191st Tank Battalion were to make one of the most grisly discoveries of the entire war—the Nazi extermination camp at Dachau. Located twenty kilometers north and east of Munich, the Dachau camp was one of Germany's most infamous and brutal. On 29 April, as the Thunderbirds approached the camp, they "picked up a clawing stink." Forty boxcars filled with human corpses were on the railroad tracks leading into the camp. The fields on each side of the track were littered with dead. All had been starved to skeletons. More horror awaited the troops inside the camp. Bodies were stacked like cordwood awaiting disposal, and, as one witness described the scene, the "various gas chambers, the crematorium, [and] instruments of torture all showed signs of recent use."[61]

Later, according to Sergeant First Class Jake Pricer of Perry, Oklahoma, who was one of the first Thunderbirds to enter Dachau, local Germans, most of whom claimed to know nothing of what was going on inside the camp, were required to visit Dachau and view the atrocities. Confronted with such scenes of horror, some of the Germans committed suicide. After the occupation, local citizens were required to view movie films of the camp before being allowed to purchase bread ration coupons.[62]

While the 157th was liberating Dachau, the 179th attacked along the autobahn toward Munich. Most of the Thunderbirds expected German fanatics to contest the town's capture, but the 179th encountered only spotty pockets of enemy resistance along Munich's outskirts. By 30 April, the regiment was "smashing through the battered streets" against light resistance. When the 180th was thrown into the fighting to occupy the city, it did encounter a stubborn pocket of SS troops; they were overcome, however, and by 1 May, Munich was firmly in American hands.[63]

The war was over for the Forty-fifth, and the division turned its attention to garrisoning Munich. Initially the 157th was given the north-central portion of the city, the 179th the eastern sector, and the 180th the southwestern part. Additional units were used to supplement the infantry at key points. On 2 May the Thunderbirds began constructing several camps to hold the flood of German prisoners of war. Some reshuffling of troop assignments were made the following day. The 157th Infantry and the 191st Tank Battalion took over guard duty in Munich; the 179th was dispatched to watch over Dachau; and the 180th took control of the POW camps. On 6 May the division was placed in reserve, and the following day, 7 May 1945, Germany's surrender was announced.[64]

MAPS

Oklahoma's Citizen Soldiers in Campaigns and Battles of the Spanish-American War, World War I, World War II, and the Korean Conflict

Maps for World War II from the collections of the Forty-fifth Infantry Division Museum, Oklahoma City.

Maps for the Korean Conflict prepared for this book by the Forty-fifth Infantry Division Museum. Cartographer, Jack Clapp. Legends by Major General Frederick A. Daugherty and Kenny A. Franks.

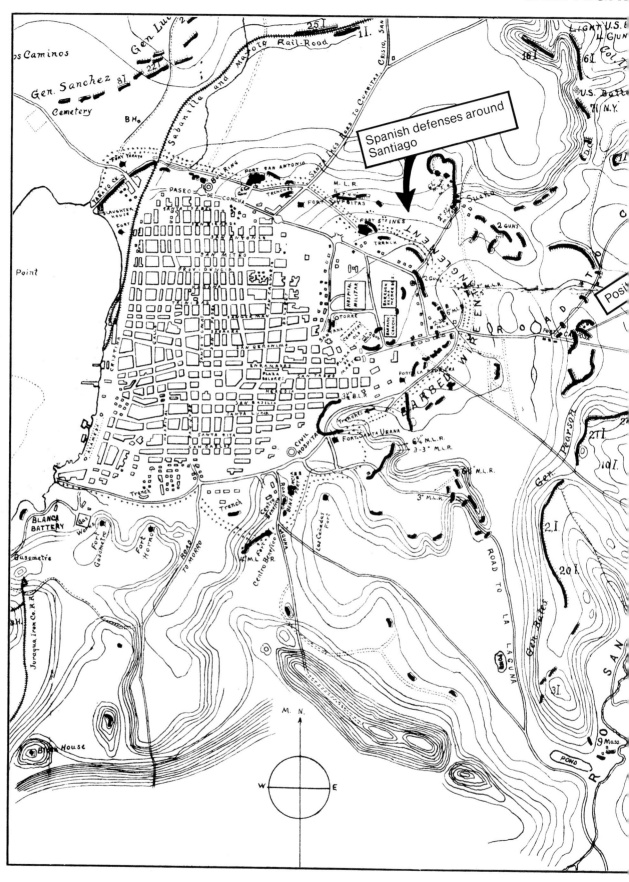

Spanish defenses around Santiago

After landing at Daiquiri, the Rough Riders began moving toward Santiago on 23 June, 1898. Wh[...] crossing the San Juan River on 1 July, they came under heavy shell fire directed at a nearby observati[...] balloon. Moving through high grass and open jungle to the right of the road, the Rough Riders storm[...]

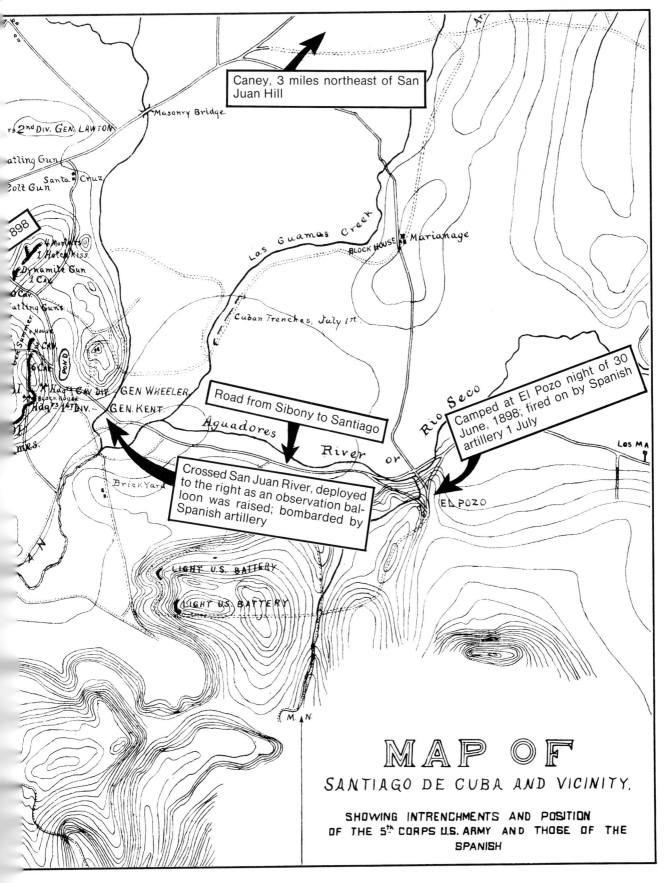

Caney, 3 miles northeast of San Juan Hill

Masonry Bridge.

rs 2nd DIV. GEN. LAWTON

atling Gun

olt Gun   Santa Cruz

.898

4 Mortars
1 Hotchkiss.

Dynamite Gun
1 Cal.

atling Guns

Las Guamas Creek

BLOCK HOUSE   Marianage

Cuban Trenches, July 1st.

Road from Sibony to Santiago

Rio Seco

Camped at El Pozo night of 30 June, 1898; fired on by Spanish artillery 1 July

LOS MA

Hqd Gen DIV GEN WHEELER.

Hqd 1st DIV. — GEN. KENT.

Aguadores

River   or

Crossed San Juan River, deployed to the right as an observation balloon was raised; bombarded by Spanish artillery

Brick Yard

EL POZO

LIGHT U.S. BATTERY

LIGHT US BATTERY

M. N.

MAP OF
SANTIAGO DE CUBA AND VICINITY.

SHOWING INTRENCHMENTS AND POSITION
OF THE 5th CORPS U.S. ARMY AND THOSE OF THE
SPANISH

Kettle Hill, to the left of San Juan Hill, and then supported the attack on San Juan Hill. Adapted from U.S. War Department *Annual Report, 1898.*

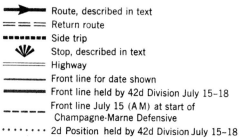

Route, described in text
=== Return route
▼▼ Side trip
▼▼ Stop, described in text
Highway
Front line for date shown
Front line held by 42d Division July 15–18
Front line July 15 (AM) at start of
 Champagne-Marne Defensive
•••••• 2d Position held by 42d Division July 15–18

All front lines are as of midnight for dates shown unless otherwise
noted; thus September 26 on a line indicates the line held at
midnight September 26/27. The dates September 26–27 on a
line indicate that the line was located at the same place at
midnight of both September 26 and September 27

Black dotted line encloses approximate area in which roads are
blocked by artillery practice at certain times

Scale $\frac{1}{200000}$

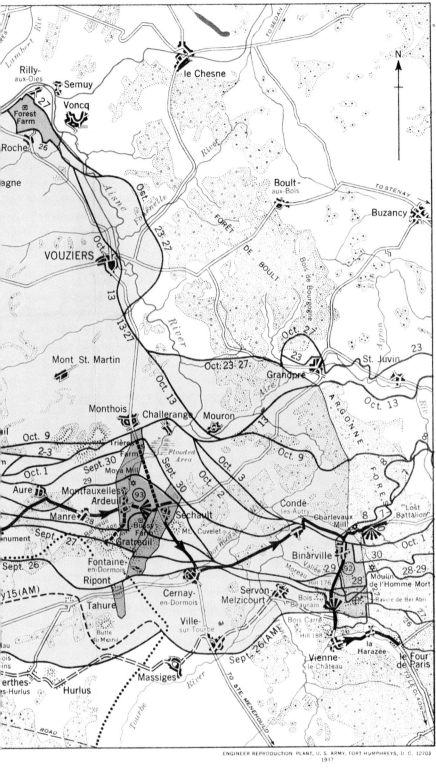

N

To Sedan

Rilly-aux-Oies

Semuy

Voncq

le Chesne

Forest Farm

27

Roche
26

agne

Aisne River

Boult-aux-Bois

To Stenay

Buzancy

FORÊT

DE

BOULT

VOUZIERS

Oct.

13

13·27

Bois de Bourgogne

23·27

Mont St. Martin

Oct. 23·27

Oct. 27

23

St. Juvin

23

Grandpré

Oct. 13

Oct. 13

Monthois

Challerange

Mouron

ARGONNE

Oct. 9

2·3

Trière Farm

Flooded Area

Sept. 30

Oct. 9

Oct. 1

Oct. 3

29

Moya Mill

Sept. 30

Aure

Montfauxelles

93

Oct. 2

Conde-les-Autry

Charlevaux Mill

8   7

"Lost Battalion"

Ardeuil

Sechault

Mt. Cuvelet

Manre

28

Bussy Farm

Gratreuil

Sept. 27

Sept. 26

Fontaine-en-Dormois

Ripont

Cernay-en-Dormois

Binarville

Vallée   29

Moreau

92

30

28·29

28

Oct. 1

Moulin de l'Homme Mort

Ravine de Bel Abri

F O R E

Tahure

Butte du Mesnil

Ville-sur-Tourbe

Hill 170

Servon-Melzicourt

Bois Beaurain

Bois Carré

Hill 188

26

la Harazée

le Four de Paris

Sept. 26(AM)

Vienne-le-Château

Hurlus

Massiges

To Ste. Menehould

Tourbe River

ROAD

ENGINEER REPRODUCTION PLANT, U. S. ARMY, FORT HUMPHREYS, D. C. 12703
1937

rican memorial

ch military cemetery

Colored areas except as indicated below show ground gained
by American units with the French Fourth Army
September 26–October 27

Ground gained by French divisions of French Fourth
Army September 26–October 27

② Large circled numeral in a colored area indicates
the American division which fought there

㊱ Small circled numeral indicates part of American
division which fought attached to another division

15 Miles

lometers

On 8 October, the Oklahoma guardsmen in the Thirty-sixth Division's 142nd Regiment launched an attack down the northern slope of Blanc Mont toward and along the sunken road to Saint-Etienne-a-Arnes. During the battle two Oklahomans, Corporal Harold L. Turner and Sergeant Samuel H. Sampler, won the Medal of Honor. On 13 October the guardsmen reached the Aisne River, where they remained for two weeks before renewing the assault.

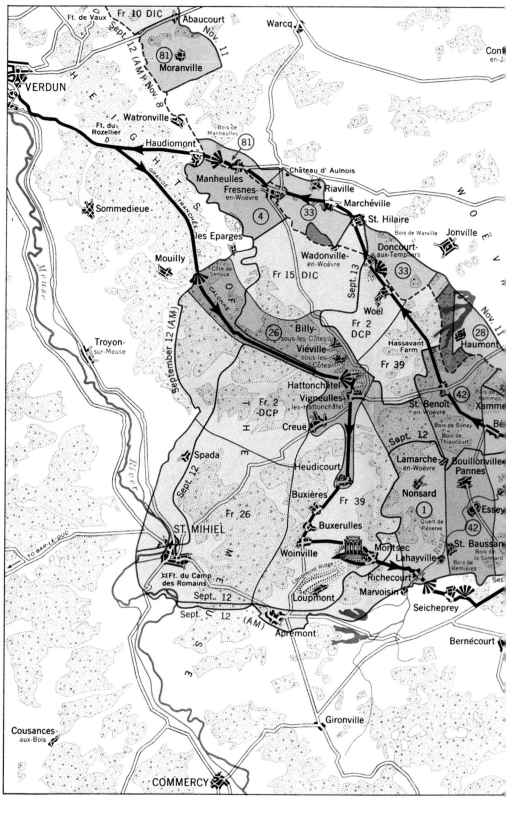

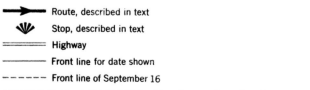

St. Mihiel
American Memorial

St. Mihiel
American Cemetery

Ruins

Scale $\frac{1}{200000}$

SAINT-MIHIEL SALIENT

ENGINEER REPRODUCTION PLANT, U.S. ARMY, FORT HUMPHREYS, D.C. 12703
1937

Colored areas except as otherwise indicated show ground gained by
American divisions in the St. Mihiel Offensive September 12–16

Ground gained September 13 and later abandoned; regained
November 10

Ground gained by American divisions Sept. 17–Nov. 8

November 9–11 Operation of American Second Army and 81st
Division American First Army

Ground gained by French divisions attached to American Army

Circled numerals indicate American divisions

Miles

On the morning of 12 September, 1918, the Oklahomans in the 357th and 358th Infantry Regiments of the Ninetieth Division launched an assault against the Saint-Mihiel salient as a part of the "big push" to end the stalemate on the Western Front. As the Americans advanced toward Villers-sous-Preny, two Oklahomans, Corporal Wilbur S. Light and Private Joseph A. Buffalo, received the Distinguished Service Cross for silencing German snipers located in the woods.

SICILY CAMPAIGN

Map showing the Thunderbird landing and advance across Sicily, July-August, 1943. Courtesy Forty-fifth Infantry Division Museum.

AMPHIBIOUS OPERATION MADE
AUGUST 15 - TO CUT OFF NAZI
FORCES

MIDAZZO

MESSINA

CEFALU

SAN STEFANO
BATTLE OF 'BLOODY RIDGE
JULY 29-30 TOUGHEST
FIGHT IN SICILY

MISTRETTA

MOUNT ETNA

CATANIA

CALTANISSETTA
JULY 18 CALTANISSETTA
FALLS TO 45th THE DIVISION
DASHES THROGH MOUNTAINS
TO THE NORTH

CALTAGIRONE

VIZZINI

SIRACUSA

BISCARI

COMISO

VITTORIO

ON JULY 11, 1943 COMISO AIRPORT IS TAKEN
180th INF RUNS HEAD ON INTO HERMAN
GORING DIVISION. BISCARI AIRPORT
TAKEN JULY 13th

RAGUSA

Y 10, 1943 - 45th LANDS IN
LY AT 0425 UNDER SUPPOR
NAVAL FIRE - MOVES INLAND
CKLY

SCOGLITA

NAPLES-FOGGIA CAMPAIGN

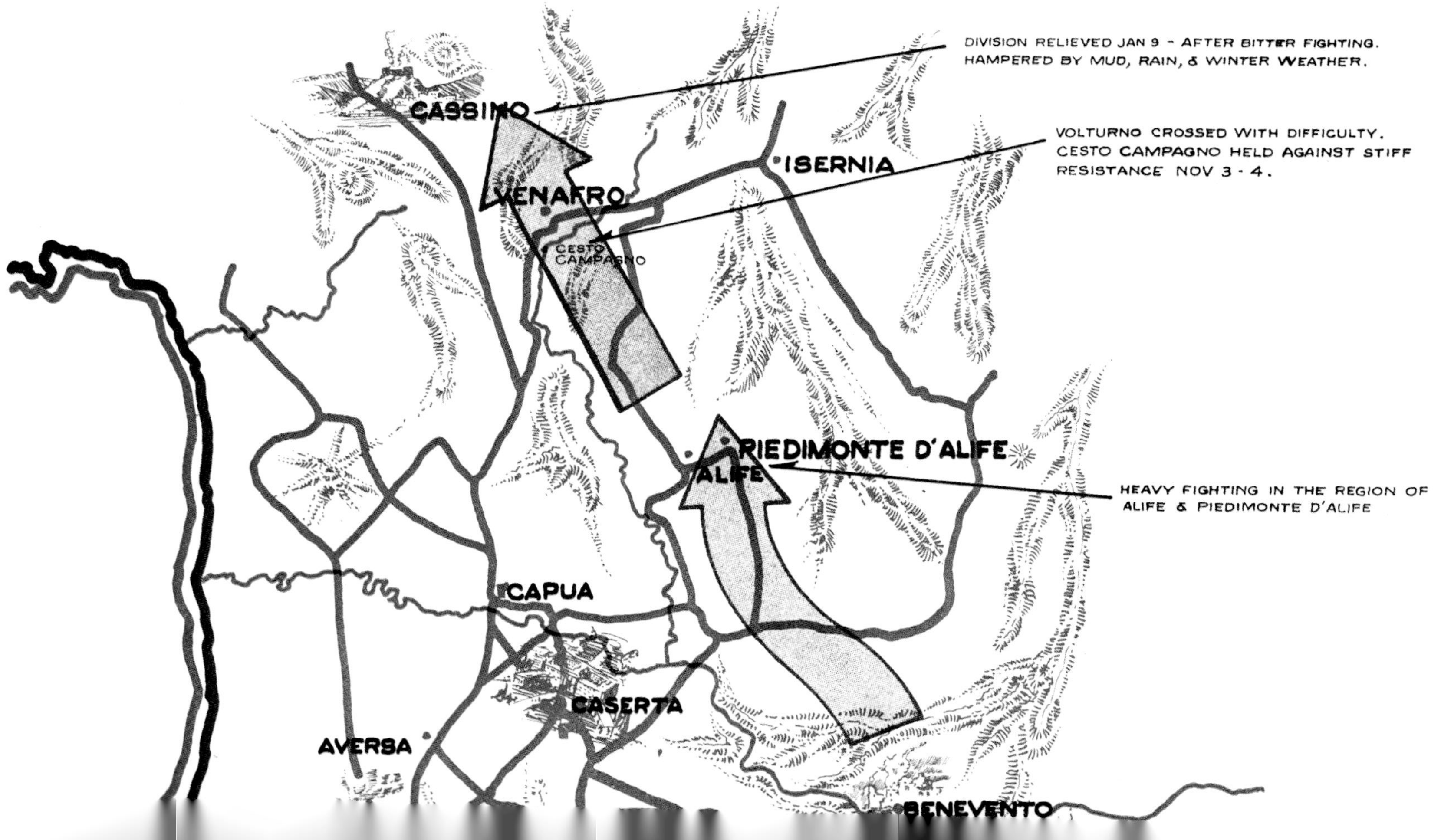

DIVISION RELIEVED JAN 9 - AFTER BITTER FIGHTING. HAMPERED BY MUD, RAIN, & WINTER WEATHER.

VOLTURNO CROSSED WITH DIFFICULTY. CESTO CAMPAGNO HELD AGAINST STIFF RESISTANCE NOV 3 - 4.

HEAVY FIGHTING IN THE REGION OF ALIFE & PIEDIMONTE D'ALIFE

CASSINO

VENAFRO

CESTO CAMPAGNO

ISERNIA

PIEDIMONTE D'ALIFE

ALIFE

BENEVENTO

CAPUA

CASERTA

AVERSA

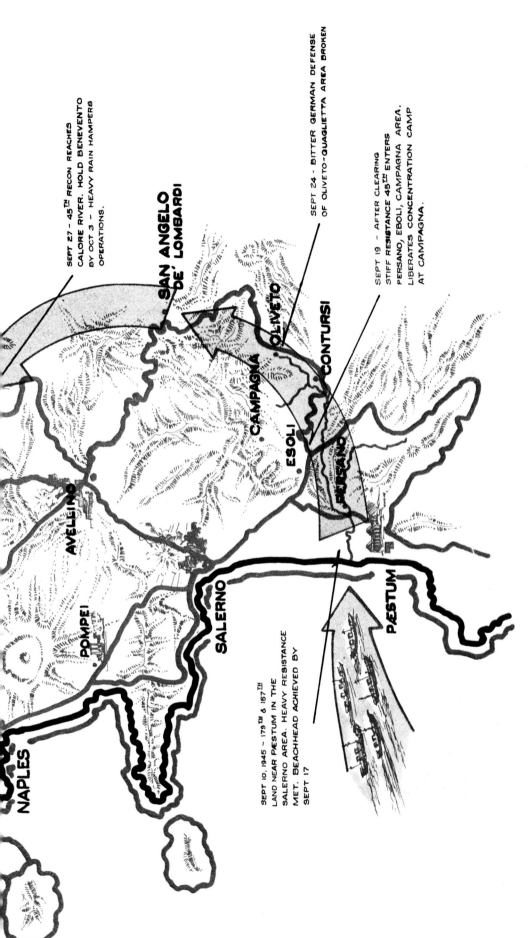

SEPT 27 - 45TH RECON REACHES
CALORE RIVER. HOLD BENEVENTO
BY OCT 3 - HEAVY RAIN HAMPERS
OPERATIONS.

SAN ANGELO
DE' LOMBARDI

OLIVETO

SEPT 24 - BITTER GERMAN DEFENSE
OF OLIVETO-QUAGLIETTA AREA BROKEN

CAMPAGNA

ESOLI

CONTURSI

PERSANO

SEPT 19 - AFTER CLEARING
STIFF RESISTANCE 45TH ENTERS
PERSANO, EBOLI, CAMPAGNA AREA.
LIBERATES CONCENTRATION CAMP
AT CAMPAGNA.

AVELLINO

POMPEI

NAPLES

SALERNO

PAESTUM

SEPT 10, 1945 - 179TH & 157TH
LAND NEAR PAESTUM IN THE
SALERNO AREA. HEAVY RESISTANCE
MET. BEACHHEAD ACHIEVED BY
SEPT 17

Naples-Foggia Campaign, September, 1943–January, 1944. Courtesy Forty-fifth Infantry Division Museum.

ROME-ARNO CAMPAIGN

FEB 16 - 19 · GERMANS LAUNCH FURIOUS FOUR
DAY ASSAULT TO SPLIT BEACHHEAD FORCES
ALONG THE ANZIO-ALBANO ROAD WITH
"FACTORY AREA" AS FOCAL POINT. ELEMENTS
OF SEVEN NAZI DIVISIONS ARE THROWN AGAINST
THE 45TH WITH LUFTWAFFE SUPPORT AT ITS
PEAK. ENEMY ARTILLERY SUPPORT IS
HEAVIEST OF ITALIAN CAMPAIGN, BUT "KRAUTS"
MANAGE TO GAIN ONLY THREE KILOMETERS
AND ATTACK WHICH WAS TO LIQUIDATE THE
BEACHHEAD BY FEB. 18 DEVELOPS INTO
A MILITARY BLUNDER. CASUALTIES HEAVY
ON BOTH SIDES. TENACITY OF 45TH SAVES
BEACHHEAD.

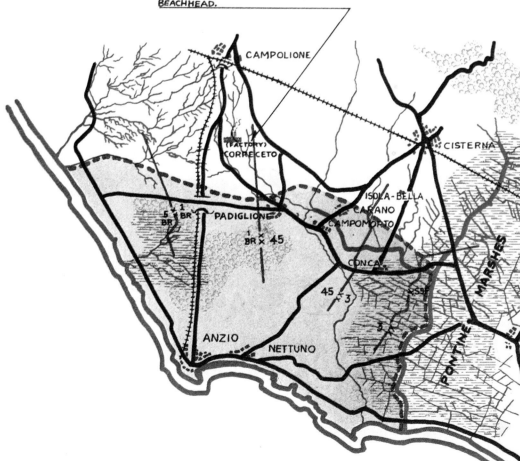

The Rome-Arno Campaign, January-June, 1944. Inset map of the Anzio beachhead. Courtesy Forty-fifth Infantry Division Museum.

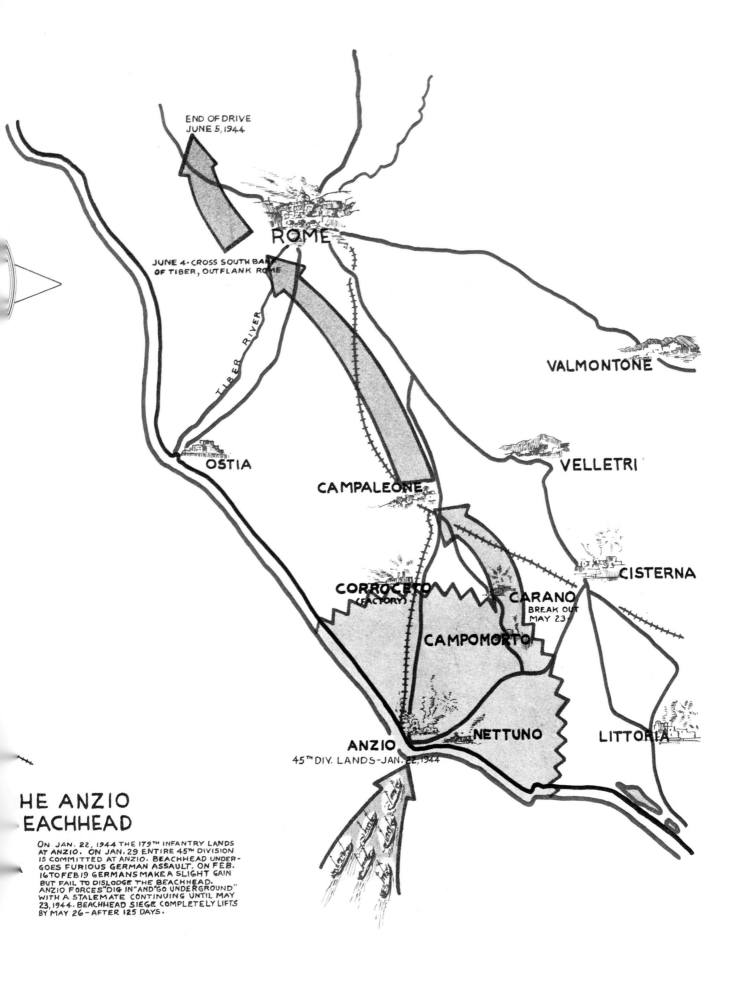

END OF DRIVE
JUNE 5, 1944

ROME

JUNE 4 - CROSS SOUTH BANK
OF TIBER, OUTFLANK ROME

TIBER RIVER

VALMONTONE

OSTIA

VELLETRI

CAMPALEONE

CORROCETO
(FACTORY)

CARANO
BREAK OUT
MAY 23

CISTERNA

CAMPOMORTO

ANZIO
45TH DIV. LANDS - JAN. 22, 1944

NETTUNO

LITTORIA

HE ANZIO
EACHHEAD

ON JAN. 22, 1944 THE 179TH INFANTRY LANDS
AT ANZIO. ON JAN. 29 ENTIRE 45TH DIVISION
IS COMMITTED AT ANZIO. BEACHHEAD UNDER-
GOES FURIOUS GERMAN ASSAULT. ON FEB.
16 TO FEB 19 GERMANS MAKE A SLIGHT GAIN
BUT FAIL TO DISLODGE THE BEACHHEAD.
ANZIO FORCES "DIG IN" AND "GO UNDERGROUND"
WITH A STALEMATE CONTINUING UNTIL MAY
23, 1944. BEACHHEAD SIEGE COMPLETELY LIFTS
BY MAY 26 - AFTER 125 DAYS.

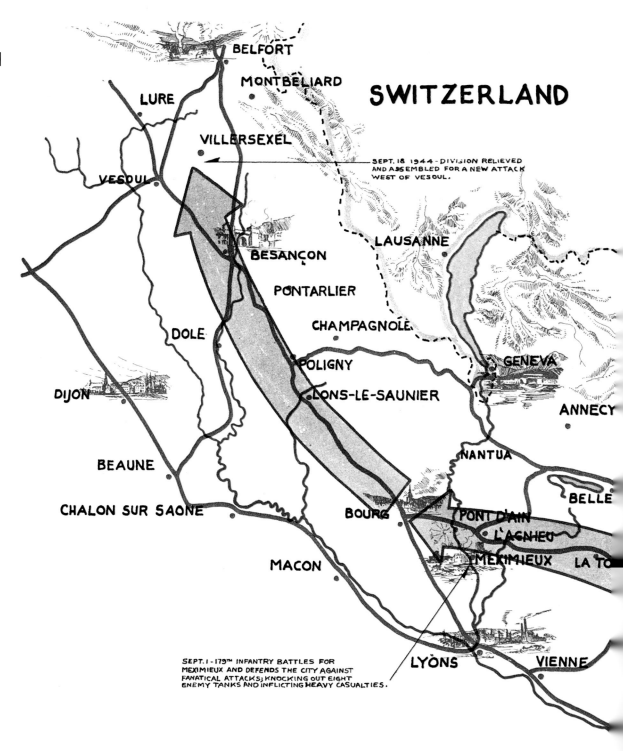

SOUTHERN
FRANCE
CAMPAIGN

SWITZERLAND

BELFORT

MONTBELIARD

LURE

VILLERSEXEL

VESOUL

SEPT. 18 1944 - DIVISION RELIEVED
AND ASSEMBLED FOR A NEW ATTACK
WEST OF VESOUL.

LAUSANNE

BESANÇON

PONTARLIER

CHAMPAGNOLE

DOLE

POLIGNY

LONS-LE-SAUNIER

GENEVA

DIJON

ANNECY

NANTUA

BEAUNE

BELLE

CHALON SUR SAONE

BOURG

PONT D'AIN

L'AGNIEU

MEXIMIEUX

LA TO

MACON

SEPT. I - 179ᵀᴴ INFANTRY BATTLES FOR
MEXIMIEUX AND DEFENDS THE CITY AGAINST
FANATICAL ATTACKS; KNOCKING OUT EIGHT
ENEMY TANKS AND INFLICTING HEAVY CASUALTIES.

LYONS

VIENNE

Forty-fifth Division
area of operations
in Southern France,
August-September,
1944. Courtesy For-
ty-fifth Infantry Di-
vision Museum.

N.

ITALY

MONACO
NICE

AMBRÉY

GRENOBLE FALLS TO UNITS OF THE
36TH DIV. THEN IS TURNED OVER TO
THE 45TH ON AUG. 23.

AUGUST 15, 1944 - 45TH DIVISION
INVADES SHORE OF SOUTHERN FRANCE
UNDER IDEAL CONDITIONS AT STE.
MAXIME - MEET ONLY SLIGHT
RESISTANCE AND RACE INLAND.

UPIN
GRENOBLE

GAP

DIGNE

ST. RAPHAËL
FREJUS

ASPRES SUR BUECH
SISTERON

DRAGUIGNAN

STE.
MAXIME

VALENCE

SEDERON

FORCALOVIER

NYONS

BARJOLES

BRIGNOLES

PEYROLLES

TOULON

PRIVAS

ORANGE

AVIGNON

MARSEILLE

ARLES

RHINELAND CAMPAIGN

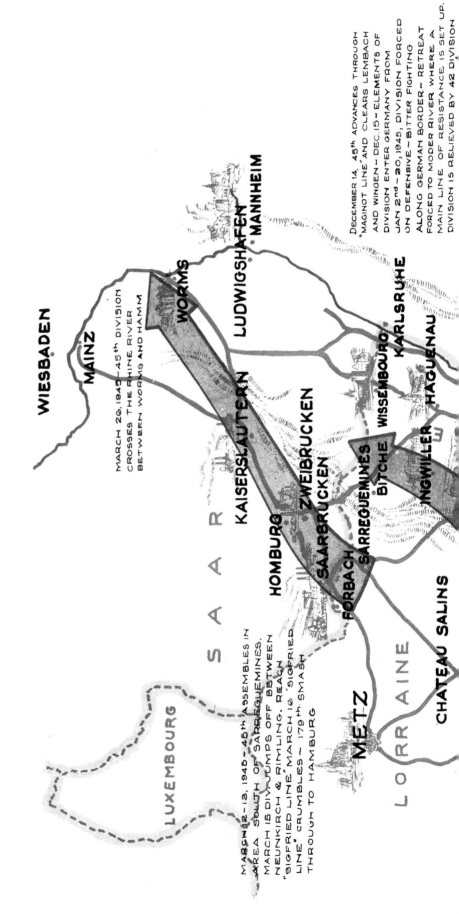

LUXEMBOURG

S A A R

MAINZ

WIESBADEN

WORMS

LUDWIGSHAFEN

MANNHEIM

KAISERSLAUTERN

HOMBURG

ZWEIBRUCKEN

SAARBRUCKEN

FORBACH

SARREGUEMINES

BITCHE

WISSEMBOURG

KARLSRUHE

INGWILLER

HAGUENAU

METZ

CHATEAU SALINS

L O R R A I N E

MARCH 20, 1945 — 45th DIVISION
CROSSES THE RHINE RIVER
BETWEEN WORMS AND HAMM

MARCH 12 - 13, 1945 ~ 45th ASSEMBLES IN
AREA SOUTH OF SARREGUEMINES.
MARCH 15 DIV. JUMPS OFF BETWEEN
NEUNKIRCH & RIMLING. REACH
"SIGFRIED LINE" MARCH 16. "SIGFRIED
LINE" CRUMBLES ~ 179th SMASH
THROUGH TO HAMBURG

DECEMBER 14, 45th ADVANCES THROUGH
"MAGINOT LINE" AND CLEARS LEMBACH
AND WINGEN ~ DEC. 15 ~ ELEMENTS OF
DIVISION ENTER GERMANY FROM
JAN 2nd - 20, 1945, DIVISION FORCED
ON DEFENSIVE ~ BITTER FIGHTING
ALONG GERMAN BORDER ~ RETREAT
FORCED TO MODER RIVER WHERE A
MAIN LINE OF RESISTANCE IS SET UP.
DIVISION IS RELIEVED BY 42 DIVISION

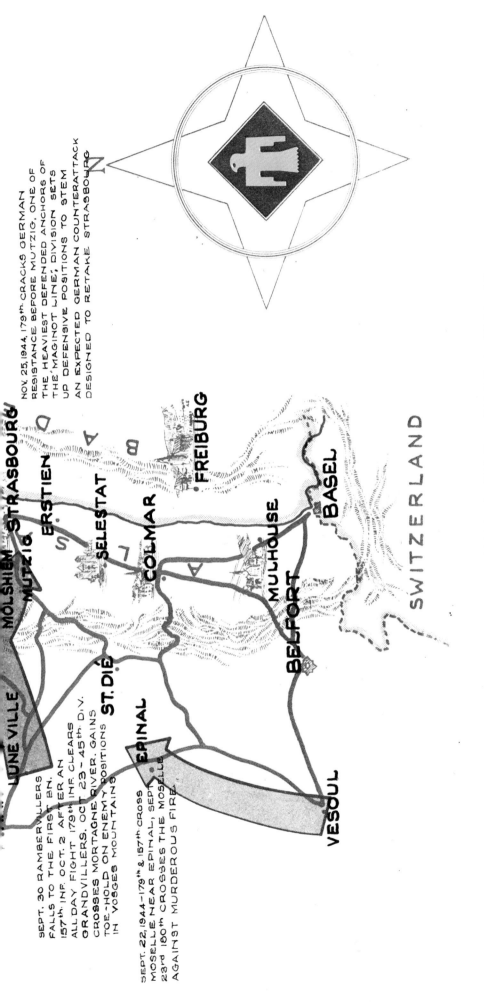

The Rhineland Campaign, October, 1944–March, 1945. Forty-fifth Infantry Division Museum.

NOV. 25, 1944, 179th CRACKS GERMAN RESISTANCE BEFORE MUTZIG, ONE OF THE HEAVIEST DEFENDED ANCHORS OF THE "MAGINOT LINE"; DIVISION SETS UP DEFENSIVE POSITIONS TO STEM AN EXPECTED GERMAN COUNTERATTACK DESIGNED TO RETAKE STRASBOURG

SEPT. 30 RAMBERVILLERS FALLS TO THE FIRST BN. 157th INF. OCT. 2 AFTER AN ALL DAY FIGHT 179th INF. CLEARS GRANDVILLERS. OCT 23 - 45th D.V. CROSSES MORTAGNE RIVER. GAINS TOE-HOLD ON ENEMY POSITIONS IN VOSGES MOUNTAINS

SEPT. 22, 1944—179th & 157th CROSS MOSELLE NEAR EPINAL, SEPT. 23rd 180th CROSSES THE MOSELLE AGAINST MURDEROUS FIRE

MARCH 28 1945 — WITH THREE REGIMENTS ABREAST, FOUR BATTALIONS CROSS MAIN RIVER 2 KMS SOUTH OF ASCHAFFENBERG. MARCH 29 · BITTER BATTLE BEGINS WITH GERMAN CIVILIANS FIGHTING OUR INFANTRY. APRIL 3 — ASCHAFFENBERG SURRENDERS TO END DIVISION'S TOUGHEST FIGHT IN GERMANY. 1500 NAZIS KILLED AND 3000 CAPTURED.

FRANKFURT

MAINZ

MAIN

DARMSTADT

WORMS

MANNHEIM

HEIDELBERG

NECKAR RI

KARLSRUHE

STUTTGART

RHINE RIVER

BODEN

N

Thunderbird operations in Central Europe, March, 1944-May 9, 1945. Courtesy Forty-fifth Infantry Division Museum.

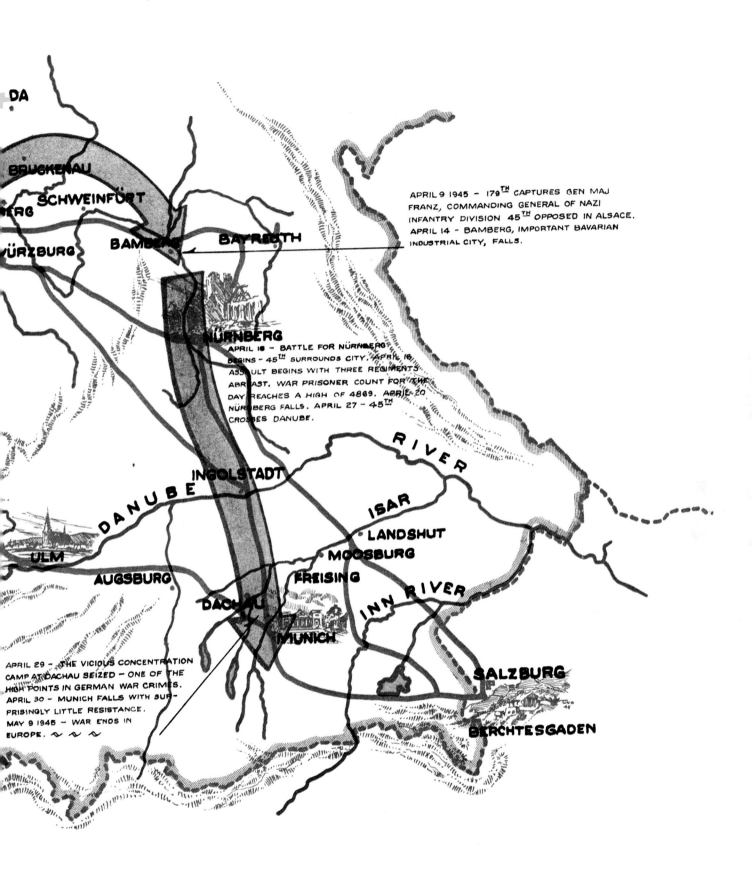

DA

BRUCKENAU

SCHWEINFÜRT

ERG

WÜRZBURG

BAMBERG   BAYREUTH

APRIL 9 1945 - 179TH CAPTURES GEN MAJ
FRANZ, COMMANDING GENERAL OF NAZI
INFANTRY DIVISION 45TH OPPOSED IN ALSACE.
APRIL 14 - BAMBERG, IMPORTANT BAVARIAN
INDUSTRIAL CITY, FALLS.

NÜRNBERG
APRIL 16 - BATTLE FOR NÜRNBERG
BEGINS - 45TH SURROUNDS CITY. APRIL 18,
ASSAULT BEGINS WITH THREE REGIMENTS
ABREAST. WAR PRISONER COUNT FOR THE
DAY REACHES A HIGH OF 4869. APRIL 20
NÜRNBERG FALLS. APRIL 27 - 45TH
CROSSES DANUBE.

INGOLSTADT

RIVER

DANUBE

ISAR

LANDSHUT

MOOSBURG

ULM

FREISING

AUGSBURG

INN RIVER

DACHAU

MUNICH

SALZBURG

APRIL 29 - THE VICIOUS CONCENTRATION
CAMP AT DACHAU SEIZED - ONE OF THE
HIGH POINTS IN GERMAN WAR CRIMES.
APRIL 30 - MUNICH FALLS WITH SUR-
PRISINGLY LITTLE RESISTANCE.
MAY 9 1945 - WAR ENDS IN
EUROPE. ∿ ∿ ∿

BERCHTESGADEN

SECOND KOREAN WINTER CAMPAIGN
Battle for Outpost Eerie

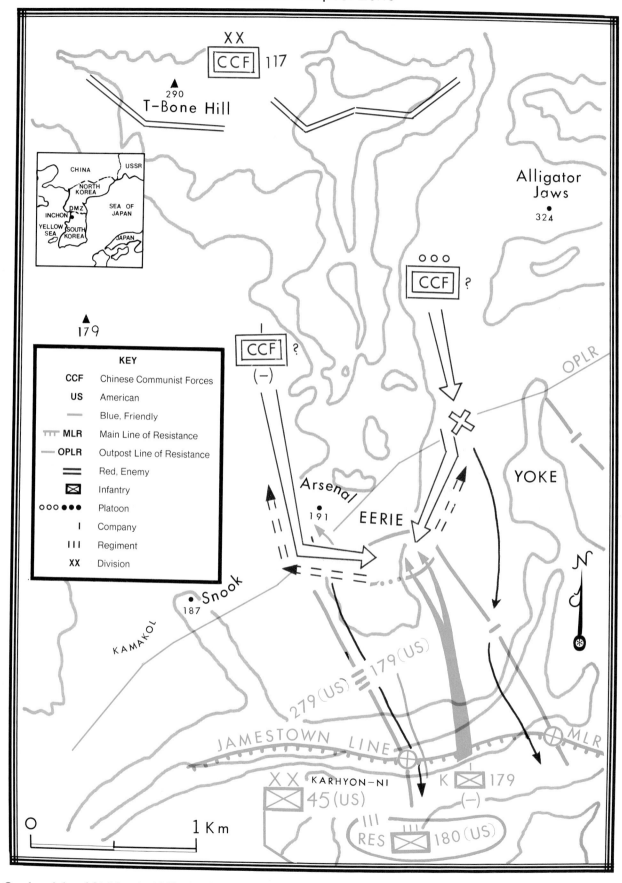

On the night of 21 March, 1952, the Chinese Communists mounted a battalion-sized attack against Outpost Eerie, manned by units of the 179th U.S. Infantry. Overwhelmed by the superior enemy force, they withdrew to their bunkers while friendly artillery fire directed at the hill drove off the Communists with heavy casualties.

KOREAN SUMMER-FALL 1952 CAMPAIGN
Assault on Hill 200

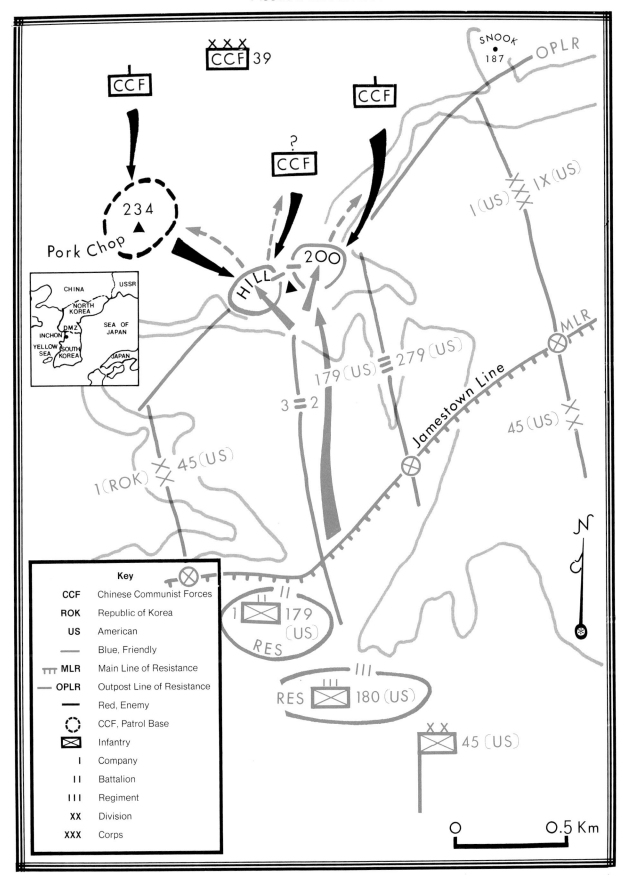

The night of 25 May, 1952, a battalion-sized enemy attack was launched on Hill 200, occupied by units of the 179th U.S. Infantry. Although assaulted from three sides, the Americans, with the aid of division artillery and illuminating flares, held the hill and inflicted heavy casualties on the Communists.

KOREAN SUMMER-FALL 1952 CAMPAIGN
Fight for Hills 812 and 854

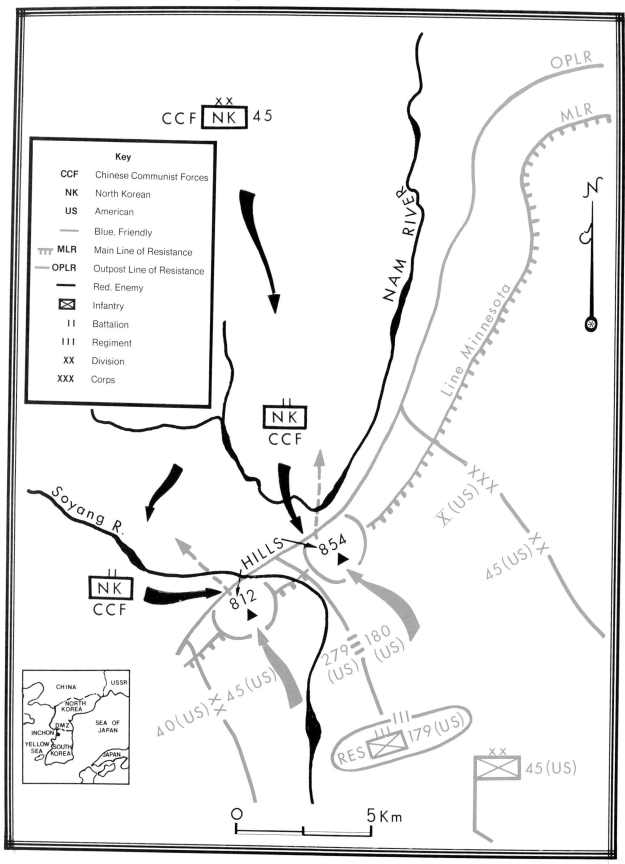

The defense of Hills 812 and 854 was a joint effort of the Eighth (ROK) Division and elements of the Forty-fifth U.S. Infantry Division. The main enemy assault fell on Hill 854, which the Communists partially occupied until drawn off by artillery fire and air strikes. The diversionary attack on Hill 812 was repulsed. By nightfall on 22 September the main line of resistance was fully restored.

THIRD KOREAN WINTER CAMPAIGN
Occupation of Heartbreak Ridge

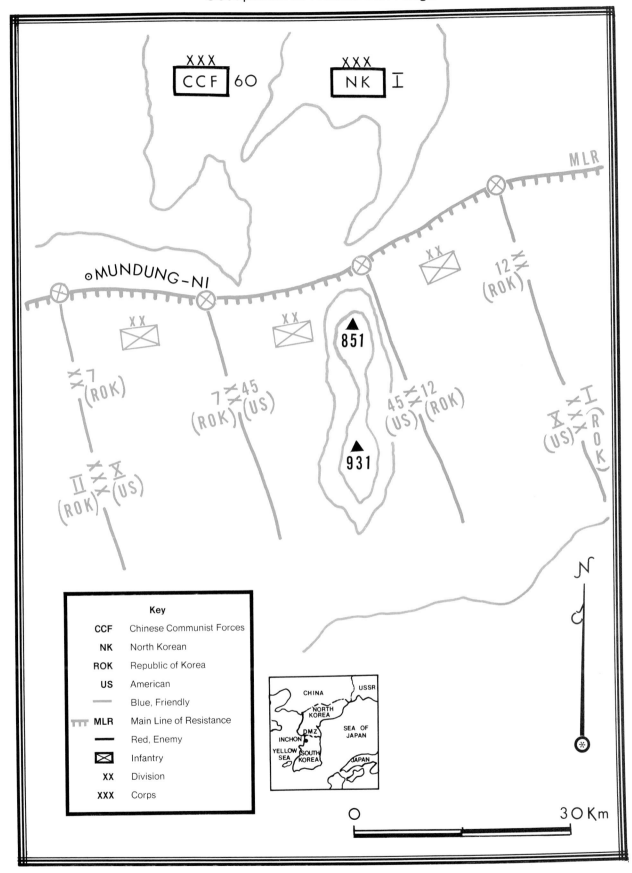

Shown here is the occupation of key terrain in the Heartbreak Ridge area by the Forty-fifth Division as of 1 February, 1953. The division manned the central front of the X (U.S.) Corps sector. The Twelfth (ROK) Division was on the left of the Forty-fifth, and the Seventh (ROK) Division was on its right.

KOREAN SUMMER-FALL 1953 CAMPAIGN
The Armistice

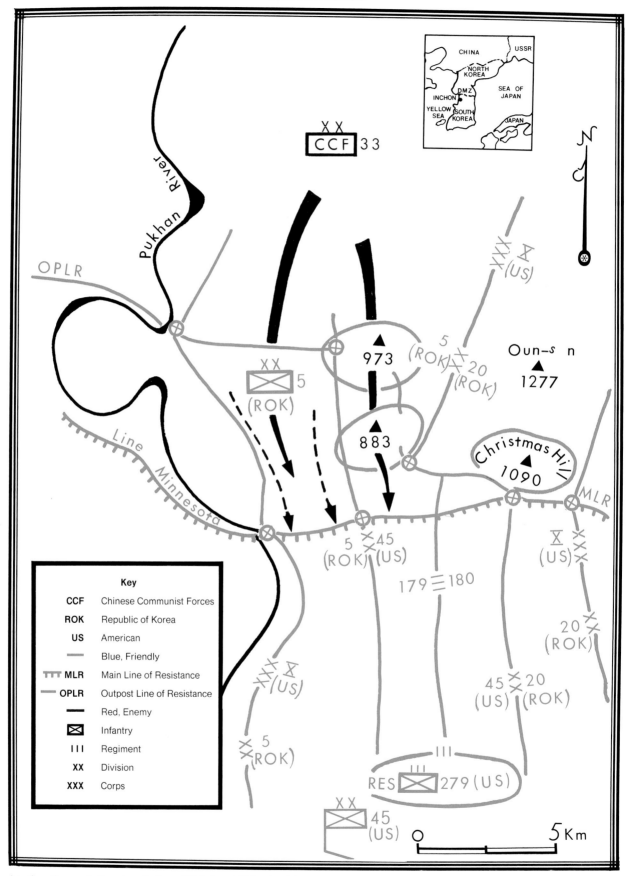

At the time of the Armistice, 27 July, 1953, the Forty-fifth Division was in position near Christmas Hill in the X (U.S.) Corps sector, facing the Thirty-third Chinese Communist Division. The Fifth (ROK) Division was on the Forty-fifth's left flank. Had the fighting not ended, it is certain that heavy combat would have ensued in this part of the front.

CHAPTER 11

THE COLD WAR

For the European countries, the horror of World War II was over. The fighting had cost the Forty-fifth Division a total of 2,540 officers and 60,023 enlisted men killed, wounded, or missing in 511 combat days. Now, with the German surrender, the Thunderbirds began the task of occupying the enemy's homeland.[1]

For nearly a month the division struggled to process a hoard of displaced persons and German prisoners of war. It was a gigantic task, and by the end of May, 1945, the total number of captured enemy soldiers held by the Forty-fifth was approaching 125,000. Although it was against official "de-Nazification policy," German officers were used to compile rosters, organize kitchens, secure rations, and serve as liaison personnel to the Allies. Employing Germans in these activities was necessary to prevent Munich from falling into chaos, and most prisoners willingly cooperated with the Americans.[2]

A simple Memorial Day service was held on 30 May in Munich's Koenigsplatz for those who had given their lives in the conflict, and then the men settled down in their new role as conquerors. In the reorganization of American forces in Europe after V-E Day, the Forty-fifth was transferred from the Seventh to the Third Army, and on 12 June 1945 the division was moved to a new camp along the autobahn on the outlying areas of Munich. Organized sports were implemented; the division's information and education section offered job training programs; and many of the men were given leaves so they could tour various parts of the Continent. Going home was, of course, foremost in everyone's mind.[3]

Many rumors circulated through the occupation camps. The morale of the men suffered when it was leaked that the Forty-fifth was to be designated as a "class two" unit, that is, the division would be transferred to the United States and then shipped to the Pacific for the war against Japan. The rumor was augmented when, during the week of 4 July, many of the division's high-point personnel, those eligible for early discharges, were reassigned to the Ninth and the 103rd infantries and the Fourteenth armored divisions. Several men deemed essential remained behind and joined a hoard of more recent inductees added to the Forty-fifth. A few of the troops with adequate service points for an early discharge were lucky enough to find space on aircraft bound for the United States by way of France, South America, and Florida.[4]

When official word of the plan was received, the division hurriedly packed records and equipment in expectation of service in the Pacific. Soon afterward, the Forty-fifth was alerted for movement to Camp Saint Louis, an assembly area command tent city near Reims, France, and on 18 July the transfer began. Most of the troops moved by rail. One thousand officers and enlisted men were loaded aboard each train of forty-four boxcars with five supply days of C or K rations for food.[5]

Fortunately, the Pacific redeployment plans ended on V-J Day in early August. Now, no one thought of anything but getting home. In mid-August the division moved to Camp Phillip Morris near the port of Le Havre, France. Three successive loading dates were canceled, however, and it was not until early September that the Thunderbirds shipped for America. During this period, on 10 September 1945, Major General Robert T. Frederick was replaced as divisional

"Autograph hounds" surround actress Rita Hayworth at Camp Saint-Louis, France, in August, after V-E Day. *Courtesy Forty-fifth Infantry Division Museum.*

commander by Brigadier General J. D. Meyer. The 180th Infantry crossed the English Channel and sailed from British seaports, while the 157th and the 179th sailed from France. Disembarking at Boston, the men were granted forty-five-day leaves before the division was to reassemble at Camp Bowie, Texas, in November. At 2400 hours on 7 December 1945, the Forty-fifth was deactivated.[6]

Almost immediately work began to reorganize the division as Oklahoma's National Guard. Throughout the war years a state headquarters had been maintained in Oklahoma City by Major General George A. Davis who had served as state adjutant-general for a dollar a year since 14 September 1940. The pre-World War II Thunderbird Division had been apportioned between Oklahoma, New Mexico, Arizona, and Colorado, it was now hoped that the new division would be located entirely within Oklahoma. The driving force behind the reorganization was Lieutenant General Raymond S. McLain, who, although a former Oklahoma national guardsman, had served in the regular army during World War II. McLain spent the first half of 1946 in Oklahoma working toward a rebirth of the Forty-fifth.[7]

In the spring of 1946 the Oklahoma National Guard Association gathered at the state capitol to lay the groundwork of the new division. Although many of those pushing for reorganization were prohibited from active participation because of their age, they worked diligently to bring about the reemergence of the Thunderbirds. It was decided that the priority for the assignment of leadership positions would be given to those men who had served during World War II in combat operations with the Forty-fifth, those who had seen combat, but who had been transferred out of the division's staff officers to other units; and staff officers who had served in combat with other units. With such a policy, many men who had fought in Sicily, Italy, France, and Germany as Thunderbirds played major roles in the revitalized division.[8]

Governors Robert S. Kerr and Roy J. Turner wholeheartedly supported the use of combat veterans for key positions, and refused to allow politics to play any role in the reorganizational effort. Colonel James C. Styron of Hobart, Oklahoma, a graduate of West Point who had later joined the Forty-fifth and served with the division for a part of World War II, was promoted to major general and given command of the new division upon McLain's recommendation. Major General Roy

W. Kenney replaced Major General Davis as adjutant-general on 7 May 1947, and held the post for the next eighteen years. Styron and McLain selected the senior officers, with Brigadier General Hal Muldrow being appointed divisional artillery officer and Adjutant-General Kenney serving as assistant division commander.[9]

Both prewar regiments, the 179th and the 180th, were reactivated. A third regiment, the 279th Infantry, was formed to replace Colorado's 157th Infantry. On 5 September 1946, the Forty-fifth became the first National Guard division reorganized after World War II, when the headquarters and headquarters detachment of the Forty-fifth Infantry Division was reorganized in Oklahoma City. Recruitment and reorganization progressed rapidly across the state.[10]

During McLain's and Styron's selection of officers in the post-World War II reorganization, Colonel Frederick A. Daugherty was given command of the 179th Infantry, located primarily in the western part of the state. Daugherty had first joined the Forty-fifth as a private in Headquarters, Headquarters Company, 1st Battalion, 179th Infantry in April of 1934. He later completed the army's ten series study course and was commissioned a second lieutenant prior to mobilization in 1940. After the call to federal service, he attended a number of command and staff schools. Later he left the division for service in Third Army Headquarters. The Third Army became the Sixth Army, and Daugherty served with distinction on the unit's staff in the Southwest Pacific theater throughout the remainder of the conflict. He then returned to Oklahoma City to resume his law practice and eventually was appointed a federal judge for the Western District of Oklahoma. Rejoining the Forty-fifth, he rose to the rank of major general and commander of the division.[11]

Besides the 179th, by the spring of 1947 many other units had been federally recognized. The 180th Infantry Regiment, under Colonel J. O. ("Cotton") Smith, in the southeastern part of the state, and the 279th Infantry, originally under Colonel Dwight Funk, in southwestern Oklahoma were among them. Funk soon accepted a slot in the regular army and was replaced by Lieutenant Colonel Thad Hummell.

In addition to the infantry, the 160th (commanded by Lieutenant Colonel Jess Todd), the 171st (commanded by Lieutenant Colonel Joseph G. Cathey), the 158th (commanded by Lieutenant Colonel Paul Scheefers), and the 189th (commanded by Lieutenant Colonel Otwa T. Autry) Field Artillery battalions, located, respectively, in Tulsa, in the southeast, in the southwest, and in the north of the state, had been formed. The 120th Medical Battalion (commanded by Lieutenant Colonel James O. Hood), located in Stillwater, and the 120th Engineer Battalion (commanded by Lieutenant Colonel Valor E. Thiessen), located in Norman, also were reorganized.[12]

That summer the reorganized Forty-fifth, with more than five thousand men, became the first postwar National Guard division to hold a field training camp. By June of 1948, the division's authorized strength was 10,532. The next month it was designated as one of the nation's eighteen divisions organized into a new mobile strike force, and its strength increased the following year to 12,500—a full wartime complement. With the increase in manpower came the organization of additional units: the 145th Antiaircraft Battalion was located in the northeast part of the state, and the 245th Heavy Tank Battalion was located in the southwest.[13]

As the Thunderbirds were reorganizing, the "cold war" settled over the world with chilling reality. Throughout the world the diverse ideologies of the free and the Communist worlds jockeyed for power. The United States and the Soviet Union would soon clash in Asia, and Oklahoma's guardsmen would again be called to arms.[14]

At the Potsdam Conference in 1945, President Harry S. Truman and Soviet Premier Joseph Stalin had both assured Korean leaders that their country would be granted independence once Japan was defeated and at the conclusion of a five-year trusteeship under the Soviet Union, China, and Great Britain. After World War II ended, the United States and the Soviet Union could not reach an agreement on how to implement the Potsdam accords, and Soviet troops continued to occupy Korea north of the 38th parallel, while American servicemen protected the southern part of the country. Eventually, in April of 1948, President Truman announced: "The United States should not become so irrevocably involved in the Korean situation that an action taken by any faction . . . could be considered a *casus belli* [pretext for making war] for the United States," and gave the question of reuniting Korea to the United Nations.[15]

The UN quickly called for free elections in both sections of the country. The Soviet Union, however, refused to cooperate and disqualified nearly all of the political parties recognized in the American zone. The result was the organization of the Republic of·Korea (ROK) in the region south of the 38th parallel, and the election in May of 1948 of Syngman Rhee as its leader. This was followed by the creation of the Democratic People's Republic of Korea, generally called North Korea, in the Soviet Union's sector under a Communist government headquartered at Pyongyang under Premier Kim Il Sung.[16]

Believing that its obligation was fulfilled, the United States began a military withdrawal from South Korea in September of 1948. At the same time, the Soviets announced the removal of their troops from North Korea by the end of that year. As the Russians returned home they left behind a well-equipped and excellently trained North Korean army, which, in the following years, they continued to supply with the latest military hardware. In South Korea, however, a weak military establishment was left by the Americans. It was concerned primarily with internal security and was devoid of any heavy artillery, tanks, anti-tank weapons, or airpower.[17]

The Communist hierarchy in North Korea was hesitant to use its military superiority to reunite the country because of the implied threat of the use of American troops to defend the Republic of Korea. Then in January of 1950, American Secretary of State Dean Acheson outlined the nation's defense perimeter in a speech that omitted South Korea. Reacting to the apparent abandonment of the Republic of Korea by America, the Communist leaders of North Korea sent their troops south across the 38th parallel on 25 June 1950.[18]

The North Koreans quickly overpowered the ROK army and hurried southward with little opposition. It was obvious that the South Koreans were incapable of defending themselves, and in response, President Truman, on 27 June, ordered the United States Navy and Air Force to help throw back the North Korean invaders. Within a short time American ships and aircraft were bombarding enemy positions and blockading the North Korean coast. It was clear, however, that air and naval forces would not be enough to stem the North Korean advance, and on 28 June, some American occupation troops in Japan were placed on combat readiness status. Two days later, President Truman authorized General of the Army Douglas MacArthur, the American commander in the Far East, to use ground forces to stem the Communists' advance.[19]

By 5 July 1950, the first American ground troops were in action in Korea. Nevertheless, the invasion of the south continued as the ROK and American troops were overwhelmed by superior North Korean manpower. Shortly afterward, the UN voted to support the American action and authorized the sending of troops under its banner to oppose the North Korean invasion. On 8 July MacArthur was named UN commander. Finally, by September, 1950, Lieutenant General Walton H. Walker, commander of the Eighth Army, managed to stem the North Korean advance and establish relatively stable defense lines around the Pusan perimeter in southeastern South Korea. This vital staging area became the center for a UN buildup to drive the Communists back across the 38th parallel.[20]

When the fighting broke out in Korea the Thunderbirds were preparing for their annual summer camp at Fort Hood, Texas. It had become apparent to many that the escalation in the Korean fighting would necessitate the federalization of several National Guard units to augment the regular army. The Selective Service Act of 1950 authorized the calling of the National Guard to active duty for a period not to exceed twenty-one months. In 1953 this was extended to twenty-four months. As the UN forces were being driven back toward the Pusan perimeter in July of 1950, Oklahoma's Forty-fifth Division and California's Fortieth Division were alerted for possible call to federal service. Later, Alabama's and Mississippi's Thirty-first Division, Illinois's Forty-fourth Division, Ohio's Thirty-seventh Division, and Minnesota's and North Dakota's Forty-seventh Division also were alerted for possible federal duty.[21]

Throughout the remainder of the summer, preparations were made in case the Forty-fifth was federalized. The guardsmen were given thorough physical examinations; detailed property inventories were taken; equipment maintenance was brought to the highest level; and the multitude of other details were taken care of in preparation for active duty. It came as no surprise when the Thunderbirds were one of the first four National Guard divisions activated for duty during the Korean War. On 22 August several of the Forty-fifth's service elements were activated in preparation for the federalization of the remainder of the division. The call for the rest of the division came ten days later on 1 September 1950.[22]

With the mobilization the division was ordered to Camp Polk, deep in the pine forest of Vernon Parish, Louisiana. Two motorized columns of men and materiel left Oklahoma for Camp Polk, while most of the division's heavy equipment was shipped by railroad. Within ten days, the entire division was on its way to the mobilization center. Major General Styron asked for and was given Brigadier General Robert L. Dulaney, who had previously been with the division in the Second World War, to serve as assistant division commander.[23]

Since World War II, Camp Polk had been used chiefly for a summer camp by the region's various National Guard units. Because of its inactivation, the post's permanent party had been reduced to a small housekeeping detail. Although for several weeks before the mobilization of the Thunderbirds, the Department of Defense had hurried to prepare Camp Polk to receive federalized National Guard units and draftees, the work was far from complete when the division arrived. As a result, for the first several weeks of active duty, the guardsmen worked hard at renovating and repairing buildings and constructing training aids. It was not until early 1951 that the post was fully restored to its proper condition.[24]

In addition to the problems of restoring the post to a fulltime training establishment, many of the division's junior officers faced a serious housing problem. Major General John Coffey, Jr., who would be Oklahoma's adjutant-general between January, 1975 and November, 1978, had joined the Forty-fifth in 1946 after serving with the regular army during World War II. As the executive officer of Battery C, 160th Field Artillery at the time of the Korean mobilization, Coffey was struck by the lack of housing in the area around Camp Polk. According to Coffey, when he arrived at Camp Polk it had the appearance of a ghost town, and, with the huge influx of Thunderbirds, housing was in short supply.

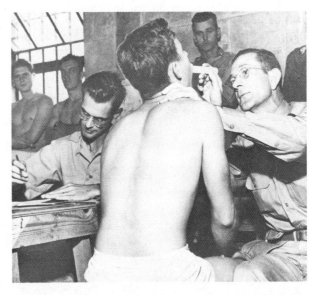

Alerted for possible mobilization in July, 1950, for duty in Asia, Oklahoma Thunderbirds are given medical examinations. *Courtesy Forty-fifth Infantry Division Museum.*

In nearby towns, numerous small dwellings—chicken houses, garages, and such—were hurriedly converted into apartments available for rent to the soldiers. As many as eighteen people would often crowd into a six-room house.[25]

Despite the condition of the post, the Forty-fifth's official army training program began on 7 November 1950. At the same time, draftees poured into Camp Polk to fill out the division's ranks. Ironically, some of the draftees were Oklahomans. The largest single group, four thousand men, arrived in January of 1951, and they were hurriedly worked into the Thunderbirds' machinery. So quickly were the men added to the ranks that some spent only twenty-four hours in replacement companies before being moved to their permanent assignments. Major General Styron tried to meet every incoming contingent and personally welcome them to the Forty-fifth.[26]

Numerous schools were established for both officers and enlisted men to sharpen their combat skills. The training was greatly aided by the fact that 75 percent of the division's officers above the grade of second lieutenant, and 50 percent of the NCOs had seen combat in World War II. By November a twenty-eight-week training program was under way, and late the following month a specialized unit, the Forty-fifth Ranger Company, was organized. The busy schedule allowed little time for relaxation. As Christmas and New Year's approached, it became apparent that there would be no leaves granted for visits home; however, every effort was made to see that each man had at least a seventy-two-hour pass for one or the other holiday.[27]

On 24 February 1951, in the midst of the intense training schedule, the Thunderbirds were alerted for shipment to Japan. The move was a surprise to most of the troops. The formal training schedule was abolished as the men hurriedly prepared for overseas duty. Medical records were brought up to date, the required shots were taken, battle indoctrination courses were established, military and personal equipment was prepared for the move, and nearly every man given ten days of leave.[28]

As the materiel and equipment were prepared for shipment overseas, they were dispatched to New Orleans, Louisiana. Once the materiel arrived it was hurriedly loaded aboard United States Army transport ships and dispatched to the Far East. In late March of 1951 the various units of the division entrained for the port, and by 1 April the division sailed. All departed except the recently received four thousand draftees and a cadre of older men who remained behind at Camp Polk where the new recruits were to complete their training under the cadre's direction. These men later rejoined the division in Japan.[29]

The decision to send Oklahoma's guardsmen to Japan had been under discussion for some time. When the United States rushed to Korea's defense, most of the American units committed to the defense of Japan were hurriedly thrown into the battle. So thoroughly were the occupation forces depleted that by January of 1951 there were no American divisions left in the Japanese home islands.[30]

To offset this serious gap in the American defenses, General MacArthur, on 18 December 1950, requested that the four National Guard divisions called to active duty in September of that year be ordered to Japan at once. The request was turned down by the Joint Chiefs of Staff. MacArthur again asked for National Guard troops on 30 December 1950 and on 9 January

1951, but was rejected both times. The Joint Chiefs of Staff did hint that if the Eighth Army's lines could be held against the North Korean onslaught, two National Guard divisions might be sent to defend Japan. But, if the Eighth Army was forced to evacuate Korea, any troops needed for the defense of Japan would have to come from the withdrawn men. When the Eighth Army established a firm line around Pusan, the Joint Chiefs agreed on 30 January to order the Forty-fifth and the Fortieth divisions to the Far East.[31]

The Thunderbirds' convoy sailed down the Mississippi River and into the Gulf of Mexico for the month-long trip to Japan. When the ships reached the Panama Canal, most of the troops were allowed a few hours leave at the Pacific end of the waterway. Some of the ships then sailed directly across the Pacific, while others paused at San Francisco, California, before embarking for Japan. Colonel Daugherty, commander of the 179th Infantry in Korea, and other officers utilized the time aboard ship to implement training programs.[32]

Preceding the division was an advance detail consisting of Colonel John H. McCasland, who was the Forty-fifth's provost marshal, and nine other men, which landed at Otaru, on the west coast of Hokkaido, the northernmost of the Japanese home islands. What they found amazed everyone. The Thunderbirds had been ordered to Camp Crawford, and although the post had been home for American occupation troops on Hokkaido, it was too small to handle more than one-third of the Thunderbirds at a time. Plans were hurriedly made to create another camp at Chitose to house the remainder of the guardsmen. Eventually a third camp, Eniwa, also was built. Unfortunately, when Colonel McCasland and the remainder of the advance party arrived, there was nothing at Chitose but forest, and there was fifteen to twenty feet of snow atop the volcanic ash. It was only a matter of weeks before the rest of the division arrived, and most of the advance party simply did not believe that the Japanese could build a tent city in the short amount of time available. Thousands of workers were brought in from throughout the islands, though, and everything was in order when the bulk of the guardsmen arrived.[33]

Beginning on 25 April 1951 and throughout the following weeks the Thunderbirds poured ashore at Otaru or at Muroran, on the island's southwestern shore. Here the guardsmen boarded Japanese trains for the trip to their various training camps. Chitose, the tent city, was just to the south of Sapporo, the prefecture capital, which was a few miles inland from Otaru Bay. Located next to an abandoned airfield that had been used to train kamikaze pilots during World War II, Chitose was surrounded by woods. Camp Crawford, about forty miles northwest of Chitose, offered more pleasant surroundings with permanent buildings and recreational facilities, which, although old, were still serviceable. Two other tent cities also were built, Camp Monte Strong, southwest of Chitose, and Camp Conrady, about half way between Chitose and Crawford near the town of Eniwa. The divisional headquarters, the 279th Infantry, and several independent companies were stationed at Camp Crawford, while the 179th and 180th infantry regiments and the divisional artillery (minus the 158th Field Artillery) were in the tent cities. Later, the regiments rotated living assignments.[34]

Almost immediately the Thunderbirds began an extensive training and conditioning program that was designed to bring the troops to the highest state of combat readiness. In June of 1951, most of the four thousand draftees that had been left behind at Camp Polk rejoined the division and were integrated into the ranks. In the meantime, much work was under way to make the tent cities more livable. Throughout the spring and summer the regular training phases were carried on with the utmost speed. As winter neared, the Thunderbirds entered a post-cycle training period. Landing exercises, air transportability, and small-arms training was emphasized, and as the weather turned colder more physical conditioning exercises were scheduled. At this time, Major General Styron was greatly concerned about the possibility of a Soviet invasion of Japan from their bases on Sakhalin, the next island north of Hokkaido. In fact, Styron had been ordered to prepare contingency plans to oppose any Soviet attack.[35]

At the end of the intensive training period, most of the officers agreed with artillery Major John Coffey, who declared that there was no doubt in his mind that when the Forty-fifth Division completed its preparation for action in Korea, it "was the best trained . . . [division] that ever took the field in a combat situation."

Thunderbirds training with an M-2A1-7 portable flame thrower at Hokkaido, Japan, in 1951. *Courtesy Forty-fifth Infantry Division Museum.*

Shortly afterward, the Thunderbirds moved to rest camps at Noboribetsu and Jozankei where life was a little easier. Taking advantage of the lull, many of the men used their leave time to visit Honshu and the other Japanese islands. Others simply relaxed.[36]

When the Forty-fifth had first been ordered to the Far East most of the men knew that they would eventually be shipped to Korea, and now that the training cycle was completed it was only a matter of time until the division was ordered to the front. As early as October, 1951, Thunderbird volunteers were being accepted for Korean duty. It was late November of that year when alert warnings were issued, preparing the Forty-fifth to replace the First Cavalry Division in the war zone's First Corps. By Thanksgiving of 1951, the advance elements of the division were landing in Korea.[37]

The move to Korea was different from those of World War II. The First Cavalry and the Thunderbirds simply traded places—The Forty-fifth took over the cavalrymen's positions in Korea, and the First Cavalry moved to Hokkaido's training area. To facilitate the transfer, all of the First Cavalry's equipment, vehicles, and armor were left in place for the Thunderbirds to use.

Christmas in Korea, 1951. The Forty-fifth was the first National Guard division to enter the Korean fighting. *Courtesy Forty-fifth Infantry Division Museum.*

Likewise, the Forty-fifth left its materiel behind when it left for Korea. This applied to all equipment except for individual arms, clothing, and kitchen trucks. The idea was that such a move would allow the use of the same shipping for both the relieving and the relieved units. In theory, by swapping all the heavy equipment there would be no need for the on- and off-loading of divisional supplies, and this would speed up the entire operation. Unfortunately, the materiel received from a unit that had been in combat was not the same quality as that left behind by the Thunderbirds.[38]

Shortly after the Oklahoma guardsmen had been called to active duty, the UN command in Korea had outflanked the North Korean invasion force by an amphibious landing at Inchon. The offensive began on 15 September 1950, and the rapid inland advance of the UN troops quickly threatened to isolate the Communist forces opposing the Pusan perimeter. At the same time the UN troops at Pusan launched their own offensive.[39]

By 27 September, the Inchon landing force and the troops pushing north from Pusan linked up. The trap was closed and the North Korean Army began to disintegrate, with thousands of enemy troops surrendering and the remainder hurrying north in an effort to escape. On 19 October, ROK troops captured the North Korean capital at Pyongyang, and the Communists were obviously defeated. MacArthur pursued the fleeing North Koreans almost to the Manchurian border before the Chinese Communists entered the fighting. Although the Chinese first claimed to be "volunteers" fighting on the side of the North Koreans, in late November of 1950 they launched a full-scale offensive that overwhelmed the UN forces and sent them reeling southward.[40]

By early January of 1951 the UN command had once again abandoned Seoul and were pushed below the 38th parallel. The UN troops then began to stiffen their lines, and the Chinese advance was halted. Later that same month the UN took the offensive, and in some furious fighting retook the South Korean capital on 14–15 March. By late March they were once again on the 38th parallel.[41]

When the Forty-fifth first arrived in Japan, the front had been pretty well established along a line running from northwest of Seoul, across the 38th parallel, to Toep'o-ri on the east coast of North Korea. With the stabilization of the battle lines, cease-fire negotiations began on 10 July 1951, and for the next few months the fighting alternated between boring lulls and bloody battles as both sides tried to strengthen their positions. Eventually, on 12 October 1951, the United States' First Corps and the western elements of its Ninth Corps opened a drive to the Jamestown line. Stretching from the west bank of the Imjin River northwest of Seoul, the new defensive line ran northeast to Sami-ch'on, Kyeho-dong, Yokkok-chon, and Chut'oso before ending eight kilometers northeast of Chorwon. This was the Korean battlefront when the Thunderbirds began landing.[42]

The Forty-fifth was the first National Guard division to enter the Korean fighting when elements of the 180th Infantry disembarked at Inchon on 5 December 1951. The 179th Infantry followed twelve days later, and on 29 December, the 279th Infantry came ashore. Actually, according to Brigadier General Hal Muldrow,

146

B Battery, 158th Field Artillery firing a 105-mm. M-101 howitzer on an enemy position. *Courtesy Forty-fifth Infantry Division Museum.*

commander of the Forty-fifth Division Artillery, all of the division's artillery had landed several days before the infantry did to provide artillery support for the Eighth ROK Division.[43]

After disembarking at Inchon, the Thunderbirds boarded railroad cars for transport to an assembly area near Yonchon. From here the Forty-fifth moved into the First Corps' sector of the Jamestown line near Chorwon. By 10 December 1951, advance units of the division were in the front lines. After an early Christmas dinner, two regiments, the 179th and the 180th, were ordered into battle. The Thunderbirds entered the front lines on Christmas Eve and on Christmas Day assumed responsibility for their section of the front. The 279th was held in reserve, and by the time it had landed on December 29, the others had already received their baptism of fire.[44]

CHAPTER 12

KOREA

When the Forty-fifth replaced the First Cavalry Division in the Jamestown line in early 1952, the fighting in Korea had become static. It was a "monotonous war of position," consisting of limited offensive actions designed to seize better defensive positions, or to regain lost territory, or to establish outpost lines. Artillery duels, night patrols, deadly ambushes, and bloody raids were characteristic of this so-called "active defense." In fact, the Forty-fifth was prohibited from sending out any reconnaissance force larger than a platoon. For any larger action Major General Styron had to get prior approval from First Corps, which sometimes had to clear the operation with officials in Washington, D.C. As a result, according to Brigadier General William E. Mayberry, who was then serving as the executive officer of the Third Battalion, 179th Infantry, the majority of actions were on the platoon or smaller level.[1]

The lack of actual combat was of major concern to some of the top-ranking divisional officers, and Major General Styron worried that the Chinese would launch a determined attack against the inexperienced American troops. A different view was that the extensive training given the Thunderbirds before their landing in Korea, coupled with the high rate of World War II combat experience among the division's officers and NCOs, would, according to Colonel Frederick Daugherty, commander of the 179th Infantry, make them more than a match for any Communist troops.[2]

While the infantry fighting was virtually static, divisional artillery often played havoc with the Communists during this period. In one instance, the Forty-fifth's gunners sighted a Chinese infan-

try battalion crossing a rice paddy from one hilltop position to another. Although it was night, an air force illumination plane was in the area, and, after flares lit up the scene, six battalions of artillery opened fire on the Chinese. Caught in the open crossing the rice paddy, the Communist unit was decimated.[3]

Augmenting the boredom of trench warfare was the bitter Korean weather. Although new winter boots and underwear were issued to keep the men warm, the intense cold often was worse than enemy activity. Offensive patrols often were conducted in −17° weather. Colonel John H. McCasland, divisional provost marshal, recalled that the temperature dropped so low that the steel in his jeep would pop like a gunshot whenever it received the slightest jolt, and Warrant Officer Richard E. ("Dick") Frazier, the Forty-fifth's bandmaster, had trouble keeping the band's instruments from freezing whenever it greeted a new group of replacements.[4]

Lieutenant Colonel Bruce Rey, the division quartermaster, remembered water settling on the floor of his tent and freezing because the diesel-burning stoves issued by the army heated only the top half of the structure. To solve the problem, Rey adopted the Korean method of heating their homes to his GI tent, with some minor modifications. First, he dug four trenches, spaced across the tent floor. He then covered the trenches with flat stones. Next he formed a new floor over the stones with mud. The trenches were connected to a firebox outside the tent on one side and to a smokestack outside on the other side. A fire was built in the box and the top was covered with a piece of metal. The heat was then drawn through the trenches by the draft from the smokestack. This in turn warmed the stones and radiated heat throughout the tent. Using this method, he was able to sleep comfortably in the coldest of weather. Others built stoves using 60-mm. or 81-mm. mortar or .50-caliber metal ammunition boxes.[5]

Because of the harsh weather, long periods of inactivity were frequent on the battlefront. Although the troops in the rear had difficulty keeping warm, those living in front-line bunkers struggled to keep from freezing. Because of the extreme cold, front-line troops often went three to four weeks at a time without being able to bathe. According to Major General Daugherty, the infantry regiments usually spent about forty-five days in the front lines and then were sent to the rear for fifteen days of rest. Nonetheless, the inactivity and what some called a "no-win policy" drastically affected morale. To counteract this, as early as March of 1952, five hundred men from the division were sent to Japan every nine days for five days of rest and recuperation.[6]

Although adequate supplies generally were available for the troops, it sometimes was difficult to get them to the front. Often supplies had to be carried up the steep hills by hand, for the terrain was often as harsh as the climate. Lieutenant Colonel Rey recalled that in one instance the 179th had to send details to the rear to bring supplies forward. To enable the men to reach the hilltops with their loads, ropes were strung along the crude trail so the men could pull themselves forward with their hands as they inched their way up the hill.[7]

Despite the harsh climate, the Forty-fifth wasted little time in launching a limited offensive operation of its own. In January of 1952 the Thunderbirds sent a series of deep probes toward the Chinese lines in an effort to uncover enemy troop concentrations and supply dumps, but the Communists generally refused to accept battle during the day, preferring instead to fight at night. In one instance, Company E, Second Battalion, 180th Infantry, in −2° weather, conducted a company-sized raid on a Communist-held hill. After climbing the hill, which was "so steep in some places that the men had to pull themselves up with their hands while heavy enemy mortar and small arms fire burst around them," the Thunderbirds had a four-hour firefight with enemy troops and then withdrew.[8]

Such raids were followed in February, 1952, with Operation Snatch, one of the first major encounters between the Thunderbirds and the Chinese Communists. Because of the limitations placed on the United Nations' offensive operations, Operation Snatch's purpose was to draw the Chinese into attacking the Americans, thereby forcing a battle. To lure the enemy into leaving their bunkers, all possible movement was stopped during the daylight hours, and most firing was prohibited. As hoped for, when the front fell silent, the Communists began to probe the Forty-fifth's line. The result was several sharp firefights in which the Chinese were thrown back with heavy losses.[9]

Another tactic to force the enemy to fight was the "fire attack." In a fire attack, a small but heavily armed force launched a brief but vicious assault on nearby enemy positions to provoke a Chinese reaction. One such operation took place on 1 March 1952 near Pork Chop Hill when a company-size force of Thunderbirds, with close artillery, mortar, and recoilless rifle fire inflicted heavy casualties on the enemy. It was not an efficient way to run a war, but it was the only way possible under the limitations placed on the troops by the Truman administration's policies.[10]

Such tactics required a series of forward outposts, well in front of the main line of defense, from which nightly patrols could be launched to keep track of enemy movement and maintain an offensive option. In addition, such advance outposts provided early warning against an attacking enemy and helped delay and disorganize any attacking force. Eventually a string of outposts stretched across the no man's land separating the two armies. One of these, Outpost Eerie, was in the Forty-fifth Division's sector.[11]

Located about ten miles west of Chorwon, Outpost Eerie was built on the southern tip of a two-mile-long ridge about a mile north of the Forty-fifth's main line of resistance and a mile and a half south of the enemy's outpost line. The position was separated from the remainder of the division by a valley floor covered with rice paddies. The rocky hill had been battered by artillery fire, but there were still a few scrub trees and bushes standing and several patches of thin grass. The defensive installations encircled the peak of the ridge, which was about a hundred and twenty feet above the rice paddies.[12]

Eerie's defensive positions were well-constructed and designed to withstand a heavy enemy assault. There were nine bunkers, each of which could hold two or three men, built just below the crest of the hill. Each bunker was constructed of a layer of sandbags and a layer of logs on the sides, and a triple layer of sandbags and logs on the top. The bunkers were for shelter only. Firing positions were in a trench that encircled the hilltop. The trench ran just above or below six bunkers, and through the other three. Fifty yards below the peak of the hill were three barbed-wire obstacles, with a gate leading from the trail to the American lines to the top of the hill. Sound-powered telephones connected all the bunkers. There were four separate telephone lines to the 179th's headquarters and a two-way radio.[13]

On the northern end of the T-shaped ridge which held Outpost Eerie, the Chinese Communists had established their outpost line. The enemy positions were on higher ground than the Americans', thus dominating the entire region and giving the Chinese a decided advantage.[14]

Usually Eerie was manned with two rifle squads, reinforced with a light machine-gun and a 60-mm. mortar crew. The afternoon of 21 March 1952, twenty-six men of the Third Platoon, Company K, 179th Infantry, under the command of Second Lieutenant Omar Manley of Edmond, Oklahoma, moved into the outpost for a five-day tour of duty. After climbing the peak, Manley quickly positioned his men in the defensive bunkers. The most important part of Eerie's defenses were the bunkers on the north part of the hill. Here Manley assigned a three-man machine-gun crew to one bunker and an automatic rifle and two riflemen to each of the other two. Immediately behind these positions was the command post bunker. In an arc running from northwest to southeast along the southern part of the outpost, Manley placed an automatic rifle and one rifleman in the first and last bunker, and two riflemen in the two bunkers between them. At the south end of the arc was the 60-mm. mortar bunker with five men.[15]

At the same time that Manley was occupying Eerie, the Americans had scheduled two patrols —Raider Patrol and King Company Patrol—to probe the enemy's lines during the night of 21-22 March. Both were sent out as scheduled, and at 2300 King Company Patrol reported enemy activity to the front of the outpost. At about the same time Raider Patrol reported a platoon-sized enemy force moving toward Manley's position. Although Raider Patrol opened fire in an effort to disrupt the attack, the Chinese moved on without pausing. Not wanting to get caught in the middle of a firefight, both patrols reported to Manley that they were returning to friendly lines; however, neither group gave their route. This oversight cost Eerie's defenders valuable time when, after hearing noises in the wire entanglements, they were unsure whether they were being made by the friendly patrols returning to the American lines or by enemy troops probing the outpost's defenses.[16]

While the American patrols were making their way back and Manley was preparing for an enemy assault, the Chinese moved into position along the ridge Outpost Eerie occupied. Of the two groups of approximately sixty men each, one was on the north and the other was on the west edge of the hill. After being told by their commander that their mission was to capture some Americans, the Chinese positioned their support weapons—machine guns and grenade launchers—and began to crawl through the wire obstacles.[17]

The confusion among the Americans as to who was making the noises in the wire surrounding their position ended at 2330 when the Chinese set off two trip flares as they tried to creep forward. Almost immediately the Thunderbirds opened fire. This was answered by heavy enemy machine-gun fire from the high ground to the north. The fighting was now in earnest as the Chinese pressed the attack against the north and northeast parts of the American perimeter. Although one defender was killed during the early fighting, for forty-five minutes the Thunderbirds held off the attack.[18]

Captain Max Clark, K Company's commander, watched the fighting start from his observation post at the main line of resistance. Immediately Clark ordered .50-caliber machine-gun and mortar fire directed toward the attackers. Friendly artillery fire also was called in on the Chinese assembly points. With this help the Americans held their positions.[19]

At midnight Manley reported that the outpost was holding out, but the Chinese were still pressing their assault. Things began to go wrong, however, when shortly before 0100 on 22 March the

American illuminating fire failed, and the Chinese were able to advance undetected. In addition, several more defenders had been hit by enemy fire. By 0100 the enemy had breached the wire in two places and were closing in on the bunkers. Manley urged his men to fight on, but the Chinese poured through the holes and began crawling up to the Thunderbirds' positions. To complicate a bad situation, the Americans also were running short of grenades and ammunition, and communications with the main line of resistance were cut shortly after the enemy had penetrated the wire.[20]

Slowly the Chinese drove the Thunderbirds out of the northern bunkers and forced them to seek shelter, either by sliding down the hillside or running to other bunkers on the southern edge of the outpost. At the same time the enemy began closing in on Eerie's west side. As the fighting shifted toward the south end of the outpost, the Americans attempted to make a stand.

As soon as the fighting had started, Colonel Daugherty had hurried to the nearest observation post so he could analyze the situation. When it became clear to him that the Chinese were overrunning the outpost, he ordered artillery fire directly on top of the bunkers and along any possible enemy withdrawal routes.[21]

The Chinese had pushed to the 60-mm. mortar bunker when the American artillery fire began to fall. The 105-mm. proximity-fused shells burst over the positions, and within a few minutes the Chinese began to withdraw without having the opportunity to search for the remaining defenders. At 0130 Daugherty ordered Clark to take Company K and relieve Manley as quickly as possible. By 0400 the reinforcements were on the scene, and the outpost remained safely in American hands.[22]

In the fighting eight American defenders had been killed, and four others were wounded. Two, including Lieutenant Manley, were missing. Captured by the Chinese, Manley was held as a prisoner of war, and after the armistice he was repatriated. Both of the patrols that had been outside the American lines when the fighting began returned safely.[23]

At daylight, the area around Eerie was searched for the missing and enemy dead or wounded left behind. Several were located in the immediate vicinity, and when Lieutenant Manley was repatriated he reported that the enemy had carried off many of their dead and wounded, which were therefore missed in the initial count. Eventually a total of thirty-one dead Chinese were accounted for, and one was captured. After completing the search, the Americans abandoned the outpost and returned to the main line.[24]

As winter ended, the Korean climate did not improve. Instead, when the ground, frozen to a depth of fourteen inches, began to thaw, the region's dry, dusty roads became rivers of mud. Adding to the thaw was an average rainfall that totaled eighteen inches for May, June, and July. Despite working around the clock building drainage ditches and culverts and laying a new rock base for the roads, it seemed to the men of the 120th Engineer Battalion that nothing stopped the spreading quagmire. Roads were not the only problem. As the ground thawed many bunkers collapsed, pinning their occupants inside. Moreover, Chinese box mines, which were not detectable with mine detectors but which had been inactivated by the frozen ground, once again became dangerous.[25]

Major Coffey, who served with the 160th Field Artillery in Korea, recalled that the mud was a real problem for the gunners, especially during periods of Communist activity when it was not uncommon for a battery to fire a thousand rounds a day. Resupplying the guns with ammunition over the muddy roads required considerable effort. The situation got so bad on one occasion that, in addition to every truck in the service battery hauling ammunition, all the unit's kitchen trucks and even a captured North Korean vehicle were pressed into service.[26]

Throughout the spring and summer of 1952, First Corps continued to hold the western half of the Korean battlefront, and, on First Corps' right flank, the Thunderbirds occupied the UN's main line of resistance, the Jamestown line. During this period, the fighting was more like frontier-style Indian campaigns than modern warfare. Employing ambushes and listening posts at various places in no man's land, the Forty-fifth fought many brief engagements with the enemy. Usually, the skirmishes involved small units, generally squads, and because the Chinese habitually abandoned their positions in the no man's land during the day, the firefights most often occurred at night.[27]

Although it was clearly limited warfare, such encounters were often bloody affairs. On 21

May, Major General Styron rotated home, and his place as divisional commander was taken by Major General David L. Ruffner. Almost as if to test the new commander, on the night of 25 May the Chinese Communists launched a heavy assault against the Thunderbirds. Penetrating the division's outpost line, the Chinese reached the main line of resistance before they were thrown back.[28]

The attack began at 2245 when the Chinese poured a heavy concentration of artillery fire on hills 200, 334, and 347, which contained outposts manned by the 179th RCT. It quickly became obvious that the enemy was directing its main thrust at the outpost on Hill 200, to the southeast of Pork Chop Hill, which was manned by F Company of the 179th. Attacking simultaneously from three directions—the north, the east, and the west—the Chinese obviously hoped to overrun the Americans as quickly as possible. The strongest assault, however, fell on the left flank, or western edge, of the American line.[29]

Before this enemy attack, Hill 200 had been strengthened with fences and fougasse and Daisy Cutter-type picket bombs had been planted at strategic places along the hill's perimeter. In addition, a master fire plan was established in which the fire of twenty-three machine guns, located on the main line of resistance, completely encircled the hill. When the Chinese attack began, Major General Daugherty, commanding the 179th Infantry at the time, directed heavy concentrations of artillery and mortar fire on the attackers to break the onslaught. All available firepower from the main line was poured on the attacking Chinese, and heavy illumination fire was maintained to expose enemy movements. When the attack began, reinforcements were dispatched to the outpost, and the combination of superior firepower and additional defenders drove the Chinese back after heavy fighting. Six Americans were killed and another twenty-one wounded in the battle, but the next morning 132 enemy dead were counted around the outpost. Three Chinese prisoners also were taken.[30]

Three nights later, on 28 May, two companies of Chinese ambushed a patrol from the 179th Infantry in no-man's-land. For awhile the American troops were surrounded and in danger of being overrun. The attackers were held off, though, and three hours later reinforcements reached the besieged Thunderbirds. In the face of the strengthened patrol, the Chinese withdrew.[31]

Almost as soon as the Thunderbirds had landed in Korea, they received word that all national guardsmen who did not wish to remain in the regular army would rotate home at the end of twenty-four months of active duty. The phaseout of enlisted personnel began in April of 1952, and the rotation of officers started in May of that same year. Major General Styron established criteria based on family, World War II service, and job performance to determine the order of rotation for officers; he was concerned that qualified officers would be available when the division was reorganized in Oklahoma. Of course, the speed with which the guardsmen returned home corresponded with how quickly the division received replacements.[32]

As their term of active duty neared an end, the first guardsmen left Korea for Oklahoma in late March of 1952; the rotation proceeded on a regular schedule with the priority of the enlisted returnees left to the discretion of company commanders and section leaders in the ensuing months. By the end of May most of the guardsmen had returned home, and only those holding key positions remained in Korea. Finally, on 6 June 1952, Sergeant First Class Bennie Zuniga of Tulsa became the last enlisted national guardsman to rotate home. The enlisted personnel of the Forty-fifth Division in Korea was now composed entirely of draftees or regular army troops; however, several National Guard officers remained behind.[33]

When members of the original Forty-fifth Division returned to Oklahoma, a new Thunderbird Division was formed and placed under the command of Major General Hal L. Muldrow on 10 September 1952. It was granted federal recognition five days later. Thus for nearly twenty months there were two Forty-fifth divisions: one fighting in Korea and the other serving as Oklahoma's National Guard unit. The division stationed in Korea retained the unit's designation, colors, and standards.[34]

While a National Guard Thunderbird Division was being created in Oklahoma, the Forty-fifth Division in Korea continued to play a major role in the fighting. Beginning on 19 June 1952, another series of limited attacks against enemy outposts were launched by the UN command. One of the assaults, Operation Counter, took place in the Forty-fifth's sector. Designed to neutralize several Chinese positions that threatened the division's main line, it was one of the most ambitious and successful operations of the entire war.[35]

The Forty-fifth held that portion of the UN's line running from Hill 281, or Arrowhead, about eight kilometers northwest of Chorwon to the village of Togun-gol about seventeen kilometers northeast of Chorwon. With the exception of Hill 281, all of the division's positions were south of the Yokkok-ch'on River. Occupying the dominant terrain to the north of the American lines were the Chinese Communists' Thirty-eighth and Thirty-ninth armies. From the higher ground the enemy could easily observe all movement inside the UN lines. The ridges also offered an excellent base from which to launch raids.[36]

Major General Ruffner hoped to offset the enemy's advantage by seizing eleven outpost sites at strategic locations across the division's front. Because he expected a strong Chinese reaction, Ruffner ordered his regimental commanders to begin the attacks after dark on 6 June, and, once the objectives were seized, to quickly follow up the attack with enough reinforcements to have the outpost heavily fortified before daylight. Once the positions were taken, Ruffner stressed, they were to be abandoned only under extreme enemy pressure.[37]

There were eleven different objectives. On the eastern part of the divisional front, the 279th, commanded by Colonel Preston J. C. Murphy, was ordered to seize objectives 1 through 6. The 180th RCT, on the west, was commanded by Lieutenant Colonel Ellis B. Ritchie, and was ordered to take objectives 7, 9, 10, and 11. Objective 8, the previously abandoned Outpost Eerie, was to be seized later.[38]

To soften up the targets, air strikes were flown against known enemy positions throughout the daylight hours of 6 June. Once night fell, the actual infantry assaults began. The size of the attacking forces ranged from single squads to companies, and little enemy opposition was encountered except at Outpost 10 on Hill 234, or Pork Chop Hill, and Outpost 11 on Hill 275, known as Old Baldy. Pork Chop was finally seized by two platoons from I Company, 180th, after nearly an hour of battle, and Old Baldy fell shortly after midnight to two platoons of A Company, 180th Infantry.[39]

After taking the objectives the Americans quickly established defensive positions around the crests of the hills. To allow friendly artillery to use proximity fuse shells against any enemy counterattack, bunkers with overhead protection were hurriedly constructed. Individual rifle and machine-gun pits also were dug. By the morning of 7 June, the main assault forces withdrew, leaving behind eighteen and forty-four men, respectively, to garrison each newly won outpost. During the next few days several efforts were made by the enemy to retake the hills, but all counterattacks were repulsed.[40]

Once the first ten objectives had been captured, plans were made for phase 2 of the operation—the seizure of Outpost Eerie on Hill 191. Behind an air strike and heavy artillery bombardment, the Second Battalion of the 180th Infantry began the attack at 0600 on 12 June. The fighting was bitter. To dislodge the Chinese defenders, 43,600 artillery shells were thrown against the outpost. In addition, fifty-eight close-support air missions were called in by the assault units. Even after the enemy had been forced off Eerie's heights, the Chinese launched four successive counterattacks to regain the hill. All failed, and the following morning, 13 June, the assault troops were relieved by the Third Battalion, which was to garrison the post.[41]

The Chinese struck back viciously. On 16 June the 179th Infantry under Lieutenant Colonel Joseph C. Sandlin relieved the 180th on Old Baldy, Pork Chop, and Eerie, and for the next ten days, the Chinese Communists launched a series of attacks to retake the ridges. Almost as soon as the 179th was in position, two enemy battalions tried to storm Eerie. Then on the night of 20–21 June the enemy sent a regiment, supported by five thousand rounds of artillery fire, against Outpost 9 (Snook) and Outpost 10 (Pork Chop). All enemy counterattacks failed.[42]

The fighting was especially bitter on Old Baldy on 26 June. In an attempt to neutralize the American outpost, the enemy had heavily fortified nearby Hill 223. In retaliation, Colonel Sandlin ordered Company C, 179th Infantry, and Company F, 180th Infantry, to seize the new Chinese strongpoints. After stubbornly resisting the American attack, the Chinese suddenly withdrew and called in artillery fire on their former positions. As soon as the fire lifted the Chinese rushed forward. Another company from the 179th was dispatched to Hill 223 as reinforcements, and for two hours the fighting was extremely heavy. Eventually the enemy was forced to abandon the ridge.[43]

Despite all this, the battle was not over. Through the night of the twenty-sixth and the following day, the Americans quickly strengthened Hill 223's defenses in anticipation of a Chinese counterattack. In addition, that afternoon Company L, Third Battalion, 179th Infantry, relieved F Company, Second Battalion, which took up a position to support the hill's defenders. By nightfall the preparations were barely completed when the enemy began to bombard the Americans with mortar and artillery fire. At 2200 the Chinese Communists counterattacked with a reinforced battalion. Although the initial assault was thrown back, a second and a third attack were launched early in the morning of 28 June. These also failed, and the Forty-fifth retained possession of the ridge. In the fighting, the enemy suffered between 250 and 350 casualties, while the 179th lost 6 men killed and 61 wounded.[44]

Late that same evening, the American outpost on Old Baldy came under heavy enemy artillery fire. Anticipating a Chinese attack, the Thunderbirds took up defensive positions, and at about 2300 two reinforced battalions of Chinese rushed forward behind a heavy artillery and mortar barrage. The enemy managed to penetrate the defensive perimeter and hand-to-hand fighting broke out. It was not until after midnight that the Thunderbirds gained the upper hand and, the enemy soon began to withdraw. This assault cost the Chinese approximately seven hundred men. Old Baldy was attacked again on the night of 3-4 July, in three separate, unsuccessful assaults. In mid-July the Thunderbirds on Old Baldy were relieved by the Second Infantry Division.[45]

Withdrawn from the front in July of 1952 after 209 days in the line, the Forty-fifth was assigned to Tenth Corps. The division operated as a reserve force to block any sudden enemy push to the south and provided security for the Tenth Corps' rear area. During this time the 180th was

stationed at Hwachon, the 179th at Yanggu, and the 279th at Inje. Their positions were taken by new replacements and by more than twenty-five hundred Korean Augmentation to United States Army (KATUSA) troops, many of which were assigned to the division.[46]

On 21 September 1952, after several weeks' rest, the Korean-based Forty-fifth Division began to relieve the Eighth ROK Division that held the extremely mountainous sector of the U.S. Tenth Corps' right flank on the Minnesota line. The sector was one of the most critical on the entire main line of resistance, and just as the guardsmen began to occupy their new positions the enemy attacked. The ROK units still in the line were quickly broken, and for the next twelve hours fighting raged along the division's front as two Chinese battalions threatened to overrun the American positions. It was not until the next day that the South Koreans counterattacked, and, with the support of the Forty-fifth's tanks, restored the main line of resistance. The Thunderbirds then completed their relief of the ROK troops and held the line until the end of December, when they were replaced by the Twelfth ROK Division.[47]

The Thunderbirds spent the rest of 1952 along the Minnesota line, and several new entries were added to the division's list of battles. Heartbreak Ridge ran north and south between the Mundung-ni Valley on the west and the Sat'ae-ri Valley on the east, and was a heavily fortified, seven-mile-long hill mass that earned its name in blood. Four or five miles straight east of Heartbreak Ridge and about forty kilometers north of Inje was a circular valley that the troops called the Punch Bowl. The So-ch'on River and one of its tributaries separated the Punch Bowl from the next series of ridges, and the Communists, who controlled the rim, exacted a fearful toll from any unit moving through the valley. "Luke the Gook's Castle," or "Luke's Castle," a rocky hill about five miles north of the Punch Bowl, also cost the Americans dearly.[48]

As the fighting slowed down, higher headquarters began to place great emphasis on the taking of prisoners. Patrols were constantly sent out in the harsh climate in an attempt to seize enemy soldiers, but it was a hopeless effort. The men made so much noise walking across the frozen ground that it was impossible to approach the enemy undetected. Other methods were tried.

It was rumored that bear traps were placed forward of the Forty-fifth's positions in an attempt to snare members of enemy patrols, and an electrified fence was strung across the division's front in hopes of stunning any Chinese soldier that stumbled into it.[49]

The bitter fighting did not cease. On Christmas Day, 1952, the Communists launched an attack against Hill 812, held by Company K, Third Battalion, 179th Infantry, under Captain Andrew J. Gatsis. The ridge was approximately five miles north of the Punch Bowl, and the Americans had occupied positions on its northern face. Following a 250-round artillery and mortar barrage, a reinforced enemy company advanced from its position on nearby "Luke's Castle" and overran Company K's forward positions. Gatsis immediately called for artillery and mortar fire, which broke the enemy assault, and then he ordered the Second Platoon, commanded by Second Lieutenant Russell J. McCann, to counterattack. After vicious hand-to-hand fighting in the trenches, McCann's men pushed the enemy back.[50]

Upon learning of the attack, Colonel Jefferson J. Irvin, the 179th Infantry Regiment's commander, dispatched A and L companies to Hill 812 as reinforcements. Despite the increased American strength, the enemy struck again in the early morning hours of the next day. Three platoon-size assault units, supported by more than two thousand rounds of artillery and mortar fire, rushed the American defenders. The enemy was again thrown back.[51]

In late January of 1953, the Forty-fifth relieved the Fortieth Division in the Tenth Corps' area. For a welcome change, the front remained relatively quiet during the following months, with most of the troops' actions confined to active defense, patrols, and raids. To strengthen the overall UN front in Korea, on 1 July the Thunderbirds, now commanded by Brigadier General Philip D. Ginder, who had replaced Major General Ruffner in March, were moved to the right flank of the Second ROK Corps on the mideastern front. The division remained there until the signing of the armistice on 27 July 1953.[52]

The cease-fire agreement climaxed a total of 429 accumulated combat days and four campaigns, designated the second Korean winter; spring-summer, 1952; the third Korean winter; and spring-summer, 1953—in which the Forty-fifth participated. For their heroism in these campaigns, the following units received the distinguished service citation: Of the 180th Infantry, the Third Battalion; Company G; the Third Platoon, Medical Company; the Fourth Platoon, Tank Company (Medium); the Automatic Weapons Section, Tank Company (Medium); the Third Platoon, Heavy Mortar Company; and the chaplain, headquarters. The award also was presented to the First Squad, Company B, 120th Engineer Battalion (Combat); the Fourth Platoon, Company B, 245th Tank Battalion; the First Platoon, Battery A, 145th Anti-aircraft Battalion. Forward observer teams 1, 2, and 3 and the liaison team, 171st Field Artillery Battalion, each received distinguished unit citations.[53]

The Forty-fifth Division remained in Korea until it sailed for the United States in groups that embarked between 15 February and 15 March 1954. The following month, the division was released from federal service. During this time the division was commanded by Major General Paul D. Harkins, 1 December 1953 to 15 March 1954, and Brigadier General Harvey H. Fischer, 18 March to 27 April 1954. The divisional colors were returned to the Oklahoma National Guard in a special ceremony called Operation Colors Back, held at the state fair in Oklahoma City on 25 September 1954.[54]

CHAPTER 13

THE OKLAHOMA AIR NATIONAL GUARD: THE 1940s

Although the Oklahoma Air National Guard (OKANG) did not come into existence until the late 1930s, shortly before the outbreak of World War II, the move to create citizen-soldier aviation units began shortly after the first successful flight of an aircraft in 1903. The effort began on the East Coast, where several members of the Aero Club of America also were New York national guardsmen who often donated their aircraft for training purposes. As a result, on 1 May 1908, the twenty-five men of the First Signal Company, New York National Guard, began their first airborne training with a borrowed 35,000-cubic-foot balloon.[1]

Later these guardsmen built their own airplane and took it to Pine Camp, in upstate New York for the summer encampment of 1910. Unfortunately, the plane crashed. By August of 1912, the unit was back in the air with another plane, which, during maneuvers between national guardsmen and the regular army, proved its value by successfully locating the enemy camps and troop concentrations. The First Signal Company's Private First Class Beckworth Haven (air license number 127), who first flew in August of 1912, became the first Air National Guard pilot.[2]

At this same time, having seen Eugene Ely land his Curtiss biplane on the U.S.S. *Pennsylvania* in March of 1911, Major General E. A. Forbes, California's adjutant-general, organized an Aeronautical Detachment, Seventh Company, Coast Artillery Corps, California National Guard. Later, on 11 December 1915, this unit was transferred to an aeronautical section of the state's naval militia, and, on 6 April 1917, it was called to active duty with the U.S. Navy. After World War I, however, the California Naval Militia was not reorganized and the unit disbanded.[3]

Back east in New York the actual formation of what would become the Air National Guard got under way. The state adjutant-general had been convinced by the 1912 maneuvers of the need for a separate aeronautical unit. As a result, the First Aero Company, New York National Guard, was organized by Lieutenant, later colonel, Raynauld C. Bolling, on 1 November 1915. The Second Aero Company was formed at Buffalo, New York, the following year.[4]

Both units were called to active duty in July of 1916 for service on the Mexican border; however, the New York guardsmen never saw actual combat. Instead, they went into training at Mineola Aviation Field on Long Island. Mustered out on 8 September 1916, the Second Aero Company was never reorganized at its home station. On 2 November 1916 the First Aero Company was returned to state control.[5]

Although several National Guard units had taken the lead in adding aircraft to their inventory, their efforts received no support from the regular army. Moreover, when the United States entered World War I, the War Department decreed that there would be no National Guard aviation units. As a result, the remaining Aero Company of the New York National Guard was disbanded.[6]

The reorganization of the National Guard under the National Defense Act of 1920 ignored the question of aviation units. Nonetheless, Brigadier General Walter F. Rhinow of the Minnesota National Guard was determined to add an air observation squadron to the Thirty-fourth Infantry Division. As a result, the state of Minnesota formed the 109th Observation Squadron at Saint Paul and equipped it with a rented three-place Curtiss Oriole. Rhinow was then sent to Washington to plead his case, and on 17 January 1921, the unit became the first National Guard aviation detachment to receive federal recognition.[7]

Minnesota was quickly followed by other states: the 104th Observation Squadron of the Twenty-ninth Division was formed in Baltimore, Maryland, on 29 June 1921; the 113th Observation Squadron of the Thirty-eighth Division was organized at Indianapolis, Indiana, on 1 August 1921; the 101st Observation Squadron of the Twenty-sixth Division was created at Boston, Massachusetts, on 18 November 1921; the 105th Observation Squadron was formed in Nashville, Tennessee, on 4 December 1921, for service in the Thirtieth Division; the 106th Observation Squadron of the Thirty-first Division was organized at Birmingham, Alabama, on 21 June 1922; and the 102nd Observation Squadron was formed by the Twenty-seventh Division of the New York National Guard on 4 November 1922. Although the many observation squadrons were a valuable addition to the National Guard structure, a major organizational change occurred in 1925, when the 154th Observation Squadron was formed in Arkansas. Instead of being organized as a divisional unit, it was assigned to the Seventh Corps. This was the beginning of a trend that saw many future National Guard aviation units listed as corps aviation troops.[8]

As war loomed on the horizon in the late 1930s, the War Department hurriedly organized additional National Guard aviation units. It was under this impetus that, on 30 July 1940, the 125th Observation Squadron was allotted to the Oklahoma National Guard. Six months later, the unit was organized in Tulsa under the command of Major Robert O. Lindsay. Hurriedly completing the organizational process, Lindsay's unit was granted federal recognition on 31 January 1941 and activated ten days later. Within the year, on 15 September 1941, the Guard's 125th Observation Squadron was called into federal service.[9]

When the National Guard was mobilized for World War II, the observation squadrons, like the divisional tank units, were separated from their parent organizations. All the National Guard aviation units retained their original numbers but were given new names and assignments. The observation squadrons soon were organized for specific tasks—tactical reconnaissance, fighter, bombardment, photo reconnaissance, or long-range weather reconnaissance. Oklahoma's air guardsmen were no different. On 13 January 1942 the 125th became the 125th Observation Squadron (Light). However, within six months, on 4 July, the unit was given back its original name and number, the 125th Observation Squadron.[10]

Five days after being mobilized, the 125th was assigned to the Sixty-eighth Observation Group and transferred from Tulsa to Fort Sill, where the Forty-fifth Infantry Division of the Oklahoma National Guard was training at that time. While at Fort Sill, the 125th was joined by other Air National Guard units, which flew simulated strafing and bombing missions against the infantrymen, dropping paper sacks filled with flour. Any of the ground troops marked by the bursting flour "bombs" were told that they had been hit by shrapnel from an exploding bomb. Although it was make-believe war, the infantry learned valuable lessons about the use of airpower in modern warfare. Six months later, on 12 March, the Oklahoma guardsmen were transferred to the Seventy-seventh Observation (later Reconnaissance) Group, and on 15 April moved to Brownwood, Texas. Brownwood was but the first of a rapid succession of bases for the Oklahomans: they were in Abilene, Texas in June, at DeRidder Army Air Base in Louisiana in July, and back to Abilene in September.[11]

Throughout the fall and winter of 1942, the 125th participated in maneuvers in Louisiana and trained for a series of observation and artillery-spotting missions. When first called into federal duty, the 125th was equipped with the older O-38 observation aircraft; however, during this training period the O-38s were replaced by the more modern O-47s, O-49s, O-52s, O-57s, O-58s, O-59s, and YO-50s. A high-wing, retractable-gear monoplane, the Curtiss O-52 Owl was one of the army's newest observation aircraft.[12]

On 2 April 1943, the Oklahoma guardsmen were redesignated the 125th Liaison Squadron and would remain as such throughout the war. For an emblem, the unit adopted a white disk with a black border. On the white background was a caricatured beaver in its proper color,

World War I era captive observation balloon at Post Field, Fort Sill, Oklahoma. The original aviation unit of the National Guard, the First Signal Company, New York National Guard, organized in 1903, trained with a 35,000-cubic-foot observation balloon. *Courtesy Forty-fifth Infantry Division Museum.*

but dressed in a white shirt, blue coat, and a top hat. The beaver mascot had a swagger stick in its left hand, and supposedly, its right hand originally displayed three playing cards, an ace, a deuce, and a five, respectively, from left to right, representing the 125th squadron. After mobilization, however, the cards were changed to the ace of diamonds, hearts, and spades, left to right, respectively, in order to maintain security concerning the unit's identity.[13]

The 125th moved to Alamo Field, Texas, on 1 July 1943, and forty-one days later, on 11 August, the unit was assigned to the Second Air Force Support Command, which later became the Second Tactical Air Division. By 1943 the Oklahomans had been primarily equipped with the L-5 Sentinel artillery spotter. A small, two-seat aircraft, the L-5 was used in several versions for light liaison, air ambulance, and recon-

naissance missions. Training and preparation for overseas duty continued throughout 1943. First, on 11 October, the men were sent to Desert Center Army Air Field in California and assigned to the Third (later the First) Tactical Air Division, and then a month later went to Thermal Army Air Field, California, where they remained until 18 May 1944. During the final three months of 1943, the Oklahoma guardsmen participated in the California-Arizona maneuvers. In January of 1944, the 125th was transferred to the Seventy-sixth Tactical Reconnaissance Group.[14]

By the spring of 1944, the guardsmen had completed their training and were ordered to the European battlefront. On D day, 6 June 1944, the 125th arrived at Liverpool, England, and was assigned to the U.S. Strategic Air Forces (Eighth Air Force) in Europe; however, the following day it was reassigned to the Ninth Air

Force, the tactical air arm supporting American ground forces. The unit later moved to Cheltenham, in the southeastern part of England, between the Cotswold Hills and the Avon River. On 12 June, the 125th was transferred first to Chedworth and then, on 9 July 1944, to Erlestokes, where final preparations were made for dispatch to the Continent. During its service with the Ninth Air Force, the 125th worked primarily with the headquarters command of the European theater of operations, but on 17 June it was reassigned to the Ninth Army for liaison and messenger duty.[15]

The first detachments of the 125th Observation Squadron landed in France on 23 August 1944. For the remainder of the European war the squadron occupied a series of stations beginning at Saint-Sauveur-Lendelin and Rennes, France, then across Belgium to Arlon, and through the Netherlands to Masstricht, as the Allied armies pushed the Germans back toward their own frontier. While stationed in the Netherlands the squadron suffered its first casualties on 11 November, when Staff Sergeant Fred Stoecker and Sergeant William H. Hunt left Heerlen on a mission and were never heard from again.[16]

On 15 November 1944, the 125th was transferred to the Twenty-ninth Tactical Air Command (Provisional), and two weeks later to the Ninth Fighter Command, which was a part of the former command. Seventeen days later, B Flight became the first unit of the squadron to operate on German soil when it established itself at Kornelimunster. Two weeks later, on 1 January 1945, staff sergeants William D. Fletcher and Owen Stafford were wounded when their aircraft, piloted by First Lieutenant Donald K. Neill, was attacked by two ME-109s. Then on 12 January, Technical Sergeant Jack S. Pridgen was injured in a crash near Heerlen in the Netherlands.[17]

The guardsmen continued to operate with the Twelfth Army Group until 8 June 1945 when the 125th was shifted to the Sixth Army Group. On 7 March the unit lost its last aircraft during the war, when Staff Sergeant Richard J. Schempf and his passenger were forced to bail out at 4,000 feet because of inclement weather. Fortunately, neither man was injured.[18]

As the Allied armies continued to advance, so did the 125th: first to Haltern, Germany, on

A rare photograph of aircraft from the 125th Observation Squadron, Oklahoma National Guard flying over Fort Sill's Post Field shortly after mobilization in September, 1941. *Courtesy Forty-fifth Infantry Division Museum.*

4 April, then to Gütersloh the following day, and finally, to Brunswick on 24 April. The unit was still at Brunswick on V-E Day, 8 May 1945. Although the 125th was transferred to the Twelfth Tactical Air Command as part of the Army of Occupation on 20 June 1945, and remained with the command until deactivation, they were attached to the headquarters command, U.S. Forces, European theater between 25 July and 15 December. During this period the unit moved first to Heidelberg and then to Frankfurt am Main, where it was deactivated on 15 December 1945. Throughout its service in World War II, the 125th Liaison Squadron served in four campaigns —northern France, the Rhineland, Ardennes-Alsace, and central Europe; it was cited for its service in the Order of the Day by the Belgian Army and the unit was awarded the Belgian Fourragere.[19]

In the post-World War II reorganization of the National Guard, more emphasis was placed on nondivisional and support elements. Throughout the period between 1946 and 1949, one of the areas of greatest growth was in aviation units. The post-World War II Air National Guard included twelve Wing Headquarters, twenty-four fighter groups, three light bomb groups, twelve aircraft control and warning groups, twelve aircraft control squadrons, twenty-four aircraft control and warning squadrons, seventy-two fighter squadrons, twelve communication squadrons, twenty-seven air service squadrons, eighty-four air service detachments, twelve signal light construction companies, twelve radar calibration detachments, eighty-four weather stations, eighty-four utility flights, four engineer aviation battalions, twelve engineer aviation companies, and twelve bands.[20]

During this reorganizational era, the nation's defense structure was redesigned through the elimination of the War Department and the creation of the Departments of the Army, Navy, and Air Force under the broad control of the Defense Department. Enacted into law by the National Security Act of 1947, the separation of the three military services was implemented on 27 July of that year. On 1 October 1948 the National Guard Bureau in Washington, D.C., was reorganized to have both an army and an air force department.[21]

Although before World War II, the 125th was Oklahoma's only Air National Guard unit, the first to organize after the fighting ended was the 185th Fighter Squadron S.E. (Single Engine). Located at Norman, Oklahoma's Max Westheimer Field, the 185th was formed by Lieutenant Colonel James E. Hill, a native of Stillwater and a World War II ace. Hill had first entered the military as an aviation cadet in the army air corps in March of 1942. Commissioned a second lieutenant after winning his wings in February of 1943, Hill was shipped to the European theater at the end of 1943 as a P-47 pilot. By V-E Day, he had completed 127 combat missions and been credited with shooting down five enemy aircraft. After being released from active duty in December of 1945, Hill came to Oklahoma and organized the 185th, which was granted federal recognition on 13 February 1947. He later returned to active duty and retired at the end of 1979 as a full general—the highest rank attained by any Oklahoman at that time.[22]

Hill had strict entrance requirements for the 185th and initially selected only those pilots with fighter-plane combat experience. Because of his stringent criteria for pilots, the squadron had well-qualified pilot officers. Eight of the pre-Korean mobilization pilots assigned to the 185th eventually became general officers: General

James E. Hill; major generals Ray A. Robinson, Grover H. Isbell, and Stanley F. H. Newman; and brigadier generals Walter F. Daniel, Doyle W. Hastie, George N. Masterson, and Robinson Risner.

Risner became a jet ace during his combat tour in Korea, shooting down eight enemy aircraft. Later, in the Vietnam conflict, Risner was shot down twice in two days. He was captured and survived eight years as a prisoner of war of the North Vietnamese. For his heroism in Vietnam, both before and after being captured, he was awarded the Air Force Cross, the nation's second highest award for air force personnel. Two other distinguished alumni of the 185th were Fred Haise, an astronaut on the Apollo XIII mission, who flew F-80s with the unit during the late 1950s while attending engineering school at the University of Oklahoma, and Walter F. Daniels, who set a world's speed record while testing the SR-71.[23]

Although the 185th Fighter Squadron of the Oklahoma Air National Guard was not established until 1947, the historical lineage of the unit could be traced to the 185th Aero Squadron formed on 11 November 1917 at Kelly Field No. 2, South San Antonio, Texas, around a nucleus drawn from the 24th Aero Squadron. Six days later the 185th was designated a service squadron and began preparing for duty on the western front in World War I. Preliminary training was completed by January of 1918, and on the 18th of that month, the 185th was ordered to France.[24]

By 16 February, the unit was disembarking in England and began training with the famous Sopwith Camel fighter plane. On 5 May 1918, the unit was reorganized as the 185th Night Pursuit Squadron and in August shipped to France, where its training was completed. Assigned to the First Pursuit Group, commanded by Captain Eddie Rickenbacker, on 7 October, the 185th was the first and only night pursuit group of the American Expeditionary Force operating on the western front. Twelve days later the 185th entered combat in the Meuse-Argonne offensive. After the end of the war, the 185th Night Pursuit Squadron was disbanded on 30 June 1919.[25]

On 25 January 1943, the forerunner of the Oklahoma National Guard's 185th Fighter Squadron was reconstituted as the U.S. Army Air

Corps' 620th Bombardment Squadron (Dive) of the 404th Bombardment Group, which was activated on 4 February 1943. Originally equipped with Douglas A-24 dive bombers, the army's version of the navy's SBD Dauntless dive bomber, the 620th trained at Key Field, Mississippi, and Congaree Field, South Carolina, before being redesignated as the 506th Fighter-Bomber Squadron of the 404th Fighter-Bomber Group in August of 1943. With the reorganization, the 506th exchanged its A-24s for more modern Bell P-39 Airacobras and Republic P-47 Thunderbolts, tough, hard-hitting fighter-bomber aircraft. Early in September, the unit was transferred to Burns Army Air Field in Oregon.[26]

At about the same time, in August, 1943, the 506th adopted as its insignia a rampaging brown bull snorting two bombs from its nostrils. The animal's tail was erect and his hooves threw a cloud of dust. Beneath the bull were several lines representing the ground and trees. The circle was outlined with two brown lines. This same emblem was carried over as the original insignia of the 185th Fighter Squadron of the Oklahoma Air National Guard.[27]

On 13 November 1943, the 506th returned to South Carolina and resumed its training at Myrtle Beach Army Air Field, where it remained until 12 March of 1944, when it was ordered overseas. Stationed at Winkton, England, the 506th Fighter-Bomber Squadron was assigned to the Ninth Air Force. The 404th was reorganized as a fighter group in May of 1944. Equipped with P-47s, the 506th Fighter Squadron began flying combat missions over France to prepare the way for the Normandy invasion. When the Allies stormed ashore on D day, 6 June 1944, the unit was a part of the air cover for the ground troops.[28]

Shortly afterward the unit moved its operations to the Continent and provided close air support for ground troops until the end of the war. The 506th provided cover for the Allied breakout at Saint-Lô and for the drive through Holland, and it helped blunt the German onslaught at the Battle of the Bulge. In addition to its ground-support role, the unit also flew interdictory and escort missions against enemy troop concentrations, railroads, bridges, ammunition and fuel dumps, and other targets during the fighting. Following the Allied advance across

Europe, the 506th was stationed at Capelle, Bretigny, and Juvincourt in France; at Saint-Trond, Belgium; and at Keltz, Fritzlar, and Stuttgart in Germany.[29]

After the war in Europe ended on 8 May 1945, the 506th helped disarm and dismantle the German aircraft industry before being returned to Drew Field, Florida, for inactivation in November, 1945. For its participation in World War II, the 506th was awarded the distinguished unit citation, the French croix de guerre with palm, and a citation from the Belgian government for its actions. On 24 May 1946, allotted to the Oklahoma Air National Guard, it was reformed as the 185th Fighter Squadron. Four months later, on 1 October 1947, it was assigned to the newly formed 137th Fighter Group commanded by Lieutenant Colonel Hill.[30]

About the same time that the 185th Fighter Squadron was being formed in Norman, the 125th Fighter Squadron, the direct descendant of the pre-war 125th Observation Squadron, was reorganized under the direction of Lieutenant Colonel Joseph W. Turner. Based in Tulsa, the 125th was granted federal recognition on 15 February 1947. Originally the 185th and the 125th both were equipped with the North American P-51D fighter, which became known as the F-51 in 1948. Officially known as the Mustang, the aircraft was affectionately dubbed the "Spam can" by many of its pilots.[31]

The F-51D was derived from the P-51 single-seat fighter, which was one of the most widely acclaimed aircraft developed during World War II. The original versions, the P-51 and the P-51A, were powered by Allison V-1710-F3R engines and carried four .50-caliber and four .30-caliber machine guns. A dive bomber version, the A-36, also was equipped with "dive brakes," which allowed it to plunge almost vertically without gaining excess speed. The later and more widely produced models used in World War II were the B, C, and D versions. These Mustangs were equipped with Packard-manufactured Rolls-Royce engines and four-bladed propellers, which enabled the aircraft to move from its original ground-attack mission to high altitude bomber escort, where it excelled in conquering the luftwaffe.[32]

In addition to the Mustangs, the Oklahoma national guardsmen had several North Ameri-

P-51D fighter plane of the 185th Fighter Squadron stationed at Max Westheimer Field in Norman, Oklahoma. Against all regulations, in 1949 the squadron removed the national insignia from the fuselage of the aircraft and replaced them with th Oklahoma "Indian" insignia. The markings were ordered removed by the air corps. *Courtesy Dennis R. Lindsey Collection.*

can T-6 Texans, Douglas C-47 Skytrains, and Martin B-26 Marauders. The T-6s were basically a training aircraft that had first flown in 1935 and saw use throughout World War II as AT-6 advance trainers. The Skytrain, a cargo transport, was an outgrowth of the world-famous Douglas DC-3 airliner. The Marauder, however, had been developed as a tough World War II twin-engine bomber. The Oklahoma guardsmen used the aircraft for utility flights, such as towing targets or for transport.[33]

In June of 1949, the 185th received the more modern D version of the Mustang series. The D, like the B and the C, was powered by the Packard-built Rolls-Royce V-1650-7 engine. This engine developed 1,590 horsepower and reached a maximum speed of 437 miles per hour; with drop tanks it had a range of 1,650 miles. Its rate of climb to twenty thousand feet was 7.3 minutes. The P-51D was armed with six (two more than the B and the C models) .50-caliber machine guns, three in each wing, and was equipped to carry two 500 or 1,000-pound bombs or six 5-inch rockets. The most obvious difference between the D model and the earlier B and C versions was a sliding bubble canopy and a cut-down rear fuselage on the later model. This gave the pilot a full 360° view, and was considered by most pilots to be well worth the slight decrease in performance.[34]

In 1948 the 185th and the 125th held a joint summer camp at Vance Air Force Base, adjacent to Enid, Oklahoma. Although the facility had been abandoned by the military after World War II and housed only a caretaker command, the Oklahoma guardsmen did the best they could with what was available. By the end of their two-week camp, they had been successful in reactivating much of the base, including the facility's swimming pool. Because of the proximity to civilian property, air-to-air gunnery was out of the question, but air-to-ground practice was extensively carried out at the nearby Great Salt Plains.[35]

The 185th continued to meet at Max Westheimer Field throughout this period, with the

137th Fighter Group providing the unit with its necessary immediate command and logistical support. In late 1949 a tornado destroyed much of the Norman facility. Almost miraculously, the fighter planes, tied down in a row only a few hundred feet from the hangar and building areas, were spared. Nonetheless, because of the extensive damage to the airport and the need for more space and longer runways, in early 1951 the squadron was relocated to Will Rogers Airport—Will Rogers Air National Guard Base—in Oklahoma City. The new installation had better facilities for jet aircraft, which the air guardsmen hoped to be receiving soon, and because of its proximity to a large population center, it offered a more ready supply of personnel.[36]

As hoped for, while the 185th was moving from Norman to Oklahoma City, the Oklahoma Air National Guard entered the jet age. On 15 March 1950, the 125th Fighter Squadron in Tulsa was reorganized as the 125th Fighter Bomber Squadron (Jet), and equipped with F-84 Thunderjet fighter-bombers. Developed by Republic Aircraft, the F-84 had been test-flown on 28 February 1946. The first production model, the F-84B, was not ordered by the air force until September of 1947.[37]

The original plane was armed with six .50-caliber machine guns and hard-points under the wings that could carry bombs and rockets; the initial order was for five hundred of the aircraft. As happens with developing programs, beginning with the production of the 227th of the planes the F-84B was given a new jet engine and redesignated the F-84C. Before the run could be completed, another modification, called the F-84D, was introduced, beginning with airframe number 191, which introduced an even more powerful engine and restressed wings. From the 154th Thunderjet, another completely restressed model, the F-84E, was produced. Despite the many efforts to redesign the F-84 into a better aircraft, by 1950 it was no longer considered a top of the line, air-superior fighter.[38]

Within a relatively short time of the reformation of the Oklahoma Air National Guard at the end of World War II, the United States was once again fighting in the Pacific. On 25 June 1950 the Korean War erupted when Communist troops invaded the Republic of Korea. Two days later, President Harry S. Truman ordered the air force and the navy to support the ROK gov-

F-51Ds over the Oklahoma countryside in 1950, after the 185th Fighter Squadron had moved to Will Rogers Air National Guard Base in Oklahoma City. The pilots of these planes (*top to bottom*) are Glenn Skinner, Stanley F. H. Newman, E. E. Scott and Bob Auison. *Courtesy of Stanley F. H. Newman Collection.*

ernment, and by early July, American ground troops were entering the battle. Both the army and the air force eventually relied on National Guard units to supply the manpower needed to throw the Communist invaders back.[39]

When the fighting began, America's Air National Guard consisted of twelve tactical air wings, twenty-four combat fighter groups, three combat bomb groups, twenty-seven air service groups, and eighty-seven squadrons. Among them were Oklahoma's 125th and 185th fighter squadrons, based at Tulsa and Oklahoma City, respectively. Both were summoned to active duty.[40]

CHAPTER 14

THE OKLAHOMA AIR NATIONAL GUARD: 1950 TO THE PRESENT

When it became obvious that the Korean peace-keeping mission was becoming a war, the Oklahoma Air National Guard began to be called to active duty in a piecemeal fashion. In the fall of 1950, the Air Service Group, Detachment C, and the Headquarters 137th Fighter Group based in Oklahoma City were mobilized, but the 185th Fighter Squadron remained under state control. On 10 October of that year Tulsa's 125th Fighter-Bomber Squadron, now under the command of Major Staryl C. Auston, Jr., was federalized. The 125th was sent first, in November, to Alexandria Air Force Base, Louisiana, along with the 137th Fighter Group, for duty with the Tactical Air Command. It was planned for the Oklahoma air guardsmen to participate in field problems with the state's Forty-fifth Infantry Division. Later, in May, 1952, the unit was moved to Chaumont, France, where it completed its tour of active duty.[1]

Although the 185th Fighter Squadron was not mobilized at the same time as the other units, part of its aircraft were federalized. Because of a pressing need for ground-attack replacement aircraft, some of the P-51Ds were hurriedly shipped to Korea. On 1 April 1951 the 185th was called for twenty-one months of active duty; it was reorganized as the 185th Tactical Reconnaissance Squadron and assigned to the 118th Tactical Reconnaissance Group and Wing of the Ninth Air Force. During the following summer and fall the squadron was gradually re-equipped with FR-51Ds, the tactical reconnaissance version of the venerable Mustang, to replace the aircraft sent to Korea. At first the guardsmen remained at Will Rogers Air National Guard Base, but by late summer of 1951 the unit's pilots slowly began to be reassigned. Most were sent to Korea, but some were assigned to Europe and North Africa, as well as to other bases within the United States.[2]

In January, 1952, the 185th was transferred from Will Rogers to Shaw Air Force Base, Sumter, South Carolina, and began to train with the RF-80A Photo Star—the reconnaissance version of the F-80 Shooting Star. Within a month most of the remaining Oklahoma Air National Guard pilots were on their way to the Far East as replacements. To their disappointment, the pilots did not go as a unit but as individual replacements. Although this was not the ideal situation, it eventually proved to be highly beneficial. Because of their experience the air guardsmen were usually assigned to command or supervisory slots once they arrived in the battle zone; this helped alleviate the inexperience of the many newly commissioned second lieutenant pilots also arriving as replacements. Almost half of the 185th's pilots found themselves assigned to the Fifth Air Force and stationed at Kimpo (K-14) Air Base near Seoul. Here they were once again assigned RF-51Ds. As the members of the 185th were rotated to the Far East, their places at Shaw Field were taken by pilots from other units who had already completed their Korean tour.[3]

At about the same time, in February of 1952, the 185th Tactical Reconnaissance Squadron began receiving the Lockheed RF-80A. New in World War II, the P-80, as it was first called, had initially flown in January of 1944 and entered service the following year. A total of 1,717 Shooting Stars were built before production was stopped. The original P-80s were given several modifications after the end of World War II.[4]

When the Air National Guard pilots arrived in Korea most were assigned to the Forty-fifth Tactical Reconnaissance Squadron where they initially flew the RF-51D; later, they also piloted RF-80As and F-80Cs. The planes usually were paired together for missions, with the wingman providing protective cover for the leader, who completed the visual reconnaissance assignment. As the unit received jet aircraft, the wingman flew the F-80C, which carried six .50-caliber machine guns in its nose, and the leader flew the RF-80A, which carried cameras instead of guns. The arrangement prompted a saying among the RF-80A pilots of being "alone, unarmed, and underpaid, but scared spitless." Although the F-80s (as the P-80s were now designated) were relatively old aircraft, they could hold their own against the Communists' MiG-15 in a turning dogfight if flown by experienced pilots. During the jet air-to-air combat over North Korea an F-80C shot down a MiG-15—history's first jet-over-jet combat victory.[5]

Even so, the early RF-80As used in Korea by the Oklahoma air guardsmen lacked much of the more advanced equipment generally associated with jet-powered aircraft. Some Oklahoma Air National Guard pilots were astounded when, after reaching Korea, they were assigned RF-80s that did not even contain automatic ejection seats. Instead, should the pilot be forced to abandon his aircraft in the air, he had to jettison the canopy manually, release himself from his straps, and climb out of the cockpit to jump or roll free of the aircraft before parachuting to earth.[6]

Major General Newman, who had first joined the 185th in 1948 and later became commander of the 137th Military Airlift Wing, was among the first four Oklahoma air guardsmen to report to the Forty-fifth Tactical Reconnaissance Squadron in March of 1952. Newman was somewhat dismayed to learn that the only thing that separated the Kimpo Air Base from North Korea was the Han River and a rather thin line of ROK infantry. Although the river was a formidable natural barrier when it was flowing, when Newman arrived it was frozen solid, and only a few ROK troops patrolled its banks. It was not until some U.S. Marines were assigned to hold the ground between the base and the river that the pilots felt secure. The Oklahoma guardsmen

were frequently harassed at night by an enemy PO-2 biplane, which would fly over the base and merely "putt-putt" back and forth just enough to alert the defenses and ruin their sleep.[7]

The reconnaissance pilots were assigned specific zones to patrol day after day. Although it became almost routine, the repetitious missions familiarized the pilots with the terrain and made the task of spotting enemy targets easier. Often the routine was broken by Communist flak or by being assigned to fly alternate missions adjusting naval gunfire on the coast of North Korea.[8]

The reconnaissance pilots agreed that the greatest drawback to their missions was the limitation placed on the use of their weapons; they could fire only in self-defense. Thus, whenever the opportunity to fly a strike mission presented itself, the guardsmen were eager to go. Once Newman was walking to the operations room when he received word that another reconnaissance pilot had spotted a group of camouflaged Communist tanks but was running too low on fuel and had to return to base. Hurriedly briefed by intelligence and quickly airborne, Newman located the tanks parked in a valley along with antiaircraft guns on the valley floor and in the surrounding hills. The hillside weapons were able to spread a network of tracer fire across the valley. Nonetheless, Newman led two flights of fighter-bombers on their bombing runs and marked the targets with his machine guns. After the fighters completed their work, Newman recorded the destruction with his reconnaissance camera and returned to base.[9]

When the 125th Fighter Bomber Squadron was released from active duty and returned to state control in July of 1952, its F-84 Thunderjets were initially replaced with F-51 Mustangs. Then, through the summer and the fall of that year, the 125th also began receiving F-80s. At about that same time the 138th group was organized in Tulsa to provide immediate command and logistical support for the fighter-bomber squadron. The Shooting Stars remained with the Tulsa Air National Guard unit for the next five years.[10]

The 185th, minus its pilots and some other key personnel, continued to serve as a tactical-reconnaissance squadron at Shaw Air Force Base until 31 December 1952. At that time the 185th designation was returned to Oklahoma City, and

"Talking Bird" or "Miss Oklahoma City," a Boeing C-97E equipped as a special airborne command post assigned to the OKARNG between 1961 and 1972. During its eleven years of service, the aircraft and its Oklahoma Guardsmen were deployed throughout the world on many occasions. *Courtesy Dennis R. Lindsey.*

the unit was reorganized as the 185th Fighter Bomber Squadron. To avoid having two 185th squadrons, the unit at Shaw was given a new designation.[11]

After their tour in the Korean War, only a quarter or less of the 185th pilots returned to the Air National Guard. The rest chose to remain on active duty and complete their careers. When first reorganized as a fighter-bomber squadron, the 185th had one F-51H, one C-47, and one T-6 with which to train. Nevertheless, the unit quickly qualified its new pilots in the T-6, and soon it was granted federal recognition. The final production version of the P-51 aircraft, the H-series, was superior to any of the previous Mustang editions. Powered by a V-1650-9 engine, it had a top speed of 487 miles per hour at 25,000 feet.[12]

The aircraft shortage was alleviated somewhat about six months later when four additional P-51Ds were assigned to the unit and the F-51H transferred out. By the summer of 1953, however, when the 185th's first post-Korea training camp was scheduled for Casper, Wyoming, the unit still had only four of its fighter aircraft avail-

able for duty. Fortunately, the 185th was able to arrange with another Air National Guard unit at Albuquerque, New Mexico, which had a similar shortage, to combine the two squadrons' planes so that each would have eight aircraft available for their summer camps that were scheduled to be held in succession at Casper. That summer the 185th went to camp with four of the "old gang" and four newly assigned pilots.[13]

The 185th returned to the jet age in July of 1953, when the F-51Ds were phased out in favor of the F-80B, and the command redesignated as the 185th Fighter Squadron (Single Engine) Jet. A year later the Oklahoma guardsmen flew their F-80Bs to the Lockheed Aircraft plant at Burbank, California, where they were modified into F-80Cs by installation of a more powerful engine and more efficient fuel control. Powered by an Allison J33-A-23 turbojet engine rated at 5,400 pounds of static thrust, the F-80C had a top speed of 580 miles per hour, a service ceiling of 48,000 feet, and a range of 1,380 miles. Later F-80C models were equipped with J33-A-35 engines, with water injection, which produced 5,400 pounds of static thrust. The planes' basic

166

F-80C Shooting Stars of the Oklahoma Air National Guard over western Oklahoma. White dots on a blue background were the markings of the Forty-fifth Tactical Reconnaissance Squadron, to which many Oklahoma air guardsmen were assigned. *Courtesy Forty-fifth Infantry Division Museum.*

armament was still six .50-caliber machine guns. The F-80C continued to be the 185th Fighter Squadron's main aircraft for five more years.[14]

Until this time the 185th's insignia had remained the rampaging bull first adopted in 1943; however, it was never very popular with the unit's guardsmen. As a result, on 3 October 1953, the 185th's commander, Captain Doyle W. Hastie, later a brigadier general, petitioned the National Guard Bureau for permission to design a new emblem that would adequately reflect the 185th's mission and jet aircraft. The new insignia was largely the work of Captain George N. Masterson, who later rose to the rank of brigadier general, and Jim Lange, the political cartoonist for the Oklahoma Publishing Company.[15]

The 185th's new insignia was an Indian warrior dressed in a red breech-cloth and moccasins, sitting atop a flaming jet engine. The warrior held a tomahawk topped with a bomb in one hand, and in the other he held onto the engine as it sped downward to the attack. The Indian held a machine gun in his teeth. The insignia was in a blue circle outlined with black. Shortly thereafter the proposed emblem was registered by the heraldic branch of the air force.[16]

In 1957 the Oklahoma Air National Guard was given a major role as fighter-interceptors in America's Air Defense Command. One reason for the interceptor mission was the seasonal flow of the upper jet stream from Siberia down across the Great Plains into the Southwest, and then toward the industrialized northeastern United

Flight line of F-86D Sabre Dogs at Will Rogers Air National Guard Base in Oklahoma City. The F-86D formed the backbone of both the Tulsa-based 125th Fighter Squadron and the Oklahoma City-based 185th Fighter Squadron during the height of the Cold War. *Courtesy Forty-fifth Infantry Division Museum.*

States. Some air force defense strategies reasoned that by utilizing the powerful west to east jet stream over Siberia, Soviet bombers could sweep diagonally across the Pacific, and stay in the flow northeast across Baja California, New Mexico, Texas, and Oklahoma to targets on the East Coast. Although the flight would be over a longer ground track than would a direct attack across the North Pole, it would be as efficient because of the added speed that could be gained from riding the high-velocity upper jet stream.[17]

On 1 August 1957, the 125th Fighter-Bomber Squadron's Shooting Stars were replaced by the North American F-86D Sabre. The following year, on 1 May 1958, the Oklahoma City-based 185th Fighter Squadron was given a similar mission and also issued F-86Ds. After becoming combat ready in the aircraft, the units were placed on 24-hours-a-day, seven-days-a-week alert.[18]

This version of the Sabre, commonly called "the Dog," was the interceptor version of the F-86 Sabre jet that had proved its value in Korea as an air-superior fighter. It had first flown in 1949 and entered service in 1951. Powered by a J47-GE-33 engine developing 7,650 pounds of static thrust (with its afterburner), it was a major departure from the basic F-86. It was originally designated the YF-93, but because of its deriva-

tion from the original F-86, it was redesignated the F-86D.

Designed as a single-seat interceptor with enough electronic aids to give the plane all-weather intercept capability, the F-86D had an autopilot and a sophisticated electronic engine control, as well as an all-flying tail in which the horizontal surfaces moved as one, thus giving the pilot better control of the aircraft at high speed. In addition, the aircraft had an eighteen-inch search radar system housed in a plastic dome protruding over a refashioned air intake below the radome. The F-86D was equipped with an afterburner to give it a greater climb and closure rate, and was armed with twenty-four 2.75-inch "Mighty Mouse" rockets in a retractable tray, which could be fired in salvos of six, twelve, or twenty-four. It was strictly an interceptor aircraft designed to destroy enemy bombers, and it was unable to cope with enemy fighters in combat. Once equipped with the "Dogs," the Oklahoma guardsmen began to conduct their summer training camps at Gulfport, Mississippi, where they could actually fire the rockets in special ranges over the Gulf of Mexico.[19]

The F-86D continued to be the workhorse of both the 125th and the 185th until 1960. On 15 January of that year, Tulsa's 125th Fighter Squadron, along with the 138th Air Transport

In the early 1960s, when the Oklahoma Air National Guard became an air transport unit, the F-86Ds were replaced with the KC-97 Stratocruisers, *left. Courtesy Forty-fifth Infantry Division Museum.*

Group, was converted to the 125th Air Transport Squadron, both to become a part of the Military Air Transport Command. With its new mission, the unit was assigned C-97 Stratocruiser cargo aircraft.[20]

In April of 1960, Oklahoma City's 185th also was reequipped with different aircraft; it received F-86Ls and, for a short time, remained a fighter-interceptor unit. The F-86L was a version of the F-86D designed to have improved high altitude performance and a data link ground-to-air control system. This system was designed to eliminate the need for voice ground-to-air intercept control and thus avoid possible voice jamming by enemy bombers. The F-86Ls were slightly slower than the D models, but they carried the same armament.[21]

At approximately the same time in 1958 that the Oklahoma Air National Guard was assigned an air defense role, the air force began a program to centralize its electronics installation resources. Before, each command had its own centralized electronics installation-engineering structure. To eliminate the duplicated facilities, several ground electronics engineering and installation squadrons, better known as GEEIAs, sub-

ordinate to the U.S. Air Force Logistics Command, were formed. Two of the squadrons, the 205th and 219th, were eventually assigned to the Oklahoma Air National Guard.[22]

Later, on 1 April 1970, Oklahoma's GEEIAs were reassigned to the Air Force Communications Systems. In May of that year all GEEIA squadrons were redesignated as electronic installation squadrons, or EIs, with the 205th and the 219th squadrons stationed at Will Rogers Air National Guard Base. Made up of highly trained specialists, the EI squadrons were responsible for erecting antennas, installing cable systems and ground radios, or reconstituting and repairing communication facilities anywhere in the world.[23]

In April of 1961 the Oklahoma City Air National Guard unit also was reorganized as the 185th Air Transport Squadron, an element of the Air Transport Command, which later evolved into the Military Airlift Command. Both the 125th and the 185th now were air transport squadrons, and both flew Stratocruisers. Initially, the two squadrons had different versions of the aircraft. Originally, from April of 1961 through February of 1963, the 185th was equipped with the KC-

97F model of the Boeing-built cargo plane. Derived from Boeing's B-50, an outgrowth of the B-29, the KC-97, like the C-97, had been created by adding a second fuselage, of a much greater diameter, to the top of the existing B-50 fuselage. The mating of the two fuselages created a "whale-like body . . . [that] had a section like a figure 8." Like the B-50, the Stratocruiser was powered by four R-4360 engines.[24]

The aircraft had first flown in January of 1945, but by the time the Oklahoma guardsmen received the plane it had undergone several modifications, and the addition of the prefix "K" indicated that the aircraft had been altered from cargo configuration to a tanker for air-refueling missions. Later, in February and October of 1963, the guardsmen were assigned the more advanced KC-97Gs. Although both planes had originally been built to serve as tankers, the 185th Air Transport Squadron used the aircraft only as a cargo carrier by removing the refueling boom and refueling tanks that were installed in the cargo compartment of the tanker version. In October of 1963, the unit's KC-97Gs were converted to C-97Gs through the addition of clam-shell doors, improved avionics, and a cargo-configured interior. Equipped with four Pratt & Whitney R-4360 Wasp Major engines, the C-97G had a peacetime gross weight of 153,000 pounds, which, in wartime emergencies, could be expanded to 175,000 pounds. Designed specifically as a cargo aircraft, its maximum speed was 375 miles per hour.[25]

During the switchover to C-97s, the 185th was given a specially equipped C-97E, the "Miss Oklahoma City"—better known as "Talking Bird"—for utilization as an airborne command post. From 1961 to 1972, Talking Bird was deployed throughout the world on various communication missions. Capable of both voice and teletype command communications, the aircraft had a range of more than twenty-five hundred miles, and was under the direct command of the USAF Command Post in the Pentagon.[26]

To fulfill its mission, Talking Bird's nine-man air crew and ten-man communications team were on constant four-hour alert to fly to any point on earth. In 1961 alone, the aircraft was deployed to twenty-two foreign countries. It was used to maintain constant secure communications between the nation's capital and President John F. Kennedy during the chief executive's visits

to Venezuela in 1961; to Mexico in 1962; and to Costa Rica, Ireland, and Rome in 1963. Later, in the mid-1960s, Talking Bird's mission was altered to that of testing communications facilities at American military bases throughout the world. The aircraft was not retired until 29 December 1972.[27]

When the United States and the Soviet Union clashed over Berlin in 1961, the 138th Air Transport Group, under the command of Lieutenant Colonel Gerald W. Stevenson, and five of its subordinate Tulsa Air National Guard units, including the 125th Air Transport Squadron, were called into federal service on 1 October. Although it remained at its Tulsa base, the 138th was assigned to the Military Air Transport Service's 146th Air Transport Wing (Heavy), activated from the California Air National Guard, and provided airlift for the Western Transport Air Force. The Tulsa guardsmen remained on active duty until 31 August 1962.[28]

Although the 185th was not called to active duty during the Berlin crisis, it flew numerous support missions, often lasting five or six days, to resupply American bases in Europe and seven-day missions to Japan. At the same time, Oklahoma City's Talking Bird was rushed to Iceland to monitor the deployment of two hundred Air National Guard aircraft to Europe as part of America's military buildup. Later, in 1965, Talking Bird was similarly scrambled when President Lyndon Johnson ordered American troops into the Dominican Republic to protect Americans caught in a civil disorder. In fact, it was among the first air force aircraft to land in that country during the crisis.[29]

In the early 1960s the squadron was assigned a wartime support role under Western Transport Air Force, now the Twenty-second Air Force, which had under its control all airlift capability from the Mississippi River westward to India. With this assignment the Oklahoma Air National Guard began to play an active role in the American involvement in South Vietnam, as both the 125th and the 185th Air Transport Squadrons began flying missions to Southeast Asia. A typical mission might originate in Oklahoma City or Tulsa, fly to the West Coast, load supplies, and then make its way across the Pacific to one of the major air bases in Vietnam. Once on the ground in Vietnam, however, the guardsmen were not scheduled to remain longer than four

Governor Henry Bellmon congratulates members of the Oklahoma Air National Guard who took part in the 1965 airlift of Christmas presents to American troops serving in Vietnam. *Left to right, front row:* Captain Dale Sawyer, Master Sergeant Jimmy Connell, Master Sergeant Charles Martz, Sergeant Ray Overton, Lieutenant Colonel Louis G. Barnett, Jr., Governor Bellmon. *Back row:* Lieutenant Colonel Roger Dabney and Captain Frank Lane. *Courtesy Forty-fifth Infantry Division Museum.*

hours and normally were turned around as quickly as possible. The large cargo aircraft made tempting targets, and if they remained stationary for any length of time it increased the chance of drawing enemy fire. As a result, the Oklahoma guardsmen were always certain of expeditious handling during their Vietnam ground times.[30]

By the mid-1960s four or five missions each month were being routinely flown to Vietnam by each Oklahoma Air National Guard squadron. The number continued to grow until in 1966 the 185th, for example, flew 119 overseas flights, with 85 of the missions terminating in Southeast Asia. As a result of the missions, 95 percent of the personnel then assigned to Will Rogers Air National Guard Base were awarded the Vietnam Service Medal. On 1 January 1966, the Air Transport Command was reorganized as the Military Command, and the 137th wing and group became military airlift wing and group, respectively. The 185th was redesignated a military airlift squadron. Two years later, on 1 April 1968, the 137th and the 138th Aerial Port Flights were formed as a part of the Oklahoma Air National Guard, and added to their groups.[31]

So that the cargo aircraft of Tulsa's 138th and Oklahoma City's 137th groups could be used to their maximum capabilities in wartime, aeromedical evacuation flights were assigned to both. These specially planned flights carried teams of flight nurses and aeromedical technicians, which gave the aircraft the ability to transport wounded. Thus, in case of an all-out war, the C-97s and the C-124s could carry cargo into a combat zone and on their return flights airlift either retrograde cargo or evacuate wounded troops. The aeromedical evacuation flights operated as a part of the Oklahoma Air National Guard until Tulsa's 138th converted to fighters in 1972. Oklahoma City's 137th Aeromedical Evacuation Squadron was inactivated on 17 August 1973.[32]

The guardsmen continued to fly C-97s until February of 1968, when both the 125th and the 185th were reequipped with the Douglas C-124C Globemaster. Nicknamed "Old Shakey," the Globemaster was developed in the late 1940s, and in its day was "the most capable transport in the world." It could seat up to 220 troops with equipment. For its cargo-carrying role, the

Douglas C-124C Globemaster, called "Old Shaky" by its crew, of the 137th Military Airlift Group, Oklahoma Air National Guard. *Courtesy Dennis R. Lindsey Collection.*

items to more remote bases with austere facilities. Because much of the nation's military hardware had grown too large to be air transported by anything other than the C-5 or the C-124, the Oklahoma guardsmen and two other Air National Guard units that were still flying the C-124s were called upon many times for missions involving cargo too large for the C-141 or the C-130 aircraft, or too uneconomical for the C-5, but suitable for the C-124. The Oklahomans flew several missions involving cargo too large for anything but a Globemaster to DEW-line installations along the Arctic Circle where primitive landing strips ruled out using the C-5s. The huge carrying capacity of the C-124s also came in handy when, in 1969, the 185th was called upon to ferry the Apollo VIII mission exhibit from place to place in Europe, including from West Berlin, Germany, to Zagreb, Yugoslavia. Mission planners believed that two Air National Guard C-124s would be ideal for the mission and because of its part in it, the 185th became the first Air National Guard unit to visit a Communist nation.[34]

C-124 was equipped with huge clam-shell doors and an aft elevator which greatly facilitated the loading of large bulky items.[33]

During this era the air force began development of its massive C-5 cargo plane. While this aircraft was unsurpassed at carrying huge loads of cargo, it was often expedient to use the C-124 for missions carrying only one or two very large

The guardsmen also were heavily involved in disaster relief missions and riot duty during this decade. When Hurricane Camille struck the

Loadmaster Larry Chilton, *right*, and Staff Sergeant Don Shephard, dropping bales of hay from a C-124C during Operation Haylift, which fed thousands of starving cattle caught in a blizzard in western Oklahoma. *Courtesy Forty-fifth Infantry Division Museum.*

Foreground, F-100 Super Sabres; *background,* A-7D Corsair II, of the Tulsa-based 138th Tactical Fighter Group at the Tulsa Air National Guard Base, September, 1977. *Courtesy Dennis R. Lindsey Collection.*

Gulf Coast in August of 1969, the 185th flew 101 members of the Mennonite Disaster Service to Mississippi to aid in the cleanup campaign. When western Oklahoma was struck by a severe blizzard in the early 1970s, the guardsmen flew missions during Operation Hay Lift to carry feed to stranded cattle. When the inmates of the State Penitentiary at McAlester rioted in the summer of 1973, both army and Air National Guard troops were called in to quell the disturbance, and members of the Oklahoma Air National Guard spent several weeks patrolling the corridors of the penitentiary.[35]

By the early 1970s the C-124s were being phased out by the air force in favor of more modern transport aircraft. As part of the modernization program, the Tulsa Air National Guard began training in October of 1972 with Lockheed T-33 jet trainer versions of the F-80C in preparation for converting to North American F-100 Super Sabres. Reorganized to include the

Headquarters, 138th Tactical Fighter Group; the 125th Tactical Fighter Squadron; the 138th Consolidated Aircraft Maintenance Squadron; the 138th Combat Support Squadron; the 138th Tactical Clinic; the 138th Civil Engineering Flight; the 138th Weapons System Security Flight; the 138th Communications Flight; the 138th Resource Management Squadron; and the 125th Weather Flight, the unit was federally recognized as the 138th Tactical Fighter Group on 25 January 1973.[36]

The F-100 had exceeded the speed of sound on its first flight on 25 May 1953—the first aircraft to do so in level flight—and was quickly added to the air force's inventory. From the original YF100A-NA through the F-100F-20NA series, 2,294 were built. Basically the Super Sabres were armed with four forward-firing 20-mm. cannon and underwing pylons for six 1,000-pound bombs, and two Sidewinder or Bullpup missiles. The F-100C was a more advanced ver-

A-7Ds of Tulsa's 125th Tactical Fighter Squadron, 1978. These aircraft bear the squadron's beaver insignia. *Courtesy Forty-fifth Infantry Division Museum.*

sion of the Super Sabre and was the model assigned to the Oklahoma Air National Guard. In addition to its superior performance, the F-100C carried eight external stores pylons and a flight refueling probe.[37]

The F-100s remained with the 138th until April of 1978 when the Tulsa guardsmen began receiving the Vought Corsair II A-7D, the air force's tactical fighter version of a successful navy design. It was commonly called "SLUF" for "Slow Little Ugly Fella." A subsonic single-seat tactical fighter, the A-7D was capable of all-weather radar bomb delivery. Although the A-7 first flew in 1965, the D model was developed soon afterward, first taking to the air on 5 April 1968. Powered by one Allison TF41-A-1, a non-afterburning turbofan engine with 14,250 pounds of thrust, the A-7D's maximum speed was 698 miles per hour with a ferry range of 3,340 miles. Its

tactical radius was 700 miles. The Corsair II carried up to 15,000 pounds of external armaments, including air-to-air missiles, air-to-ground missiles, general purpose bombs, rockets, gun pods, and auxiliary fuel tanks. Mounted in the aircraft's fuselage was a M61-A1 Vulcan 20-mm. cannon, which fired 4,000 to 6,000 rounds per minute.[38]

Another phase of the modernization program of the 1970s was the reorganization of the 137th wing and its units from a strategic to a tactical airlift mission on 10 December 1974. This was an outgrowth of the discovery by the 137th's non-destructive inspection technicians of a fleet-wide main wing spar crack that, except for a one-time flight to the air force's disposal facility, permanently grounded America's entire C-124 fleet. At the same time the 185th traded its C-124s for the Lockheed C-130A, officially known

Company E, OKARNG officer candidates during field training under the watchful eye of Tactical Officer First Lieutenant S. O. Yates (*right rear*), at Fort Chaffee, Arkansas, August, 1961. *Courtesy Forty-fifth Infantry Division Museum.*

as the Hercules and affectionately known as "Herky Birds." Together with the 185th Tactical Airlift Squadron, the 137th Consolidated Aircraft Maintenance Squadron, the 137th USAF Clinic, the 137th Combat Support Squadron, the 137th Civil Engineering Flight, the 137th Weapons System Security Flight, the 137th Mobile Aerial Port Flight, and the 137th Communications Flight were grouped under the 137th Tactical Airlift Wing, which also exercised supervision over the training of three other tactical airlift groups—two in West Virginia and one in Missouri. Later the 137th Resources Management Squadron was added to the wing.[39]

The C-130A first flew in 1954, and was designed as "an outstanding military airlifter, with a level truck-bed height floor, full-section rear doors [which could be opened in flight], soft-field retractable gear, efficient high-lift wing,

turboprop engines and full pressurization." The A version of the aircraft was powered with four Allison T56 single-shaft turboprops. With the reorganization and arrival of newer aircraft, the 137th's mission was changed to short range, low-level air drop and assault landings in support of ground combat forces.[40]

The C-130As were replaced on 23 June 1979 by C-130Hs, which were flown by Oklahoma guardsmen directly from the factory to Will Rogers Air National Guard Base. In so doing, the 137th became the first Air National Guard unit ever to be issued factory-fresh transport planes. The C-130H was a greatly improved and more powerful version of the C-130, which by this time had been in service for a quarter of a century. The H model had a maximum speed of 384 miles per hour and a service ceiling of 33,000 feet. Its maximum payload range was

2,487 miles with a loaded weight of 175,000 pounds.[41]

As a part of America's tactical airlift capabilities, the 185th has a global mission to resupply any military post by either conventional landings, air drop, or assault landings. The unit's main concern is with getting badly needed equipment and personnel into forward positions occupied by ground troops where landing strips are either primitive or nonexistent. If no landing facilities are available, the cargo can be parachuted from the aircraft into the perimeter occupied by friendly troops. If a landing strip is available, the guardsmen would make assault landings, in which the aircraft comes in at an altitude of about three hundred feet to protect it from small-arms fire, dives at the landing strip, and comes to a stop within 2,500 feet. After the cargo is unloaded, sometimes while the aircraft is still rolling, the plane turns around, or backs up, and immediately takes off.[42]

At the beginning of the 1980s, the Oklahoma Air National Guard consisted of four major units: the 138th Tactical Fighter Group at the Tulsa Air National Guard Base, and the 137th Tactical Airlift Wing and the 205th and the 219th electronic installations squadrons stationed at Will Rogers Air National Guard Base in Oklahoma City. These units, with their subordinate units, are a part of the total force concept of the air force. Their training, maintenance, and inspection criteria adhere to the same standards as active duty units. Their readiness for almost instant deployment is certified by inspections and operational readiness tests administered by teams from the air force's training commands, using the same basic criteria as those maintained by active duty and reserve components.[43]

The importance of these units to the defense of the United States is stressed by Major Joe E. Blackwell, the senior air adviser to the 137th, who points out that approximately one-third of the tactical airlift capabilities of the air force are relegated to the Air National Guard. The units maintain such a high state of readiness that within seventy-two hours the 137th Tactical Airlift Wing would be ready to deploy anywhere in the world. To maintain this rapid deployment capability, approximately 15 to 20 percent of the air national guardsmen are fulltime personnel assigned to aircraft maintenance. The remaining two thousand members train at least once a month, while pilots and navigators fly a minimum of 150 hours annually to maintain their proficiency and combat readiness. The Oklahoma Air National Guard units, citizen soldiers all, are a part of America's front-line defense; they are ready and willing, in peace or war, to provide for the common defense.[44]

CHAPTER 15

THE TOTAL FORCE

The 429 days of combat duty accumulated in the Korean War added to the 511 days of combat in World War II allowed the Forty-fifth Division to boast of more days of combat than any other army division to that time. With the return of the division to state control, the process of building it into a fully prepared and trained fighting unit assumed new importance. Some progress already had been made with the establishment of the Forty-fifth Division of the Oklahoma National Guard while the Forty-fifth Division of the U.S. Army was still fighting in Korea, but now that there was just one Thunderbird Division the progress was more rapid. Many Korean War veterans had rejoined the National Guard after they were rotated home during that conflict, and now that the fighting was over even more enlisted. Unlike World War II, after Korea there was no lapse of time from the end of the fighting to the formation of a new National Guard division for Oklahoma.[1]

Major General Hal L. Muldrow, Jr., who had commanded the division's artillery during the fighting in Korea, was named the new commander of the Thunderbirds on 15 September 1952. Colonel, later major general, Daugherty, was promoted to brigadier general one month later and named assistant division commander. Under their leadership, within a short time the Oklahoma National Guard was heavily involved in training and weekend drills. The division retained its three regimental combat team organization until 1959, when it was reorganized under the pentomic concept.[2]

Under the pentomic organization, the Forty-fifth was formed around five battle groups. The number of units within the division were reduced from 110 to 88, with the greatest reduction being in the infantry. The reorganization was part of the changing military strategy that developed because of the increase in nuclear weapons. Many military leaders believed that any future warfare would be "done in the round." That is, American troops might find themselves surrounded by the enemy. Thus, an organization of five battle groups, instead of three regiments, by a division headquarters would allow it to deploy troops on a five-sided, enclosed front. From such positions it was believed that it would be easier to rescue troops from a surrounding enemy by the limited use of nuclear weapons.[3]

Another reason, it was argued, was that the pentomic reorganization would allow the National Guard to achieve a higher state of readiness by concentrating many of the personnel and priority units, which were to be maintained at 80 percent of war strength. These divisions would be given first priority in the allotment of equipment and increased training. Although the Forty-fifth Infantry was not given priority, it was still reorganized, as were all of the nation's National Guard divisions, along the pentomic lines.[4]

Soon after the reorganization, Brigadier General Daugherty was named commander of the Thunderbirds on 1 September 1960, and promoted to major general twenty-five days later. He held the post until retiring in 1964 to accept a federal judgeship in Oklahoma City. One of Daugherty's main goals was to raise the division's manpower and rebuild the Forty-fifth to its full authorized strength. He also was instrumental in shifting the Thunderbirds' summer training camp from Fort Hood, Texas, to Fort Chaffee, Arkansas. Such a move not only re-

M-48A3 medium tank of the Clinton (Oklahoma) National Guard unit, participating in a mock assault at Fort Chaffee, Arkansas, during summer camp, 1965. *Courtesy Forty-fifth Infantry Division Museum.*

duced travel time, thereby making more time available for training, but it allowed more of the guardsmen's families to visit them during summer camp. After he retired, Major General Daugherty played an important role in the creation of the Forty-fifth Infantry Division Museum, which is dedicated to the preservation of the heritage of Oklahoma's citizen soldiers.[5]

The pentomic concept for the National Guard lasted only a few years. Within a short time Staff College war games underlined the fact that divisions reorganized with five battle groups, while perfectly equipped for fighting in a defensive situation, lacked any offensive striking power. In addition, after the Berlin crisis of 1960-1961, it was discovered that the priority divisions that had been called to active duty suffered so much from personnel losses that their priority status was dropped.[6]

In place of the pentomic concept, the Forty-fifth Division was reorganized again in April of 1963 along the lines of a three-brigade unit. The

plan, designated ROAD for Reorganization Objectives Army Divisions, basically returned the National Guard units to the triangular divisions of the World War II and Korean War eras. The basic alteration was in the number of battalions attached to the brigade, which differed with each brigade's mission. For example, an infantry division, such as the Forty-fifth, might be assigned only eight combat battalions combining infantry and armor within its brigade organization for a certain mission. At another time, it might have as many as fifteen battalions divided between infantry, mechanized infantry, and armor for a different assignment. Obviously such a formation allowed great flexibility. On 21 November 1964, Major General Jasper N. Baker assumed command of the Forty-fifth Infantry Division. Baker, who at the time of his appointment was serving as assistant division commander, had begun his National Guard career as an enlisted man in the unit at Atoka.[7]

With the phasing out of priority status units

The phase-out of the Forty-fifth Infantry Division in favor of the Forty-fifth Infantry Brigade was begun in September, 1968. The Thunderbirds were issued more modern equipment, such as the M-16 assault rifles and PRC-25 radios. *Courtesy Forty-fifth Infantry Division Museum.*

after the Berlin crisis, the army created a series of selected reserve forces (SRF) units in July, 1965. The SRF organization was to be the most ready reserve component in the nation's history, and was composed of three infantry divisions, five separate infantry brigades, a mechanized infantry brigade, an armored cavalry regiment, and numerous combat support and service units. The development of such units would give the nation greater options in reacting to international situations. Eighty-five percent of the manpower, 130,000 troops, was to come from National Guard units, which were to be manned and equipped at full strength. Among the major components were the Twenty-eighth, the Thirty-eighth, and the Forty-seventh infantry divisions, and the Twenty-ninth Infantry Brigade.[8]

Oklahoma's National Guard SRF force was to form a part of the Forty-seventh Infantry Division. Under the SRF organization, a division base and three infantry battalions were provided by Minnesota's Forty-seventh Infantry Division. In addition, an infantry brigade formed from three infantry battalions, one direct support artillery battalion, an armored cavalry troop, an airmobile cavalry troop, and a medical company were provided by the Forty-fifth Infantry Division. A direct support artillery battalion, an airmobile company, an armored cavalry troop, and a medical company came from Wisconsin's Sixty-seventh Infantry Division.[9]

While the Oklahoma National Guard units that were a part of the SRF force received priority in training and equipment, the remainder of the Thunderbirds were reduced to 46 percent of their strength. Reorganization of the Forty-

Specialist Fourth Class Aaron McGee of Hugo, Oklahoma, a member of the First Battalion, 180th Infantry, linking M-60 machine-gun ammunition. *Courtesy Forty-fifth Infantry Division Museum.*

fifth began almost immediately, and by November of 1965, the division had created twenty-three SRF units with a total of 3,926 men. In addition to added training assemblies, which were increased by 50 percent, and a higher standing in equipment procurement, a special one-week course for SRF infantry brigade and battalion commanders and staff officers was held at Fort Benning, Georgia, in November of 1965, at the initiative of the Oklahoma National Guard. With the increased drill schedule, by the summer of 1966 all units had completed their concentrated training program. According to Adjutant-General Robert M. Morgan, Jr., who commanded Company A, Second Battalion, 279th Infantry, an SRF unit in the late 1960s, the high-priority guardsmen were the best-trained troops of America's reserve force. The SRF concept lasted through a series of modifications—

SRF, SRF I, SRF I-A, SRF II—until it was discontinued on 30 September 1969.[10]

The long line of post-Korea reorganizations continued into the mid-1960s. Perhaps the most important of them was the one that called for the creation of high-priority National Guard units. It grew out of the so called "Cantwell Plan" developed by the Roles and Missions Committee of the National Guard Association of the United States. Although Major General James F. Cantwell was president of the association, the chairman of the committee that produced the report was Major General Daugherty, commanding general of the Forty-fifth Division. The plan basically called for the establishment of one high-priority and two low-priority brigades in each of the National Guard's seventeen infantry and six armored divisions. Under such an organization, the high-priority brigades would be assembled into their assigned priority divisions at mobilization. The low-priority brigades would serve as a source of replacements for the high-priority divisions and as nuclei for additional divisions, should they be needed.[11]

The Defense Department implemented a slightly different plan, however. The plan reflected the intent of the Roles and Missions Committee to preserve all of the twenty-three division structures then existing. Recognizing that it is far more difficult to organize a division from a low beginning point, the committee recommended that all National Guard divisions be retained, with each supporting one high-priority brigade that could be used to round out a committed division. The remaining divisions would fill their ranks with volunteers and draftees following the initial stages of any conflict.[12]

According to Major General Daugherty, during negotiations with Secretary of Defense Robert McNamara about the plan, it became evident that he had other ideas in mind. "McNamara first insisted on maintaining all National Guard divisions at 100 percent manpower," Daugherty recalled. In replying to McNamara, the Roles and Missions Committee "informed him that such a goal was not only impossible to maintain for the National Guard, but that the National Guard had never been at such a level before and it was not needed based on past experience." The committee recommended a 65 percent manning level, but McNamara refused to accept anything less than a 90 percent level.[13]

Army aircraft demonstration held for the Forty-fifth Infantry Brigade at Fort Chaffee, Arkansas, 20 June 1969. *Left to right:* Major General LaVern E. Weber, adjutant-general of Oklahoma; Brigadier General Harry W. Barnes, commanding general of the Special Headquarters Brigade of OKARNG; Brigadier General David C. Matthews, commander of the Forty-fifth Infantry Brigade; Major General Frederick A. Daugherty (Ret.), former commander of the Forty-fifth Infantry Division and later chairman of the board of directors of the Forty-fifth Infantry Division Museum; and Captain Don LeMonier, 291st Aviation Company, Fort Sill, Oklahoma. *Courtesy Forty-fifth Infantry Division Museum.*

"It became evident," Daugherty explained, "that speculation that had surfaced at the time that the Secretary wanted to abolish most of the divisions in the National Guard was a fact, and that he was looking for a mechanism to implement his plan." Many believed that McNamara did not like the National Guard concept because as a state militia it was not totally under the control of the federal government, a condition that apparently chafed him because of the necessity of having to consult with state and territorial governors. Still, according to Daugherty, "the Committee's effort was not entirely in vain." Although McNamara's Defense Department implemented a different plan, it did preserve some National Guard divisional structures. Thus the Roles and Missions Committee did achieve partial success.[14]

Eight National Guard combat divisions and sixteen separate brigades would be brought up to strength and tailored for specific tasks instead of being "type" organizations. For example, the Thirty-eighth Infantry Division would be specifically trained to reinforce the Panama Canal

Zone. Each of the eight divisions was divided among three states to minimize the effects of a nuclear attack and avoid the possibility of any one of the divisions being totally destroyed.

In preparation for any European conflict, most of the divisions were located east of the Mississippi River. Individual brigades within the divisions, each commanded by a colonel, were authorized to have from 2,500 to 3,700 men, to be divided between two to four maneuver battalions. Each brigade would be supported by an armored cavalry troop; an aviation unit; an engineer unit with forward support maintenance and medical companies; military police and truck platoons; forward support, supply and services, and administrative sections; and a 105-mm. howitzer battalion.[15]

The separate brigades were strengthened to more appropriately resemble scaled-down divisions. Given a total strength of from 4,000 to 4,700 men, the brigades, each commanded by a brigadier general, were almost one-half divisional strength. In addition to their maneuver battalions, each brigade had an armored cavalry troop; a composite aviation company; an engineer company; a 105-mm. howitzer battalion; and a support battalion, with medical, supply, transportation, maintenance, and administrative companies. Each state was to be given "a National Guard force sufficient to meet . . . [its] anticipated internal needs," with America's total National Guard force pegged at 400,000 men. The deactivation of the Forty-fifth Division on 1 February 1968 resulted in a reorganization of the Oklahoma Air National Guard.[16]

Replacing the division was the Forty-fifth Artillery Group, which was comprised of three artillery battalions. Also created was the Forty-fifth Support Center (Rear Area Operations), composed of five support battalions, as well as the Forty-fifth Infantry Brigade (Separate), which had three infantry battalions, a direct-support artillery battalion, a support battalion, an aviation company, an engineer company, an armored cavalry troop, a military police platoon, and a brigade headquarters. The Forty-fifth Infantry Brigade (Separate) was the only new line organization authorized a general officer and was commanded by Brigadier General David C. Matthews.[17]

Matthews had first enlisted in the Forty-fifth as a private in 1932. In World War II he had received a navy commission, and commanded an LST at Iwo Jima. After the war he returned to the division, served in Korea, and was appointed assistant division commander on 15 September 1965.[18]

When the Forty-fifth Infantry Division was phased out, the diamond-shaped shoulder patch with its thunderbird of Indian myth was lost to many members of the former division because only the Forty-fifth Infantry Brigade was authorized to wear the familiar patch. It was not until September of 1980 that Major General Robert M. Morgan, Oklahoma's adjutant-general, authorized the Forty-fifth Artillery Brigade, the Forty-fifth Troop Command, and the Forty-fifth Infantry Brigade to once again wear the Thunderbird patch. Members of the headquarters and headquarters detachment, the general staff, and the adjutant-general's personal staff continued to wear the Indian head patch.[19]

At the time of the 1968 reorganization, the state's headquarters and headquarters detachment and the adjutant-general were given greater responsibilities. Major General L. E. Weber, state adjutant-general at the time, had to assume responsibility for many duties that previously had been assigned to the divisional commander and his staff. To many officers this was a serious mistake, for the removal of a divisional command structure greatly restricted the National Guard's ability to maintain its readiness. As Major General Daugherty explained, a division is the basic army unit capable of independent operations; any smaller unit requires a number of support groups. Thus, the reduction, of the Forty-fifth from a division to brigade-size units greatly reduced its ability to function. It requires far less time to detach brigade-size units from divisions for separate service, Daugherty pointed out, than it does to create a functioning divisional staff.[20]

Weber also was concerned that Oklahoma's reorganized National Guard would be unable to complete its state mission in its reorganized form. Fortunately, Weber and Governor Dewey Bartlett received assurances from Secretary of Defense Robert McNamara that Oklahoma would retain most of its National Guard units. In fact, according to Major General Morgan, the difference in manpower between the Forty-fifth Infantry Division, which was maintained at 50 to 60 percent strength, and the Forty-fifth Infantry

Members of the Oklahoma National Guard practicing an assault boat crossing of a river during training exercises. *Courtesy Forty-fifth Infantry Division Museum.*

Brigade, which was authorized full strength, was minimal. Nevertheless, one of Oklahoma's greatest traditions, the Forty-fifth Infantry Division, was lost. The following year, on 30 September 1969, the SRF status of the Forty-fifth Infantry Brigade was phased out as part of an overall army restructuring.[21]

The United States withdrew from its involvement in Vietnam in 1972 and the regular army changed to an all-volunteer concept in 1973. In line with this policy, Secretary of Defense Melvin Laird greatly increased the role of the National Guard in America's defense posture in lieu of conscription. Beginning in November of 1970, the National Guard, regular army, and army reserve were combined into a "one army" or "total force" concept.[22]

Military strategists recognized that the luxury of an extended period of mobilization, in which the regular army could be strengthened by the draft, would no longer be present. With this line of planning, the Department of Defense announced an increase in the readiness, reliability, and timely responsiveness of the nation's National Guard units, and an increase in priority for the updating of equipment and material. This made the National Guard an integral part of America's national security and made it available to meet early military requirements.[23]

As the Oklahoma National Guard entered a new era as a full partner in America's defense

readiness, Major General LaVern E. Weber, Oklahoma's adjutant-general since 8 March 1965, was named director of the Army National Guard in the National Guard Bureau in October of 1971. Later, in July of 1974, he became chief of the National Guard Bureau, and in June, 1979, he became the second former Oklahoma national guardsman to be promoted to lieutenant general. Weber had enlisted in the U.S. Marines in 1943 while attending the University of Oklahoma, and, after completing officers candidate school, was commissioned a second lieutenant on 21 November 1945. Three years later, he joined the Oklahoma National Guard at the request of then Adjutant-General Roy W. Kenney.[24]

A month later Weber received a commission as second lieutenant in the Oklahoma Army National Guard and was given command of Headquarters Company, 180th Infantry. Called to active duty during the Korean War, he served with the Second Battalion of the 180th and was promoted to major. In 1952 he returned to the Oklahoma National Guard and held a number of positions in the division before becoming chief of staff in 1964. He was named Oklahoma's adjutant-general in March of 1965, and two years later in December, 1967, received federal recognition as a major general. Weber previously had served on the Army Reserve Forces Policy Committee and the Reserve Forces Policy Board of the Secretary of Defense. He also served as a member of the executive council of the National

The author, Specialist Fourth Class Kenny A. Franks, Co. C, 120th Engineers, at Annual Field Training, Camp Gruber, Oklahoma, in 1971. Removal of enlisted men's insignia from the sleeves to the shirt collar was a modification of the uniform resulting from the conflict in Vietnam. Officers' rank had always been worn on their shirt collars, a fact quickly learned by the Viet Cong and North Vietnamese, who looked for the collar insignia when picking their targets. Placing their rank on their collars for both enlisted men and officers made it more difficult for the enemy to distinguish officers and enlisted men in combat. *Courtesy Forty-fifth Infantry Division Museum.*

Guard Association of the United States between 1966 and 1968, and received the association's distinguished service medal for heading an ad hoc committee on the purposes and organization of the nation's National Guard.[25]

Weber was replaced by Major General David C. Matthews, the former commander of the Forty-fifth Infantry Brigade. Matthews served as adjutant-general from 1 October 1971 until 12 January 1975. During Matthews's tenure, the army, after determining that "battalions and brigades had a higher potential for early deployment" than divisions, began training individual National Guard battalions to deploy as part of regular army divisions. Likewise, National Guard brigades were prepared for early deployment to trouble spots around the world. The total regular army, reserve army, and National Guard troops available under this plan were to be organized into sixteen regular army and eight National Guard divisions. Within these twenty-four divisions, 80 percent of the affiliated units and 46 percent of the total combat force was represented by the National Guard.[26]

According to Weber and Morgan, one of the greatest problems facing the National Guard in the 1970s and 1980s was a drop in enlistments. During the Vietnam War the National Guard had functioned in a different environment. Where previously the makeup of the National Guard had been that of volunteers who wanted to serve, during the Vietnam conflict many young men joined the National Guard to escape the draft. As a result the National Guard "forgot how to recruit," and once the draft was dropped, the National Guard had to relearn how to attract volunteers. It was not until 1979 that the National Guard registered its first net gain in manpower after five successive years of net losses. By 1980, though, National Guard enlistments were once again on the upswing, and, according to Adjutant-General Morgan, in 1981 the Oklahoma National Guard was approaching a net gain in manpower of seven hundred.[27]

On 13 January 1975 Major General John Coffey, Jr. was named adjutant-general and remained in the post until 19 November 1978. On the following day, Major General Robert M. Morgan, Jr. was named to the position by Governor David Boren. Morgan had started his military career in 1953, at the age of eighteen, as a private in the Medical Company, 180th Infantry. After spending twenty-one months on active duty from 1955 to 1957, he returned to the Oklahoma National Guard, completed the army's ten series, and received his commission. Originally assigned as a second lieutenant to A Company, First Battle Group, 279th Infantry, Morgan served in a variety of company command and staff assignments with the Second Battalion, 279th Infantry until 1 February 1968. On that date, he was trans-

Firing high explosive rounds from a 90-mm. antitank weapon during the 1978 annual field training held at Fort Chaffee, Arkansas. *Courtesy Forty-fifth Infantry Division Museum.*

ferred to the 120th Supply and Service Battalion, and held a series of unit commands and staff and command battalion positions until he was assigned as comptroller of the Headquarters-Headquarters Detachment, Oklahoma Army National Guard, in 1977. Sixteen months later, in the fall of 1978, he was appointed the twelfth adjutant-general of Oklahoma since statehood.[28]

With the greater dependence upon the National Guard in time of emergencies, both Coffey and Morgan were especially concerned with maintaining the highest degree of readiness. At the same time, the fighting capabilities of Oklahoma guardsmen were greatly increased. A highlight of this program occurred in the summer of 1977 when the Second Battalion, 180th Infantry became the first reserve unit assigned the XBGM-71A TOW missile.[29]

A "tube launched, optically tracked, wire-guided" antitank missile, the TOW was designed to offset the superiority of Communist-bloc countries in armored forces. To qualify the troops in its handling, a special intensified program was conducted at Fort Benning, Georgia, in July of that year. So successful was the adaption of Oklahoma's guardsmen to the TOW concept that, according to Major General Morgan, the unit is considered fully combat-capable. Under the army's Capstone concept, the guardsmen would be used to reinforce the regular army in the front lines. In addition, the Oklahoma TOW units are in line to receive the new ad-

vanced infantry fighting vehicle, currently under development, which will greatly increase their combat capabilities.[30]

In 1978, Morgan said, the National Guard began training with first-line regular army troops, and the following year units of the Oklahoma National Guard, that is, the 445th Military Police Company, conducted its annual training in Germany. Computer-assisted war games have been conducted by various National Guard staffs to increase their proficiency. By 1979, 28 percent of the army's 105-mm. gun tanks, 31 percent of all aircraft, 35 percent of tube artillery, and 33 percent of all M113 armored personnel carriers were in the National Guard's inventory.[31]

In fiscal year 1980, more than seven thousand national guardsmen from across America trained in Europe under the army's OCONUS (Outside Continental Limits of the United States) training program. Many of the OCONUS troops were Oklahoma guardsmen, half of which were "considered essential in the first 30 days of war." In addition, portions of the Forty-fifth's MPs were sent to Panama for OCONUS training.[32]

In 1980 one-third of the army's combat divisions, more than half of its artillery battalions, 29 percent of the standard aviation assets, more than 70 percent of the army's separate brigades, 60 percent of its armored cavalry regiments, and one-third of the special forces groups were in the nation's National Guard. Four National Guard brigades had been designated to deploy as part of regular army divisions, and eight of the army's twenty-four divisions were National Guard units. Of the total major combat units of the United States Army, two—the Forty-fifth Separate Infantry Brigade and the Forty-fifth Field Artillery Brigade—were part of the Oklahoma National Guard.[33]

By 1980 modernization of equipment had reached the point that 97 percent of the National Guard's materiel was considered deployable. The National Guard was no longer equipped with hand-me-downs from the regular army. Instead, under the total force concept, the guardsmen utilize the same equipment as their regular army counterparts. In fact, in some instances the regular army borrows equipment from National Guard units to conduct training exercises.[34]

At the same time that the National Guard was given a greater burden of America's defense, it was called upon to assume another role, that of controlling civil disorder. In the late 1960s, when much of the nation was being subjected to antiwar marches and campus protests, the National Guard was relied on time and again to reinforce local police as an emergency law enforcement agency. Nationwide, between 1965 and 1969, national guardsmen were called to duty 242 times for civil disturbance duty. In addition, much of their training schedule was given over to riot control. Although no major civil disorders or campus riots occurred in Oklahoma during this period, when campus unrest threatened Governor Dewey Bartlett placed several hundred guardsmen on training alert between 5 and 9 May and on 11 May 1970, and warned local students that he would not condone violence.[35]

The situation was more critical when the inmates of the Oklahoma State Penitentiary in McAlester rioted on Friday, 27 July 1973, a week before the Forty-fifth Infantry Brigade and its support units were scheduled to attend annual training at Fort Carson, Colorado. The trouble began in the prison mess hall during lunch, when between twenty-five and thirty inmates seized several guards and began urging the other inmates to riot. Within a short time many of the prison's buildings were on fire, and the situation was beyond the control of prison guards as about six hundred inmates gained control of the inner

Air national guardsmen deploying for riot duty at the Oklahoma State Penitentiary in July, 1973. *Courtesy Forty-fifth Infantry Division Museum.*

prison grounds. To help the prison's guards, Highway Patrol officers and local police patrolled the prison walls, and between forty and sixty MPs from the local 445th Military Police Company were quickly ordered to the prison.[36]

Realizing that the available manpower was unable to prevent the taking of additional hostages, Warden Park Anderson requested additional National Guard units to help restore order. Responding immediately, the adjutant-general began gathering troops. Throughout Friday night and the following day guardsmen arrived at the prison until nearly one thousand men were on duty, including the First Battalion, 180th Infantry; the 2120th Supply and Services Battalion; Company B (Medical), 700th Support Battalion; the 745th Military Police Company; and units of the 445th Aviation Company. As quickly as they

Flak-jacketed, riot-equipped Oklahoma national guardsmen patrolling the burned-out state prison during the July, 1973, riot. *Courtesy Forty-fifth Infantry Division Museum.*

arrived the men were briefed, issued live ammunition, and hurried to the prison's walls.[37]

Early the next morning, helicopters were sent over the prison yard to drop tear gas canisters and to place police officers and guardsmen atop buildings from which they could cover the rioters. At the same time, the First Battalion, 180th Infantry, under the command of Lieutenant Colonel Buster Smith, who later rose to the rank of brigadier general and commanded the Forty-fifth Infantry Brigade, seized the prison rodeo grounds and began preparations for entering the prison yard. Just as the guardsmen were ready to move against the rioters, the prisoners set fire to debris piled along the 20-feet-high chain-link gate leading into the prison grounds, thus blocking the guardsmen. Although the sortie was postponed, the rioters, knowing they could not keep the guardsmen out indefinitely, requested several National Guard noncommissioned officers to act as negotiators between themselves and prison officials.[38]

The negotiators secured the release of the rioters' hostages, and, in exchange for withdrawing the troops from the rodeo grounds, the seven hundred nonrioting inmates were allowed to seek shelter there and in the prison's industrial grounds. Once the nonviolent inmates were segregated, medics were sent to treat those who had been injured in the fighting. Although the situation had calmed somewhat, that afternoon renewed rioting broke out inside the prison. The next morning, on Sunday, more national guardsmen were deposited on rooftops, while others swept through the cell blocks forcing the remaining prisoners into the prison yard. Once the cell blocks were cleared, workmen began repairing the locks on individual cells. Other guardsmen protected firefighters attempting to extinguish the many fires.[39]

At 11:00 A.M. on Sunday, several MPs and Highway Patrol officers, supported by an armored personnel carrier, entered the prison yard and began pushing the more violent rioters toward the southeast corner of the prison and the other inmates toward the rodeo grounds. At the same time a cell-by-cell search for weapons was launched. As some prisoners were returned to the cell blocks, national guardsmen were assigned to guard them. It was not an easy task for the only thing separating the troops from the inmates was one row of bars. Worse still was guard duty in the prison yard, where only a hurriedly built, high chain-link fence and barricade stood between the guards and prisoners.[40]

Although order was being restored, there was still the problem of getting the nonrioters back into their cells along with the rioters. Moreover, the presence of a large number of troops was needed to prevent renewed violence. On Monday, 30 July, the First Battalion, 180th was relieved by the 120th Engineer Battalion; the 2120th Supply and Services Battalion was replaced by the First Battalion, 158th Field Artillery; and Company B (Medical), 700th Support Battalion was exchanged for the 145th Medical Company, 120th Medical Battalion. The troops again were rotated on 1 August 1973 when the First Battalion, 171st Field Artillery and the First

Battalion, 189th Field Artillery relieved the First Battalion, 158th Field Artillery and the 120th Engineers. Their medical platoons replaced the 145th Medics. Searchlight units from the 138th Fighter Squadron of the Air National Guard also were activated.[41]

Complete order was restored on 4 August, when the guardsmen and civilian authorities swept through the last of the rioters and forced them back into their cells. Forming a skirmish line that moved west to east through the rubble, the flak-jacketed, visor-helmeted guardsmen pushed the rioters into the rotunda between cell blocks. Although medics stood by in case of trouble, they were not needed.

Once the rioters had been locked up, the guardsmen made one final sweep through the prison yard tossing CS grenades. CS is a powerful riot-control agent that produces the same effects as tear gas—reactions such as involuntary closing of the eyes, nasal drip, severe coughing, tightness of the chest, and difficulty in breathing. The CS grenades were thrown into burrows, manholes, and bunkers the inmates had built during their week of rioting. A nearly completed tunnel was discovered at the north edge of the prison, and if the guardsmen had not cleared the area on that day, one official expressed the fear that there would have been a mass escape that night. The last guardsmen finally were withdrawn from the prison on 24 September 1975, after putting down the worst prison riot in Oklahoma history without causing a single death.[42]

Within five years, in the spring of 1980, portions of the Oklahoma National Guard again were involved in riot duty. When America threw open its doors to those Cubans wishing to flee Fidel Castro's regime, thousands of refugees made their way to Florida where they quickly overtaxed existing facilities. To relieve the pressure, the federal government moved nearly twenty thousand Cubans from Florida to Fort Chaffee, Arkansas. Innumerable delays in resettling the refugees, coupled with the resentment of many local inhabitants to such an influx of outsiders, produced a volatile situation at the post that threatened to erupt into violence.[43]

Nine days after the Cubans were shipped to Fort Chaffee, units of the Oklahoma National Guard—the First Battalion, 179th Infantry, Forty-fifth Infantry Brigade; the Forty-fifth Artillery

Among the members of the Judge Advocate General section of the Oklahoma National Guard called to active duty to provide legal counsel during the Fort Chaffee Cuban exile riot of 1980 were, *from left to right:* Specialist Fifth Class Mark L. ("Beau") Cantrell, later second lieutenant; Lieutenant Colonel John Howard, Oklahoma's Judge Advocate General; and Captain Tom Walker. *Courtesy Forty-fifth Infantry Division Museum.*

Brigade; several units of the Forty-fifth Troop Command, and the Judge Advocate General (JAG) Section, Headquarters, Headquarters Detachment—arrived at the post for their annual summer training. Because the Cubans were housed in the post's barracks, some of the guardsmen bivouacked in the field or stayed at a "tent city" west of the refugee internment area. The First Battalion, 179th Infantry, however, was located along Donahue Ridge, just south and west of the Cuban internment area, and the JAG Section, commanded by Lieutenant Colonel John Howard, which had been detailed to serve as legal counsel for both the Oklahoma, Arkansas, and Puerto Rican national guardsmen and federal troops ordered to Fort Chaffee to support the refugee operation, were housed within the Cuban internment area.[44]

According to Specialist Fifth Class, later second lieutenant, Mark L. Cantrell, of the JAG Section, who was sergeant of the guard in the internment area on the day the riot started, the Oklahomans in the JAG unit were the only legal advisers available to the military during most of the Cuban operation. They were confronted with a variety of problems, the main one being the question of who had jurisdiction over the refugees, local or federal authorities. Because of the jurisdictional question, the Oklahoma guardsmen, with the exception of the JAG Section, which was working with the refugees, were ordered "not to come into contact with the Cubans under any circumstances," and if a confrontation developed, "[use only] the minimum force necessary to protect lives and property."[45]

On 26 May 1980 the First Battalion, 179th Infantry was undergoing its annual field training exercise. The battalion commander, Lieutenant Colonel Peter E. Wheeler, had gone to Fort Smith to visit a guardsman who had become ill, and the battalion's executive officer, Major Grant Cable, was commanding the troops. Almost without warning the Cubans rioted.[46]

At the time Major Cable was inspecting the battalion's mortar and training area near Donahue Ridge. Major Timothy E. Martin, the operations and training officer for the First Battalion, was in the field with the troops supervising the training. Martin first learned of the riot over the battalion radio network. The initial reports coming from the battalion's ammunition supply point were sketchy.[47]

The supply point, which stored the 179th's supply of ammunition for summer training, was located in an open field of approximately five acres, on the south of the Cuban internment area and a mile east of Donahue Ridge. South of the ammunition supply point was a road that led away from the post. The supply area was guarded by a detachment of twelve guardsmen and surrounded by a barbed-wire fence. The guards were armed but had not been issued ammunition.[48]

When the riot broke out, many of the Cubans began to try to leave by the road leading off the post. At first it appeared that they were trying to seize the ammunition and weapons. Reacting to the threat, Major Martin contacted Lieutenant Colonel Wheeler, who had returned to his command when he learned of the riot, and recommended that the troops in the field stand down and return to their bivouac on Donahue Ridge, northwest of the supply point and near the refugee internment area. Such a move would place the troops in a position to respond quickly to any situation in the internment area or near the ammunition supply if the need arose.[49]

Wheeler replied that because many of his staff were in the field with the troops, he was forming a temporary staff from available officers. Martin should hold his position in the field training area. As more reports arrived, it became apparent that the Cubans were not attacking the supply point but were simply trying to flee off post. Later a detachment of military police and federal marshals reinforced the supply point guard, and Lieutenant Colonel Wheeler ordered the guardsmen in the vicinity of Donahue Ridge to establish a security perimeter around the battalion's bivouac.[50]

At the same time the 179th's ground surveillance radar sections were ordered to establish a ground radar perimeter around the bivouac area. Throughout the night, as Cubans attempted to escape the internment area, the radar discovered them and directed the 179th's reconnaissance platoon to their location. Once captured, the Cubans were detained for federal marshals. The following morning, May 27, Major Martin and those guardsmen who had been participating in the field exercise also were moved to Donahue Ridge to reinforce the perimeter.[51]

The activity of the guardsmen helped stabilize the situation. Once the initial rioting was contained, the guardsmen completed their two weeks of training and returned home. On the day the Oklahoma guardsmen left, the Cubans rioted again and burned several buildings on the post; however, this and other Cuban riots were contained by the regular army troops, the Arkansas and Puerto Rico national guardsmen, and by federal officers.[52]

In addition to national defense and riot duty, Oklahoma guardsmen assisted in civil disaster aid on many occasions in the post-Korean War era. Often the assistance was given spontaneously. For example, in February of 1972, two Oklahoma guardsmen of the Forty-fifth Infantry Brigade, Aviation Section, Captain Robert C. Armstrong and Specialist Fifth Class Gerald E. Taylor, were flying their OH-23D helicopter across northeastern Oklahoma when they spotted a burning house near Vinita. Landing near a toll gate on the Will Rogers Turnpike, they notified the local fire department and then flew back to the burning structure to search for possible victims. Once Armstrong and Taylor determined that the house was unoccupied, they saved as much furniture and other possessions as they could.[53]

A member of the Forty-fifth Field Artillery Group helping to clean up after rampaging floodwaters swept through a part of Enid, Oklahoma in October, 1973. *Courtesy Forty-fifth Infantry Division Museum.*

Most often, though, the guardsmen responded to help others recover from some of Oklahoma's severe weather. In early 1973, when a mobile home park near Ada was swept by a tornado, the local guardsmen of the Headquarters and Headquarters Company, 120th Support and Service Battalion, quickly began patrolling the area to protect property and aid victims. Later, on 10 October, when a record sixteen-inch rainfall hit five Oklahoma counties, the National Guard was called to help. For four days, members of the Forty-fifth Field Artillery Group evacuated Enid residents stranded by rampaging floodwaters that drove two thousand persons from their homes. At the same time nearly a thousand bales of hay were dropped from helicopters to cattle stranded by high waters. The following month, on 19 November, tornadoes struck Moore, Blackwell, Blanchard, and Tonkawa, and several guardsmen were called upon to provide security and traffic control.[54]

Flooding was again the crisis in November of 1974 when guardsmen were called upon to help the residents of Chandler, Kingfisher, Guthrie, Yukon, Skiatook, and Sperry as the Cimarron

River spilled over its banks. A few months later, in February of 1975, the communities of Altus and Duncan were hit by tornadoes and the Tonkawa-Ponca City area was devastated by a snowstorm. Once more the National Guard rushed to the rescue. Again in April of 1981, when Bixby and Kiefer were struck by tornadoes, local guardsmen responded with badly needed aid. These are but a few examples of the many occasions throughout its history that the Oklahoma National Guard provided rescue forces to help local residents cope with natural disasters.[55]

In looking to the future of the National Guard in America's defense posture, both Lieutenant General Weber and Major General Morgan point out that the United States Constitution called for the establishment of community militias that could be used in times of national emergencies. Moreover, because these reserve forces would be controlled by the individual states, they served to offset any large regular army controlled by the federal government. The State National Guard units, then, are an important part of the checks and balances system of American government. Presently, under the strategy of the total force restructuring, in any future national emergency the country would rely on the National Guard and the army reserves as immediate backups for the regular army. As the result of this planning, by early 1981 70 percent of the nationwide National Guard was combat ready.[56]

According to Weber, many of the National Guard reorganizations of the 1960s and 1970s were in response to a changing national strategy and the development of new weapons systems. The most dramatic change resulted from the adaptation of nuclear weapons to the battlefield. In the future, the impact of further changing strategy and weapons systems is likely to be even greater.[57]

Weber believes that the principal concern of the National Guard in the early 1980s is not manpower but equipment. On a dollar-for-dollar basis, the National Guard has about 75 percent of the authorized equipment required for peacetime and 69 percent of the authorized equipment needed for war. There is not the same feeling of urgency for modernization in the Army National Guard as there is in the Air National Guard. Even so, Weber, Major General Styron, and Major General Daugherty, all former commanders of the Forty-fifth believe that the National Guard is the one military element that produces the greatest return for the amount of dollars invested of any under the U.S. Defense Department. The same sentiment is echoed by Major General Morgan, who points out that for approximately 5 percent of the nation's total defense budget the National Guard furnishes two-thirds of America's combat power.[58]

Just as important to the people of Oklahoma, Morgan stresses, is the economic impact of the state's 77 National Guard units, spread among 109 communities. To maintain these units, the Oklahoma legislature budgeted approximately $3 million in 1980-1981. In exchange, nearly $50 million was returned to the state's economy through local payrolls, purchases, and maintenance expenses. In many of Oklahoma's smaller towns the local National Guard unit is the community's largest industry. As a result, there are strong sentiments of local support, pride, and involvement across the state—support that has done much to help the Oklahoma National Guard attain the success it has enjoyed. It is this local support, according to Morgan, together

A member of the Second Battalion, 180th Infantry, TOW unit, the first reserve unit assigned the anti-tank weapon. Members of the unit also were issued experimental camouflage fatigues. Note the subdued Thunderbird shoulder patch, ordered reinstated in 1980. *Courtesy Forty-fifth Infantry Division Museum.*

with pride and tradition that make the Oklahoma National Guard a vital part of America's defense system and an integral part of Oklahoma's heritage.[59]

The preservation of this heritage is the goal of the Forty-fifth Infantry Division Museum. Although named for Oklahoma's Army National Guard division, the museum is concerned with the entire history of Oklahoma's citizen soldiers. The museum was initiated in 1967-1968 when a committee, chaired by Major General Daugherty, was appointed to gather artifacts and to investigate the possibility of establishing a permanent museum. Later the state legislature formally established the Forty-fifth Infantry Division Museum.[60]

Eventually, the Lincoln Park Armory in Okla-

A part of the Forty-fifth Infantry Division Museum in Oklahoma City, Oklahoma. *Courtesy Forty-fifth Infantry Division Museum.*

homa City was declared surplus, and the museum moved into the vacated structure. With the aid of state and private funding, and with the support of both the Forty-fifth Infantry Division Association and the National Guard Association of Oklahoma, the museum began to expand following a five-phase development plan. Phase I dealt with the renovation of the Lincoln Park Armory and the opening of the main gallery, which is dedicated to the chronological history of the citizen soldier in Oklahoma. Phase II was a continuation of exhibits in the Lincoln Park Armory, with rooms dedicated to the infantry and the artillery and a memorial chapel. Phase III was the renovation of a second nearby museum building for the supporting forces and vehicles. Phase IV called for connecting the first two buildings by a third structure, which also held the Jordan and Ruby Reaves Collection of Military Weapons and the Bill Mauldin Collection. Phase V was the development of an outdoors display of military weapons, vehicles, and aircraft, on 12.65 acres of adjacent land. When the entire project is completed, Oklahoma will have one of the finest military history museums in America.[61]

TABLES OF ORGANIZATION: OKLAHOMA NATIONAL GUARD

Throughout its history, in both war and peace, the Oklahoma National Guard was constantly undergoing expansion or reorganization. For example, during one period of the Korean Conflict there were two Forty-fifth Infantry Divisions, one serving in Korea and one in Oklahoma. These lists present the general table of organization for the Oklahoma National Guard, or the parent organization of which they were a part at the time; however, there may be other units than those indicated.

NINETIETH INFANTRY OR T-O DIVISION
ca. 1918

Division Headquarters
179th Infantry Brigade
   Headquarters
   357th Infantry Regiment
   358th Infantry Regiment
   344th Machine Gun Battalion
180th Infantry Brigade
   Headquarters
   359th Infantry Regiment
   360 Infantry Regiment
   345th Machine Gun Battalion
343rd Field Artillery Regiment
344th Field Artillery Regiment
345th Field Artillery Regiment
343rd Machine Gun Battalion
315th Engineer Regiment
315th Train Headquarters
315th Ammunition Train
315th Supply Train
315th Sanitary Train
315th Field Signal Battalion
Ninetieth Division Military Police Company
315th Mobile Ordnance Repair Shop
315th Mobile Veterinary Section
Sanitary Squad No. 40
Mobile Field Laboratory
Salvage Unit No. 310
Machine Shop Truck Unit No. 391
Sales Commissary Unit No. 17

THIRTY-SIXTH INFANTRY DIVISION
ca. 1918

Division Headquarters
Seventy-first Infantry Brigade
   141st Infantry Regiment
   142nd Infantry Regiment
   132nd Machine Gun Battalion
Seventy-second Infantry Brigade
   143rd Infantry Regiment
   144th Infantry Regiment
   133rd Machine Gun Battalion
61st Field Artillery Brigade
   131st Field Artillery Regiment
   132nd Field Artillery Regiment
   133rd Field Artillery Regiment
   111th Trench Mortar Battery
111th Engineer Regiment
131st Machine Gun Battalion
111th Field Signal Battalion

OKLAHOMA NATIONAL GUARD
1923-1941

State Staff
State Detachment
Forty-fifth Infantry Division (square division)
   Headquarters
   Eighty-ninth Infantry Brigade
      157th Infantry Regiment
      158th Infantry Regiment

Ninetieth Infantry Brigade
  179th Infantry Regiment
  180th Infantry Regiment
Seventieth Field Artillery Brigade
  160th Field Artillery Regiment
  189th Field Artillery Regiment
  Forty-fifth Tank Battalion
  Forty-fifth Signal Battalion
  120th Ordnance Battalion
  120th Medical Regiment
  120th Engineer Regiment
  120th Transportation Regiment
  Forty-fifth Military Police Company
125th Observation Squadron

OKLAHOMA NATIONAL GUARD
1941 to 1945

Headquarters Headquarters Detachment
Forty-fifth Infantry Division (triangular division)
  Headquarters
  157th Infantry Regiment
  179th Infantry Regiment
  180th Infantry Regiment
  Forty-fifth Divisional Artillery
    158th Field Artillery Battalion
    160th Field Artillery Battalion
    171st Field Artillery Battalion
    189th Field Artillery Battalion
  120th Engineer Battalion
  120th Medical Battalion
  120th Transportation Battalion
  645th Tank Battalion (Attached)
  Forty-fifth Military Police Company
  Forty-fifth Signal Company
  120th Ordnance Company

OKLAHOMA NATIONAL GUARD
ca. 1947

Headquarters Detachment
Forty-fifth Infantry Division
  Headquarters and Headquarters Company (including band)
    179th Infantry Regiment
      First Battalion
      Second Battalion

  Third Battalion
  180th Infantry Regiment
    First Battalion
    Second Battalion
    Third Battalion
  279th Infantry Regiment
    First Battalion
    Second Battalion
    Third Battalion
  Forty-fifth Divisional Artillery
    158th Field Artillery Battalion
    160th Field Artillery Battalion
    171st Field Artillery Battalion
    189th Field Artillery Battalion
    145th Antiaircraft Artillery Battalion
  245th Tank Battalion
  120th Engineer Battalion
  120th Medical Battalion
  Forty-fifth Administration Company
  Forty-fifth Replacement Company
  Forty-fifth Signal Company
  Forty-fifth Military Police Company
  120th Transportation Company
  700rd Ordnance Company
125th Fighter Squadron
185th Fighter Squadron

FORTY-FIFTH INFANTRY DIVISION
ca. 1951

Headquarters and Headquarters Company
179th Infantry Regiment
180th Infantry Regiment
279th Infantry Regiment
Divisional Artillery
  158th Field Artillery Battalion
  160th Field Artillery Battalion
  171st Field Artillery Battalion
  189th Field Artillery Battalion
  145th Antiaircraft Artillery Battalion
245th Tank Battalion
120th Engineer Battalion
120th Medical Battalion
Forty-fifth Reconnaissance Company
Forty-fifth Quartermaster Company
Forty-fifth Signal Company
Forty-fifth Military Police Company
Forty-fifth Replacement Company
Forty-fifth Band
700rd Ordnance and Maintenance Company

FORTY-FIFTH DIVISION INFANTRY REGIMENT
ca. 1951

Headquarters and Headquarters Company
First Battalion
    Headquarters and Headquarters Company
    Company A
    Company B
    Company C
    Company D
Second Battalion
    Headquarters and Headquarters Company
    Company E
    Company F
    Company G
    Company H
Third Battalion
    Headquarters and Headquarters Company
    Company I
    Company K
    Company L
    Company M
Service Company
Heavy Mortar Company
Tank Company
Medical Company

OKLAHOMA ARMY NATIONAL GUARD
ca. 1982

Headquarters and Headquarters Detachment, Oklahoma Army National Guard
    145th Public Affairs Detachment
    145th Band
Forty-fifth Infantry Brigade
    Headquarters and Headquarters Company
    First Battalion, 179th Infantry
    First Battalion, 180th Infantry
    First Battalion, 279th Infantry
    First Battalion, 160th Field Artillery
    700th Support Battalion
        Company A, Administration
        Company B, Medical
        Company C, Supply and Services
        Company D, Ordnance
    Company E, 145th Cavalry
    245th Engineer Company

Forty-fifth Artillery Brigade
    Headquarters and Headquarters Battery
    First Battalion, 158th Field Artillery
    First Battalion, 171st Field Artillery
    First Battalion, 189th Field Artillery
Forty-fifth Troop Command
    Headquarters and Headquarters Company
    Second Battalion, 179th Infantry
    Second Battalion, 180th Infantry (TOW)
    Second Battalion, 279th Infantry
    120th Medical Battalion
    120th Supply and Services Battalion
    120th Engineer Battalion
    120th Transportation Battalion
    Forty-fifth Military Police Battalion
    145th Aviation Battalion (Provisional)
    149th Ordnance Company
    Forty-fifth Support Center, Rear Area Operations
    Army National Guard Training Camp Detachment

OKLAHOMA AIR NATIONAL GUARD
ca. 1982

Headquarters Air National Guard
137th Tactical Airlift Wing
    Headquarters 137th Tactical Airlift Wing
    137th Consolidated Aircraft Maintenance Squadron
    137th Combat Support Squadron
    137th Tactical Hospital
    137th Resources Management Squadron
    137th Aerial Port Flight
    137th Civil Engineering Flight
    137th Weapons Security Flight
    137th Communications Flight (support)
    185th Tactical Airlift Squadron
    205th Electronics Installation Squadron
    219th Electronics Installation Squadron
138th Tactical Fighter Group
    Headquarters 138th Tactical Fighter Group
    125th Tactical Fighter Squadron
    125th Weather Flight (fixed)
    138th Resources Management Squadron
    138th Communications Flight (support)
    138th Weapons Security Flight
    138th Civil Engineer Flight
    138th Tactical Clinic
    138th Combat Support Squadron
    138th Consolidated Aircraft Maintenance Squadron

NOTES

1

THE TERRITORIAL MILITIA

1. Gaston Litton, *History of Oklahoma at the Golden Anniversary of Statehood,* vol. 1, pp. 241-85, 379-90.

2. Ibid., pp. 451-55.

3. Ibid., vol. 2, p. 415; Will T. Little, L. G. Pitman, and R. J. Barker, *The Statutes of Oklahoma, 1890,* p. 692.

4. Little, Pitman, and Barker, *The Statutes of Oklahoma, 1890,* pp. 692-93; Litton, *History of Oklahoma,* vol. 2, p. 415.

5. Litton, *History of Oklahoma,* vol. 2, p. 415.

6. Ibid., vol. 1, pp. 458-66; Territory of Oklahoma, *Session Laws of 1895* (n.p., 1895), pp. 165-66, 173-74.

7. Territory of Oklahoma, *Session Laws of 1895,* pp. 165, 169-71.

8. Ibid., pp. 166-68.

9. Ibid., pp. 166, 169.

10. Ibid., pp. 169-70, 172-73.

11. Ibid., pp. 167, 170.

12. Ibid., pp. 167-68, 170-71, 173.

13. Ibid., p. 173.

14. Ibid., p. 168.

15. Ibid., pp. 171-72.

16. Ibid., p. 172.

17. Ibid., pp. 167-68.

18. Ibid., pp. 171, 174.

19. Ibid., p. 173.

20. Litton, *History of Oklahoma,* vol. 2, p. 415; Joseph B. Thoburn, *A Standard History of Oklahoma,* vol. 2, p. 821.

21. Thoburn, *Standard History of Oklahoma,* vol. 2, p. 821; Litton, *History of Oklahoma,* vol. 2, p. 415; Woodrow Wilson, *A History of the American People,* vol. 5, pp. 274-75; Theodore Roosevelt, *The Rough Riders,* pp. 6-7, 265-69; U.S., War Department, Report of the Inspector General, November 1, 1898, *Annual Report, 1898,* House Doc. 2, 55th Cong., 3d Sess., 1898, p. 564; U.S., War Department, Annual Report of the Adjutant-General to the Major-General Commanding the Army, October 25, 1899, Report of the Major-General Commanding the Army, 3 parts, *Annual Report, 1899,* House Doc. 2, 56th Cong., 1st Sess., 1899, pt. 1, p. 364.

22. U.S., War Department, Annual Report of the Adju-tant-General to the Major-General Commanding the Army, October 25, 1899, *Annual Report, 1899,* pt. 1, p. 364; U.S., War Department, Report of the Inspector General, No-vember 1, 1898, *Annual Report, 1898,* p. 564; Wilson, *His-tory of the American People,* vol. 5, pp. 274-75; Thoburn, *Standard History of Oklahoma,* vol. 2, p. 821; Litton, *His-tory of Oklahoma,* vol. 2, p. 415.

23. Litton, *History of Oklahoma,* vol. 2, p. 415; Roose-velt, *Rough Riders,* pp. 6-46, 54, 265-69; Reader's Com-ments, Oklahoma Military Collection, Archives, Oklahoma Heritage Association, Oklahoma City, Oklahoma (here-after cited as OMC).

24. Roosevelt, *Rough Riders,* pp. 6-46, 54, 265-69, pp. 46-70; Litton, *History of Oklahoma,* vol. 2, p. 415; Tho-burn, *Standard History of Oklahoma,* vol. 1, p. 821; U.S., War Department, [Major] General [William R.] Shaffer's Report, September 13, 1898, *Annual Report, 1898,* p. 151; U.S., War Department, [Major] General [Joseph] Wheeler's Report, June 26, 1898, *Annual Report, 1898,* p. 163; U.S., War Department, Colonel Leonard Wood to Adjutant-General, July 6, 1898, *Annual Report, 1898,* pp. 342-43.

25. Wood to Adjutant-General, July 6, 1898, pp. 342-43; Thoburn, *Standard History of Oklahoma,* vol. 1, p. 821; Litton, *History of Oklahoma,* vol. 2, p. 415; [Major] General [William R.] Shaffer's Report, September 13, 1898, *Annual Report, 1898,* p. 151; [Major] General [Joseph] Wheeler's Report, June 26, 1898, p. 163.

26. Roosevelt, *Rough Riders,* pp. 73-82; U.S., War De-partment, Brigadier General S.B.M. Young to Adjutant-General, Cavalry Division, June 29, 1898, *Annual Report, 1898,* pp. 331-32; Reader's Comments, OMC.

27. Young to Adjutant-General, Cavalry Division, June 29, 1898, *Annual Report, 1898,* pp. 331-32; Roosevelt, *Rough Riders,* pp. 73-87.

28. Roosevelt, *Rough Riders,* pp. 73-87, pp. 84-87; Young to Adjutant-General, Cavalry Division, June 29, 1898, *An-nual Report, 1898,* pp. 332-33.

29. Young to Adjutant-General, Cavalry Division, June 29, 1898, *Annual Report, 1898,* pp. 332-33; Roosevelt, *Rough Riders,* pp. 87-104.

30. Roosevelt, *Rough Riders,* pp. 102-15; Young to Ad-jutant-General, Cavalry Division, June 19, 1898, *Annual Report, 1898,* pp. 332-33; U.S., War Department, Briga-dier General Leonard Wood to Adjutant-General, Cavalry Division, July 22, 1898, *Annual Report, 1898,* p. 341.

31. Wood to Adjutant-General, Cavalry Division, July 22, 1898, *Annual Report, 1898,* p. 341; Roosevelt, *Rough Riders,* pp. 112-15.

32. Roosevelt, *Rough Riders,* pp. 115-19; U.S., War Department, Brigadier General H. W. Lawton to Adjutant-General, Fifth Army Corps, July 3, 1898, *Annual Report, 1898,* p. 378; Colonel Leonard Wood to Adjutant-General, Fifth Army Corps, July 6, 1898, *Annual Report, 1898,* pp. 342-43; Wood to Adjutant-General, Cavalry Division, July 22, 1898, *Annual Report, 1898,* pp. 341-42.

33. Wood to Adjutant-General, Cavalry Division, July 22, 1898, *Annual Report, 1898,* pp. 341-42; Roosevelt, *Rough Riders,* pp. 119-22; Wood to Adjutant-General, Fifth Army Corps, July 6, 1898, *Annual Report, 1898,* pp. 341-42.

34. Wood to Adjutant-General, Fifth Army Corps, July 6, 1898, *Annual Report, 1898,* pp. 341-42; Roosevelt, *Rough Riders,* pp. 122-33; Wood to Adjutant-General, Cavalry Division, July 22, 1898, *Annual Report, 1898,* pp. 341-42; U.S., War Department, Lieutenant Colonel Theodore Roosevelt to Colonel Leonard Wood, July 4, 1898, *Annual Report, 1898,* pp. 684-86.

35. Roosevelt to Wood, July 4, 1898, *Annual Report, 1898,* pp. 684-86; Roosevelt, *Rough Riders,* pp. 133-43; Wood to Adjutant-General, Fifth Army Corps, July 6, 1898, *Annual Report, 1898,* pp. 342-43; Wood to Adjutant-General, Cavalry Division, July 22, 1898, *Annual Report, 1898,* pp. 341-42.

36. Wood to Adjutant-General, Cavalry Division, July 22, 1898, *Annual Report, 1898,* pp. 341-42; Wood to Adjutant-General, Fifth Army Corps, July 6, 1898, *Annual Report, 1898,* pp. 342-43; Roosevelt to Wood, July 4, 1898, *Annual Report, 1898,* pp. 684-86; Roosevelt, *Rough Riders,* pp. 143-98; Wilson, *History of the American People,* vol. 5, p. 288.

37. Wilson, *History of the American People,* vol. 5, pp. 288-92; Roosevelt, *Rough Riders,* pp. 198-237; Annual Report of the Adjutant-General to the Major-General Commanding the Army, October 25, 1899, *Annual Report, 1899,* pt. 1, p. 369.

38. Annual Report of the Adjutant-General to the Major-General Commanding the Army, October 25, 1899, *Annual Report, 1899,* pt. 1, p. 364; Litton, *History of Oklahoma,* vol. 2, pp. 415-16; Wilson, *History of the American People,* vol. 5, p. 292; Thoburn, *Standard History of Oklahoma,* vol. 2, pp. 821-22.

39. Thoburn, *Standard History of Oklahoma,* vol. 2, pp. 821-22; Annual Report of the Adjutant General to the Major-General Commanding the Army, October 25, 1899, *Annual Report, 1899,* pt. 1, p. 369; U.S., War Department, Annual Report to the Adjutant-General to the Major-General Commanding the Army, October 17, 1898, *Annual Report, 1898,* pt. 1, p. 5; Litton, *History of Oklahoma,* vol. 2, p. 416.

40. Litton, *History of Oklahoma,* vol. 2, pp. 416-17; Wilson, *History of the American People,* vol. 5, p. 275; Little, Pitman, and Barker, *Statutes of Oklahoma, 1890,* pp. 692-93; Territory of Oklahoma, *Session Laws of 1895,* pp. 165-74.

2
THE MEXICAN BORDER

1. Gaston Litton, *History of Oklahoma at the Golden Anniversary of Statehood,* vol. 1, p. 528; State of Oklahoma, *Session Laws of 1907-1908* (Guthrie: Oklahoma Printing Company, 1908), pp. 562-72.

2. State of Oklahoma, *Session Laws of 1907-1908,* pp. 562, 572.

3. Ibid., p. 565.

4. Ibid., pp. 564, 566.

5. Ibid., pp. 568-70.

6. Ibid.

7. Ibid., pp. 563-65.

8. Litton, *History of Oklahoma,* vol. 1, p. 528; Angie Debo, *Road to Disappearance* (Norman: University of Oklahoma Press, 1941), p. 376.

9. Debo, *Road to Disappearance,* p. 375; Joseph B. Thoburn and Muriel H. Wright, *Oklahoma: A History of the State and Its People,* vol. 2, p. 618; Litton, *History of Oklahoma,* vol. 1, p. 528.

10. Litton, *History of Oklahoma,* vol. 1, p. 528; Debo, *Road to Disappearance,* p. 376.

11. Debo, *Road to Disappearance,* pp. 376-77; Litton, *History of Oklahoma,* vol. 1, pp. 528-29.

12. Litton, *History of Oklahoma,* vol. 1, pp. 528-29.

13. Litton, *History of Oklahoma,* vol. 1, pp. 529-30; Ralph L. Jones and Colonel John H. McCasland (Ret.), Notes, Oklahoma Military Collection, Archives, Oklahoma Heritage Association, Oklahoma City, Oklahoma (OMC).

14. U.S., *Statutes at Large,* vol. 39, National Defense Act of 1916, pp. 197-98.

15. Ibid., pp. 198-200.

16. Ibid., pp. 200-202.

17. Ibid., pp. 202-203.

18. Ibid., pp. 203-205.

19. Ibid., pp. 205-10.

20. Ibid., pp. 207-209.

21. Ibid., pp. 209-11.

22. Jim D. Hill, *The Minute Man in Peace and War,* pp. 221-22, 231.

23. Litton, *History of Oklahoma,* vol. 2, p. 416; Herbert M. Mason, Jr., *The Great Pursuit,* pp. 23-39.

24. Mason, *The Great Pursuit,* pp. 38-39.

25. Ibid., pp. 39-42.

26. Ibid., pp. 42-52.

27. Ibid.

28. Ibid., pp. 52-55.

29. Ibid., pp. 55-59.

30. Ibid., pp. 2-4, 59-64.

31. Ibid., pp. 4-21; Donald E. Houston, "The Oklahoma National Guard on the Mexican Border, 1916," *Chronicles of Oklahoma,* 53 (Winter, 1975-76):447.

32. Mason, *The Great Pursuit,* pp. 21-85.

33. Ibid., pp. 85-222; Litton, *History of Oklahoma,* vol. 2, p. 416; Houston, "The Oklahoma National Guard on the Mexican Border," pp. 447-48.

34. Houston, "The Oklahoma National Guard on the Mexican Border," pp. 447-48; Mason, *The Great Pursuit,* pp. 173-222; Litton, *History of Oklahoma,* vol. 2, p. 416.

35. Litton, *History of Oklahoma,* vol. 2, p. 416; Houston,

"The Oklahoma National Guard on the Mexican Border," pp. 447-49.

36. Houston, "The Oklahoma National Guard on the Mexican Border," pp. 447-49; Litton, *History of Oklahoma,* vol. 2, p. 416.

37. Litton, *History of Oklahoma,* vol. 2, p. 416; Houston, "The Oklahoma National Guard on the Mexican Border," pp. 447-49.

38. Houston, "The Oklahoma National Guard on the Mexican Border," pp. 448-53; Guy Nelson, *Thunderbird: A History of the 45th Infantry Division,* p. 5; Litton, *History of Oklahoma,* vol. 2, p. 416.

39. Houston, "The Oklahoma National Guard on the Mexican Border," pp. 453-56.

40. Ibid.

41. Ibid., pp. 456-57; Mason, *The Great Pursuit,* p. 222.

42. Mason, *The Great Pursuit,* p. 222; Houston, "The Oklahoma National Guard on the Mexican Border," pp. 456-57.

43. Houston, "The Oklahoma National Guard on the Mexican Border," pp. 456-57; Mason, *The Great Pursuit,* p. 222.

44. Houston, "The Oklahoma National Guard on the Mexican Border," pp. 457-59.

45. Ibid., p. 459.

46. Ibid.

47. Mason, *The Great Pursuit,* pp. 222-31.

48. Ibid., pp. 231-32.

49. Houston, "The Oklahoma National Guard on the Mexican Border," pp. 459-62; Nelson, *Thunderbird,* p. 5; Litton, *History of Oklahoma,* vol. 2, p. 416.

50. Mason, *The Great Pursuit,* pp. 233-34.

51. Houston, "The Oklahoma National Guard on the Mexican Border," pp. 459-62; Nelson, *Thunderbird,* p. 5; Litton, *History of Oklahoma,* vol. 2, p. 416.

52. Litton, *History of Oklahoma,* vol. 2, p. 416; Houston, "The Oklahoma National Guard on the Mexican Border," pp. 459-61; Nelson, *Thunderbird,* p. 5.

3
WORLD WAR I: THE THIRTY-SIXTH DIVISION

1. Gaston Litton, *History of Oklahoma at the Golden Anniversary of Statehood,* vol. 2, pp. 416-21; James G. Harbord, *American Army in France, 1917-1919,* pp. 1-16.

2. Harbord, *American Army in France, 1917-1919,* pp. 1-16; Litton, *History of Oklahoma,* vol. 2, pp. 416-21.

3. Maurice de Castelbled, *History of the A.E.F.,* pp. 103-104; Ben H. Chastaine, *Story of the 36th,* pp. 1-7; C. H. Barnes, *History of the 142nd Infantry of the Thirty-sixth Division,* pp. 1-14.

4. Barnes, *History of the 142nd,* pp. 1-14; de Castelbled, *History of the A.E.F.,* pp. 103-104; Chastaine, *Story of the 36th,* pp. 1-7.

5. Chastaine, *Story of the 36th,* pp. 8-15.

6. Ibid.; Barnes, *History of the 142nd Infantry,* p. 19.

7. Barnes, *History of the 142nd Infantry,* pp. 19-24; Chastaine, *Story of the 36th,* pp. 15-23.

8. Chastaine, *Story of the 36th,* pp. 23-33; Barnes, *History of the 142nd Infantry,* pp. 24-25.

9. Barnes, *History of the 142nd Infantry,* pp. 25-27; Chastaine, *Story of the 36th,* pp. 33-37.

10. Chastaine, *Story of the 36th,* pp. 37-44; Barnes, *History of the 142nd Infantry,* p. 27.

11. Barnes, *History of the 142nd Infantry,* pp. 27-28; Chastaine, *Story of the 36th,* pp. 44-56.

12. Chastaine, *Story of the 36th,* pp. 44-56, 251-57.

13. Ibid., pp. 56-74; Barnes, *History of the 142nd Infantry,* pp. 28-29.

14. Barnes, *History of the 142nd Infantry,* p. 29; Chastaine, *Story of the 36th,* p. 61; American Battle Monuments Commission, *American Armies and Battlefields in Europe,* p. 333; U.S., War Department, *Battle Participation of Organizations of the American Expeditionary Forces in France, Belgium and Italy, 1917-1918,* p. 24.

15. Laurence Stallings, *The Doughboys: The Story of the AEF, 1917-1918,* pp. 280-86; Barnes, *History of the 142nd Infantry,* pp. 28-29.

16. Barnes, *History of the 142nd Infantry,* p. 29; Chastaine, *Story of the 36th,* pp. 61-88.

17. Chastaine, *Story of the 36th,* pp. 88-99, 111-16; Barnes, *History of the 142nd Infantry,* pp. 29-31; American Battle Monuments Commission, *American Armies and Battlefields in Europe,* pp. 333-57.

18. American Battle Monuments Commission, *American Armies and Battlefields in Europe,* pp. 333-57; Chastaine, *Story of the 36th,* pp. 61-88; Barnes, *History of the 142nd Infantry,* pp. 29-31.

19. Barnes, *History of the 142nd Infantry,* pp. 30-31; Chastaine, *Story of the 36th,* pp. 111-16.

20. Chastaine, *Story of the 36th,* pp. 114-31; Barnes, *History of the 142nd Infantry,* pp. 31-32.

21. Chastaine, *Story of the 36th,* p. 131; Public Information Division, Department of the Army, *The Medal of Honor of the United States Army,* pp. 263-64.

22. Chastaine, *Story of the 36th,* pp. 131-32; Public Information Division, Department of the Army, *The Medal of Honor,* p. 263.

23. Chastaine, *Story of the 36th,* pp. 132-63.

24. Ibid., pp. 163-76.

25. Ibid.

26. Ibid., pp. 217-20; Stallings, *The Doughboys,* p. 288; Barnes, *History of the 142nd Infantry,* pp. 37-38.

27. Barnes, *History of the 142nd Infantry,* pp. 37-38; Chastaine, *Story of the 36th,* pp. 220-27.

28. Chastaine, *Story of the 36th,* pp. 220-27; Barnes, *History of the 142nd Infantry,* pp. 37-38.

29. Barnes, *History of the 142nd Infantry,* pp. 38-39; Chastaine, *Story of the 36th,* pp. 227-35.

30. Chastaine, *Story of the 36th,* pp. 231-32; Barnes, *History of the 142nd Infantry,* p. 39.

31. Barnes, *History of the 142nd Infantry,* p. 39; Chastaine, *Story of the 36th,* pp. 231-32.

32. Chastaine, *Story of the 36th,* pp. 232-49; Barnes, *History of the 142nd Infantry,* pp. 39-42.

33. Barnes, *History of the 142nd Infantry,* pp. 42-48; Chastaine, *Story of the 36th,* pp. 259-72.

34. Chastaine, *Story of the 36th,* pp. 259-72; Barnes, *History of the 142nd Infantry,* pp. 42-48.

35. Barnes, *History of the 142nd Infantry,* pp. 48-55; Litton, *History of Oklahoma,* vol. 2, p. 421; Chastaine, *Story of the 36th,* pp. 272-78.

36. Chastaine, *Story of the 36th*, pp. 131-32, 277; de Castelbled, *History of the A.E.F.*, p. 104; U.S., War Department, *Battle Participation of Organizations of the American Expeditionary Forces in France, Belgium and Italy, 1917-1918*, p. 24.

37. U.S., War Department, *Battle Participation of Organizations of the American Expeditionary Forces in France, Belgium and Italy, 1917-1918*, pp. 36, 37, 104; de Castelbled, *History of the A.E.F.*, pp. 149-50; Litton, *History of Oklahoma*, vol. 2, pp. 421-22.

4
WORLD WAR I: THE NINETIETH (TEXAS-OKLAHOMA) DIVISION

1. James G. Harbord, *The American Army in France, 1917-1919*, pp. 22-27; Maurice de Castelbled, *History of the A.E.F.*, pp. 7, 149.

2. Gaston Litton, *History of Oklahoma at the Golden Anniversary of Statehood*, vol. 2, pp. 421-22; George Wythe, *A History of the 90th Division*, pp. 6-7.

3. Wythe, *History of the 90th Division*, p. 6; Litton, *History of Oklahoma*, vol. 2, p. 421.

4. Litton, *History of Oklahoma*, vol. 2, p. 421; Harbord, *American Army in France, 1917-1919*, p. 31; de Castelbled, *History of the A.E.F.*, p. 149; Wythe, *History of the 90th Division*, p. 3.

5. Wythe, *History of the 90th Division*, p. 7.

6. Ibid., pp. 7-8.

7. Ibid., pp. 8-9; de Castelbled, *History of the A.E.F.*, p. 149.

8. Wythe, *History of the 90th Division*, pp. 9-13.

9. Ibid., p. 13.

10. Ibid., p. 14.

11. Ibid., pp. 14-16.

12. Ibid., pp. 16-26.

13. Ibid.

14. Ibid., pp. 24-26.

15. Ibid., p. 26.

16. Ibid., pp. 26-32, 38-41.

17. Ibid., pp. 32-33; American Battle Monuments Commission, *American Armies and Battlefields in Europe*, pp. 105-106.

18. American Battle Monuments Commission, *American Armies and Battlefields in Europe*, pp. 106-107.

19. Wythe, *History of the 90th Division*, pp. 33-38.

20. Ibid., pp. 38-45.

21. Ibid., pp. 45-52.

22. Ibid., pp. 52-55.

23. Ibid., pp. 55-57.

24. Ibid.

25. Ibid., pp. 67-73.

26. Ibid., pp. 69-73.

27. Ibid., pp. 73-79.

28. Ibid., pp. 77-88.

29. Ibid., p. 88.

30. Ibid., pp. 88-92.

31. Ibid., pp. 92-96.

32. Ibid.

33. Ibid., pp. 96-114.

34. Ibid., pp. 114-20.

35. Ibid., pp. 120-29.

36. Ibid., pp. 129-31.

37. Ibid., pp. 129-79.

38. Ibid., pp. 179-89.

39. Ibid.

40. Ibid., pp. 189-94.

41. Ibid., pp. 194-99; de Castelbled, *History of the A.E.F.*, pp. 149-50.

42. De Castelbled, *History of the A.E.F.*, pp. 149-50; Wythe, *History of the 90th Division*, pp. 194-99; Litton, *History of Oklahoma*, vol. 2, pp. 423-24; Guy Nelson, *Thunderbird: A History of the 45th Infantry Division*, p. 5.

43. Litton, *History of Oklahoma*, vol. 2, pp. 423-24.

5
THE FORTY-FIFTH INFANTRY DIVISION

1. Guy Nelson, *Thunderbird: A History of the 45th Infantry Division*, p. 5; Joseph B. Thoburn and Muriel H. Wright, *Oklahoma: A History of the State and Its People*, vol. 2, pp. 691-92; Gaston Litton, *History of Oklahoma at the Golden Anniversary of Statehood*, vol. 2, p. 416.

2. Litton, *History of Oklahoma*, vol. 2, p. 424; Nelson, *Thunderbird*, pp. 5-7; U.S., *Statutes at Large*, vol. 41, National Defense Act of 1920, pp. 758-812.

3. National Defense Act of 1920, pp. 759-60; Nelson, *Thunderbird*, pp. 5-7; Jim D. Hill, *The Minute Man in Peace and War: A History of the National Guard*, pp. 310-15.

4. Hill, *The Minute Man*, pp. 310-15; National Defense Act of 1920, pp. 759-65, 782, 784-85.

5. National Defense Act of 1920, pp. 780-84; Hill, *The Minute Man*, pp. 310-15; Interview, Colonel John H. McCasland (Ret.), October 15, 1980, Oklahoma Military Collection (OMC).

6. Hill, *The Minute Man*, p. 314.

7. Nelson, *Thunderbird*, pp. 7-8; Litton, *History of Oklahoma*, vol. 2, p. 424; Ralph W. Jones and Colonel John H. McCasland (Ret.), Notes, OMC.

8. Nelson, *Thunderbird*, pp. 9, 12-14, 130.

9. Ibid., p. 8.

10. Jones and McCasland, Notes, OMC; Interview, McCasland, October 15, 1980, OMC.

11. Interview, McCasland, October 15, 1980, OMC.

12. Jack T. Conn, *One Man in His Time*, pp. 60-63.

13. Ibid.

14. Nelson, *Thunderbird*, p. 6; Litton, *History of Oklahoma*, vol. 1, p. 537; Orben J. Casey, "Governor Lee Cruce and Law Enforcement, 1911-1915," *Chronicles of Oklahoma*, 54 (Winter, 1976-1977):435-36.

15. Casey, "Governor Lee Cruce and Law Enforcement," pp. 436-37; Nelson, *Thunderbird*, p. 6; Litton, *History of Oklahoma*, vol. 1, pp. 534-37.

16. Litton, *History of Oklahoma*, vol. 1, p. 527; Nelson, *Thunderbird*, p. 6; Casey, "Governor Lee Cruce and Law Enforcement," pp. 449-51.

17. Casey, "Governor Lee Cruce and Law Enforcement," pp. 436-47; Nelson, *Thunderbird*, p. 6.

18. Nelson, *Thunderbird*, p. 6; Litton, *History of Oklahoma*, vol. 1, p. 537; Casey, "Governor Lee Cruce and Law Enforcement," pp. 454-55.

19. Casey, "Governor Lee Cruce and Law Enforcement," pp. 454-56; Nelson, *Thunderbird;* Litton, *History of Oklahoma,* vol. 1, p. 537.

20. Litton, *History of Oklahoma,* vol. 1, p. 537; Casey, "Governor Lee Cruce and Law Enforcement," pp. 454-56; Nelson, *Thunderbird,* p. 6.

21. Nelson, *Thunderbird,* p. 6; Litton, *History of Oklahoma,* vol. 1, pp. 548-49.

22. Litton, *History of Oklahoma,* vol. 1, p. 548 and vol. 2, pp. 418-19; Nelson, *Thunderbird,* p. 6; James R. Scales and Danney Goble, *Oklahoma Politics: A History,* p. 95.

23. Nelson, *Thunderbird,* p. 6; Scales and Goble, *Oklahoma Politics,* p. 95; *Daily Oklahoman* (Oklahoma City), February 12, 1928; *Drumright News* (Drumright), September 26, 1919; *Drumright Derrick* (Drumright), September 23, 1919; Litton, *History of Oklahoma,* vol. 1, p. 548.

24. Litton, *History of Oklahoma,* vol. 1, p. 548; Nelson, *Thunderbird,* p. 6; *Daily Oklahoman,* February 12, 1928.

25. *Daily Oklahoman,* February 12, 1928; Litton, *History of Oklahoma,* vol. 2, pp. 168-69.

26. Litton, *History of Oklahoma,* vol. 1, p. 549; Nelson, *Thunderbird,* p. 6; Jimmie Lewis Franklin, *Journey Toward Hope,* p. 144; *Daily Oklahoman,* February 12, 1928; Rudie Halliburton, Jr., *The Tulsa Race War of 1921,* p. 3; Lieutenant Colonel Peter E. Wheeler, Comments, OMC.

27. Halliburton, *Tulsa Race War of 1921,* pp. 3-6; Nelson, *Thunderbird,* p. 6; Wheeler, Comments, OMC.

28. Franklin, *Journey Toward Hope,* pp. 142-49; Halliburton, *Tulsa Race War of 1921,* pp. 9-10; Wheeler, Comments, OMC.

29. Halliburton, *Tulsa Race War of 1921,* pp. 10-12; Nelson, *Thunderbird,* p. 6; Wheeler, Comments, OMC.

30. Halliburton, *Tulsa Race War of 1921,* pp. 12-15; Wheeler, Comments, OMC.

31. Halliburton, *Tulsa Race War of 1921,* pp. 12-15; Wheeler, Comments, OMC.

32. Halliburton, *Tulsa Race War of 1921,* pp. 13-15; Nelson, *Thunderbird,* p. 6; Wheeler, Comments, OMC.

33. Litton, *History of Oklahoma,* vol. 1, pp. 557-58; Sheldon Neuringer, "Governor Walton's War on the Ku Klux Klan: An Episode in Oklahoma History, 1923-1924," *Chronicles of Oklahoma,* 45 (Summer, 1967) 153-58; Howard A. Tucker, *History of Governor Walton's War on Ku Klux Klan: The Invisible Empire,* pp. 6-7.

34. Tucker, *History of Governor Walton's War on Ku Klux Klan,* pp. 7-11; Litton, *History of Oklahoma,* vol. 1, pp. 557-58; Neuringer, "Governor Walton's War on the Ku Klux Klan," pp. 158-61.

35. Neuringer, "Governor Walton's War on the Ku Klux Klan," pp. 158-61; Litton, *History of Oklahoma,* vol. 1, pp. 557-58; Tucker, *History of Governor Walton's War on Ku Klux Klan,* pp. 11-12.

36. Tucker, *History of Governor Walton's War on Ku Klux Klan,* pp. 12-15; Litton, *History of Oklahoma,* vol. 1, pp. 557-58; Neuringer, "Governor Walton's War on the Ku Klux Klan," pp. 161-63.

37. Neuringer, "Governor Walton's War on the Ku Klux Klan," pp. 163-67; Litton, *History of Oklahoma,* vol. 1, pp. 557-59; Tucker, *History of Governor Walton's War on Ku Klux Klan,* pp. 12-15; Scales and Goble, *Oklahoma Politics,* pp. 123-25.

38. Tucker, *History of Governor Walton's War on Ku Klux Klan,* p. 61; Litton, *History of Oklahoma,* vol. 1, pp. 557-59; Scales and Goble, *Oklahoma Politics,* p. 123-24; Neuringer, "Governor Walton's War on the Ku Klux Klan," pp. 166-67.

39. Neuringer, "Governor Walton's War on the Ku Klux Klan," pp. 166-67; Litton, *History of Oklahoma,* vol. 1, pp. 557-59; Tucker, *History of Governor Walton's War on Ku Klux Klan,* p. 61; Scales and Goble, *Oklahoma Politics,* pp. 124-25.

40. Tucker, *History of Governor Walton's War on Ku Klux Klan,* pp. 61-62; Litton, *History of Oklahoma,* vol. 1, pp. 557-59; Neuringer, "Governor Walton's War on the Ku Klux Klan," pp. 167-68.

41. Neuringer, "Governor Walton's War on the Ku Klux Klan," pp. 168-69; Litton, *History of Oklahoma,* vol. 1, pp. 557-59; Tucker, *History of Governor Walton's War on Ku Klux Klan,* pp. 61-62; Scales and Goble, *Oklahoma Politics,* p. 124.

42. Tucker, *History of Governor Walton's War on Ku Klux Klan,* pp. 61-67; Litton, *History of Oklahoma,* vol. 1, pp. 559-60; Scales and Goble, *Oklahoma Politics,* p. 124; Neuringer, "Governor Walton's War on the Ku Klux Klan," pp. 169-79.

43. Litton, *History of Oklahoma,* vol. 1, pp. 567-78; Keith L. Bryant, Jr., *Alfalfa Bill Murray,* pp. 200-201; Scales and Goble, *Oklahoma Politics,* pp. 167-70.

44. Litton, *History of Oklahoma,* vol. 1, pp. 567-78; Bryant, *Alfalfa Bill Murray,* pp. 200-201; Scales and Goble, *Oklahoma Politics,* pp. 167-70.

45. Bryant, *Alfalfa Bill Murray,* pp. 200-201; Litton, *History of Oklahoma,* vol. 1, p. 577; Gordon Hines, *"Alfalfa Bill": An Intimate Biography,* pp. 288-89.

46. Hines, *"Alfalfa Bill,"* pp. 288-89; Litton, *History of Oklahoma,* vol. 1, p. 577; Bryant, *Alfalfa Bill Murray,* pp. 200-201; Scales and Goble, *Oklahoma Politics,* p. 170.

47. Bryant, *Alfalfa Bill Murray,* pp. 200-201; Litton, *History of Oklahoma,* vol. 1, p. 577; Hines, *"Alfalfa Bill,"* pp. 288-89.

48. Hines, *"Alfalfa Bill,"* pp. 288-89; Litton, *History of Oklahoma,* vol. 1, p. 577; Bryant, *Alfalfa Bill Murray,* pp. 200-201; Wheeler, Comments.

49. Kenny A. Franks, *The Oklahoma Petroleum Industry,* pp. 127-47; Carl C. Rister, *Oil! Titan of the Southwest,* pp. 248-55.

50. Rister, *Oil!,* pp. 255-63; Franks, *Oklahoma Petroleum Industry,* p. 127; Scales and Goble, *Oklahoma Politics,* p. 169.

51. Franks, *Oklahoma Petroleum Industry,* pp. 147-48; Litton, *History of Oklahoma,* vol. 1, p. 577; Rister, *Oil!,* pp. 263-64.

52. Rister, *Oil!,* pp. 263-64; Litton, *History of Oklahoma,* vol. 1, pp. 577-78; Franks, *Oklahoma Petroleum Industry,* pp. 147-48; Scales and Goble, *Oklahoma Politics,* p. 169.

53. Franks, *Oklahoma Petroleum Industry,* pp. 166-67; Litton, *History of Oklahoma,* vol. 1, pp. 577-78; Rister, *Oil!,* pp. 263-64.

54. Rister, *Oil!,* pp. 264-65; Interview, Command Sergeant Major Arthur E. Peters (Ret.), January 22, 1981, OMC; Litton, *History of Oklahoma,* vol. 1, pp. 577-78; Franks, *Oklahoma Petroleum Industry,* pp. 166-67.

55. Franks, *Oklahoma Petroleum Industry,* pp. 166-68;

Litton, *History of Oklahoma,* vol. 1, pp. 577-78; Rister, *Oil!,* pp. 264-65.

56. Rister, *Oil!,* pp. 265-66; Roy P. Stewart, *Born Grown: An Oklahoma City History* (Oklahoma City: Fidelity Bank National Association, 1974), pp. 217-18.

57. Stewart, *Born Grown,* pp. 217-18; Rister, *Oil!,* pp. 265-66.

58. Rister, *Oil!,* pp. 265-66; Stewart, *Born Grown,* pp. 217-18.

59. Jones and McCasland, Notes, OMC; Interview, McCasland, October 15, 1980, OMC.

60. Interview, McCasland, October 15, 1980, OMC.

61. Ibid.

62. Nelson, *Thunderbird,* p. 9; Hill, *The Minute Man,* pp. 347-80.

6
MOBILIZATION, 1940

1. Operational Order, AG. 421.7, 45th Division, 12-15-38 Misc., 5-22-39, Archives, Forty-fifth Infantry Division Museum, Oklahoma City, Oklahoma; Interview, Colonel John H. McCasland (Ret.), November 12, 1980, Oklahoma Military Collection (OMC); Guy Nelson, *Thunderbird: A History of the 45th Infantry Division,* p. 20.

2. Nelson, *Thunderbird,* p. 10; Gaston Litton, *History of Oklahoma at the Golden Anniversary of Statehood,* vol. 2, pp. 424-25; Jim D. Hill, *The Minute Man in Peace and War: A History of the National Guard,* p. 430.

3. Hill, *The Minute Man,* pp. 430-31; Nelson, *Thunderbird,* pp. 12-13.

4. Nelson, *Thunderbird,* pp. 12-13; Hill, *The Minute Man,* pp. 430-31.

5. Hill, *The Minute Man,* p. 430; Nelson, *Thunderbird,* pp. 10-12; Litton, *History of Oklahoma,* vol. 2, pp. 424-25.

6. Nelson, *Thunderbird,* p. 12; Interview, Colonel Roy P. Stewart (Ret.), February 4, 1981, OMC.

7. Litton, *History of Oklahoma,* vol. 2, pp. 424-25; Nelson, *Thunderbird,* pp. 10-12; Ralph W. Jones and Colonel John H. McCasland, Notes, OMC; Hill, *The Minute Man,* p. 430.

8. Hill, *The Minute Man,* pp. 430-31; Jones and McCasland, Notes, OMC; Nelson, *Thunderbird,* pp. 12-13, 131; Interview, Colonel John H. McCasland, October 15, 1980, OMC; Interview, Major General Frederick A. Daugherty (Ret.), November 18, 1976, Archives, Forty-fifth Infantry Division Museum, Oklahoma City, Oklahoma.

9. Hill, *The Minute Man,* pp. 430-31; Jones and McCasland, Notes, OMC; Nelson, *Thunderbird,* pp. 12-13; 131; Interview, Major General Hal L. Muldrow, Jr. (Ret.), February 13, 1981, OMC; Interview, McCasland, October 15, 1980, OMC.

10. Interview, McCasland, October 15, 1980, OMC; Nelson, *Thunderbird,* pp. 12-13; Hill, *The Minute Man,* p. 430.

11. Hill, *The Minute Man,* pp. 430-33; Nelson, *Thunderbird,* pp. 12-13; "Reader's Comments," OMC.

12. Nelson, *Thunderbird,* pp. 12-13; Maurer Maurer, *Combat Squadrons of the Air Force, World War II,* p. 350; Litton, *History of Oklahoma,* vol. 2, pp. 424-25.

13. Litton, *History of Oklahoma,* vol. 2, pp. 424-25; Nelson, *Thunderbird,* pp. 12-13; Colonel W.D. McGlasson, "Mobilization 1940!," *Soldiers,* 36, No. 1 (January, 1981): 13-15; Hill, *The Minute Man,* pp. 367-80.

14. Hill, *The Minute Man,* pp. 367-80, 532-43; Nelson, *Thunderbird,* pp. 12-13; Litton, *History of Oklahoma,* vol. 2, pp. 424-25.

15. Litton, *History of Oklahoma,* vol. 2, pp. 424-25; Maurer, *Combat Squadrons of the Air Force,* p. 350; Nelson, *Thunderbird,* pp. 12-13; Hill, *The Minute Man,* pp. 367-80, 532-43.

16. Hill, *The Minute Man,* p. 407; McGlasson, "Mobilization 1940," p. 15; Nelson, *Thunderbird,* pp. 12-13, 131; Interview, McCasland, October 15, 1980, OMC; Litton, *History of Oklahoma,* vol. 2, pp. 424-25.

17. Hill, *The Minute Man,* p. 407; Nelson, *Thunderbird,* pp. 12-13; Interview, McCasland, October 15, 1980, OMC; Litton, *History of Oklahoma,* vol. 2, pp. 424-25.

18. Litton, *History of Oklahoma,* vol. 2, p. 425; Roy P. Stewart, "Thunderbird Mobilization: 1940," Roy P. Stewart Papers, Archives, Forty-fifth Infantry Division Museum, Oklahoma City, Oklahoma; Interview, Sergeant Major Jack Clapp (Ret.), February 6, 1981; OMC; *Edmond Evening Sun* (Edmond), July 17, 1980; *45th Division News* (45th Infantry Division), October 11, 1940, November 1, 1940, November 8, 1940, and November 15, 1940. Publication of the *45th Division News* started with mobilization in 1940. Although it also was titled *The 45th Division News, Camp Barkeley News, 45th Division Daily News,* and *The Thunderbird News,* it is cited as *45th Division News* throughout this work. The Forty-fifth Infantry Division Museum in Oklahoma City has a complete set of the newspaper.

19. Litton, *History of Oklahoma,* vol. 2, p. 425; Nelson, *Thunderbird,* pp. 13-14; Roy P. Stewart, "Thunderbird Mobilization: 1940," Roy P. Stewart Papers; *45th Division News,* October 11, 1940; Hill, *The Minute Man,* pp. 407-408; Interview, Clapp, February 6, 1981, OMC; *Edmond Evening Sun,* July 17, 1980.

20. Hill, *The Minute Man,* p. 408; Nelson, *Thunderbird,* pp. 14-15; Litton, *History of Oklahoma,* vol. 2, p. 425; Jones and McCasland, Notes, OMC; Interview, Muldrow, February 13, 1981, OMC; Stewart, "Thunderbird Mobilization: 1940"; *45th Division News,* October 4, 1980; George A. Fisher, *The Story of the 180th Infantry Regiment,* unpaged.

21. Hill, *The Minute Man,* p. 408; Nelson, *Thunderbird,* pp. 14-15; Litton, *History of Oklahoma,* vol. 2, p. 425; Jones and McCasland, Notes, OMC; Interview, Muldrow, February 13, 1981, OMC; Stewart, "Thunderbird Mobilization: 1940"; Interview, McCasland, October 15, 1980, OMC; McGlasson, "Mobilization 1940!" p. 15; Fisher, *The 180th.*

22. Hill, *The Minute Man,* p. 408; Nelson, *Thunderbird,* pp. 14-15; Litton, *History of Oklahoma,* vol. 2, p. 425; Jones and McCasland, Notes, OMC; Stewart, "Thunderbird Mobilization: 1940"; Fisher, *The 180th.*

23. Litton, *History of Oklahoma,* vol. 2, p. 425; Nelson, *Thunderbird,* pp. 14-15; Fisher, *The 180th;* Hill, *The Minute Man,* p. 408; *45th Division News,* October 12, 1940.

24. Interview, Stewart, February 4, 1981, OMC; Stewart, "Thunderbird Mobilization: 1940"; *45th Division News,* October 4, 1940 and June 6, 1944; Don Robinson, *News of the 45th,* pp. 1-43 passim.

25. Interview, Stewart, February 4, 1981; Stewart, "Thunderbird Mobilization: 1940"; Robinson, *News of the 45th,* passim; "Reader's Comments," OMC.

26. Interview, Roy P. Stewart, February 4, 1981, OMC; Stewart, "Thunderbird Mobilization: 1940"; Robinson, *News of the 45th,* pp. 18-26, 73-77, 125-43; Nelson, *Thunderbird,* pp. 49-50; Interview, Warrant Officer George F. Tapscott (Ret.), May, 1978, Archives, Forty-fifth Infantry Division Museum, Oklahoma City, Oklahoma.

27. Hill, *The Minute Man,* p. 408; Nelson, *Thunderbird,* p. 15; Litton, *History of Oklahoma,* vol. 2, p. 425; *45th Division News,* February 7, 1941 and March 7, 1941.

28. Litton, *History of Oklahoma,* vol. 2, p. 425; Nelson, *Thunderbird,* p. 15; Hill, *The Minute Man,* pp. 408-23.

29. *45th Division News,* March 21 and 28, April 4, 11, 18, and 25, May 2 and 30, June 6 and 12, 1941.

30. Hill, *The Minute Man,* pp. 423-27; Nelson, *Thunderbird,* p. 15; Litton, *History of Oklahoma,* vol. 2, p. 425.

31. *45th Division News,* July 18 and 25, 1945.

32. Fisher, *The 180th;* Roy P. Stewart, "Raymond S. McClain, America's Greatest Citizen Soldier," pp. 4-6, Roy P. Stewart Papers; Robinson, *News of the 45th,* pp. 22-24; Nelson, *Thunderbird,* p. 10; Warren P. Munsell, Jr., *The Story of a Regiment: A History of the 179th Regimental Combat Team,* p. 2.

33. Fisher, *The 180th.*

34. Ibid.; Munsell, *The 179th,* p. 2.

35. Munsell, *The 179th,* p. 2; Fisher, *The 180th.*

36. Fisher, *The 180th;* Interview, McCasland, October 15, 1980, OMC; Munsell, *The 179th,* p. 2; Reader's Comments, OMC.

37. Munsell, *The 179th,* p. 2; Interview, McCasland, October 15, 1980, OMC; Fisher, *The 180th; 45th Division News,* January 10, 1941.

38. Munsell, *The 179th,* p. 2; Interview, McCasland, October 15, 1980, OMC; Fisher, *The 180th; 45th Division News,* March 13, 1942.

39. Fisher, *The 180th;* Nelson, *Thunderbird,* p. 18; Jones and McCasland, Notes, OMC; Robert L. Dulaney, *45th Infantry Division,* unpaged; Munsell, *The 179th,* pp. 2-3; Interview, Colonel Herbert C. O'Neil (Ret.), January 7, 1981, OMC; Interview, Lieutenant Colonel Bruce E. Rey (Ret.), February 27, 1981, OMC; *45th Division News,* February 27, 1942.

40. Interview, O'Neil, January 7, 1981.

41. Ibid.

42. Ibid.

43. Interview, Rey, February 27, 1981, OMC.

44. Ibid.

45. Ibid.

46. Ibid.

47. Munsell, *The 179th,* p. 2.

48. Ibid., pp. 2-3; Fisher, *The 180th;* Nelson, *Thunderbird,* p. 18; Dulaney, *45th Infantry Division.*

49. Dulaney, *45th Infantry Division;* Fisher, *The 180th;* Munsell, *The 179th,* pp. 2-3; Nelson, *Thunderbird,* p. 18.

50. Nelson, *Thunderbird,* p. 18; Jones and McCasland, Notes, OMC; Fisher, *The 180th;* Munsell, *The 179th,* pp. 2-3; Dulaney, *45th Infantry Division; 45th Division News,* November 21, 1942.

51. Nelson, *Thunderbird,* p. 18; Jones and McCasland, Notes, OMC; Fisher, *The 180th;* Munsell, *The 179th,* pp. 2-3; Dulaney, *45th Infantry Division.*

52. Dulaney, *45th Infantry Division;* Fisher, *The 180th;* Munsell, *The 179th,* pp. 2-4; Nelson, *Thunderbird,* p. 18.

53. Nelson, *Thunderbird,* pp. 18-19; Fisher, *The 180th;* Munsell, *The 179th,* pp. 4-5; Dulaney, *45th Infantry Division.*

54. Dulaney, *45th Infantry Division;* Jones and McCasland, Notes, OMC; Fisher, *The 180th;* Munsell, *The 179th,* pp. 4-5; Nelson, *Thunderbird,* pp. 18-19.

55. Dulaney, *45th Infantry Division;* Fisher, *The 180th;* Munsell, *The 179th,* pp. 4-5; Nelson, *Thunderbird,* pp. 18-19.

56. Nelson, *Thunderbird,* pp. 18-19; Fisher, *The 180th;* Munsell, *The 179th,* pp. 5-6; Dulaney, *45th Infantry Division.*

57. Dulaney, *45th Infantry Division;* Fisher, *The 180th;* Munsell, *The 179th,* pp. 6-7.

58. Munsell, *The 179th,* map between pages 10-11; Albert N. Garland and Howard M. Smyth, *United States Army in World War II: The Mediterranean Theater of Operations, Sicily and the Surrender of Italy,* pp. 1-105.

59. Fisher, *The 180th;* Munsell, *The 179th,* p. 7; Nelson, *Thunderbird,* p. 20; Dulaney, *45th Infantry Division;* 45th Infantry Division, *The Fighting Forty-Fifth: The Combat Report of an Infantry Division,* p. 7.

60. 45th Infantry Division, *The Fighting Forty-Fifth;* Fisher, *The 180th;* Munsell, *The 179th,* pp. 7-8; Dulaney, *45th Infantry Division;* Interview, Clapp, February 6, 1981, OMC; Nelson, *Thunderbird,* p. 20.

61. Nelson, *Thunderbird,* p. 20; Fisher, *The 180th;* Munsell, *The 179th;* Dulaney, *45th Infantry Division;* 45th Infantry Division, *The Fighting Forty-Fifth,* p. 7.

62. 45th Infantry Division, *The Fighting Forty-Fifth,* pp. 7, 13; Fisher, *The 180th;* Munsell, Jr., *The 179th,* pp. 8-10; Dulaney, *45th Infantry Division;* Jones and McCasland, Notes, OMC; Nelson, *Thunderbird,* pp. 20-27.

63. Nelson, *Thunderbird,* pp. 24-27; Fisher, *The 180th;* Munsell, *The 179th,* pp. 9-10; Dulaney, *45th Infantry Division;* Interview, Clapp, February 6, 1981, OMC; 45th Infantry Division, *The Fighting Forty-Fifth,* pp. 7, 13.

64. 45th Infantry Division, *The Fighting Forty-Fifth,* pp. 7, 13; Fisher, *The 180th;* Munsell, *The 179th,* pp. 9-11; Interview, Clapp, February 6, 1981, OMC; Nelson, *Thunderbird,* pp. 24-27; Dulaney, *45th Infantry Division.*

7

BAPTIZED IN BLOOD: THE INVASION OF SICILY

1. Guy Nelson, *Thunderbird: A History of the 45th Infantry Division,* pp. 26-28; Warren P. Munsell, Jr., *The Story of a Regiment: A History of the 179th Regimental Combat Team,* p. 11; George A. Fisher, *The Story of the 180th Infantry Regiment;* Robert L. Dulaney, *45th Infantry Division,* passim; 45th Infantry Division, *The Fighting Forty-Fifth: The Combat Report of an Infantry Division,* pp. 13-15.

2. 45th Infantry Division, *The Fighting Forty-Fifth,* pp. 15-18; Nelson, *Thunderbird,* pp. 28-29; Munsell, *The 179th,* pp. 11-12; Fisher, *The 180th;* Dulaney, *45th Infantry Division.*

3. Dulaney, *45th Infantry Division;* Nelson, *Thunder-*

bird, pp. 28-29; Munsell, *The 179th*, pp. 11-12; Fisher, *The 180th;* 45th Infantry Division, *The Fighting Forty-Fifth*, p. 16.

4. 45th Infantry Division, *The Fighting Forty-Fifth*, p. 16; Dulaney, *45th Infantry Division;* Fisher, *The 180th.*

5. Fisher, *The 180th;* 45th Infantry Division, *The Fighting Forty-Fifth*, p. 16; Dulaney, *45th Infantry Division.*

6. Munsell, *The 179th*, p. 11.

7. *History of the 157th Infantry Regiment (Rifle)*, pp. 21-22.

8. Nelson, *Thunderbird*, pp. 28-29; Munsell, *The 179th*, pp. 11-12; Fisher, *The 180th; The 157th*, pp. 21-23; Dulaney, *45th Infantry Division.*

9. Dulaney, *45th Infantry Division;* Nelson, *Thunderbird*, pp. 28-29.

10. Albert N. Garland and Howard M. Smyth, *United States Army in World War II: The Mediterranean Theater of Operations, Sicily and the Surrender of Italy*, pp. 148-49; Fisher, *The 180th.*

11. Fisher, *The 180th.*

12. Ibid.

13. Ibid.; Munsell, *The 179th*, p. 13; *The 157th*, pp. 23-24; Nelson, *Thunderbird*, p. 29; *45th Division News*, September 1, 1943.

14. Nelson, *Thunderbird*, p. 29; Fisher, *The 180th.*

15. Fisher, *The 180th;* 45th Infantry Division, *The Fighting Forty-Fifth*, pp. 21-22; Interview, Sergeant Major Jack Clapp, February 6, 1981, OMC; Dulaney, *45th Infantry Division.*

16. Fisher, *The 180th;* Nelson, *Thunderbird*, pp. 29-31; *45th Division News*, September 1, 1943.

17. Nelson, *Thunderbird*, pp. 30-31; Fisher, *The 180th; 45th Division News*, September 1, 1943.

18. Munsell, *The 179th*, pp. 12-13; Nelson, *Thunderbird*, pp. 30-32.

19. Nelson, *Thunderbird*, pp. 31-32; Garland and Smyth, *United States Army in World War II: The Mediterranean Theater of Operations, Sicily and the Surrender of Italy*, Map, "The Final Landing Plans"; 45th Infantry Division, *The Fighting Forty-Fifth*, pp. 24-25.

20. Nelson, *Thunderbird*, p. 32; *The 157th*, pp. 25-27; Fisher, *The 180th; 45th Division News*, September 1, 1943; Lieutenant Colonel Peter E. Wheeler, Comments, OMC.

21. Fisher, *The 180th; The 157th*, pp. 25-27; Nelson, *Thunderbird*, p. 32.

22. Nelson, *Thunderbird*, p. 32; Fisher, *The 180th;* 45th Infantry Division, *The Fighting Forty-Fifth*, pp. 26-27; *45th Division News*, September 1, 1943.

23. 45th Infantry Division, *The Fighting Forty-Fifth*, pp. 26-27; Fisher, *The 180th;* Nelson, *Thunderbird*, pp. 32-33.

24. 45th Infantry Division, *The Fighting Forty-Fifth*, pp. 26-27; Fisher, *The 180th;* Nelson, *Thunderbird*, pp. 32-33.

25. 45th Infantry Division, *The Fighting Forty-Fifth*, p. 27; *The 157th*, pp. 26-27.

26. *The 157th*, p. 27; Fisher, *The 180th;* Nelson, *Thunderbird*, p. 33.

27. *45th Division News*, September 1, 1943.

28. Ibid.

29. Nelson, *Thunderbird*, p. 33; Fisher, *The 180th.*

30. Fisher, *The 180th; The 157th*, pp. 26-27; Nelson, *Thunderbird*, pp. 33-34.

31. Nelson, *Thunderbird*, pp. 33-34; Fisher, *The 180th; The 157th*, pp. 26-28.

32. *The 157th*, p. 28; Nelson, *Thunderbird*, pp. 33-34; *45th Division News*, September 1, 1943.

33. Nelson, *Thunderbird*, pp. 33-34; Fisher, *The 180th.*

34. Fisher, *The 180th;* Nelson, *Thunderbird*, pp. 33-34.

35. Nelson, *Thunderbird*, pp. 33-34; *The 157th*, pp. 28-29.

36. Nelson, *Thunderbird*, pp. 34-35; Fisher, *The 180th;* Munsell, *The 179th*, pp. 18-19; 45th Infantry Division, *The Fighting Forty-Fifth*, p. 27; Dulaney, *45th Infantry Division.*

37. Ibid.; *The 157th*, pp. 28-29.

38. Dulaney, *45th Infantry Division*, pp. 28-30; Garland and Smyth, *United States Army in World War II: The Mediterranean Theater of Operations, Sicily and the Surrender of Italy*, pp. 374-417; Nelson, *Thunderbird*, pp. 34-35.

39. Nelson, *Thunderbird*, pp. 34-35; Dulaney, *45th Infantry Division.*

40. Dulaney, *45th Infantry Division;* 45th Infantry Division, *The Fighting Forty-Fifth*, pp. 38-39; Garland and Smyth, *United States Army in World War II: The Mediterranean Theater of Operations, Sicily and the Surrender of Italy*, pp. 435-553.

41. Garland and Smyth, *United States Army in World War II: The Mediterranean Theater of Operations, Sicily and the Surrender of Italy*, pp. 435-553; Dulaney, *45th Infantry Division;* 45th Infantry Division, *The Fighting Forty-Fifth*, pp. 38-39.

42. U.S., War Department, *Salerno: American Operations from the Beaches to the Volturno*, pp. 1-12; Nelson, *Thunderbird*, pp. 38-40.

43. Nelson, *Thunderbird*, p. 36; 45th Infantry Division, *The Fighting Forty-Fifth*, p. 39.

44. Dulaney, *45th Infantry Division;* U.S., War Department, *Salerno*, pp. 1-12; Nelson, *Thunderbird*, pp. 36-37.

45. Nelson, *Thunderbird*, pp. 36-37; U.S., War Department, *Salerno*, pp. 1-12; 45th Infantry Division, *The Fighting Forty-Fifth*, pp. 39-40.

46. 45th Infantry Division, *The Fighting Forty-Fifth*, pp. 40-41; Nelson, *Thunderbird*, pp. 37-38; Munsell, *The 179th*, pp. 20-22; Fisher, *The 180th; The 157th*, pp. 31-34.

47. *The 157th*, pp. 32-33; Munsell, *The 179th*, pp. 21-22; 45th Infantry Division, *The Fighting Forty-Fifth*, pp. 40-41.

48. 45th Infantry Division, *The Fighting Forty-Fifth*, pp. 40-41; U.S., War Department, *Salerno*, pp. 14-15.

49. U.S., War Department, *Salerno*, pp. 14-15; *The 157th*, p. 33; Nelson, *Thunderbird*, pp. 40-41.

50. Nelson, *Thunderbird*, pp. 40-41; U.S., War Department, *Salerno*, pp. 14-15; Ralph W. Jones and Colonel John H. McCasland, Notes, OMC; *The 157th*, p. 33.

51. *The 157th*, pp. 33-34; 45th Infantry Division, *The Fighting Forty-Fifth*, p. 42.

52. 45th Infantry Division, *The Fighting Forty-Fifth*, p. 42; Munsell, *The 179th*, pp. 21-23; *The 157th*, pp. 33-34; Nelson, *Thunderbird*, pp. 40-41.

53. Nelson, *Thunderbird*, pp. 40-41; 45th Infantry Division, *The Fighting Forty-Fifth*, p. 42; Munsell, *The 179th*, pp. 21-23; *The 157th*, pp. 33-34.

8
SALERNO

1. Warren P. Munsell, Jr., *The Story of a Regiment: A History of the 179th Regimental Combat Team*, p. 23; George A. Fisher, *The Story of the 180th Infantry Regiment; History of the 157th Infantry Regiment (Rifle)*, pp. 34-37; Lieutenant Colonel Peter E. Wheeler, Comments, OMC.

2. *The 157th*, p. 34; Munsell, *The 179th*, p. 23; Guy Nelson, *Thunderbird: A History of the 45th Infantry Division*, p. 41.

3. Nelson, *Thunderbird*, pp. 40-42; *The 157th*, pp. 34-35; Munsell, *The 179th*, pp. 23-24, 140.

4. Nelson, *Thunderbird*, pp. 40-42; *The 157th*, pp. 34-35; Munsell, *The 179th*, pp. 23-24, 140.

5. Munsell, *The 179th*, pp. 24-25; *The 157th*, pp. 34-35; Nelson, *Thunderbird*, pp. 41-43.

6. Nelson, *Thunderbird*, pp. 41-43; *The 157th*, pp. 34-35; Munsell, *The 179th*, pp. 24-26.

7. Interview, Major General Hal L. Muldrow, Jr., February 13, 1981, OMC.

8. Ibid.

9. Munsell, *The 179th*, pp. 24-26; *The 157th*, pp. 34-35; Nelson, *Thunderbird*, pp. 41-43.

10. Nelson, *Thunderbird*, pp. 41-43; *The 157th*, pp. 34-35; Munsell, *The 179th*, pp. 25-26.

11. Munsell, *The 179th*, pp. 25-26; *The 157th*, pp. 34-35; Nelson, *Thunderbird*, pp. 41-43.

12. Nelson, *Thunderbird*, pp. 41-43; *The 157th*, pp. 34-37.

13. *The 157th*, pp. 34-37; Ralph W. Jones and Colonel John H. McCasland, Notes, OMC; Nelson, *Thunderbird*, pp. 41-43, 132.

14. Nelson, *Thunderbird*, pp. 41-43; *The 157th*, pp. 36-37; Munsell, *The 179th*, pp. 27-28; Wheeler, Comments, OMC.

15. Martin Blumenson, *United States Army in World War II, The Mediterranean Theater of Operations, Salerno to Cassino*, pp. 85-132; 45th Infantry Division, *The Fighting Forty-Fifth: The Combat Report of an Infantry Division*, pp. 42-49; Nelson, *Thunderbird*, p. 43.

16. Fisher, *The 180th*; Munsell, *The 179th*, pp. 28-29; *The 157th*, pp. 37-38; Nelson, *Thunderbird*, pp. 43-44.

17. Nelson, *Thunderbird*, pp. 44-45; 45th Infantry Division, *The Fighting Forty-Fifth*, pp. 49-50.

18. 45th Infantry Division, *The Fighting Forty-Fifth*, pp. 49-50; Nelson, *Thunderbird*, pp. 44-45; 45th Infantry Division, *The Fighting Forty-Fifth*, pp. 49-50.

19. Nelson, *Thunderbird*, pp. 44-45; 45th Infantry Division, *The Fighting Forty-Fifth*, pp. 49-50.

20. Nelson, *Thunderbird*, p. 45; Public Information Division, Department of the Army, *The Medal of Honor of the United States*, p. 276; *45th Division News*, April 15, 1944.

21. Nelson, *Thunderbird*, pp. 45-47; 45th Infantry Division, *The Fighting Forty-Fifth*, pp. 50-51.

22. 45th Infantry Division, *The Fighting Forty-Fifth*, p. 52; *The 157th*, p. 42; Nelson, *Thunderbird*, pp. 44-45.

23. Nelson, *Thunderbird*, p. 46; Fisher, *The 180th*; Munsell, *The 179th*, p. 42.

24. Munsell, *The 179th*, p. 42; Fisher, *The 180th*; Nelson, *Thunderbird*, p. 42.

25. Nelson, *Thunderbird*, pp. 46-47; Interview, Muldrow, February 13, 1981, OMC; Munsell, *The 179th*, pp. 31-33.

26. Munsell, *The 179th*, p. 33.

27. Ibid., pp. 32-33; 45th Infantry Division, *The Fighting Forty-Fifth*, pp. 53-55.

28. Ibid.; Munsell, *The 179th*, pp. 32-33; *The 157th*, pp. 54-55; Wheeler, Comments, OMC.

29. Nelson, *Thunderbird*, pp. 47-48; 45th Infantry Division, *The Fighting Forty-Fifth*, p. 56.

30. 45th Infantry Division, *The Fighting Forty-Fifth*, p. 56; *The 157th*, p. 45; Nelson, *Thunderbird*, pp. 47-48.

31. Nelson, *Thunderbird*, pp. 50-51; 45th Infantry Division, *The Fighting Forty-Fifth*, p. 56; Wheeler, Comments, OMC.

32. 45th Infantry Division, *The Fighting Forty-Fifth*, p. 56; Interview, Muldrow, February 13, 1981, OMC; Nelson, *Thunderbird*, pp. 50-52.

33. Nelson, *Thunderbird*, pp. 50-51; 45th Infantry Division, *The Fighting Forty-Fifth*, pp. 56-57.

34. 45th Infantry Division, *The Fighting Forty-Fifth*, pp. 56-57; Nelson, *Thunderbird*, pp. 50-51.

35. Fisher, *The 180th*; Munsell, *The 179th*, pp. 35-37; 45th Infantry Division, *The Fighting Forty-Fifth*, pp. 56-57.

36. 45th Infantry Division, *The Fighting Forty-Fifth*, pp. 57-59; Munsell, *The 179th*, pp. 35-38.

37. Munsell, *The 179th*, pp. 35-38; Fisher, *The 180th*; 45th Infantry Division, *The Fighting Forty-Fifth*, pp. 59-61; *45th Division News*, April 14, 1944.

38. 45th Infantry Division, *The Fighting Forty-Fifth*, pp. 59-61; Fisher, *The 180th*; Munsell, *The 179th*, pp. 35-38.

39. Munsell, *The 179th*, pp. 38-41; *The 157th*, pp. 45-50; Fisher, *The 180th*; 45th Infantry Division, *The Fighting Forty-Fifth*, pp. 51-65.

40. 45th Infantry Division, *The Fighting Forty-Fifth*, pp. 51-65; *The 157th*, pp. 45-50; Interview, Clapp, February 6, 1981, OMC; Fisher, *The 180th*; Munsell, *The 179th*, pp. 38-41.

41. 45th Infantry Division, *The Fighting Forty-Fifth*, pp. 51-65; *The 157th*, pp. 45-50; Interview, Clapp, February 6, 1981, OMC; Fisher, *The 180th*, Munsell, *The 179th*, pp. 38-41.

42. Interview, Clapp, February 6, 1981, OMC.

43. Munsell, *The 179th*, pp. 42-43; *The 157th*, pp. 48-50; Fisher, *The 180th*; 45th Infantry Division, *The Fighting Forty-Fifth*, pp. 65-70; Nelson, *Thunderbird*, pp. 52-53.

44. Nelson, *Thunderbird*, pp. 52-53; Munsell, *The 179th*, p. 45.

45. Chester G. Starr, *From Salerno to the Alps: A History of the Fifth Army, 1943-1944*, p. 127; Blumensen, *United States Army in World War II, The Mediterranean Theater of Operations, Salerno to Cassino*, pp. 293-404.

46. Blumensen, *United States Army in World War II, The Mediterranean Theater of Operations, Salerno to Cassino*, pp. 293-404; Starr, *From Salerno to the Alps*, p. 127; Jones and McCasland, Notes, OMC; Historical Division, Department of the Army, *Anzio Beachhead, 22 January-25 May 1944*, pp. 1-26.

47. Historical Division, Department of the Army, *Anzio Beachhead, 22 January-25 May 1944*, pp. 1-26; Blumensen, *United States Army in World War II, The Mediterranean Theater of Operations, Salerno to Cassino*, pp. 293-404.

48. Historical Division, Department of the Army, *Anzio Beachhead, 22 January-25 May 1944*, pp. 3-5; Blumensen,

United States Army in World War II, The Mediterranean Theater of Operations, Salerno to Cassino, pp. 293-404.

49. Blumensen, *United States Army in World War II, The Mediterranean Theater of Operations, Salerno to Cassino,* pp. 293-404; Historical Division, Department of the Army, *Anzio Beachhead, 22 January-25 May 1944,* p. 5.

50. Fisher, *The 180th;* Munsell, *The 179th,* pp. 46-48; *The 157th,* p. 50; 45th Infantry Division, *The Fighting Forty-Fifth,* pp. 68-70.

51. 45th Infantry Division, *The Fighting Forty-Fifth,* pp. 68-70; Munsell, *The 179th,* pp. 47-49; Fisher, *The 180th; The 157th,* p. 50.

52. Starr, *From Salerno to the Alps,* pp. 84-85; Historical Division, Department of the Army, *Anzio Beachhead, 22 January-25 May 1944,* pp. 12-17.

53. Fisher, *The 180th; The 157th,* p. 51; Munsell, *The 179th,* pp. 48-49; Nelson, *Thunderbird,* pp. 55-59; 45th Infantry Division, *The Fighting Forty-Fifth,* pp. 70-72.

54. 45th Infantry Division, *The Fighting Forty-Fifth,* pp. 71-86; Nelson, *Thunderbird,* pp. 55-64; Historical Division, Department of the Army, *Anzio Beachhead, 22 January-25 May 1944,* pp. 11-104.

9

ANZIO

1. *History of the 157th Infantry Regiment (Rifle),* p. 52.

2. George A. Fisher, *The Story of the 180th Infantry Regiment;* Lieutenant Colonel Peter E. Wheeler, Comments, OMC.

3. Ibid.; Warren P. Munsell, Jr., *The Story of a Regiment: A History of the 179th Regimental Combat Team,* pp. 50-51; 45th Infantry Division, *The Fighting Forty-Fifth: The Combat Report of an Infantry Division,* pp. 71-72; Lieutenant Colonel Peter E. Wheeler, Comments, OMC.

4. 45th Infantry Division, *The Fighting Forty-Fifth,* pp. 71-72; *The 157th,* pp. 51-53; Fisher, *The 180th;* Munsell, *The 179th,* pp. 50-51.

5. Munsell, *The 179th,* pp. 50-52; William L. Allen, *Anzio: Edge of Disaster,* pp. 41-82; Wynford Vaughan-Thomas, *Anzio,* pp. 47-92; Interview, Brigadier General William R. Wilson, January 7, 1977, Archives.

6. Interview, Colonel H.A. Meyers (Ret.), Colonel Preston J.C. Murphy (Ret.), and Colonel William P. Grace (Ret.), August 22, 1980, OMC; Interview, Colonel John H. McCasland, October 29, 1980, OMC.

7. Munsell, *The 179th,* p. 51; *The 157th,* p. 54; Guy Nelson, *Thunderbird: A History of the 45th Infantry Division,* pp. 57-58.

8. Nelson, *Thunderbird,* pp. 57-58; Munsell, *The 179th,* p. 51; *The 157th,* p. 54.

9. Historical Division, Department of the Army, *Anzio Beachhead, 22 January-25 May 1944,* p. 111; Ralph W. Jones and Colonel John H. McCasland, Notes, OMC; Christopher Hibbert, *Anzio: The Bid for Rome,* pp. 70-71; Vaughan-Thomas, *Anzio,* pp. 132-33.

10. Vaughan-Thomas, *Anzio,* pp. 132-33; Interview, Sergeant Major Jack Clapp, February 6, 1981, OMC; Munsell, *The 179th,* pp. 50-53.

11. Munsell, *The 179th,* pp. 50-53; Vaughan-Thomas, *Anzio,* pp. 132-33.

12. *The 157th,* pp. 54-56.

13. Munsell, *The 179th,* p. 53; Historical Division, Department of the Army, *Anzio Beachhead, 22 January-25 May 1944,* pp. 54-56.

14. Historical Division, Department of the Army, *Anzio Beachhead, 22 January-25 May 1944,* pp. 54-56; Munsell, *The 179th,* p. 53.

15. Munsell, *The 179th,* pp. 53-54.

16. Ibid., pp. 54-55; Historical Division, Department of the Army, *Anzio Beachhead, 22 January-25 May 1944,* pp. 64-65; Wheeler, Comments, OMC.

17. Historical Division, Department of the Army, *Anzio Beachhead, 22 January-25 May 1944,* pp. 64-65; Munsell, *The 179th,* pp. 54-55.

18. Munsell, *The 179th,* pp. 54-55; Historical Division, Department of the Army, *Anzio Beachhead, 22 January-25 May 1944,* pp. 64-65.

19. Historical Division, Department of the Army, *Anzio Beachhead, 22 January-25 May 1944,* pp. 64-65; Munsell, *The 179th,* pp. 54-55.

20. Allen, *Anzio: Edge of Disaster,* pp. 104-105; Historical Division, Department of the Army, *Anzio Beachhead, 22 January-25 May 1944,* pp. 64-65, 87.

21. Historical Division, Department of the Army, *Anzio Beachhead, 22 January-25 May 1944,* pp. 68-70; Nelson, *Thunderbird,* p. 56; Munsell, *The 179th,* pp. 54-55; Fisher, *The 180th; The 157th,* p. 57.

22. Historical Division, Department of the Army, *Anzio Beachhead, 22 January-25 May 1944,* pp. 71-72.

23. Ibid.; *The 157th,* pp. 57-58; Allen, *Anzio: Edge of Disaster,* pp. 1-7, 105-107.

24. Allen, *Anzio: Edge of Disaster,* pp. 1-7, 105-107; *The 157th,* pp. 57-58; Historical Division, Department of the Army, *Anzio Beachhead, 22 January-25 May 1944,* pp. 71-72.

25. Historical Division, Department of the Army, *Anzio Beachhead, 22 January-25 May 1944,* pp. 72-75; *The 157th,* pp. 57-58; Nelson, *Thunderbird,* p. 132; *45th Division News,* September 6, 1944.

26. *The 157th,* pp. 57-58; Historical Division, Department of the Army, *Anzio Beachhead, 22 January-25 May 1944,* pp. 72-75.

27. Nelson, *Thunderbird,* p. 132; *45th Division News,* September 6, 1944 and November 15, 1944.

28. Historical Division, Department of the Army, *Anzio Beachhead, 22 January-25 May 1944,* pp. 70-75; Jones and McCasland, Notes, OMC; Munsell, *The 179th,* pp. 54-55.

29. Munsell, *The 179th,* pp. 54-56; Fisher, *The 180th;* Historical Division, Department of the Army, *Anzio Beachhead, 22 January-25 May 1944,* pp. 70-75.

30. Historical Division, Department of the Army, *Anzio Beachhead, 22 January-25 May 1944,* pp. 75-77; Fisher, *The 180th; The 157th,* pp. 60-62; Munsell, *The 179th,* pp. 55-56.

31. Munsell, *The 179th,* pp. 55-56; Fisher, *The 180th; The 157th,* pp. 60-62; Historical Division, Department of the Army, *Anzio Beachhead, 22 January-25 May 1944,* pp. 75-77.

32. Historical Division, Department of the Army, *Anzio Beachhead, 22 January-25 May 1944,* pp. 77-79; Fisher, *The 180th; The 157th,* pp. 62-68; Munsell, *The 179th,* pp. 55-56.

33. Munsell, *The 179th,* pp. 55-56; Fisher, *The 180th;* Historical Division, Department of the Army, *Anzio Beachhead, 22 January-25 May 1944,* pp. 62-68, 77-80.

34. *The 157th,* pp. 66-67.

35. *45th Division News,* June 10, 1944.

36. Ibid.; Nelson, *Thunderbird,* p. 132.

37. Nelson, *Thunderbird,* pp. 65-66; Fisher, *The 180th;* Munsell, *The 179th,* pp. 55-56; Historical Division, Department of the Army, *Anzio Beachhead, 22 January-25 May 1944,* pp. 79-81.

38. Historical Division, Department of the Army, *Anzio Beachhead, 22 January-25 May 1944,* pp. 79-82; *The 157th,* pp. 65-68; Allen, *Anzio: Edge of Disaster,* p. 111; Fisher, *The 180th;* Munsell, *The 179th,* pp. 55-56.

39. Munsell, *The 179th,* pp. 55-56; Fisher, *The 189th; The 157th,* pp. 66-68; Historical Division, Department of the Army, *Anzio Beachhead, 22 January-25 May 1944,* pp. 81-84.

40. Historical Division, Department of the Army, *Anzio Beachhead, 22 January-25 May 1944,* pp. 84-87; Fisher, *The 180th; The 157th,* pp. 68-69; Munsell, *The 179th,* pp. 56-57.

41. *45th Infantry News,* March 22, 1944.

42. Historical Division, Department of the Army, *Anzio Beachhead, 22 January-25 May 1944,* pp. 87-91.

43. Nelson, *Thunderbird,* pp. 62-66; Interview, Clapp, February 6, 1981, OMC; Interview, Major General Hal L. Muldrow, Jr. (Ret.), February 13, 1981, OMC; 45th Infantry Division, *The Fighting Forty-Fifth,* pp. 80-83; *45th Division News,* April 4, 1944 and May 6, 1944; Interview, Wilson, January 7, 1977, Archives.

44. Interview, Colonel Bruce E. Rey, March 22, 1981, OMC; Letter, Ralph W. Jones to Kenny A. Franks, October 16, 1980, OMC.

45. Nelson, *Thunderbird,* pp. 62-66; Interview, Clapp, February 6, 1981, OMC; Interview, Muldrow, February 13, 1981, OMC; 45th Infantry Division, *The Fighting Forty-Fifth,* pp. 80-83.

46. Public Information Division, Department of the Army, *The Medal of Honor of the United States,* p. 334.

47. Ibid.

48. Ibid.; *45th Infantry News,* August 6, 1944.

49. 45th Infantry Division, *The Fighting Forty-Fifth,* pp. 80-83; Interview, Muldrow, February 13, 1981, OMC; Munsell, *The 179th,* pp. 57-65; Nelson, *Thunderbird,* pp. 62-66; Fisher, *The 180th; The 157th,* pp. 68-81.

50. 45th Infantry Division, *The Fighting Forty-Fifth,* pp. 80-83; Munsell, *The 179th,* pp. 57-65; Nelson, *Thunderbird,* pp. 62-66; Fisher, *The 180th; The 157th,* pp. 68-81.

51. *The 157th,* pp. 79-80; Fisher, *The 180th.*

52. Fisher, *The 180th; The 157th,* pp. 79-80; Interview, Command Sergeant Arthur E. Peters, January 22, 1981, OMC.

53. Nelson. *Thunderbird,* p. 59; Interview, Colonel Roy P. Stewart (Ret.), February 4, 1981, OMC; Jones and McCasland, Notes, OMC.

54. Interview, Forrest G. Munson, January 22, 1981, OMC.

55. Ibid.; Nelson, *Thunderbird,* p. 59.

56. Nelson, *Thunderbird,* p. 59.

57. Ibid.

58. Ibid.

59. Ibid.; Interview, Meyers, Murphy, and Grace, August 22, 1980, OMC; Jones and McCasland, Notes, OMC; Interview, McCasland, October 29, 1980, OMC; Reader's Comments, OMC.

60. Munsell, *The 179th,* p. 65; Nelson, *Thunderbird,* p. 58; 45th Infantry Division, *The Fighting Forty-Fifth,* pp. 84-85.

61. 45th Infantry Division, *The Fighting Forty-Fifth,* pp. 83-86; Nelson, *Thunderbird,* pp. 65-66.

62. *The 157th,* pp. 84-89; Fisher, *The 180th;* Munsell, *The 179th,* pp. 64-65.

63. Munsell, *The 179th,* pp. 65-67; 45th Infantry Division, *The Fighting Forty-Fifth,* pp. 86-89; Nelson, *Thunderbird,* pp. 65-66; *The 157th,* pp. 89-94; Fisher, *The 180th; 45th Division News,* May 27, 1944.

64. Interview, Meyers, Murphy, and Grace, August 22, 1980, OMC; Interview, McCasland, October 29, 1980, OMC.

65. Interview, McCasland, October 29, 1980, OMC.

66. Nelson, *Thunderbird,* pp. 65-66; *The 157th,* pp. 94-96; Fisher, *The 180th;* Munsell, *The 179th,* pp. 67-68; 45th Infantry Division, *The Fighting Forty-Fifth,* pp. 89-92.

67. 45th Infantry Division, *The Fighting Forty-Fifth,* pp. 89-92; *The 157th,* pp. 96-98; Fisher, *The 180th;* Munsell, *The 179th,* pp. 68-70; Nelson, *Thunderbird,* pp. 65-71.

68. 45th Infantry Division, *The Fighting Forty-Fifth,* pp. 89-92; *The 157th,* pp. 96-98; Fisher, *The 180th;* Munsell, *The 179th,* pp. 68-70; Interview, Clapp, February 6, 1981, OMC; Nelson, *Thunderbird,* pp. 65-71.

69. Nelson, *Thunderbird,* pp. 71-72; 45th Infantry Division, *The Fighting Forty-Fifth,* pp. 92-93; *The 157th,* pp. 98-100; Fisher, *The 180th,* Munsell, Jr., *The 179th,* pp. 68-70.

70. Nelson, *Thunderbird,* p. 72.

10
VICTORY IN EUROPE

1. Robert L. Dulaney, *45th Infantry Division;* Guy Nelson, *Thunderbird: A History of the 45th Infantry Division,* pp. 74-75; 45th Infantry Division, *The Fighting Forty-Fifth: The Combat Report of an Infantry Division,* p. 99.

2. 45th Infantry Division, *The Fighting Forty-Fifth,* pp. 94-95; *Report of Operations: The Seventh United States Army in France and Germany, 1944-1945,* vol. 1, pp. 57-58, map following p. 56; Lieutenant Colonel Peter E. Wheeler, Comments, OMC.

3. George A. Fisher, *The Story of the 180th Infantry Regiment;* Warren P. Munsell, Jr., *The Story of a Regiment: A History of the 179th Regimental Combat Team,* pp. 71-76; *History of the 157th Infantry Regiment (Rifle),* pp. 99-103; 45th Infantry Division, *The Fighting Forty-Fifth,* pp. 99-100.

4. 45th Infantry Division, *The Fighting Forty-Fifth,* pp. 99-100; Fisher, *The 180th; The 157th,* pp. 99-103; Interview, Sergeant Major Jack Clapp (Ret.), February 3, 1981, OMC; Munsell, *The 179th,* pp. 71-76.

5. 45th Infantry Division, *The Fighting Forty-Fifth,* pp. 99-100; Fisher, *The 180th; The 157th,* pp. 99-103; Munsell, *The 179th,* pp. 71-76.

6. Munsell, *The 179th,* pp. 71-76; 45th Infantry Divi-

sion, *The Fighting Forty-Fifth*, pp. 99-101; Fisher, *The 180th; The 157th*, pp. 103-108; Interview, Brigadier General William R. Wilson (Ret.), January 7, 1977, OMC; Wheeler, Comments, OMC.

7. Nelson, *Thunderbird*, p. 84; Wheeler, Comments, OMC.

8. Munsell, *The 179th*, pp. 76-78; 45th Infantry Division, *The Fighting Forty-Fifth*, pp. 99-100; Wheeler, Comments, OMC.

9. 45th Infantry Division, *The Fighting Forty-Fifth*, pp. 99-100; Munsell, *The 179th*, pp. 76-78; Wheeler, Comments, OMC.

10. Munsell, *The 179th*, pp. 78-83; Fisher, *The 180th; The 157th*, pp. 105-107; 45th Infantry Division, *The Fighting Forty-Fifth*, pp. 101-102; Wheeler, Comments; Nelson, *Thunderbird*, p. 77.

11. 45th Infantry Division, *The Fighting Forty-Fifth*, pp. 102-105; Munsell, *The 179th*, pp. 83-87; Fisher, *The 180th; The 157th*, pp. 108-11.

12. Nelson, *Thunderbird*, pp. 77-79; 45th Infantry Division, *The Fighting Forty-Fifth*, p. 105.

13. 45th Infantry Division, *The Fighting Forty-Fifth*, pp. 105-107; Nelson, *Thunderbird*, p. 79.

14. Munsell, *The 179th*, p. 87; Fisher, *The 180th; The 157th*, pp. 108-10; Dulaney, *45th Infantry Division;* 45th Infantry Division, *The Fighting Forty-Fifth*, pp. 106-107.

15. 45th Infantry Division, *The Fighting Forty-Fifth*, pp. 107-108; *The 157th*, p. 109; Fisher, *The 180th*.

16. Fisher, *The 180th;* Nelson, *Thunderbird*, pp. 79-80; 45th Infantry Division, *The Fighting Forty-Fifth*, p. 109.

17. 45th Infantry Division, *The Fighting Forty-Fifth*, pp. 109-11; *The 157th*, pp. 110-15; Fisher, *The 180th;* Munsell, *The 179th*, pp. 88-91.

18. Munsell, *The 179th*, pp. 88-91; 45th Infantry Division, *The Fighting Forty-Fifth*, pp. 109-11; *The 157th*, pp. 110-15; Fisher, *The 180th*.

19. Munsell, *The 179th*, pp. 89-90.

20. Ibid., pp. 90-92; *The 157th*, pp. 113-15; Fisher, *The 180th;* Nelson, *Thunderbird*, pp. 80-81; 45th Infantry Division, *The Fighting Forty-Fifth*, pp. 111-17.

21. 45th Infantry Division, *The Fighting Forty-Fifth*, pp. 111-18; Fisher, *The 180th;* Nelson, *Thunderbird*, pp. 80-81, 132; Munsell, *The 179th*, pp. 91-94.

22. Munsell, *The 179th*, pp. 92-95; Nelson, *Thunderbird*, pp. 81-82; Fisher, *The 180th; The 157th*, pp. 115-20; 45th Infantry Division, *The Fighting Forty-Fifth*, pp. 118-21.

23. 45th Infantry Division, *The Fighting Forty-Fifth*, pp. 121-22; Munsell, *The 179th*, p. 96; Dulaney, *45th Infantry Division*.

24. Dulaney, *45th Infantry Division;* Munsell, *The 179th*, pp. 96-98; 45th Infantry Division, *The Fighting Forty-Fifth*, pp. 122-25.

25. 45th Infantry Division, *The Fighting Forty-Fifth*, pp. 122-25; Interview, Clapp, February 6, 1981, OMC; Dulaney, *45th Infantry Division;* Munsell, *The 179th*, pp. 96-98.

26. Munsell, *The 179th*, pp. 98-100; Nelson, *Thunderbird*, pp. 85-87; Fisher, *The 180th; The 157th*, pp. 121-32; Dulaney, *45th Infantry Division;* 45th Infantry Division, *The Fighting Forty-Fifth*, pp. 125-27.

27. 45th Infantry Division, *The Fighting Forty-Fifth*, pp. 125-27; Munsell, *The 179th*, pp. 98-100; Nelson, *Thunder-*

bird, pp. 85-87; Fisher, *The 180th; The 157th*, pp. 121-32; Dulaney, *45th Infantry Division; 45th Division News*, December 23, 1944.

28. Dulaney, *45th Infantry Division;* Nelson, *Thunderbird*, pp. 86-89; Fisher, *The 180th;* 45th Infantry Division, *The Fighting Forty-Fifth*, pp. 127-28.

29. 45th Infantry Division, *The Fighting Forty-Fifth*, pp. 128-30; Nelson, *Thunderbird*, pp. 87-89, 132; Fisher, *The 180th;* Dulaney, *45th Infantry Division*.

30. Dulaney, *45th Infantry Division;* Nelson, *Thunderbird*, pp. 88-89; Munsell, *The 179th*, pp. 101-103; 45th Infantry Division, *The Fighting Forty-Fifth*, pp. 129-33.

31. 45th Infantry Division, *The Fighting Forty-Fifth*, pp. 129-31; *The 157th*, pp. 122-28; Dulaney, *45th Infantry Division*.

32. Dulaney, *45th Infantry Division; The 157th*, pp. 122-28; 45th Infantry Division, *The Fighting Forty-Fifth*, pp. 129-31.

33. Ibid., pp. 133-35; *Report of Operations: The Seventh United States Army in France and Germany, 1944-1945*, vol. 2, p. 572; Dulaney, *45th Infantry Division*.

34. Dulaney, *45th Infantry Division;* Munsell, *The 179th*, pp. 104-106; 45th Infantry Division, *The Fighting Forty-Fifth*, pp. 136-37; *45th Division News*, February 9, 1945; Wheeler, Comments, OMC.

35. 45th Infantry Division, *The Fighting Forty-Fifth*, pp. 136-37; Dulaney, *45th Infantry Division;* Munsell, *The 179th*, pp. 105-109; Fisher, *The 180th; The 157th*, pp. 129-32.

36. *The 157th*, pp. 129-33, 146; 45th Infantry Division, *The Fighting Forty-Fifth*, pp. 142-45; *45th Division News*, July 10, 1945; Wheeler, Comments, OMC.

37. 45th Infantry Division, *The Fighting Forty-Fifth*, pp. 142-45; *The 157th*, pp. 133-34; *45th Division News*, July 10, 1945, OMC.

38. *The 157th*, pp. 133-34; 45th Infantry Division, *The Fighting Forty-Fifth*, pp. 144-46; *45th Division News*, July 10, 1945.

39. 45th Infantry Division, *The Fighting Forty-Fifth*, pp. 144-46; *The 157th*, pp. 134-36; *45th Division News*, July 10, 1945.

40. *The 157th*, pp. 134-41; Dulaney, *45th Infantry Division;* Fisher, *The 180th;* Munsell, *The 179th*, pp. 107-12; Interview, Clapp, February 6, 1981, OMC; 45th Infantry Division, *The Fighting Forty-Fifth*, pp. 146-49.

41. *The 157th*, pp. 134-41; Dulaney, *45th Infantry Division;* Fisher, *The 180th;* Munsell, *The 179th*, pp. 107-12; 45th Infantry Division, *The Fighting Forty-Fifth*, pp. 146-49.

42. 45th Infantry Division, *The Fighting Forty-Fifth*, pp. 149-53; Munsell, *The 179th*, pp. 107-12; *The 157th*, pp. 134-41; Dulaney, *45th Infantry Division*.

43. Dulaney, *45th Infantry Division; The 157th*, pp. 141-46; 45th Infantry Division, *The Fighting Forty-Fifth*, pp. 143-55.

44. Public Information Division, Department of the Army, *The Medal of Honor of the United States Army*, pp. 346-47; Reader's Comments, OMC.

45. Ibid.

46. 45th Infantry Division, *The Fighting Forty-Fifth*, pp. 154-56; Dulaney, *45th Infantry Division;* Wheeler, Comments, OMC.

47. Dulaney, *45th Infantry Division;* 45th Infantry Division, *The Fighting Forty-Fifth,* pp. 154-56.

48. 45th Infantry Division, *The Fighting Forty-Fifth,* pp. 156-57; *The 157th,* pp. 145-46; Dulaney, *45th Infantry Division.*

49. Dulaney, *45th Infantry Division;* Fisher, *The 180th;* Munsell, *The 179th,* pp. 114-15; 45th Infantry Division, *The Fighting Forty-Fifth,* p. 157.

50. 45th Infantry Division, *The Fighting Forty-Fifth,* pp. 157-60; Fisher, *The 180th;* Munsell, *The 179th,* pp. 115-17; Dulaney, *45th Infantry Division.*

51. Dulaney, *45th Infantry Division; The 157th,* pp. 149-50, 154-55; 45th Infantry Division, *The Fighting Forty-Fifth,* pp. 160-64.

52. 45th Infantry Division, *The Fighting Forty-Fifth,* pp. 161-64; *The 157th,* pp. 149-55; Dulaney, *45th Infantry Division.*

53. Dulaney, *45th Infantry Division; The 157th,* pp. 149-55; 45th Infantry Division, *The Fighting Forty-Fifth,* pp. 161-68; Mary H. Williams, comp., *United States Army in World War II, Special Studies, Chronology, 1941-1945,* p. 471.

54. Williams, comp., *United States Army in World War II, Special Studies, Chronology, 1941-1945,* p. 471; *The 157th,* pp. 149-55; Dulaney, *45th Infantry Division;* 45th Infantry Division, *The Fighting Forty-Fifth,* pp. 164-68.

55. 45th Infantry Division, *The Fighting Forty-Fifth,* pp. 164-68; Williams, comp., *United States Army in World War II, Special Studies, Chronology, 1941-1945,* p. 494; Fisher, *The 180th;* Dulaney, *45th Infantry Division.*

56. Dulaney, *45th Infantry Division;* Munsell, *The 179th,* p. 121; 45th Infantry Division, *The Fighting Forty-Fifth,* pp. 164-68; Reader's Comments, OMC.

57. 45th Infantry Division, *The Fighting Forty-Fifth,* pp. 165-80; Dulaney, *45th Infantry Division;* Fisher, *The 180th; The 157th,* pp. 157-60; Munsell, *The 179th,* pp. 121-23.

58. Munsell, *The 179th,* pp. 121-23; Dulaney, *45th Infantry Division;* Fisher, *The 180th; The 157th,* pp. 157-60; 45th Infantry Division, *The Fighting Forty-Fifth,* pp. 165-80; Nelson, *Thunderbird,* pp. 98-99, 132.

59. 45th Infantry Division, *The Fighting Forty-Fifth,* pp. 180-85; Munsell, *The 179th,* pp. 123-26; Fisher, *The 180th; The 157th,* pp. 160-62; Dulaney, *45th Infantry Division.*

60. Dulaney, *45th Infantry Division;* Munsell, *The 179th,* pp. 123-26; Fisher, *The 180th; The 157th,* pp. 160-62; 45th Infantry Division, *The Fighting Forty-Fifth,* pp. 180-85.

61. 45th Infantry Division, *The Fighting Forty-Fifth,* p. 185; *The 157th,* pp. 162-67; Interview, Clapp, February 6, 1981, OMC; Dulaney, *45th Infantry Division; 45th Division News,* May 13, 1945.

62. 45th Infantry Division, *The Fighting Forty-Fifth,* p. 185; *The 157th,* pp. 162-67; Interview, Clapp, February 6, 1981, OMC; Dulaney, *45th Infantry Division; 45th Division News,* May 13, 1945; Wheeler, Comments, OMC.

63. Dulaney, *45th Infantry Division; The 157th,* pp. 167-73; Fisher, *The 180th;* Munsell, *The 179th,* pp. 127-29; 45th Infantry Division, *The Fighting Forty-Fifth,* pp. 185-88.

64. 45th Infantry Division, *The Fighting Forty-Fifth,* pp. 187-88; Dulaney, *45th Infantry Division; The 157th,* pp. 169-73; Fisher, *The 180th;* Munsell, *The 179th,* pp. 129-31.

11
THE COLD WAR

1. Guy Nelson, *Thunderbird: A History of the 45th Infantry Division,* pp. 103-105; 45th Infantry Division, *The Fighting Forty-Fifth,* pp. 193-95.

2. 45th Infantry Division, *The Fighting Forty-Fifth,* pp. 195-98; Lieutenant Colonel Peter E. Wheeler, Comments, OMC.

3. 45th Infantry Division, *The Fighting Forty-Fifth,* pp. 195-96; Nelson, *Thunderbird,* pp. 104-105; *History of the 157th Infantry Regiment (Rifle),* p. 176; George A. Fisher, *The Story of the 180th Infantry Regiment; 45th Division News,* March 9, May 20, May 31, June 9, June 17, and June 28, 1945.

4. Fisher, *The 180th;* Interview, Command Sergeant Major Arthur E. Peters, January 22, 1981, OMC; Interview, Sergeant Major Jack Clapp (Ret.), February 6, 1981, OMC; *The 157th,* pp. 176-77; *The Thunderbird News,* November 1, 1947.

5. *The 157th,* p. 177; Fisher, *The 180th; The Thunderbird News,* November 1, 1947.

6. Fisher, *The 180th;* Nelson, *Thunderbird,* pp. 105, 130; *The 157th,* pp. 177-78; Dulaney, *45th Infantry Division; The Thunderbird News,* November 1, 1947.

7. Robert L. Dulaney, *45th Infantry Division;* Ralph W. Jones and Colonel John H. McCasland, Notes, OMC; Nelson, *Thunderbird,* p. 105; *The Thunderbird News,* November 1, 1947; TAG (The Adjutant-General), Letter, Ralph W. Jones to Kenny A. Franks, April 21, 1981, OMC.

8. Nelson, *Thunderbird,* p. 105; Interview, Major General Hal L. Muldrow, Jr. (Ret.), February 13, 1981; Dulaney, *45th Infantry Division;* Interview, Major General James C. Styron (Ret.), September, 1973, Archives; TAG, Jones to Franks, April 21, 1981; Interview, Major General Frederick A. Daugherty (Ret.), November 18, 1976, Archives.

9. Nelson, *Thunderbird,* p. 105; Interview, Muldrow, February 13, 1981, OMC; Dulaney, *45th Infantry Division;* Interview, Styron, September, 1973, Archives; TAG, Jones to Franks, April 21, 1981; Interview, Daugherty, November 18, 1976, Archives.

10. Dulaney, *45th Infantry Division;* Nelson, *Thunderbird,* pp. 105-106; *The Thunderbird News,* November 1, 1947; Interview, Daugherty, November 18, 1976, Archives.

11. Dulaney, *45th Infantry Division;* Nelson, *Thunderbird,* pp. 105-106, 131; *The Thunderbird News,* November 1, 1947; Interview, Daugherty, November 18, 1976, Archives.

12. Dulaney, *45th Infantry Division;* Nelson, *Thunderbird,* pp. 105-106; *The Thunderbird News,* November 1, 1947; Interview, Daugherty, November 18, 1976, Archives.

13. Dulaney, *45th Infantry Division;* Nelson, *Thunderbird,* pp. 105-106; *The Thunderbird News,* November 1, 1947, March 1 and July 26, 1948, and January 1 and February 1, 1949.

14. Nelson, *Thunderbird,* pp. 106-107; Dulaney, *45th Infantry Division;* Matthew B. Ridgeway, *The Korean War,* pp. 1-7.

15. Ridgeway, *Korean War,* pp. 1-8; Nelson, *Thunderbird,* pp. 106-107; Dulaney, *45th Infantry Division.*

16. Ridgeway, *Korean War,* pp. 8-9.

17. Ibid., pp. 9-11.

18. Ibid., pp. 11-17; War Compilation Committee, *History of the United Nations Forces in the Korean War,* vol. 3, p. 568.

19. War Compilation Committee, *History of the United Nations Forces in the Korean War,* vol. 3, p. 568; Ridgeway, *Korean War,* pp. 17-26; R. L. Lapica, et al., eds., *Facts on File Yearbook, 1950,* pp. 201-209.

20. Lapica, et al., eds., *Facts on File Yearbook, 1950,* pp. 109-225; Ridgeway, *Korean War,* pp. 26-29; War Compilation Committee, *History of the United Nations Forces in the Korean War,* vol. 3, pp. 568-69.

21. Jim D. Hill, *The Minute Man in Peace and War: A History of the National Guard,* pp. 506-507; Nelson, *Thunderbird,* p. 107; Dulaney, *45th Infantry Division.*

22. Dulaney, *45th Infantry Division;* Nelson, *Thunderbird,* p. 107; *45th Division News,* September 6, 1950; Interview, Daugherty, January 6, 1977, Archives.

23. Nelson, *Thunderbird,* p. 107; Dulaney, *45th Infantry Division; 45th Division News,* September 6, 1950; Interview, Styron, September, 1973, Archives.

24. Dulaney, *45th Infantry Division;* Nelson, *Thunderbird,* p. 107.

25. TAG, Jones to Franks, April 21, 1981; Interview, Major General John Coffey, Jr. (Ret.), undated, Archives.

26. Nelson, *Thunderbird,* pp. 107-108; Interview, Colonel John H. McCasland (Ret.), October 19, 1980, OMC; Dulaney, *45th Infantry Division; 45th Division News,* September 28 and October 12, 1950.

27. Dulaney, *45th Infantry Division;* Nelson, *Thunderbird,* pp. 107-108; *45th Division News,* November 9, November 16, November 30, December 14, and December 28, 1950, and January 4, 1951; Interview, Styron, September, 1973, Archives.

28. Nelson, *Thunderbird,* pp. 107-108; Dulaney, *45th Infantry Division; 45th Division News,* August 30, 1951; Interview, Styron, September, 1973, Archives.

29. Dulaney, *45th Infantry Division;* Nelson, *Thunderbird,* p. 108; Interview, McCasland, October 29, 1980, OMC; *45th Division News,* March 15, 1951.

30. James F. Schnable, *Policy and Direction: The First Year,* vol. 3, in *United States Army in the Korean War,* ed. Stetson Conn, pp. 344-45.

31. Ibid.

32. Dulaney, *45th Infantry Division;* Ralph W. Jones and John H. McCasland, Notes, OMC; Nelson, *Thunderbird,* p. 108; Interview, Coffey, undated, Archives; Interview, Daugherty, January 6, 1977, Archives.

33. Nelson, *Thunderbird,* pp. 108-10; Jones and McCasland, Notes, OMC; Interview, McCasland, October 15, November 12, 1980, OMC; Dulaney, *45th Infantry Division;* Reader's Comments, OMC.

34. Interview, McCasland, November 12, 1980, and October 29, 1980; Nelson, *Thunderbird,* pp. 108-10; McCasland, December 10, 1980, OMC; Dulaney, *45th Infantry Division; 45th Division News,* May 10, May 17, June 7, and August 30, 1951; Interview, Styron, September, 1973, Archives.

35. Dulaney, *45th Infantry Division;* Nelson, *Thunderbird,* p. 110; *45th Division News,* June 28 and July 12, 1951; Interview, Styron, September, 1973, Archives.

36. Nelson, *Thunderbird,* pp. 110-11; Jones and McCasland, Notes, OMC; Dulaney, *45th Infantry Division;* Walter G. Hermes, *Truce Tent and Fighting Front,* vol. 3 in *United States Army in the Korean War,* ed. Stetson Conn, p. 203; Interview, Coffey, undated, Archives.

37. Hermes, *Truce Tent and Fighting Front,* p. 203; Interview, McCasland, November 12, 1980, OMC; Nelson, *Thunderbird,* pp. 110-11; Dulaney, *45th Infantry Division; 45th Division News,* October 11 and October 25, 1951; Interview, Coffey, undated, Archives.

38. Dulaney, *45th Infantry Division;* Hermes, *Truce Tent and Fighting Front,* p. 202-203; Interview, McCasland, November 12, 1980, OMC; Nelson, *Thunderbird,* pp. 110-11; Reader's Comments, OMC.

39. Ridgeway, *Korean War,* pp. 29-31; Lapica, et al., eds., *Facts on File Yearbook, 1950,* pp. 225-97; War Compilation Committee, *History of the United Nations Forces in the Korean War,* vol. 3, p. 569.

40. War Compilation Committee, *History of the United Nations Forces in the Korean War,* vol. 3, pp. 568-74; Ridgeway, *Korean War,* pp. 30-78.

41. Ridgeway, *Korean War,* pp. 78-204; War Compilation Committee, *History of the United Nations Forces in the Korean War,* vol. 3, pp. 569-72, 580.

42. War Compilation Committee, *History of the United Nations Forces in the Korean War,* vol. 3, pp. 569-72, 580; Ridgeway, *Korean War,* pp. 78-204.

43. Nelson, *Thunderbird,* pp. 110-11; Interview, Muldrow, February 13, 1981, OMC; Hermes, *Truce Tent and Fighting Front,* p. 203; Interview, Coffey, undated, Archives; Interview, Daugherty, January 6, 1977, Archives; Reader's Comments, OMC.

44. Nelson, *Thunderbird,* pp. 110-11; Interview, Muldrow, February 13, 1981, OMC; Hermes, *Truce Tent and Fighting Front,* p. 203; Interview, Coffey, undated, Archives; Interview, Daugherty, January 6, 1977, Archives.

12
KOREA

1. Walter G. Hermes, *Truce Tent and Fighting Front,* pp. 204-205; Guy Nelson, *Thunderbird: A History of the 45th Infantry Division,* pp. 113-14; Interview, Major General James C. Styron, September, 1973, Archives; Interview, Brigadier General William E. Mayberry (Ret.), January 7, 1977, Archives.

2. Interview, Styron, September, 1973; Interview, Major General Frederick A. Daugherty (Ret.), May 8, 1981, OMC.

3. Interview, Major General Hal L. Muldrow, Jr. (Ret.), February 13, 1981, OMC.

4. Nelson, *Thunderbird,* pp. 114-15; Interview, Colonel John H. McCasland (Ret.), November 12, 1980, OMC; Ralph W. Jones and John H. McCasland, Notes, OMC; *45th Division News,* December 18, 1951, and January 4, 1952; Interview, Daugherty, May 8, 1981, OMC.

5. Letter, Lieutenant Colonel Bruce E. Rey (Ret.), to Kenny A. Franks, March 13, 1981, OMC; *45th Division News,* December 28, 1951.

6. Hermes, *Truce Tent and Fighting Front,* p. 376; The War History Compilation Committee, *The History of the*

United Nations Forces in the Korean War, vol. 5, p. 383; Russel A. Gugeler, *Combat Actions in Korea,* pp. 215, 236; Nelson, *Thunderbird,* p. 120; Interview, McCasland, November 12, 1980, OMC; *45th Division News,* February 15, 1952; Interview, Daugherty, January 6, 1977, Archives.

7. Interview, Rey, February 27, 1981, OMC; Interview, Styron, September, 1973, Archives.

8. Nelson, *Thunderbird,* pp. 114-15; War History Compilation Committee, *History of the United Nations Forces in the Korean War,* vol. 5, p. 285; *45th Division News,* January 18, 1952.

9. Nelson, *Thunderbird,* pp. 114-15; War History Compilation Committee, *History of the United Nations Forces in the Korean War,* vol. 5, p. 285.

10. War History Compilation Committee, *History of the United Nations Forces in the Korean War,* vol. 5, p. 285; Nelson, *Thunderbird,* pp. 114-15.

11. Gugeler, *Combat Actions in Korea,* pp. 222, 234-35.

12. Ibid., p. 222; War History Compilation Committee, *History of the United Nations Forces in the Korean War,* vol. 5, pp. 285-86.

13. War History Compilation Committee, *History of the United Nations Forces in the Korean War,* vol. 5, pp. 285-86; Gugeler, *Combat Actions in Korea,* pp. 222-24.

14. Gugeler, *Combat Actions in Korea,* p. 224.

15. Ibid., pp. 222-25; Interview, McCasland, December 17, 1980, OMC; War History Compilation Committee, *History of the United Nations Forces in the Korean War,* vol. 5, pp. 285-86.

16. Gugeler, *Combat Actions in Korea,* pp. 225-26.

17. Ibid., p. 234.

18. Ibid., pp. 226-28.

19. Ibid., pp. 222, 228-29.

20. Ibid., pp. 222, 228-32; War History Compilation Committee, *History of the United Nations Forces in the Korean War,* vol. 5, pp. 285-86.

21. War History Compilation Committee, *History of the United Nations Forces in the Korean War,* vol. 5, pp. 285-86; Gugeler, *Combat Actions in Korea,* pp. 229-32; Interview, Daugherty, May 8, 1981, OMC.

22. Gugeler, *Combat Actions in Korea,* pp. 232-33; War History Compilation Committee, *History of the United Nations Forces in the Korean War,* vol. 5, pp. 285-86; Interview, Styron, September, 1973, Archives.

23. War History Compilation Committee, *History of the United Nations Forces in the Korean War,* vol. 5, pp. 285-86; Gugeler, *Combat Actions in Korea,* pp. 232-33; Interview, Daugherty, May 8, 1981, OMC.

24. Gugeler, *Combat Actions in Korea,* pp. 233-34; War History Compilation Committee, *History of the United Nations Forces in the Korean War,* vol. 5, pp. 285-86; Interview, Daugherty, May 8, 1981, OMC.

25. *45th Division News,* March 21, March 28, and April 18, 1952.

26. Interview, Major General John Coffey, Jr., undated, Archives.

27. War History Compilation Committee, *History of the United Nations Forces in the Korean War,* vol. 5, pp. 306-307.

28. Ibid., p. 230; Nelson, *Thunderbird,* pp. 116-17; Interview, Daugherty, May 8, 1981, Archives.

29. War History Compilation Committee, *History of the*

United Nations Forces in the Korean War, vol. 5, p. 320; Interview, Daugherty, May 8, 1981, Archives; "An After Action Report of a Battalion Size Attack on Hill '200,' Night 25-26 May 52, 179th Infantry Regiment," Archives, 45th Infantry Division Museum, Oklahoma City, Oklahoma.

30. War History Compilation Committee, *History of the United Nations Forces in the Korean War,* vol. 5, p. 320; Interview, Daugherty, May 8, 1981, OMC; "An After Action Report of a Battalion Size Attack on Hill '200,' Night 25-26 May 52, 179th Infantry Regiment," Archives.

31. Nelson, *Thunderbird,* pp. 116-17.

32. Ibid., pp. 119-22; *45th Division News,* March 21, March 28, May 30, and June 6, 1952; Interview, Styron, September, 1973, Archives.

33. Nelson, *Thunderbird,* pp. 119-22; *45th Division News,* March 21, March 28, May 30, and June 6, 1952; Interview, McCasland, November 12, 1980, OMC; Interview, Daugherty, May 8, 1981, OMC.

34. Nelson, *Thunderbird,* pp. 119-22, 131; *45th Division News,* February 1 and February 22, 1952.

35. Nelson, *Thunderbird,* p. 117; War History Compilation Committee, *History of the United Nations Forces in the Korean War,* vol. 5, pp. 340-42.

36. War History Compilation Committee, *History of the United Nations Forces in the Korean War,* vol. 5, pp. 340-43; Nelson, *Thunderbird,* pp. 117-18.

37. Nelson, *Thunderbird,* pp. 117-18; War History Compilation Committee, *History of the United Nations Forces in the Korean War,* vol. 5, pp. 340-42.

38. War History Compilation Committee, *History of the United Nations Forces in the Korean War,* vol. 5, pp. 342-43.

39. Ibid., pp. 343-44; Nelson, *Thunderbird,* pp. 117-18.

40. Nelson, *Thunderbird,* pp. 117-18; War History Compilation Committee, *History of the United Nations Forces in the Korean War,* vol. 5, pp. 343-44.

41. War History Compilation Committee, *History of the United Nations Forces in the Korean War,* vol. 5, p. 344; Nelson, *Thunderbird,* pp. 118-19.

42. Nelson, *Thunderbird,* pp. 118-19; War History Compilation Committee, *History of the United Nations Forces in the Korean War,* vol. 5, pp. 343-45.

43. War History Compilation Committee, *History of the United Nations Forces in the Korean War,* vol. 5, pp. 345-46.

44. Ibid., p. 346.

45. Ibid., pp. 346-47, 349.

46. Nelson, *Thunderbird,* pp. 119-22.

47. Ibid., p. 120; War History Compilation Committee, *History of the United Nations Forces in the Korean War,* vol. 5, p. 383.

48. War History Compilation Committee, *History of the United Nations Forces in the Korean War,* vol. 5, pp. 124-25, 172; Gugeler, *Combat Actions in Korea,* pp. 215, 236; Nelson, *Thunderbird,* p. 120; Hermes, *Truce Tent and Fighting Front,* p. 376; Reader's Comments, OMC.

49. Interview, McCasland, November 12, 1980, OMC.

50. Hermes, *Truce Tent and Fighting Front,* pp. 376-77.

51. Ibid., p. 377.

52. Ibid., pp. 389n.; War History Compilation Committee, *History of the United Nations Forces in the Korean War,* vol. 5, pp. 413-14, 460-61, 474-75; Interview, Ralph

W. Jones, December 18, 1980, OMC; Nelson, *Thunderbird*, pp. 120-21; Fred McGhee, ed., *Facts on File Yearbook, 1953*, p. 255; *45th Division News*, August 10, 1953.

53. Hermes, *Truce Tent and Fighting Front*, pp. 389n.; War History Compilation Committee, *History of the United Nations Forces in the Korean War*, vol. 5, pp. 413-14, 460-61, 474-75; Interview, Jones, December 18, 1980, OMC; Nelson, *Thunderbird*, pp. 120-22, 131; Interview, McCasland, November 12, 1980, OMC; *45th Division News*, February 1, 1954.

54. Hermes, *Truce Tent and Fighting Front*, pp. 389n.; War History Compilation Committee, *History of the United Nations Forces in the Korean War*, vol. 5, pp. 413-14, 460-61, 474-75; Interview, Jones, December 18, 1989, OMC; Nelson, *Thunderbird*, pp. 120-22, 131; Interview, McCasland, November 12, 1980; *45th Division News*, February 1, 1954; "Operation Color Back," September 25, 1954, Archives, Forty-fifth Infantry Division Museum, Oklahoma City, Oklahoma.

13
THE OKLAHOMA AIR NATIONAL GUARD: THE 1940s

1. Jim D. Hill, *The Minute Man in Peace and War: A History of the National Guard*, pp. 517-20.

2. Ibid.; Letter, Master Sergeant Dennis R. Lindsey to Kenny A. Franks, March 9. 1981, OMC.

3. Hill, *The Minute Man in Peace and War*, p. 522.

4. Ibid., pp. 517-21, 522n.; Major General Stanley F. H. Newman, Notes, OMC.

5. Hill, *The Minute Man in Peace and War*, pp. 517-20; Anthony Robinson, ed., *The Encyclopedia of American Aircraft*, pp. 152-53.

6. Hill, *The Minute Man in Peace and War*, pp. 517-20.

7. Ibid., pp. 521-26.

8. Ibid., pp. 526-27.

9. Ibid., pp. 527-28; Maurer Maurer, ed., *Combat Squadrons of the Air Force, World War II*, p. 350; "Historical Record of the 138th Tactical Fighter Group—Tulsa IAP OK for the period ending 31 December 1977," Historical Records, Oklahoma Air National Guard, Oklahoma Military Department, Oklahoma City, Oklahoma, unpaged; *125th Air Transport Squadron Yearbook*, Historical Records, Oklahoma Air National Guard, Oklahoma Military Department, Oklahoma City, Oklahoma, unpaged.

10. Hill, *The Minute Man in Peace and War*, pp. 531-43; Maurer, ed., *Combat Squadrons of the Air Force, World War II*, p. 350.

11. Maurer, ed., *Combat Squadrons of the Air Force, World War II*, p. 350; Guy Nelson, *Thunderbird: A History of the 45th Infantry Division*, pp. 13-14; Interview, Colonel Roy P. Stewart (Ret.), February 4, 1981, OMC; David Mondey, *The Complete Illustrated Encyclopedia of the World's Aircraft*, p. 136; "Historical Record of the 138th Tactical Fighter Group"; *125th Air Transport Squadron Yearbook;* Robinson, ed., *Encyclopedia of American*

Aircraft, p. 166; *45th Division News*, October 4, 1940.

12. Maurer, ed., *Combat Squadrons of the Air Force, World War II*, p. 350; Mondey, *Complete Illustrated Encyclopedia of the World's Aircraft*, p. 136; "Historical Record of the 138th Tactical Fighter Group"; *125th Air Transport Squadron Yearbook;* Robinson, ed., *Encyclopedia of American Aircraft*, p. 166.

13. Maurer, ed., *Combat Squadrons of the Air Force, World War II*, pp. 350-51.

14. Ibid., p. 350; Robinson, ed., *Encyclopedia of American Aircraft*, p. 392; "Historical Record of the 138th Tactical Fighter Group"; *125th Air Transport Squadron Yearbook*.

15. Maurer, ed., *Combat Squadrons of the Air Force, World War II*, p. 350; Robinson, ed., *Encyclopedia of American Aircraft*, p. 356; Newman, Notes, OMC; "Historical Record of the 138th Tactical Fighter Group"; *125th Air Transport Squadron Yearbook*.

16. Maurer, ed., *Combat Squadrons of the Air Force, World War II*, p. 350; "Historical Record of the 138th Tactical Fighter Group"; *125th Air Transport Squadron Yearbook*.

17. Maurer, ed., *Combat Squadrons of the Air Force, World War II*, p. 350; "Historical Record of the 138th Tactical Fighter Group"; *125th Air Transport Squadron Yearbook;* Lindsey to Franks, March 9, 1981.

18. Maurer, ed., *Combat Squadrons of the Air Force, World War II*, p. 350; "Historical Record of the 138th Tactical Fighter Group"; *125th Air Transport Squadron Yearbook;* Lindsey to Franks, March 9, 1981.

19. "Historical Record of the 138th Tactical Fighter Group"; *125th Air Transport Squadron Yearbook*.

20. Maurer, ed., *Combat Squadrons of the Air Force, World War II*, p. 350; Hill, *The Minute Man in Peace and War*, pp. 498-99.

21. Hill, *The Minute Man in Peace and War*, p. 500n.

22. "Historical Record of the 138th Tactical Fighter Group"; *125th Air Transport Squadron Yearbook;* Dennis R. Lindsey, "Brief History of the 137th Tactical Airlift Wing (1947-1980)," Master Sergeant Dennis R. Lindsey, Historian, 137th Tactical Airlift Wing, OKANG, Personal Collection, Del City, Oklahoma, p. 1 (hereafter cited as DRLC); "Biography of General James E. Hill," DRLC; undated newspaper clipping, DRLC; Interview, Major General Stanley F. H. Newman, February 16, 1981, OMC; Lindsey to Franks, March 9, 1981.

23. Interview, Newman, February 16, 1981, OMC; Newman, Notes, OMC; Major General Stanley F. H. Newman, Comments, OMC; Lindsey to Franks, March 9, 1981.

24. Lindsey to Franks, March 9, 1981; Newman, Notes, OMC: *History of the 185th Aero Squadron*, Major General Stanley F. H. Newman, Personal Collection, Oklahoma City, Oklahoma, pp. 1-3 (hereafter cited as SFHNC); "History—185th Military Airlift Squadron—Oklahoma ANG," p. 1, SFHNC; Headquarters 137th Tactical Air Wing to National Guard Bureau, May 4, 1977, SFHNC.

25. Interview, Newman, February 16, 1981, OMC; *History of the 185th Aero Squadron*, pp. 3-20; "History—185th Military Airlift Squadron—Oklahoma ANG," Headquarters 137th Tactical Air Wing to National Guard Bureau, May 4, 1977; Newman, Comments, OMC.

26. Interview, Newman, February 16, 1981, OMC; "History—185th Military Airlift Squadron—Oklahoma ANG," pp. 1-3; "Background on 185th," pp. 1-3, SFHNC; Headquarters 137th Tactical Air Wing to National Guard Bureau, May 4, 1977; Robinson, ed., *Encyclopedia of American Aircraft,* pp. 16-18, 174-75, 344-62.

27. Lindsey to Franks, March 9, 1981.

28. Interview, Newman, February 16, 1981, OMC; "History—185th Military Airlift Squadron—Oklahoma ANG," pp. 1-3; "Background on 185th," pp. 1-3, SFHNC; HQ 137TAW to NGB, May 4, 1977.

29. Interview, Newman, February 16, 1981, OMC; "History—185th Military Airlift Squadron—Oklahoma ANG," pp. 1-3; "Background on 185th," pp. 1-3, SFHNC; HQ 137TAW to NGB, May 4, 1977.

30. Interview, Newman, February 16, 1981, OMC; "History—185th Military Airlift Squadron—Oklahoma ANG," pp. 1-3; "Background on 185th," pp. 1-3, SFHNC; HQ 137TAW to NGB, May 4, 1977.

31. "Historical Record of the 138th Tactical Fighter Group"; *125th Air Transport Squadron Yearbook;* Lindsey, "Brief History of the 137th Tactical Airlift Wing (1947-1980)," p. 1; Newman, Notes, OMC; Robinson, ed., *Encyclopedia of American Aircraft,* pp. 293-312; H. F. King, comp., and John W. R. Taylor, ed., *Milestones of the Air, Jane's 100 Significant Aircraft,* p. 101; Newman, Comments, OMC.

32. Lindsey, "Brief History of the 137th Tactical Airlift Wing (1947-1980)," p. 1; Robinson, ed., *Encyclopedia of American Aircraft,* pp. 293-312; Newman, Notes, OMC; King, comp., and Taylor, ed., *Milestones of the Air,* p. 101; Newman, Comments, OMC.

33. Interview, Newman, February 26, 1981, OMC; Robinson, ed., *Encyclopedia of American Aircraft,* pp. 172-74, 270-72, 286-88.

34. Lindsey, "Brief History of the 137th Tactical Airlift Wing (1947-1980)," p. 1; Robinson, ed., *Encyclopedia of American Aircraft,* pp. 293-312; Newman, Notes, OMC; King, comp., and Taylor, ed., *Milestones of the Air,* p. 101; Newman, Comments, OMC; *45th Division News,* May 25 and July 26, 1948.

35. Interview, Newman, February 16, 1981, OMC; Newman, Notes, OMC; Newman, Comments, OMC.

36. Lindsey, "Brief History of the 137th Tactical Airlift Wing (1947-1980)," p. 1; Miscellaneous Notes, OMC; Historical Briefs, p. 2, DRLC; *45th Division News,* July, 1949.

37. Lindsey, "Brief History of the 137th Tactical Airlift Wing (1947-1980)," p. 1; Miscellaneous Notes; Historical Briefs, p. 1, DRLC; Robinson, ed., *Encyclopedia of American Aircraft,* pp. 293-312; "Historical Record of the 138th Tactical Fighter Group"; *125th Air Transport Squadron Yearbook;* Newman, Comments, OMC.

38. Lindsey, "Brief History of the 137th Tactical Airlift Wing (1947-1980)," p. 1; Miscellaneous Notes; Historical Briefs, p. 1, DRLC; Robinson, ed., *Encyclopedia of American Aircraft,* pp. 293-312; "Historical Record of the 138th Tactical Fighter Group"; *125th Air Transport Squadron Yearbook;* Newman, Comments, OMC.

39. Lapica, et al., *Facts on File Yearbook, 1950,* pp. 201-16; Hill, *The Minute Man in Peace and War,* pp. 501-507, 534-35.

40. Hill, *The Minute Man in Peace and War,* pp. 534-35; Interview, Newman, February 16, 1981, OMC; "Brief History of the 137th Tactical Airlift Wing (1947-1980)," p. 1; "Historical Record of the 138th Tactical Fighter Group"; *125th Air Transport Squadron Yearbook.*

14
THE OKLAHOMA AIR NATIONAL GUARD: 1950 TO THE PRESENT

1. (No author), "Historical Record of the 138th Tactical Fighter Group"; *125th Air Transport Squadron Yearbook;* Major General Stanley F. H. Newman, Notes, OMC; Dennis T. Lindsey, "Brief History of the 137th Tactical Airlift Wing (1947-1980)," p. 1; Newman, Notes, OMC; Miscellaneous Notes, OMC; *45th Division News,* November 2 and November 30, 1950.

2. Interview, Major General Stanley F. H. Newman, February 16, 1981, OMC; Newman, Notes, OMC; Newman, Comments, OMC.

3. Lindsey, "Brief History of the 137th Tactical Airlift Wing (1947-1980)," p. 1; Miscellaneous Notes, OMC; Newman, Notes, OMC; Bill Gunston, *The Illustrated Encyclopedia of the World's Modern Military Aircraft,* p. 236; Enzo Angelucci, *Airplanes from the Dawn of Flight to the Present Day,* pp. 146-47; Newman, Comments, OMC.

4. Interview, Newman, February 16, 1981, OMC; Newman, Notes, OMC; Newman, Comments, OMC.

5. Lindsey, "Brief History of the 137th Tactical Airlift Wing (1947-1980)," p. 1; Miscellaneous Notes, OMC; Newman, Notes, OMC; Gunston, *Illustrated Encyclopedia of the World's Modern Military Aircraft,* p. 236; Angelucci, *Airplanes from the Dawn of Flight to the Present Day,* pp. 146-47; Newman, Comments, OMC.

6. Interview, Newman, February 16, 1981, OMC; Newman, Notes, OMC; Newman, Comments, OMC.

7. Interview, Newman, February 16, 1981, OMC; Newman, Comments, OMC.

8. Interview, Newman, February 16, 1981, OMC; Newman, Comments, OMC.

9. "Historical Record of the 138th Tactical Fighter Group"; *125th Air Transport Squadron Yearbook;* Newman, Notes, OMC; Newman, Comments, OMC.

10. Newman, Notes, OMC; Newman, Comments, OMC.

11. Lindsey, "Brief History of the 137th Tactical Airlift Wing (1947-1980)," pp. 1-2; Interview, Newman, February 16, 1981, OMC; Newman, Notes, OMC; H. F. King, comp., and John W. R. Taylor, ed., *Milestones of the Air: Jane's 100 Significant Aircraft,* p. 101; Newman, Comments, OMC.

12. Lindsey, "Brief History of the 137th Tactical Airlift Wing (1947-1980)," pp. 1-2; Interview, Newman, February 16, 1981, OMC; King, comp., and Taylor, ed., *Milestones of the Air,* p. 101; Newman, Notes, OMC; Newman, Comments, OMC.

13. Lindsey, "Brief History of the 137th Tactical Airlift Wing (1947-1980)," pp. 1-2; Newman, Notes, OMC; Interview, Newman, February 16, 1981, OMC; Newman, Comments, OMC.

14. Newman, Comments, OMC; Lindsey, "Brief History of the 137th Tactical Airlift Wing (1947-1980)," pp. 1-2; Interview, Newman, February 16, 1981, OMC; Chris Chant, ed., *The World's Air Forces,* p. 37; Interview, Newman, February 16, 1981, OMC; Robinson, ed., *Encyclopedia of American Aircraft,* pp. 255-56; Newman, Comments, OMC.

15. Letter, Master Sergeant Dennis R. Lindsey to Kenny A. Franks, March 9, 1981, OMC.

16. Ibid.

17. Lindsey, "Brief History of the 137th Tactical Airlift Wing (1947-1980)," p. 2; Interview, Newman, February 13, 1981, OMC. Chant, ed., *World's Air Forces,* p. 56; Robinson, ed., *Encyclopedia of American Aircraft,* pp. 313-18; "Historical Record of the 138th Tactical Fighter Group"; *125th Air Transport Squadron Yearbook;* Newman, Notes, OMC; Newman, Comments, OMC; Lindsey to Franks, March 9, 1981.

18. Lindsey, "Brief History of the 137th Tactical Airlift Wing (1947-1980)," p. 2; Chant, ed., *World's Air Forces,* p. 56; Robinson, ed., *Encyclopedia of American Aircraft,* pp. 313-18; "Historical Record of the 138th Tactical Fighter Group"; *125th Air Transport Squadron Yearbook;* Interview, Newman, February 16, 1981, OMC.

19. "Historical Record of the 138th Tactical Fighter Group"; *125th Air Transport Squadron Yearbook;* Robinson, ed., *Encyclopedia of American Aircraft,* pp. 64-66; Interview, Newman, February 16, 1981, OMC; Gunston, *Illustrated Encyclopedia of the World's Modern Military Aircraft,* p. 158; Newman, Notes, OMC; Newman, Comments, OMC.

20. Lindsey, "Brief History of the 137th Tactical Airlift Wing (1947-1980)," p. 2; Chant, ed., *World's Air Forces,* p. 56; Robinson, ed., *Encyclopedia of American Aircraft,* pp. 313-18.

21. Lindsey, "Brief History of the 137th Tactical Airlift Wing (1947-1980)," p. 2; Interview, Lieutenant Colonel James R. McKinney, January 29, 1981, OMC; Newman, Notes, OMC; Newman, Comments, OMC.

22. Lindsey, "Brief History of the 137th Tactical Airlift Wing (1947-1980)," p. 2; Interview, McKinney, January 29, 1981, OMC; Newman, Comments, OMC.

23. Lindsey, "Brief History of the 137th Tactical Airlift Wing (1947-1980)," p. 2; Interview, Newman, February 16, 1981, OMC; Robinson, ed., *Encyclopedia of American Aircraft,* pp. 64-66; Gunston, *Illustrated Encyclopedia of the World's Modern Military Aircraft,* p. 158; Newman, Notes, OMC.

24. Lindsey, "Brief History of the 137th Tactical Airlift Wing (1947-1980)," p. 2; Interview, Newman, February 16, 1981, OMC; Robinson, ed., *Encyclopedia of American Aircraft,* pp. 64-66; Gunston, *Illustrated Encyclopedia of the World's Modern Military Aircraft,* p. 158; Newman, Notes, OMC; Newman, Comments, OMC.

25. Lindsey, "Brief History of the 137th Tactical Airlift Wing (1947-1980)," pp. 2-3; Robinson, ed., *Encyclopedia of American Aircraft,* pp. 64-66; "Talking Bird," DRLC; Newman, Comments, OMC.

26. Lindsey, "Brief History of the 137th Tactical Airlift Wing (1947-1980)," pp. 2-3; Robinson, ed., *Encyclopedia of American Aircraft,* pp. 64-66; "Talking Bird," DRLC.

27. "Historical Record of the 138th Tactical Fighter Group"; *125th Air Transport Squadron Yearbook;* Inter-

view, Newman, February 16, 1981, OMC; Lindsey, "Brief History of the 137th Tactical Airlift Wing (1947-1980)," pp. 2-3; "Talking Bird," DRLC.

28. Interview, Newman, February 16, 1981, OMC; Lindsey, "Brief History of the 137th Tactical Airlift Wing (1947-1980)," pp. 2-3; "Talking Bird," DRLC; Newman, Notes, OMC; Newman, Comments, OMC.

29. Lindsey, "Brief History of the 137th Tactical Airlift Wing (1947-1980)," pp. 2-3; Interview, Newman, February 16, 1981, OMC; Historical Briefs, DRLC; Newman, Comments, OMC.

30. Lindsey, "Brief History of the 137th Tactical Airlift Wing (1947-1980)," pp. 2-3; Interview, Newman, February 16, 1981, OMC; Historical Briefs, DRLC; Newman, Notes, OMC; Newman, Comments, OMC.

31. Lindsey, "Brief History of the 137th Tactical Airlift Wing (1947-1980)," pp. 2-3; Historical Briefs, DRLC; Interview, Newman, February 16, 1981, OMC; "Historical Record of the 138th Tactical Fighter Group"; *125th Air Transport Squadron Yearbook;* Robinson, ed., *Encyclopedia of American Aircraft,* pp. 180-81; Newman, Notes, OMC; Newman, Comments, OMC.

32. Newman, Comments, OMC.

33. Ibid.; Lindsey, "Brief History of the 137th Tactical Airlift Wing (1947-1980)," pp. 2-3; Historical Briefs, DRLC; Interview, Newman, February 16, 1981, OMC; "Historical Record of the 138th Tactical Fighter Group"; *125th Air Transport Squadron Yearbook;* Newman, Notes, OMC.

34. Lindsey, "Brief History of the 137th Tactical Airlift Wing (1947-1980)," pp. 2-3; Historical Briefs, DRLC; Interview, Newman, February 16, 1981, OMC; "Historical Record of the 138th Tactical Fighter Group"; Newman, Notes, OMC; Newman, Comments, OMC.

35. Lindsey, "Brief History of the 137th Tactical Airlift Wing (1947-1980)," pp. 2-3; Historical Briefs, DRLC; Interview, Newman, February 16, 1981, OMC; *Daily Oklahoman* (Oklahoma City), August 5, 1973; "Historical Record of the 138th Tactical Fighter Group"; Newman, Notes, OMC; Newman, Comments, OMC.

36. "Historical Record of the 138th Tactical Fighter Group"; *125th Air Transport Squadron Yearbook;* Robinson, ed., *Encyclopedia of American Aircraft,* pp. 319-22; Interview, Lieutenant Colonel James R. McKinney, January 27, 1981, OMC; Mark Herish, et al., *Air Forces of the World: An Illustrated Directory of all the World's Military Air Powers,* p. 248; Newman, Notes, OMC.

37. Robinson, ed., *Encyclopedia of American Aircraft,* pp. 319-22; Interview, McKinney, January 27, 1981, OMC; Herish, et al., *Air Forces of the World,* p. 248; Newman, Comments, OMC.

38. Robinson, ed., *Encyclopedia of American Aircraft,* pp. 405-406; John W. R. Taylor, comp. and ed., *Jane's All the World's Aircraft,* pp. 355-56; "Historical Record of the 138th Tactical Fighter Group"; *125th Air Transport Squadron Yearbook;* Interview, McKinney, January 27, 1981, OMC.

39. Lindsey, "Brief History of the 137th Tactical Airlift Wing (1947-1980)," pp. 2-3; Interview, Colonel Raymond Sturm, January 22, 1981, OMC; Newman, Comments, OMC.

40. Robinson, ed., *Encyclopedia of American Aircraft,* pp. 257-58; Lindsey, "Brief History of the 137th Tactical Airlift Wing (1947-1980)," pp. 2-3; Gunston, *Illustrated*

Encyclopedia of the World's Modern Military Aircraft, pp. 170-72; Newman, Notes, OMC; Newman, Comments, OMC.

41. Robinson, ed., *Encyclopedia of American Aircraft,* pp. 257-58; Lindsey, "Brief History of the 137th Tactical Airlift Wing (1947-1980)," pp. 2-3; Gunston, *Illustrated Encyclopedia of the World's Modern Military Aircraft,* pp. 170-72; Newman, Notes, OMC.

42. Interview, Newman, February 16, 1981, OMC; Interview, Major Joe E. Blackwell, February 16, 1981, OMC.

43. Interview, McKinney, January 29, 1981, OMC; Interview, Newman, February 16, 1981, OMC; Interview, Blackwell, February 16, 1981, OMC; Newman, Notes, OMC; Newman, Comments, OMC.

44. Interview, McKinney, January 29, 1981, OMC; Interview, Newman, February 16, 1981, OMC; Interview, Blackwell, February 16, 1981, OMC; Newman, Notes, OMC; Newman, Comments, OMC.

15

THE TOTAL FORCE

1. Guy Nelson, *Thunderbird: The Story of the 45th Infantry Division,* pp. 103, 121-22; Walter G. Hermes, *Truce Tent and Fighting Front,* pp. 448-90.

2. Nelson, *Thunderbird,* pp. 122-23; Jim D. Hill, *The Minute Man in Peace and War,* p. 542; Interview, Major General Frederick A. Daugherty (Ret.), January 6, 1977, Archives; Lieutenant Colonel Peter E. Wheeler, Comments, OMC.

3. Nelson, *Thunderbird,* pp. 122-23; Hill, *The Minute Man in Peace and War,* pp. 542-44.

4. Hill, *The Minute Man in Peace and War,* pp. 542-44; Nelson, *Thunderbird,* p. 123; Interview, Major General Frederick A. Daugherty (Ret.), January 6, 1977, Archives.

5. Interview, Daugherty, January 6, 1977, Archives; Wheeler, Comments, OMC.

6. Hill, *The Minute Man in Peace and War,* pp. 542-44.

7. Ibid., pp. 544-45; Nelson, *Thunderbird,* p. 123; Wheeler, Comments, OMC.

8. Nelson, *Thunderbird,* p. 123; Lieutenant General William R. Peers, "Army Reserve and National Guard Meet the Test at Home and Abroad," *Army: 1969 Green Book,* vol. 19, No. 10 (October, 1969):71-74; Lieutenant General Charles W. G. Rich, "'New Look' of Reserve Reflects Eventful Year," *Army: 1968 Green Book,* vol. 18, No. 11 (November, 1968):67-68; "SRF," *The National Guardsman,* vol. 19, No. 11 (November, 1965):8-10, 48; Interview, Lieutenant General LaVern E. Weber, March 7, 1981, OMC.

9. Nelson, *Thunderbird,* p. 123; Peers, "Army Reserve and National Guard Meet the Test at Home and Abroad," pp. 71-74; Rich, "'New Look' of Reserve Reflects Eventful Year," pp. 67-68; "SRF," pp. 8-10, 48; Interview, Weber, March 7, 1981, OMC.

10. Nelson, *Thunderbird,* p. 123; Peers, "Army Reserve and National Guard Meet the Test at Home and Abroad," pp. 71-74; Rich, "'New Look' of Reserve Reflects Eventful Year," pp. 67-68; "SRF," pp. 8-10, 48; "Guard Gets 'SRF' Rolling," *The National Guardsman,* vol. 19, No. 12 (December, 1965): 24-25; "SRF, Born 27 September 1965, Dies 30 September 1969: It Accomplished its Mission," *The National Guardsman,* vol. 23, No. 9 (September, 1969):12-16; Interview, Weber, March 7, 1981, OMC; Interview, Major General Robert M. Morgan, Jr., April 27, 1981, OMC; Wheeler, Comments, OMC.

11. "One Reserve Force: The Army National Guard," *The National Guardsman,* vol. 19, No. 1 (January, 1965): 16-18.

12. Wheeler, Comments, OMC.

13. Ibid.

14. Ibid.

15. "One Reserve Force: The Army National Guard," pp. 16-18; "One Reserve Force: The New Lineup," *The National Guardsman,* vol. 19, No. 4 (April, 1965):12-16; Interview, Weber, March 7, 1981, OMC.

16. "One Reserve Force: The New Lineup," pp. 12-16; Nelson, *Thunderbird,* pp. 122-24; Interview, Ralph W. Jones, September 17, 1980, OMC; Rich, "'New Look' of Reserve Reflects Eventful Year," pp. 67-68; "The Guard-Reserve Reshuffle," *The National Guardsman,* vol. 21, No. 7 (July, 1967):2-8, 40; "1968 Photo Directory," *Army: 1968 Green Book,* vol. 18, No. 11 (November, 1968):127-29; "Major General David Crockett Matthews, The Adjutant General, Oklahoma National Guard," Public Affairs Office, Oklahoma Military Department, Oklahoma City, Oklahoma; Wheeler, Comments, OMC.

17. "One Reserve Force: The New Lineup," pp. 12-16; Nelson, *Thunderbird,* pp. 122-24; Interview, Jones, September 17, 1980, OMC; Rich, "'New Look' of Reserve Reflects Eventful Year," pp. 67-68; "The Guard-Reserve Reshuffle," pp. 2-8, 40; "1968 Photo Directory," pp. 127-29; Wheeler, Comments, OMC.

18. "One Reserve Force: The New Lineup," pp. 12-16; Nelson, *Thunderbird,* pp. 122-24; Interview, Jones, September 17, 1980, OMC; Rich, "'New Look' of Reserve Reflects Eventful Year," pp. 67-68; "The Guard-Reserve Reshuffle," pp. 2-8, 40; "1968 Photo Directory," pp. 127-29; "Major General David Crockett Matthews, The Adjutant General, Oklahoma National Guard"; Wheeler, Comments, OMC; Reader's Comments, OMC.

19. Nelson, *Thunderbird,* pp. 123-24; Interview, Ralph W. Jones, September 17, 1980, OMC; "Thunderbirds Migrate Back to Oklahoma," *The National Guardsman,* vol. 35, No. 3 (March, 1981):6; Rich, "'New Look' of Reserve Reflects Eventful Year," pp. 127-29; Peers, "Army Reserve and National Guard Meet the Test at Home and Abroad," p. 73; Interview, Weber, March 7, 1981, OMC; Reader's Comments, OMC.

20. Nelson, *Thunderbird,* pp. 123-24; Interview, Jones, September 17, 1980, OMC; "Thunderbirds Migrate Back to Oklahoma," p. 6; Rich, "'New Look' of Reserve Reflects Eventful Year," pp. 127-29; Peers, "Army Reserve and National Guard Meet the Test at Home and Abroad," p. 73; Interview, Daugherty, May 8, 1981, OMC; Interview, Weber, March 7, 1981, OMC; Interview, Morgan, April 27, 1981, OMC; Interview, Daugherty, January 6, 1977, Archives.

21. Nelson, *Thunderbird,* pp. 123-24; Interview, Jones, September 17, 1980, OMC; "Thunderbirds Migrate Back to Oklahoma," p. 6; Rich, "'New Look' of Reserve Reflects

Eventful Year," pp. 127-29; Peers, "Army Reserve and National Guard Meet the Test at Home and Abroad," p. 73; Interview, Weber, March 7, 1981, OMC; Interview, Morgan, April 27, 1981, OMC; Interview, Daugherty, January 6, 1977, Archives.

22. Lieutenant General George I. Forsythe, "The Impact of VOLAR," *Army: 1971 Green Book,* vol. 21, No. 10 (October, 1971):29-32; Lieutenant General William R. Peers, "New Priorities for Guard, Reserve," *Army: 1971 Green Book,* vol. 21, No. 10 (October, 1971): 71-77; George Fielding Eliot, "A New Day for the Guard and Reserves?", *The National Guardsman,* vol. 25, No. 1 (January, 1971): 2-6; Interview, Weber, March 7, 1981, OMC.

23. Forsythe, "The Impact of VOLAR," pp. 29-32; Peers, "New Priorities for Guard, Reserve," pp. 71-77; Eliot, "A New Day for the Guard and Reserves?", pp. 2-6; Interview, Weber, March 7, 1981, OMC.

24. "Weber New Army Guard Director," *The National Guardsman,* vol. 25, No. 10 (November, 1971):30; Interview, Weber, March 7, 1981, OMC; "Lieutenant General LaVern E. Weber," Public Affairs Office, Oklahoma Military Department, Oklahoma City, Oklahoma; Wheeler, Comments, OMC.

25. "Weber New Army Guard Director," p. 30; Interview, Weber, March 7, 1981, OMC; Reader's Comments, OMC.

26. Major General Charles A. Ott, Jr., "Affiliation is Key to Readiness," *Army: 1975 Green Book,* vol. 25, No. 10 (October, 1975):75-79, TAG, Jones to Franks, April 21, 1981; "Major General David Crockett Matthews, The Adjutant-General, Oklahoma National Guard."

27. Interview, Morgan, April 27, 1981, OMC.

28. Ibid.; TAG, Jones to Franks, April 21, 1981; Wheeler, Comments, OMC.

29. "TOW Training Slated," *The National Guardsman,* vol. 31, No. 7 (July-August, 1977):32; TAG, Jones to Franks, April 21, 1981; Interview, Coffey, undated, OMC; Interview, Morgan, April 27, 1981, OMC.

30. "TOW Training Slated," p. 32; TAG, Jones to Franks, April 21, 1981; Interview, Coffey, undated, OMC; Interview, Morgan, April 27, 1981, OMC.

31. Major General Emmett H. Walker, Jr., "U.S. Army National Guard: Working Toward 'Come as you are' Readiness," *Army: 1979 Green Book,* vol. 29, No. 10 (October, 1979):82-85; James B. Deerin, "NATO and the National Guard," *The National Guardsman,* vol. 33, No. 2 (February, 1979):8.

32. Major General Emmett H. Walker, Jr., "Guard Focuses on Total Army Picture: Progress in Training, Readiness, Manning," *Army: 1980-1981 Green Book,* vol. 30, No. 10 (October, 1980):150-55; "Major Combat Units of the U.S. Army," *Army: 1980-1981 Green Book,* vol. 30, No. 10 (October, 1980):142-43; Interview, Morgan, April 27, 1981, OMC.

33. Walker, "Guard Focuses on Total Army Picture: Progress in Training, Readiness, Manning," pp. 150-55; "Major Combat Units of the U.S. Army," pp. 142-43; Interview, Morgan, April 27, 1981, OMC.

34. Walker, "Guard Focuses on Total Army Picture: Progress in Training, Readiness, Manning," pp. 150-55; "Major Combat Units of the U.S. Army," pp. 142-43; Interview, Morgan, April 27, 1981, OMC.

35. "The Guard vs. Disorder," *The National Guardsman,* vol. 24, No. 6 (June, 1970):2-7, 9-13, 40; "The Role of the National Guard in an Age of Unrest," *The National Guardsman,* vol. 24, No. 9 (September, 1970):9-15; Interview, Brigadier General William E. Mayberry (Ret.), January 7, 1977, Archives.

36. Sergeant First Class Tom House and Captain Jim Haney, *"Guard Helps Quell Massive Prison Riot," The National Guardsman,* vol. 27, No. 8 (August-September 1973):30; *Sunday Oklahoman* (Oklahoma City), August 5, 1973; *Sunday Phoenix and Times-Democrat* (Muskogee), July 29, 1973; *Oklahoma City Times,* August 1, 1973; Wheeler, Comments, OMC.

37. House and Haney, "Guard Helps Quell Massive Prison Riot," pp. 30-31; *Sunday Oklahoman,* August 5, 1973; *Sunday Phoenix and Times-Democrat,* July 29, 1973; *Oklahoma City Times,* August 1, 1973.

38. House and Haney, "Guard Helps Quell Massive Prison Riot," pp. 30-31; *Sunday Oklahoman,* August 5, 1973; *Sunday Phoenix and Times-Democrat,* July 29, 1973; *Oklahoma City Times,* August 1, 1973; Wheeler, Comments, OMC.

39. House and Haney, "Guard Helps Quell Massive Prison Riot," pp. 30-31; *Sunday Oklahoman,* August 5, 1973; *Sunday Phoenix and Times-Democrat,* July 29, 1973; *Oklahoma City Times,* August 1, 1973.

40. House and Haney, "Guard Helps Quell Massive Prison Riot," pp. 30-32; *Sunday Oklahoman,* August 5, 1973; *Sunday Phoenix and Times-Democrat,* July 29, 1973; *Oklahoma City Times,* August 1, 1973.

41. House and Haney, "Guard Helps Quell Massive Prison Riot," pp. 30-32; *Sunday Oklahoman,* August 5, 1973; *Sunday Phoenix and Times-Democrat,* July 29, 1973; *Oklahoma City Times,* August 1, 1973.

42. House and Haney, "Guard Helps Quell Massive Prison Riot," pp. 30-32; *Sunday Oklahoman,* August 5, 1973; *Sunday Phoenix and Times-Democrat,* July 29, 1973; *Oklahoma City Times,* August 1, 1973; Wheeler, Comments, OMC.

43. Interview, Second Lieutenant Mark L. Cantrell, September 15, 1981, OMC.

44. Ibid.; Reader's Comments, OMC.

45. Interview, Cantrell, September 15, 1981; Reader's Comments, OMC.

46. Reader's Comments, OMC; Interview, Major Timothy E. Martin, December 29, 1982 and December 4, 1983, OMC.

47. Reader's Comments, OMC; Interview, Martin, December 29, 1982, OMC.

48. Reader's Comments, OMC; Interview, Martin, December 29, 1982, OMC.

49. Reader's Comments, OMC; Interview, Martin, December 29, 1982, OMC.

50. Reader's Comments, OMC; Interview, Cantrell, September 15, 1981, OMC; Interview, Martin, December 29, 1983, OMC.

51. Reader's Comments, OMC; Interview, Cantrell, September 15, 1981, OMC; Interview, Martin, December 29, 1982 and January 4, 1983, OMC.

52. Reader's Comments, OMC; Interview, Cantrell, September 15, 1981, OMC; Interview, Martin, December 29, 1982 and January 4, 1983, OMC.

53. "Chopper Fliers Save Goods from Blazing House," *The National Guardsman,* vol. 26, No. 4 (April, 1972):34;

Wheeler, Comments, OMC.

54. "The Forces of Nature," *The National Guardsman,* vol. 27, No. 6 (June, 1973):32; "Guardsmen Fight Floods, Quench Fires, Quell Convicts," *The National Guardsman,* vol. 27, No. 11 (December, 1973):42-43; "Storms and Big Blast Bring Guard to Duty," *The National Guardsman,* vol. 28, No. 2 (February, 1974):30.

55. "The Guard Responds," *The National Guardsman,* vol. 28, No. 11 (December, 1974):27; "Water, Wind and Snow," *The National Guardsman,* vol. 29, No. 4 (April, 1975):34; News Broadcast, KTOK Radio (Oklahoma City),

April 21, 1981; Interview, Morgan, April 27, 1981, OMC.

56. Interview, Weber, March 7, 1981, OMC; Interview, Morgan, April 27, 1981, OMC.

57. Interview, Weber, March 7, 1981, OMC.

58. Ibid.; Interview, Styron, September, 1973, Archives; Interview, Morgan, April 27, 1981, OMC; Interview, Daugherty, May 8, 1981, OMC.

59. Interview, Morgan, April 27, 1981, OMC.

60. Interview, Daugherty, May 8, 1981, OMC.

61. Ibid.; Interview, Jones, August 7, 1981, OMC; Interview, Morgan, May 11, 1981, OMC.

BIBLIOGRAPHY

COLLECTIONS

45th Infantry Division Museum Archives (Archives), Oklahoma City, Oklahoma. Materials from this collection include the various reports of the Oklahoma Military Department, the Adjutant-General of Oklahoma (TAG); operational orders; after-action reports; many interviews with members of the Oklahoma National Guard; and copies of the various issues of the *45th Division News, Camp Barkeley News, 45th Division Daily News,* and *The Thunderbird News.*

Dennis R. Lindsey Collection (DRLC), Del City, Oklahoma. The personal collection of Master Sergeant Dennis R. Lindsey, unit historian at Will Rogers Air National Guard Base. This collection includes unit histories, photographs, biographical information, and historical notes. Much of the material used in the Oklahoma Air National Guard chapters was taken from this fine collection.

Historical Records, Oklahoma Air National Guard, Oklahoma Military Department, Oklahoma City, Oklahoma. This collection contains many of the early records of the Oklahoma Air National Guard units, records of many of the individuals involved, unit histories discussing the organization and evolution of the 125th and 185th squadrons, squadron yearbooks, and miscellaneous documents.

Oklahoma Military Collection (OMC), Archives, Oklahoma Heritage Association, Oklahoma City, Oklahoma. Materials from the collection used in preparing this book include: personal recollections from many of the actual participants of the Oklahoma National Guard from the 1920s to the present; several written narratives of actual events they witnessed; notes of all types, based on personal experiences or on official records in the Public Information Office of the Oklahoma Military Department, made during the preparation of the manu-

script; biographical sketches; correspondence; interview tapes; comments made by various readers (military specialists who evaluated the documents for accuracy), and notes.

Public Affairs Office, Oklahoma Military Department, Oklahoma City, Oklahoma. This collection contains biographical sketches of many of the individuals involved in the Oklahoma National Guard and other information valuable in explaining the role of the state National Guard.

Stanley F. H. Newman Collection (SFHNC), Oklahoma City, Oklahoma. Major General Newman (OKANG) served with the Oklahoma Air National Guard from the time of its reorganization in the post-World War II era. His personal collection includes rare books, unit histories, biographical sketches, recollections, and notes covering nearly thirty-five years of personal experience with the Oklahoma ANG.

Stewart Papers, Forty-fifth Infantry Division Museum, Oklahoma City, Oklahoma. Roy P. Stewart joined the Oklahoma National Guard in the years between World War I and World War II and served until the post-Korean War reorganizations. In addition, he served as a newspaper correspondent with the Forty-fifth for part of World War II. His collection contains a wealth of biographical information on many national guardsmen, as well as his personal recollections.

INTERVIEWS

Archives, Forty-fifth Infantry Division Museum.

Coffey, Major General John, Jr. (Ret.), Army of the United States, undated.
Daugherty, Major General Frederick A. (Ret.), Army of the United States, November 18, 1976 and January 6, 1977.

Mayberry, Brigadier General William E. (Ret.), Army of the United States, January 7, 1977.

Styron, Major General James C. (Ret.), United States Army, September, 1973.

Tapscott, Warrant Officer George F. (Ret.) Oklahoma Army National Guard, May, 1978.

Wilson, Brigadier General William R. (Ret.), Oklahoma Army National Guard, January 7, 1977.

Oklahoma Military Collection, Oklahoma Heritage Association.

Cantrell, Second Lieutenant Mark L., Oklahoma Army National Guard, September 15, 1981.

Blackwell, Major Joe E., United States Air Force, February 16, 1981.

Clapp, Sergeant Major Jack (Ret.), Oklahoma Army National Guard, February 6, 1981.

Daugherty, Major General Frederick A. (Ret.), Army of the United States, May 8, 1981.

Jones, Ralph W., September 17, 1980 and August 7, 1981.

McCasland, Colonel John H. (Ret.), Oklahoma Air National Guard, October 15, 1980, November 12, 1980, October 29, 1980 and December 10, 1980.

McKinney, Lieutenant Colonel James R., Oklahoma Air National Guard, January 27, 1981 and January 29, 1981.

Martin, Major Timothy E., Oklahoma Army National Guard, December 19, 1982 and January 4, 1983.

Morgan, Major General Robert M., Jr., Oklahoma Army National Guard, April 27, 1981 and May 11, 1981.

Muldrow, Major General Hal L., Jr. (Ret.), Oklahoma Army National Guard, February 13, 1981.

Meyers, Colonel H. A. (Ret.), United States Army; Colonel Preston J. C. Murphy (Ret.), Army of the United States; and Colonel William P. Grace (Ret.), United States Army, August 22, 1980.

Munson, First Sergeant Forest G. (Ret.), Oklahoma Army National Guard, January 22, 1981.

Newman, Major General Stanley F. H., Oklahoma Air National Guard, February 16, 1981.

O'Neil, Colonel Herbert C. (Ret.), Oklahoma Army National Guard, January 7, 1981.

Peters, Command Sergeant Major Arthur E. (Ret.), Oklahoma Army National Guard, January 22, 1981.

Rey, Colonel Bruce E. (Ret.), Oklahoma Army National Guard, March 22, 1981 and February 22, 1981.

Stewart, Colonel Roy P. (Ret.), Oklahoma Army National Guard, February 4, 1981.

Sturm, Colonel Raymond, Oklahoma Air National Guard, January 22, 1981.

BOOKS AND AUTHORS

Allen, William L. *Anzio: Edge of Disaster.* New York: E. P. Dutton, 1978.

American Battle Monuments Commission. *American Armies and Battlefields in Europe.* Washington: Government Printing Office, 1938.

Angelucci, Enzo. *Airplanes from the Dawn of Flight to the Present Day.* New York: McGraw-Hill Book Co., 1973.

Barnes, C. H. *History of the 142nd Infantry of the Thirty-sixth Division.* N.P.: Blackwell Job Printing Co., 1922.

Blumensen, Martin. *United States Army in World War II, The Mediterranean Theater of Operations, Salerno to Cassino.* Washington: Office of the Chief of Military History, 1969.

Bryant, Keith L., Jr. *Alfalfa Bill Murray.* Norman: University of Oklahoma Press, 1968.

Casey, Orben J. "Governor Lee Cruce and Law Enforcement, 1911-1915," *Chronicles of Oklahoma,* vol. 54 (Winter, 1976-1977).

Chant, Chris, ed. *The World's Air Forces.* Secaucus, New Jersey: Chartwell Books, Inc., 1979.

Chastaine, Ben H. *Story of the 36th.* Oklahoma City: Harlow Publishing Co., 1920.

"Chopper Fliers Save Goods from Blazing House." *The National Guardsman,* vol. 26, no. 4 (April, 1972).

Conn, Jack T. *One Man in His Time.* Oklahoma City: Western Heritage Books, Inc., 1979.

Corden, Seth K., and W. B. Richards, comps. *The Oklahoma Red Book.* 2 vols., Tulsa: Democrat Printing Co.

de Castelbled, Maurice. *History of the A.E.F.* New York: Bookcraft, 1937.

Deerin, James B. "NATO and the National Guard." *The National Guardsman,* vol. 33, No. 2 (February, 1979).

Dulaney, Robert L. *45th Infantry Division.* Atlanta: Albert Love Enterprises, n.d.

Eliot, George Fielding. "A New Day for the Guard and Reserves?" *The National Guardsman,* vol. 25, No. 1 (January, 1971).

Fisher, George A. *The Story of the 180th Infantry Regiment.* San Angelo, Texas: Newsfoto Publishing Co., 1947.

Forsythe, Lieutenant General George I. "The Impact of VOLAR." *Army: 1971 Green Book,* vol. 21, No. 10 (October, 1971).

Forty-fifth Infantry Division. *The Fighting Forty-Fifth: The Combat Report of an Infantry Division.* Baton Rouge, Louisiana: Army & Navy Publishing Co., n.d.

Franklin, Jimmie Lewis. *Journey Toward Hope.* Norman: University of Oklahoma Press, 1982.

BIBLIOGRAPHY

Franks, Kenny A. *The Oklahoma Petroleum Industry.* Norman: University of Oklahoma Press, 1980.

Garland, Albert N., and Howard M. Smyth, *United
States Army in World War II: The Mediterranean
Theater of Operations, Sicily and the Surrender
of Italy.* Washington: Office of the Chief of Military History, 1965.

"Guard Gets (SRF) Rolling." *The National Guardsman,* vol. 29, No. 12 (December. 1965).

"Guardsmen Fight Floods, Quench Fires, Quell Convicts." *The National Guardsman,* vol. 27, No. 11
(December, 1973).

Gugeler, Russel A. *Combat Actions in Korea.* Washington: Government Printing Office, 1970.

Gunston, Bill. *The Illustrated Encyclopedia of the
World's Modern Military Aircraft.* New York:
Crescent Books, 1977.

Halliburton, Rudie, Jr. *The Tulsa Race War of 1921.*
San Francisco: R. & E. Associates, 1975.

Harbord, James G. *The American Army in France,
1917-1919.* Boston: Little, Brown & Co., 1936.

Herish, Mark, Bill Sweetman, Barry C. Wheeler, and
Bill Gunston. *Air Forces of the World: An Illus-
trated Directory of all the World's Military Air
Powers.* New York: Simon & Schuster, 1978.

Hermes, Walter G. *Truce Tent and Fighting Front,*
vol. 3 in *United States Army in the Korean War.*
Stetson Conn, ed. 5 vols. Washington: Government Printing Office, 1960— .

Hibbert, Christopher. *Anzio: The Bid for Rome.* New
York: Ballantine Books, 1970.

Hill, Jim D. *The Minute Man in Peace and War:
A History of the National Guard.* Harrisburg, Pennsylvania: The Stackpole Co., 1964.

Hines, Gordon. *"Alfalfa Bill": An Intimate Biography.*
Oklahoma City: Oklahoma Press, 1932.

History of the 157th Infantry Regiment (Rifle). N.p.,
n.d.

House, Sergeant First Class Tom, and Captain Jim
Haney. "Guard Helps Quell Massive Prison Riot."
The National Guardsman, vol. 27, No. 8 (August/
September 1973).

Houston, Donald E. "The Oklahoma National Guard
on the Mexican Border, 1916." *Chronicles of Oklahoma,* vol. 53 (Winter, 1975-1976).

King, H. F., comp., and John W. R. Taylor, ed.,
*Milestones of the Air, Jane's 100 Significant Air-
craft.* New York: McGraw-Hill Book Co., 1969.

Lapica, R. L., Fred McGhee, Samuel Klein, and
Lester A. Sobel, eds., *Facts on File Yearbook, 1950.*
New York: Facts on File, Inc., 1951.

Little, Will T., L. G. Pitman, and R. J. Barker. *The
Statutes of Oklahoma, 1890.* Guthrie: State Capital
Printing Co., 1891.

Litton, Gaston. *History of Oklahoma at the Golden
Anniversary of Statehood.* 4 vols., New York:

Lewis Historical Publishing Co., 1957.

"Major Combat Units of the U.S. Army." *Army: 1980-
1981 Green Book,* vol. 30, No. 10 (October, 1980).

Mason, Herbert M., Jr. *The Great Pursuit.* New York:
Random House, 1970.

Maurer, Maurer. *Combat Squadrons of the Air Force,
World War II.* Washington: Government Printing
Office, 1969.

McGhee, Fred, ed. *Facts on File Yearbook, 1953.* New
York: Facts on File, Inc., 1954.

McGlasson, Colonel W. D. "Mobilization 1940!" *Soldiers,* vol. 36, No. 1 (January, 1981).

Mondey, David. *The Complete Illustrated Encyclopedia of the World's Aircraft.* New York: A &
W Publishers, Inc., 1978.

Munsell, Warren P., Jr. *The Story of a Regiment:
A History of the 179th Regimental Combat Team.*
San Angelo, Texas: Newsfoto Publishing Co., 1946.

Nelson, Guy. *Thunderbird: A History of the 45th
Infantry Division.* Oklahoma City: Forty-fifth Infantry Division Association, 1970.

Neuringer, Sheldon. "Governor Walton's War on the
Ku Klux Klan: An Episode in Oklahoma History,
1923-1924." *Chronicles of Oklahoma,* vol. 45 (Summer, 1967).

"1968 Photo Directory." *Army: 1968 Green Book,*
vol. 18, No. 11 (November, 1968).

"One Reserve Force: The Army National Guard."
The National Guardsman, vol. 19, No. 1 (January,
1965).

"One Reserve Force: The New Lineup." *The National
Guardsman,* vol. 19, No. 4 (April, 1965).

Ott, Major General Charles A., Jr. "Affiliation is
Key to Readiness." *Army: 1975 Green Book,* vol.
25, No. 10 (October, 1975).

Peers, Lieutenant General William R. "Army Reserve and National Guard Meet the Test at Home
and Abroad." *Army: 1969 Green Book,* vol. 19,
No. 10 (October, 1969).

——. "New Priorities for Guard, Reserve." *Army:
1971 Green Book,* vol. 21, No. 10 (October, 1971).

*Report of Operations: The Seventh United States
Army in France and Germany, 1944-1945.* 3 vols.,
Heidelberg, Germany: Heidelberg Gutenberg Print-
ing Co., 1946.

Rich, Lieutenant General Charles W. G. "'New Look'
of Reserve Reflects Eventful Year." *Army: 1968
Green Book,* vol. 18, No. 11 (November, 1968).

Ridgeway, Matthew B. *The Korean War.* Garden
City, New York: Doubleday & Co., Inc., 1967.

Rister, Carl C. *Oil! Titan of the Southwest.* Norman:
University of Oklahoma Press, 1949.

Robinson, Anthony, ed. *The Encyclopedia of American Aircraft.* New York: Galahad Books, 1979.

Robinson, Don. *News of the 45th.* Norman: University of Oklahoma Press, 1944.

Roosevelt, Theodore. *The Rough Riders.* New York: Charles Scribner's Sons, 1925.

Scales, James R. and Danney Goble. *Oklahoma Politics: A History.* Norman: University of Oklahoma Press, 1982.

Schnable, James F. *Policy and Direction: The First Year,* vol. 3 in *United States Army in the Korean War,* Stetson Conn, ed. 5 vols., Washington: Government Printing Office, 1960—

Stallings, Laurence. *The Doughboys: The Story of the AEF, 1917-1918.* New York: Harper & Row Publishers, 1963.

Starr, Chester G. *From Salerno to the Alps: A History of the Fifth Army, 1943-1944.* Washington: Infantry Journal Press, 1948.

State of Oklahoma, *Session Laws of 1907-1908.* Guthrie: Oklahoma Printing Co., 1908.

Stewart, Roy. *Born Grown: An Oklahoma City History.* Oklahoma City: Fidelity Bank National Association.

"Storms and Big Blast Bring Guard to Duty." *The National Guardsman,* vol. 28, No. 2 (February, 1974).

"SRF." *The National Guardsman,* vol. 19, No. 11 (November, 1965).

"SRF, Born 27 September 1965, Dies 30 September 1969, It Accomplished its Mission." *The National Guardsman,* vol. 23, No. 9 (September, 1969).

Taylor John W. R., comp. and ed. *Jane's All the World's Aircraft.* New York: McGraw-Hill Book Co., 1972.

Territory of Oklahoma. *Session Laws of 1895.* N.p., 1895.

"The Forces of Nature." *The National Guardsman,* vol. 27, No. 6 (June, 1973).

"The Guard-Reserve Reshuffle." *The National Guardsman,* vol. 21, No. 7 (July, 1967).

"The Guard Responds." *The National Guardsman,* vol. 28, No. 11 (December, 1974).

"The Guard vs. Disorder." *The National Guardsman,* vol. 24, No. 6 (June, 1970).

"The Role of the National Guard in an Age of Unrest." *The National Guardsman,* vol. 24, No. 9 (September, 1970).

Thoburn, Joseph B. *A Standard History of Oklahoma.* 5 vols., Chicago and New York: The American Historical Society, 1916.

Thoburn, Joseph B., and Muriel H. Wright. *Oklahoma: A History of the State and Its People.* 4 vols. New York: Lewis Historical Publishing Co., 1929.

"Thunderbirds Migrate Back to Oklahoma." *The National Guardsman,* vol. 35, No. 3 (March, 1981).

"TOW Training Slated." *The National Guardsman,* vol. 31, No. 7 (July-August, 1977).

Tucker, Howard A. *History of Governor Walton's*

War on Ku Klux Klan: The Invisible Empire. Oklahoma City: Southwestern Publishing Co., 1923.

United States Army, Historical Division. *Anzio Beachhead, 22 January-25 May 1944.* Washington: Government Printing Office, n.d.

United States Army, Public Information Division. *The Medal of Honor of the United States Army.* Washington: Government Printing Office, 1948.

United States Government. *Statutes at Large,* vol. 39.

———. *Statutes at Large,* vol. 41.

United States War Department. *Annual Report, 1898.* House Doc. 2, 55th Cong., 3rd Sess.

———. *Annual Report, 1899.* House Doc. 2, 56th Cong., 1st Sess.

———. *Battle Participation of Organizations of the American Expeditionary Forces in France, Belgium and Italy, 1917-1918.* Washington: Government Printing Office, 1920.

———. *Salerno: American Operations from the Beaches to the Volturno.* Washington: Military Intelligence Division, n.d.

Vaughan-Thomas, Wynford. *Anzio.* New York: Holt, Rinehart & Winston, 1961.

Walker, Major General Emmett H., Jr. "U.S. Army National Guard: Working Toward 'Come as you are' Readiness." *Army: 1979 Green Book,* vol. 29, No. 10 (October, 1979).

———. "Guard Focuses on Total Army Picture: Progress in Training, Readiness, Manning." *Army: 1980-1981 Green Book,* vol. 30, no. 10 (October, 1980).

War Compilation Committee, The. *The History of the United Nations Forces in the Korean War.* 6 vols. The Ministry of National Defense, The Republic of Korea, 1972-1977.

"Water, Wind and Snow." *The National Guardsman,* vol. 29, No. 4 (April, 1975).

"Weber New Army Guard Director." *The National Guardsman,* vol. 25, No. 10 (November, 1971), p. 30.

Williams, Mary H., comp., *United States Army in World War II, Special Studies, Chronology, 1941-1945.* Washington: Government Printing Office, 1960.

Wilson, Woodrow. *A History of the American People.* 5 vols. New York: Harper & Brothers, Publishers, 1907.

Wythe, George. *A History of the 90th Division.* N.p.: The 90th Division Association, 1920.

NEWSPAPERS

Daily Oklahoman, Oklahoma City, Oklahoma
Drumright News, Drumright, Oklahoma
Drumright Derrick, Drumright, Oklahoma

BIBLIOGRAPHY

Oklahoma City Times, Oklahoma City
Sunday Oklahoman, Oklahoma City
Sunday Phoenix and Times-Democrat, Muskogee, Oklahoma
Edmond Evening Sun, Edmond, Oklahoma
45th Division News, Forty-fifth Infantry Division (also known as *Camp Barkeley News, 45th Division Daily News,* and *The Thunderbird News,* but cited throughout this book as the *45th Division News*)

RADIO BROADCAST

KTOK Radio. Oklahoma City. April 21, 1981.

INDEX

All military units—armies, corps, divisions, brigades, regiments, battalions, etc.—are listed under Military Units.

INDEX